China's Turbulent Quest

CHINA'S TURBULENT QUEST

*An Analysis of China's Foreign
Relations Since 1949*

NEW AND ENLARGED EDITION

HAROLD C. HINTON

*Indiana University Press
Bloomington & London*

For Mary Page and John

SECOND PRINTING 1973

Published in Canada by Fitzhenry & Whiteside Limited,
Don Mills, Ontario
Library of Congress catalog card number: 72-83700
ISBN: 253-20157-8

A clothbound edition of this book is available from
the Macmillan Company

Manufactured in the United States of America

Contents

Preface   ix

I   *The Legacy of China's Past*   1
    TRADITIONAL CHINA   2
    MODERN CHINA   8
    THE RISE OF CHINESE COMMUNISM   18
    SOME INHERITED ATTITUDES   30

PART ONE

II *Stalinism and Armed Struggle (1950–53)*   35
    THE PATTERN OF DIPLOMATIC RELATIONSHIPS   35
    THE SINO-SOVIET ALLIANCE   37
    THE ORIGINS AND OUTBREAK OF THE KOREAN WAR   40
    CHINESE INTERVENTION   44
    CHINA AND "ARMED STRUGGLE" IN SOUTHERN ASIA   49
    THE CRUNCH IN KOREA   53

III *The Road to Bandung (1953–55)*   57
    THE LIQUIDATION AND LESSONS OF THE KOREAN WAR   57
    MAO TSE-TUNG AS SENIOR COMMUNIST   59
    LIMITED VICTORY IN INDOCHINA   62
    CRISIS IN THE TAIWAN STRAIT   67
    ACCOMMODATION AND COMPETITION WITH KHRUSHCHEV   69
    "PEACEFUL COEXISTENCE" WITH NEUTRAL ASIA   73

IV *The Challenge to Mao and His Response (1956–58)*   78
    THE EAST WIND   79
    THE TWENTIETH CONGRESS   80
    CHINA AND THE EAST EUROPEAN CRISIS   82
    MAO AND THE DE-STALINIZATION QUESTION   85

PAPER TIGERS IN THE TAIWAN STRAIT   89
MAO AND HIS SKEPTICAL COLLEAGUES   94

V   *The Struggle Against Khrushchev (1959–64)*   96

THE FRACTURING OF THE SINO-SOVIET ALLIANCE   96
THE LAUNCHING OF THE SINO-SOVIET POLEMIC   102
ALBANIA AND ALL THAT   105
THE LAOTIAN CRISIS   107
BRIGHT HOPES FOR THE DARK CONTINENT   110
THE HUMBLING OF INDIA   112
THE REVOLUTIONARY TIDE IN SOUTHEAST ASIA   117
THE LAST ROUND WITH KHRUSHCHEV   120

VI   *The Foreign Policy of the Cultural Revolution (1965–68)*   127

THE CAMPAIGN AGAINST KHRUSHCHEV'S SUCCESSORS   128
THE LAUNCHING OF THE CULTURAL REVOLUTION   137
CHINA AND THE CRISIS IN VIETNAM   141
SETBACKS IN THE THIRD WORLD   146
THE RISE AND FALL OF RED GUARD DIPLOMACY   153
CHINESE FOREIGN POLICY IN 1968   156

PART TWO

VII *The Making of Foreign Policy*   165

CONCERNS AND GOALS   165
POLICY DIFFERENCES   179
MILITARY CONSIDERATIONS AND STRATEGY   182
FORMULATION OF POLICY   188
AVAILABLE STRATEGIES AND TACTICS   191
IMPLEMENTATION OF POLICY   201

VIII *Peking and World Communism*   205

SOURCES OF THE SINO-SOVIET DISPUTE   206
THE QUARREL BETWEEN THE CHINESE AND SOVIET PARTIES   208
THE CONFRONTATION BETWEEN THE CHINESE AND SOVIET
    STATES   210
PEKING AND EASTERN EUROPE   212
PEKING AND THE ASIAN PARTIES   219
PEKING, THE OTHER PARTIES, AND THE WORLD MOVEMENT   227

IX   *Peking and Asia*   231

CHINA AS AN ASIAN POWER   231
THE EASTERN FLANK   233
THE SOFT UNDERBELLY   236

X   *Peking and the Third World*   248

   GENERAL CONSIDERATIONS   248
   CHINA AND THE MIDDLE EAST   257
   CHINA AND AFRICA   259
   CHINA AND LATIN AMERICA   261

XI   *Peking and the West*   263

   THE UNITED STATES   264
   THE BRITISH COMMONWEALTH   271
   WESTERN EUROPE   275

PART THREE

XII   *Foreign Policy Since the Cultural Revolution*   283

   THE END OF THE CULTURAL REVOLUTION   283
   THE NORMALIZATION OF EXTERNAL RELATIONS   285
   THE SINO-SOVIET CRUNCH   287
   THE OPENING TO THE UNITED STATES   289
   THE REPERCUSSIONS   293
   PEKING AND JAPAN   295
   PEKING'S OTHER PROBLEM AREAS   298

XIII   *The Balance Sheet and the Outlook*   306

   ACHIEVEMENTS   306
   FAILURES   309
   THE OUTLOOK FOR FOREIGN POLICY   312
   SOME THOUGHTS ON AMERICAN CHINA POLICY   313

Sources and References   323

Suggestions for Further Reading   334

Index   339

Preface to Revised Edition

THE ENTRY OF the People's Republic of China into the United Nations and its globally televised reception of President Nixon have focused public attention on China and its growing role in the world as never before. The Nixon administration has been acting on the assumption that China, if it does not feel threatened by the United States as it has in the past, can be brought to play a constructive rather than a disruptive role in Asia, and perhaps to help design a political settlement for Vietnam. Is this assumption valid? Can the new, more positive, relationship between the United States and China survive if no solution is found to the Vietnam crisis? Are China's tense relations with the Soviet Union likely to get better or worse? Unfortunately, no certain answers can be given to questions such as these, even on the basis of a knowledge of China's foreign policy and foreign relations down to the present. But without such knowledge, there is no possibility of arriving at answers having a sufficient probability of being correct to serve as the basis of policy-making or policy judgments. This book has been written in an effort to convey this knowledge. Aimed primarily at the general reader, it has also been designed to be useful to the student and interesting to the specialist as well.

For roughly the first decade and a half after World War II, international politics appeared to be dominated by the United States and the Soviet Union and the Cold War between them. The recurrent assertiveness of China, notably during the Korean War, was generally assumed in the United States, although less widely in Asia, to be a manifestation of Soviet expansionism. But by about 1960 this assumption, which had never been really correct, became obviously untenable because of the increasingly rude remarks that were flying between Moscow and Peking. Instead, it became clear that China had independent ambitions to become a superpower equipped with nuclear weapons and all the other trappings considered appropriate to that status.

In short, the Cold War became a triangular rather than a two-sided affair, each relationship being an adversary one yet differing from the other two. To each party, its own relations with the others and theirs with each other have become perhaps its most important external problem. None wants to fight a major war with either of the others or has any real interest in seeing them fight each other, yet each dreads a reversion to a two-sided Cold War through a combination of the other two against it. In reality, as far as can be seen, this is not likely to happen. The triangle has varied in shape and will presumably continue to vary as one relationship or another becomes more or less hostile. But a reversion to a two-sided Cold War in which any two of the parties, even the Chinese and Russians, align themselves against the third appears improbable in the near future.

Contemporary China is proverbially a difficult subject to study and understand in any of its major aspects. One reason is of course China's inherent and traditional complexity, including the fabled inscrutability of the Chinese language. Another is the shortage of "hard" information and the difficulties of travel to and in China, which to a greater extent than is generally realized are the product of a decision taken in Peking in 1949 to ring down the Bamboo Curtain on most foreign contacts that cannot be made to serve Chinese propaganda purposes. Another is the typically Communist distortions and omissions that pervade what information, or propaganda, is allowed to become publicly available. (Careful work by foreign analysts employing a variety of techniques, however, including the widely but unjustly ridiculed one of "kremlinology," or the study of esoteric communications and other such evidence, has been surprisingly successful in extracting valuable metal from this low-grade ore.) Another is the peculiarly Chinese phenomenon of the cult of Mao Tse-tung and his "thought," which produces a deceptive homogeneity of public Chinese political statements that is exceptionally great even for a Communist country. Finally, there is the rather strange emotional climate, or rather climates, in which discussion of China and of policy toward China is often conducted, notably in the United States and in American academic circles. On the right, there is a surviving although probably diminishing tendency to see China as a malevolent threat. On the left, there is a growing tendency to see it as an awkward giant driven to misbehavior by uncomprehending American hostility. Neither attitude is helpful to the rational analysis that is needed or the difficult decision-making that probably lies ahead.

This revised edition incorporates significant new material that updates the original to the spring of 1972. The information in the new chapter (XII) on Chinese foreign policy since the Cultural Revolution has not to my knowledge been presented elsewhere in book form. The section (in Chapter XIII) on United States policy toward China has been rewritten to include the Nixon China policy and the President's visit to China. It appears that neither the crisis in Vietnam that erupted in the spring of 1972 nor the Nixon visit to the Soviet Union has so far made any fundamental change in the developing Sino-American relationship described here; more precisely, they have done no more than the escalation of 1965 to drive China and the United States farther apart or China and the Soviet Union closer together. As an aid to students and in response to various colleagues and reviewers, a set of notes to each chapter has been included giving specific sources for that chapter and discussing some problems of interpretation that the general reader might not care to see treated in the text.

The fact that a revised edition of this book has come into being is due to my wife, Virginia.

June 27, 1972

China's Turbulent Quest

CHAPTER I

The Legacy
of China's Past

IT IS OFTEN said that social revolution in the non-Western world is inevitable, and it is sometimes added that the policy of the United States, in effect if not by actual design, tends to oppose this revolution. Without pausing here to examine the second half of this proposition, we may content ourselves with noting the questionability of the first. Modernization is not a very scientific or fruitful concept, and even if it were there would be no assurance of its inevitability. For good or ill, the hand of the past, in the West although much more in the non-West, lies heavy on the present and the future, on the totality of local patterns of thought, feeling, and behavior that are called cultures. In Europe, it was only with the ending of the wars of religion in 1648, and the partial collapse of the cultures they symbolized, that the unprecedented intellectual and technological advances of the next two hundred and fifty years became possible. Even after that, the twentieth-century wars of the modernized nation-states of Europe and of Hitler's and Stalin's new quasi-religious despotisms threatened for a time to usher in a new Dark Age.

To no segment of an all too numerous humanity does the proposition that not all change is progress, and that the past is still a powerful influence, apply with greater force than to the most numerous segment of all, the Chinese. Of all major contemporary cultures, that of China is the oldest; of the world's primary civilizations, the Chinese is the only one that has survived unbroken, although not unchanged, into recent times.

TRADITIONAL CHINA

The area that Europeans have long called China, after the name of its first imperial dynasty, the Ch'in (221–206 B.C.), is a large land mass which, until the invention of modern means of transport, was largely although not totally isolated from other early centers of civilization not only by distance but by mountains, deserts, and the vast expanse of the Pacific. Both its size and its isolation have been crucial factors in the molding of Chinese culture and have contrasted it sharply with the ancient Mediterranean world, a collection of small land areas arranged around a central sea that provided constant and fruitful contact among cultures.

The Chinese are of course the most numerous branch of the so-called yellow or Mongoloid race, whose ancestors lived widely scattered over northeastern Asia during the Old Stone Age. After the end of the Ice Age and in the New Stone Age, perhaps about 5000 B.C., a major migration of Mongoloids from eastern Siberia and Mongolia seems to have occurred into North China, and in particular the valley of the mighty and treacherous Yellow River. Since this region contains the eastern termini of the ancient trade and caravan routes across Central Asia connecting eastern and western Asia, the Chinese (as we may now call them) undoubtedly benefited from many cultural and technological contacts with western Asia, which in the New Stone Age displaced Africa as the culturally most advanced region of the world.

It was from this direction that the Chinese evidently learned one of the major components of their justly famous agricultural technology, which a writer of a generation ago aptly named "permanent agriculture"—namely, the careful control of water. Another component, the cultivation of the high-yielding rice plant, the Chinese learned from their contact with the Thai and Malayo-Polynesian peoples who then inhabited what later became Central and South China. The third component, the careful return to the soil of all available organic waste matter, vegetable, animal, and human, the Chinese seem to have devised on their own. Permanent agriculture has provided the Chinese for the past three millennia with standards of nutrition, health, and vigor that are high by almost any measure and has made possible a rate of population growth sufficient to make the Chinese for many centuries now the most numerous cultural community on earth. To give an approximate illustration: if we assume that the population of China in A.D. 1100 was about 100 million, as seems probable, and that it was 600 million in 1900 (somewhat too high a figure, but one that is close enough to indicate the order of magnitude involved), an average annual growth rate of only 0.2 percent (roughly one-tenth of the rate at which the population of the world, and of China, is currently growing) would have been all that was required; such is the power of compound interest.

On the foundations of permanent agriculture there emerged what was probably the toughest and most durable of the world's popular cultures. By far the majority of its members were peasant farmers organized into tightly knit families, clans (groups of related families bearing the same surname), and villages. Each marketing area, consisting of a central town and the villages it served, was a very nearly self-sufficient unit, except to the extent that war and politics interwove its fluctuating fortunes with those of others. The area that was culturally Chinese, and therefore can be called China, expanded in all directions, but mainly to the south, from its original home in the Yellow River Valley through the intermediacy not only of politics and war but of migration as well. Denser populations and greater power resulting from higher organization created a kind of osmotic pressure in favor of the Chinese and to the disadvantage of their non-Chinese neighbors, who were steadily pushed back, annihilated, or assimilated, as the case might be. Thus China expanded, by conquest, migration, and political integration, until in early modern times something like its natural limits, in the shape of mountains and deserts that barred the way to peasant settlement and cultivation, were reached. Within this vast area, of continental proportions, the distances, geographical obstacles, and pre-Chinese ethnic patterns were varied enough to produce a diversity so considerable that political unity has always been difficult to achieve and even more difficult to maintain. It could never have been achieved at all if there had not emerged a common, overarching elite culture capable of counteracting to a degree what Indians, referring to their own country, call fissiparous tendencies.

As permanent agriculture is the foundation of popular Chinese culture, the main foundation of elite Chinese culture is probably the famous writing system, the despair of students. There is no Chinese spoken language, only a collection of related languages and dialects, but there is a Chinese written language, based on a unique writing system known to all educated members of the elite for the past two and a half millennia. It was devised by the priests of the Shang period (approximately 1500–1100 B.C.) for religious purposes and was then adopted for secular uses as well. Its essential feature is that it is an ideographic system. In other words, each symbol (known as character) represents, not a unit of sound (phoneme), but a unit of meaning (morpheme). Thus it can be, and to some extent has been, independent of the variations in time and space of the spoken language, or rather spoken languages. There are a number of written styles, varying from the extremely terse classical language, which is generally unintelligible even to educated Chinese if read aloud (in other words, if each character is given the pronunciation of the corresponding word in one of the spoken languages), to modern literary Chinese. The latter has virtually converged with the standard spoken language, Mandarin, which is spoken with dialectal variations throughout North China and much of Central and Southwest China. This relative independence of the written language from the spoken languages at any given time meant that it could serve as a common medium for written communication among educated men who could not communicate with each other in a common spoken language, an invaluable asset to unity.

Educated men of traditional China shared not only a common written language but a common philosophy and code of conduct, usually known as Confucianism. Although never complete, the hold of Confucianism on the elite was more secure than on the masses, to whom it was preached by their betters but who often preferred other ways, such as the interesting amalgam of magic and mysticism known as Taoism. To those capable of appreciating it, Confucianism taught the supreme importance of social stability. This was to be achieved essentially by regarding the state as an enlargement of the family, with the ruler cast in the role of the patriarchal family head. Like the latter, the ruler was supposed to exert his authority through example and precept rather than through force. But since most rulers were realistic enough to understand that it would be utopian to try to maintain China's precarious unity solely by means such as this, the actual techniques of imperial rule nearly always included a heavy admixture of regulations and force, which were rendered respectable to a degree by a philosophy usually known as Legalism. The main practitioners of Confucianism were not so much the ruling dynasties as the broader elite, or the gentry, which supported the dynasties and from which the latter often, although by no means invariably, emerged. The main common characteristic of the gentry was its mastery of the written language and the vast literature, notably the so-called Confucian classics, to which it gave rise. Its secondary characteristic was land ownership, although many members of the gentry gained their livelihood by means other than owning land and many Chinese not members of the gentry class owned land. Its tertiary characteristic was public service. Eligibility for entry into the elaborate imperial bureaucracy, although not acquired strictly on the basis of birth, was normally gained through passing an extremely difficult set of examinations on the Confucian classics, which as a rule only members of the gentry would have the incentive or the leisure to master, but as only a minority of the gentry served in the bureaucracy, it was possible to gain entry to the latter by other methods, too. In any case, it was mainly the gentry that provided the institutional cement tending to hold China together during the life cycle of a given dynasty and to carry the country, often in a temporarily fractionated condition, through the intervals between dynasties, when frequently there was a war of all against all.

Although there was of course more to traditional Chinese culture than this, the phenomena just discussed—permanent agriculture, the writing system, Confucianism, the gentry, and the bureaucracy—

came close to constituting what was distinctive about that culture and what differentiated it from its neighbors. If a person or community not of Chinese origin accepted, willingly or unwillingly, not only direct Chinese political control but also the essentials of Chinese culture, he or it could in theory be considered by the Chinese as Chinese, although as usual, practice was never more than a rough approximation of theory. Peoples and states living within the reach of Chinese power that wished to live in peace with it, and yet found it both desirable and feasible to accept Chinese control and Chinese culture only in part, generally considered it wise to fit themselves into the tributary system that the Chinese empire maintained at the times of its greatest influence. In a manner somewhat reminiscent of the Holy Roman Empire, this system to varying degrees combined a recognition of political inferiority and often nominal subordination on the part of the vassal state with trade in the guise of tribute. The Chinese found the relationship agreeable, because it confirmed their deep conviction of their own cultural superiority to all other peoples and sometimes helped to prevent threats to Chinese security; in exchange for these advantages, they were willing and able on occasion to provide protection to the ruling family of the state in question against external enemies or domestic rebels.

At one time or another, most of the states of eastern and central Asia acknowledged themselves to be vassals of the Chinese empire. Japan came very close to being an exception; a vassal relationship to China was acknowledged for only about one hundred years (the mid-fifteenth century to the mid-sixteenth), in spite of the massive cultural borrowing from China that had taken place several centuries earlier. Korea, being weaker and more accessible than Japan, was invaded several times from China and generally accepted Chinese political as well as cultural domination until it came under Japanese control at the end of the nineteenth century. In Southeast Asia there were considerable variations in the relations of the local states with China. The Vietnamese lived under direct Chinese political control, and under Chinese cultural influence, for a millennium until about 900, when they gained substantial independence but remained a tributary state until conquered by France in the late nineteenth century. The numerous and remote Malay states of insular

Southeast Asia maintained no more than token tributary relations and underwent very little Chinese cultural influence, although they were among the targets of a few naval expeditions launched from China in the late thirteenth and early fifteenth centuries. Roughly the same held true, to a lesser degree, of Burma and Siam (Thailand); the warlike Burmese turned back two invasions from China in the late eighteenth century but then found it wise to maintain tributary relations with China until they were themselves subjugated by the British in the late nineteenth century. The Himalayan states were generally protected from Chinese influence by their remoteness and topography, except for such cases as the defeat of the Gurkhas of Nepal by the Manchus in 1792. The nomadic and often warlike peoples of Chinese Central Asia, or the vast arc from Manchuria to Tibet, from time to time gave rise to empires that threatened, invaded, and even on occasion conquered China. Since their way of life rendered them almost impervious to Chinese culture as long as they remained on their own territory, the Chinese saw no way of protecting their own security against the nomads except to conquer and dominate them whenever China's strength permitted, as it did at several periods. The only significantly more fruitful relationship between Chinese and nomad developed when an army of nomadic origin not only invaded China and conquered part or all of it but then set up a Sino-barbarian state whose non-Chinese ruling elite adopted a significant portion of Chinese culture. The most notable example of this category of phenomena were the Manchus, who conquered China in the mid-seventeenth century, rounded out their control over Chinese Central Asia by the mid-eighteenth century, became highly sinicized (culturally Chinese), and established an impressive network of tributary relationships with other Asian states.

Mainly no doubt because they had no close and continuous contact with another center of power and culture comparable to their own, the Chinese early developed a huge sense of their own superiority to the rest of mankind, a feeling sometimes described with the term "ethnocentrism." Although by no means wholly unjustified, this feeling often went to excessive lengths. It tended to visualize China as a united and, culturally at least, homogeneous country, whose neighbors generally regarded it with respect and even affection. Interludes of disunity and weakness were dismissed as exceptions that proved the rule.

The outside observer is under no compulsion, unless it is self-imposed, to accept or reject such claims in their entirety. Enough has already been said in praise of the Chinese tradition so that it is now time to note a few critical deficiencies. In spite of the brilliance that a few Chinese theoretical scientists have demonstrated in recent years, the Chinese tradition was largely lacking in the scientific spirit. It developed wealthy and sometimes powerful merchants, but no free cities under bourgeois control and nothing that could be called capitalism, or a Third Estate. For a combination of reasons, after about 1000 B.C. China's cultural tradition grew increasingly conservative and resistant to new, especially foreign, influences. Its political system, although remarkably effective by traditional standards, also displayed tendencies toward rigidity, perhaps more under the non-Chinese Manchus than would have been the case under a Chinese dynasty. As a result, the political system proved almost completely unable in the nineteenth century to cope with the problems posed by the assertive and more dynamic nations of the West. Finally, as was already suggested, China is in many ways a highly disunited country, in spite of the accepted myth to the contrary. One of the evidences of this underlying disunity is the fact that, in spite of the cultural antiforeignism of the Chinese, since the decline of the Confucian empire and the full force of the Western impact began in the mid-nineteenth century, China has been able to achieve political unity only for brief periods and only under the banner of imported ideologies, although the latter have invariably been sinicized almost beyond recognizability after importation.

It was the novel tests to which the Chinese tradition was subjected in modern times that brought out these critical deficiencies.

MODERN CHINA

By the eighteenth century, China's demographic shoe was beginning to pinch. Population growth had been somewhat accelerated by a number of recent developments, notably the introduction of new food crops like sweet potatoes from the New World by way of the Philippines. Demographic expansion had proceeded to the point where there was little but marginal or uncultivable land left empty within the outer limit of agriculture traced by mountain and desert. Among the inevitable although gradual results of this tendency was a growth of rural tenancy and other sources of rural unrest. Industrialization or the acquisition of fertile new colonies might have eased the situation, as both did for Europe after population growth set in during the eighteenth century following the popularization of the Irish potato, but neither of these safety valves was then available to China. Nor, of course, was population control in any modern form.

During the first half of the nineteenth century, or perhaps a little earlier, the Manchus entered the stage of decline that had also overtaken every other dynasty in Chinese history. The causes of this aspect of the "dynastic cycle," in the case of the Manchus as in that of the others, were complex and somewhat obscure. At the basis were almost certainly deep-seated social and economic processes, apart from the population growth already mentioned, among them a tendency toward concentration of land ownership, the avoidance of taxation by powerful landowners, and the falling of a proportionately greater weight of taxation on the poorer elements of the rural population. The inability of the central government to check this process, in spite of its desire to do so, illustrates another aspect of dynastic decline, the shrinking energy and efficiency of the political system and of the court that presided over it. The Chinese imperial system was a highly centralized one, in theory at least if much less so in practice; if the trumpet from Peking gave forth an uncertain sound, one could expect self-serving vacillation on the part of the bureaucracy.

The decline of the Manchus was greatly complicated by the intrusion of Western influences, although it is impossible to be sure whether it was accelerated or slowed by them on balance. The pre-industrial West came to China in the seventeenth and eighteenth centuries to buy produce (notably tea and silk) from China and to "sell" it Christianity. After considerable initial successes, both processes were placed under severe restrictions from the Chinese side in the eighteenth century in order to prevent the undermining of the Chinese economy first by Western silver and later by Western opium and the undermining of Chinese culture by Jesuit missionaries and Catholicism. In addition, the Manchus refused to treat the European nations and the United States on any other basis except that of the tributary system and insisted on subjecting foreign nationals to the often barbarous rigors of Chinese criminal procedure. The Western countries regarded this relationship as unreasonable, but in general they were prepared to accept it as an unavoidable part of the price of the much-desired China produce as long as the latter remained their chief economic concern and they lacked the means of altering the situation.

The Industrial Revolution made alteration possible, and probably inevitable, by increasing the effectiveness of Western armies and navies and by creating exportable surpluses of manufactured goods, mainly textiles, for which markets must be sought. A tendency promptly arose in the West, one that has never entirely died out, to mistake the size of China's population for a supposedly vast absorptive power of its market. Britain, as the most industrialized and therefore the strongest state in the world, took the lead in breaking down Chinese resistance to expanded foreign contacts, although it was never able or willing to go much farther than that because of its heavy involvement in India. In 1833, at the insistence of the rising Lancashire textile manufacturers, Anglo-Chinese trade was thrown open to private enterprise on the British side instead of being confined as previously to the semiofficial British East India Company; it remained to open trade similarly on the Chinese side. This was done by the so-called Opium War of 1839–42. After that, and progressively over the ensuing half century, China was forced by military and diplomatic pressures to permit relatively free trade with the outside world subject only to a nominal tariff fixed by treaty, to tolerate the opium trade, to agree to foreign residence and business activity amounting to control in a number of "treaty ports," to allow foreigners to be subject to their own rather than to Chinese law, to legalize Christian missionary activity, and to sanction the transformation of many of its tributary states into Western or Japanese dependencies.

It is difficult to say with confidence whether China was better or worse off for this experience; in any case, something of the sort was probably inevitable. We need not accept in full the Leninist concept of imperialism in order to recognize that the power and expansiveness (not exclusively military) of the modern West have been so great that it has been impossible for any significant part of the world to avoid being affected by them. If one accepts the reasonable, but not incontestable, proposition that the best way out for an object of this process is evolution into a "modernized" nation-state and ignores the more or less insoluble question of whether China would have been better off if it had become some-one's outright colony after the manner of India, one can see that some of the effects of the Western impact on China were bene-ficial and others harmful. Through its contacts with the West, China acquired an introduction to modern science and technology, modern Western economic and political institutions and to a lesser extent the outlook that paralleled them, and Western literature and culture in general (including Christianity). Such contacts were a necessary, although not a sufficient, condition for China's evolution into a modern nation-state. On the other hand, it cannot be doubted that until the twentieth century the Western impact was so powerful as to eliminate any possibility of China's completing the transition to nationhood, because China would not have been permitted to acquire and exercise full national sovereignty even if it had been capable of doing so. In addition, the Western impact undermined the self-confidence and prestige of the Confucian tradition and engendered in nearly all politically conscious Chinese a sense of frustrating and infuriating helplessness. From being the central, and in its own eyes the only significant, unit in its own traditional world, China had been suddenly reduced to a mere object of a new set of international forces created and manipulated by the alien West and the upstart Japanese.

It was under extremely complex and difficult circumstances, then, that some members of the Chinese elite tried to evolve a creative and effective response, or adaptation, to the challenge posed by the West. The Manchu dynasty was almost foreclosed from doing so, both by its own conservatism and by the fear of losing the essential support of the largely conservative Chinese gentry. The only Chi-nese emperor to attempt something of a reform program was promptly (in 1898) deposed in all but name by his powerful and formidable aunt, the famous Empress Dowager. When she herself inaugurated a similar program a few years later, after the humiliation of another defeat by the Western powers as a consequence of the Boxer Rebellion (1900), it was too late to save the dynasty. In particular, she made what was probably a major mistake by abolishing the traditional civil service examinations (in 1905), rather than modernizing them gradually, and thus drastically weakening the politically indispensable ties between the dynasty and the gentry.

In addition to the abolition of the civil service examination system, the year 1905 witnessed a number of other important developments as well. By defeating Russia, Japan validated its credentials as the strongest power in eastern Asia and the inspiration of Asian nationalists and revolutionaries, and the Manchu government decided to send a sizable number of young Chinese to study in Japan. This was a logical but dangerous decision, since many of these students proceeded to organize and agitate against Manchu rule. In fact, it was on the foundation of anti-Manchu Chinese students in Japan that Sun Yat-sen founded, also in 1905, his first important revolutionary organization, the T'ung Meng Hui. Sun also built up sufficient support among overseas Chinese elsewhere and in China itself so that, when the Manchus collapsed in early 1912, he was elected Provisional President of the Republic of China by an assembly of revolutionaries meeting at Nanking.

The ensuing years brought the patriotic but ineffective Sun and his party, now known as the Kuomintang (National People's Party) little but frustration. Power was seized in 1913–14 by Yuan Shih-k'ai, the ablest of the remaining former high officials under the Manchus, and he exercised it ruthlessly until his death in 1916. In the meanwhile, the regions of Chinese Central Asia, notably Outer Mongolia, which had refused to pay to the Republic the allegiance that they had owed to the Manchus, had begun to drift away and come under increasing foreign influence: Manchuria under Russian and Japanese, Outer Mongolia and Sinkiang under Russian, and Tibet under British. In 1915 the Japanese, who disliked Yuan Shih-k'ai because they preferred to see China disunited and vulnerable to their pressures, compelled him to accept part of an outrageous set of conditions known as the Twenty-One Demands. China's formal entry into the First World War in 1917, at the suggestion of the

United States, entitled it to a seat at the peace conference and might have helped it to undo the Twenty-One Demands, but a pro-Japanese clique was then in control of the increasingly ineffectual Republican government in Peking. In the spring of 1919 a nationalistic student demonstration in Peking with nationwide repercussions, known as the May Fourth Movement, compelled the government despite its pro-Japanese sympathies to refuse to sign the Treaty of Versailles, which ratified the concessions that Japan had gained in 1915. China had to tolerate continued Japanese enjoyment of these concessions, nevertheless, until they were liquidated by the Washington Conference in 1922.

With the death of Yuan Shih-k'ai, China ceased to know any effective central authority. The government in Peking became a largely nominal one. The provinces were generally controlled with a heavy hand by their provincial governors, or warlords, and in some regions a particularly powerful man would succeed in dominating a group of provinces. Foreign economic and political influence persisted at a high level, not only in Chinese Central Asia but in the coastal regions of China Proper. In fact, it was mainly in and near the treaty ports that there occurred whatever constructive or progressive developments, such as the gowth of a politically conscious industrial working class, existed in the China of the warlord period. Elsewhere there was mainly stagnation, or even retrogression.

In 1917 Sun Yat-sen established a revolutionary regime at Canton in rivalry with the recognized government at Peking. He continued to experience repeated frustrations, notably a violent falling out with the local warlord in 1922. These setbacks made Sun increasingly receptive to new ideas, especially those propounded to him by certain emissaries of Lenin's Comintern (Communist International) who began to make contact with him in 1922. The Comintern had come to regard Sun's Kuomintang as a valuable potential ally in Moscow's struggle to promote a revolutionary and anti-imperialist China as a counterweight to the Western powers and Japan, which were considered by the young Soviet regime as its main enemies. Sun had grown somewhat anti-Western, although not anti-Japanese, and furthermore he saw the value of Comintern aid and support in his struggle to unite China under the control of his own party. He therefore agreed to accept Soviet advisers, funds, and arms but to form an alliance with the young Communist Party of China (CPC), as the Comintern wished, only if its members also joined the Kuomintang as individuals and agreed to accept its discipline. On this basis the alliance between the Kuomintang and the Comintern was concluded in 1923. The Kuomintang was soon overhauled, with Soviet advice, along the centralized lines of the Soviet party and equipped for the first time with an indoctrinated and reasonably effective army. In this increasingly formidable organization, Communists played a surprisingly active and effective role at all levels.

After Sun Yat-sen's death in 1925 the largest share of his power passed to the party's military commander, General Chiang Kai-shek. In spite of the Comintern's reservations, Chiang launched the so-called Northern Expedition in mid-1926 to begin the military unification of China that Sun had regarded as an essential preliminary to the political modernization of the country. By this time Chiang was seriously concerned over what he regarded as the danger of Soviet control from above and Communist-led social revolution from below and had decided to protect his party from both dangers. In the spring of 1927, when the Northern Expedition had won impressive victories over its warlord opponents with the help of a wave of antiforeign nationalism then sweeping China and had reached the Yangtze Valley, Chiang crushed the Communist-controlled unions and peasant organizations in the coastal provinces of the Yangtze region and compelled his more leftist colleagues, who were based upriver at Hankow, to break off their alliance with the Comintern and the CPC and accept his authority. In mid-1928, in spite of Japanese opposition, he took Peking and proclaimed a new Kuomintang-controlled Republic of China with its capital at Nanking.

After a decade of chaos, unity was easier to proclaim than to achieve. In reality, the new government controlled little but the provinces of the lower Yangtze Valley. Elsewhere, things remained much as they had been since the death of Yuan Shih-k'ai, except for the Communist-controlled areas and Manchuria. In the latter case, a patriotic warlord, Chang Hsueh-liang, accepted Nanking's authority and thereby enraged the Japanese military authorities who had dominated southern Manchuria since 1905. Manchuria, further-more, was filling up with Chinese immigrants, and it seemed to the Japanese Army that its powerful position in Manchuria would soon be eroded unless it struck. It therefore seized all of Manchuria in 1931–32; by this action it put an end to a Soviet sphere of influ-ence in northern Manchuria and touched off a major international crisis.

In spite of this major setback, Chiang Kai-shek's government was making some progress toward national unity and development. Communications and finances were improved. A large and expensive army, trained in part under German advisers, was used not only to fight the Communists in South China but also to overawe or dis-place some of Chiang's non-Communist rivals in that region. Some of the rights gained by the foreign powers under the "unequal treaties" of the nineteenth century were abrogated. Meanwhile, the continued presence of Chiang's German advisers began to be threatened by the conclusion of the anti-Comintern Pact between Germany and Japan, and Stalin became increasingly alarmed at Japan's expansionist tendencies and impressed by Chiang's skill at coping with his domestic rivals by political and military means. In 1936 the Soviet ambassador in Nanking began a series of secret talks that eventuated in August 1937, after Chiang had convinced Stalin that he would resist Japan, in a Sino-Soviet nonaggression pact and a military aid agreement. Most of the military aid that Chiang Kai-shek's government received from that time until Pearl Harbor was of Soviet origin.

In spite of the fact that it was by far the strongest single political entity in China, Chiang Kai-shek's government had a serious weak-ness in that it did not control most of the rural areas and was afraid of social revolution, or even social change. In the areas under its control, it dealt severely not only with suspected Communists but with any others who criticized it. In the countryside, it allowed itself to remain largely dependent on the support of local vested interests, so that it was foreclosed from doing anything effective for the peasants. These conservative tendencies, combined with growing ideological sterility, alienated the Kuomintang from many of the intellectuals and tended to drive them closer to the Communists.

Not satisfied with seizing Manchuria and beginning to build a major heavy industrial base there, the Japanese Army soon began to put pressures on the Soviet Far East and China Proper, both of which it would have liked to dominate. The Soviet Union fought back effectively, however, in a series of border clashes in 1937–39, and Japan signed a neutrality pact with the Soviet Union in April 1941 in order to free its hands for an advance into Southeast Asia. Japan's pressures on China were more effective, and its influence grew rapidly in much of North China and Inner Mongolia. On the other hand, Chinese public pressure on Chiang to stop fighting the Communists and appeasing the Japanese and to begin resisting the latter also increased. The Communists shared in this clamor and benefited from it, although it was with some reluctance that they decided in 1936 to conform to the demands of Stalin and Chinese public opinion and cooperate at least nominally with the Kuomintang in a joint resistance to Japan.

Fully aware of this trend, the Japanese Army began major military operations at key points along the China coast in the summer of 1937. Chiang's troops and those of the Communists fought bravely and even victoriously on occasion, but they could not withstand the superior firepower of the Japanese forces. By the end of 1938 the Japanese controlled the major cities of eastern China and the lines of communication linking them. They attempted in 1940 with little success to set up a puppet government at Nanking, but their real hope was that Chiang Kai-shek, who had retreated inland to Chungking, would come to terms with them. This he was unwilling to do, and after Pearl Harbor a considerable volume of American aid and support eliminated any chance that he might waver. His only moment of serious danger came in late 1944, when Japanese forces staged a last major offensive in South China. East of the Japanese lines, Communist guerrilla units operated successfully in many areas, but the Kuomintang was never able to duplicate their performance.

Occupied China suffered devastating damage at the hands of the Japanese, especially during the initial fighting. Millions of people fled to the Nationalist (Kuomintang) areas. In the latter, the regime grew more conservative, corrupt, and ineffective as the war went on. It believed that the United States would not allow it to be crushed by Japan and would in fact crush Japan sooner or later.

The Nationalists therefore made few efforts against Japan, which would have been difficult and costly but also might have validated their claim to national leadership, and husbanded their forces, the best of which were trained and equipped by the United States, for a later struggle with the Communists. Victory over Japan and a founding role in the United Nations Organization, accompanied by a permanent seat on the Security Council, were both presented to the Nationalists by the United States and could do little to offset the inflation, war-weariness, and loss of self-confidence and public support that had overtaken the Nationalists by the end of the war.

Being reasonably well aware of the weaknesses in the Nationalist position, the United States began in 1944 to bring about some sort of collaboration between them and the Communists, so as to make a more effective prosecution of the struggle with Japan possible and minimize the chances of a civil war after Japan's defeat. The collapse of Japan in August 1945 lent an urgent priority to this project, and at the end of the year President Truman sent General George C. Marshall to China to try to stave off civil war and work out a democratic coalition government embracing the Communists as well as other non-Nationalist parties. Stalin added his voice, in private conversation with Chinese Communist representatives, against civil war and in favor of a political and military coalition, mainly it appears because he did not want to risk being dragged into a confrontation with the United States over China. The idea of a coalition was doomed from the start, however; each side basically wanted to resume the struggle with the other, and even while its patron, the United States or the Soviet Union as the case might be, kept troops on Chinese soil (until the late spring of 1946), it would go only so far as to propose terms that it could feel sure the other would not accept. After the withdrawal of American and Soviet forces civil war broke out in earnest, mainly in Manchuria.

For a variety of reasons, including its strategic location and resources, Manchuria was the major initial prize for both sides. In addition to the general disadvantages suffered by a government, especially one weakened by eight years of war, in fighting an entrenched and powerful insurgent movement, the Nationalists were disadvantaged by the long distance separating Manchuria from their main bases in the Yangtze Valley. The Communists, on the other hand, had their main bases in Northwest China and could communicate with Manchuria across Inner Mongolia with reasonable ease. Superior leadership, strategy, tactics, and logistics, combined with a more flexible approach to the local population, soon gave the Communists an advantage, and by the end of 1948 it was all over in Manchuria.

Meanwhile, the Nationalist home front had been rocked by astronomical inflation and political unrest. In the spring of 1948 the Kuomintang put into effect a new and supposedly democratic constitution, but Chiang Kai-shek was elected President, the more democratic provisions were suspended on account of the emergency, and it soon became clear that little had changed. The alienation of the middle-of-the-road elements, notably the intellectuals, from the Kuomintang continued at an accelerating pace, especially as the Communists began to win major military victories in 1948.

In the early months of 1949 the military balance tipped irreversibly in favor of the Communists as they took Peking and Tientsin and cleared the way to the Yangtze Valley. The latter region fell in the spring, and the rest of mainland, except for Tibet, before the end of the year. The Chinese People's Republic (CPR) was proclaimed at Peking on October 1, 1949.

THE RISE OF CHINESE COMMUNISM

The main reasons why the Nationalists became the first major regime to be overthrown by a Communist insurgency were the Japanese invasion and their own errors, but the Communists themselves obviously played an important role.

By the time of the First World War, most politically conscious Chinese were convinced that their country badly needed economic modernization and social revolution. They further tended to conclude from the failure of Western-style parliamentary institutions in China after 1912, the concessions made by the Western powers to Japan at China's expense at the end of the war, and foreign support for various of the warlords in the 1920s that the "imperialist" powers were an unhelpful and even hostile influence and must be combatted. It is not surprising, therefore, that some of them responded favorably to the seemingly similar arguments that emanated from Moscow after 1917. To contrast Soviet policy as strongly as possible with that of the Western powers and Japan, Lenin in July 1919 renounced all special privileges that the tsarist government had gained at China's expense. The fact that the Soviet Union detached Outer Mongolia from Chinese influence a few years later and regained the tsarist government's hold over the strategic Chinese Eastern Railway across northern Manchuria did not lead many Chinese to pin the imperialist label on Moscow. For the Soviet Union was working against, not with, the "imperialist" powers, in China as elsewhere.

Lenin founded the Third, or Communist, International (Comintern) in 1919 as a means of asserting the leadership of his own party and government over other Communist parties and of implementing his program for world revolution. He visualized a revolutionary center in Moscow directing a series of "proletarian" (Communist-led) revolutions in "the West" (the developed countries) and a series of "national" (bourgeois-led) revolutions in "the East" (the underdeveloped countries). Although Communist parties were to be formed in the latter, and in many cases actually were formed, their proletariat was considered too weak, except in Japan, to lead the anti-"imperialist" revolution. They must therefore support revolutionary, anti-"imperialist," "national bourgeois" parties until the time should come, possibly as a result of a "proletarian" revolution in Japan—the only "imperialist" power among the countries of Asia—when they could assert their own leadership.

In the case of China, as we have seen, the Comintern selected the Kuomintang as the anti-"imperialist" party that would receive its support. The young Communist Party of China (CPC), formed in July 1921, was told by a Comintern representative a year later to enter the Kuomintang on Sun Yat-sen's terms and concentrate on organizing and manipulating mass organizations (labor and peasant unions). It was hoped that after building a power base in this way the Communist members of the Kuomintang could influence the latter's policies in a leftward direction and ultimately acquire a leading role in it. These trends actually made some headway by 1926, and even more during the Northern Expedition, but they were largely interrupted by Chiang Kai-shek's military coup and police terror of 1927.

In the process of being forced to break first with Chiang Kai-shek and then with the Kuomintang as a whole, the Comintern, which had been controlled by Stalin since about the time of Lenin's death in 1924, and the CPC, whose original Secretary General Ch'en Tu-hsiu was purged as a scapegoat for the break with Chiang, in-augurated a series of armed risings. Although there is no doubt that Stalin approved of them in principle, it appears that the times and places were determined by the leadership on the spot, sometimes including local representatives of the Comintern, rather than by Stalin himself or even by the central leadership of the CPC. These risings were all disastrous failures, and by the end of 1927 little remained of the Chinese Communist movement but a leadership huddled in Shanghai, still in touch with and loyal to the Comintern, and a few groups of Communist agitators and soldiers in various places in Central and South China. In time, some of these evolved into Communist-controlled base areas, or "soviets."

After appraising the debacle for a few months, Stalin summoned the main leaders of the CPC to Moscow in the spring of 1928 for a congress (the party's sixth) that he could fully control. The line that he imposed on the Chinese party, as on all other Communist parties at about the same time, was to struggle against rather than cooperate with nationalist movements and parties, to launch intense class struggle (strikes, etc.), and to prepare actively for armed revolt when the situation should permit. In the case of China, rural organization and agitation of the kind already in progress was recognized as permissible and promising; in addition, efforts were to be made to rebuild a Communist political base in the cities. Control of the party passed into the hands of the energetic and over-bearing Li Li-san, who decided prematurely in early 1930 that the time had come to recapture some of the key cities of the Yangtze Valley with Red Army units based in the hinterland of Central China. The effort was a disastrous failure, and by the end of the year the Comintern had felt compelled to remove Li and summon him to Moscow for investigation and re-education. Control over the central apparatus (the Central Committee) of the party, whose headquarters was located in Shanghai where it received instructions and funds from the Comintern, then passed into the hands of an inexperienced group of young men just back from Moscow and therefore usually known as the Returned Students. Although anxious both to please Stalin and to bring the party's rural base areas under control, they ultimately succeeded in doing neither. The Comintern press continued to shower praise on Mao Tse-tung, the party's principal rural leader, and there was no practical way for the Returned Students to bring the rural areas under control. The attempt was made beginning in 1931, when Shanghai was rendered too hot to hold the Central Committee by a series of Nationalist police raids, but with only partial success.

Mao Tse-tung, a man of activist temperament and great political intelligence, had had a fairly typical career for a Chinese Communist of that period, first as a rebellious student and then as a labor and peasant organizer during the period of the Kuomintang-Communist alliance. After the collapse of the alliance, he made his base in the hinterland of his native province of Hunan and its neighboring province of Kiangsi. He soon realized that if Communist-controlled rural base areas were to survive in a sea of hostile Nationalist and provincial generals, let alone grow so as ultimately to encompass the entire country, they must be held by armies capable of defending them. In short, the leaders of the Communist bases must play Chinese military politics much like any warlord, but do it more intelligently. He selected the province of Kiangsi as the weak point in the checkerboard of warlord holdings and accordingly made his main base there. He and his colleagues defended his base successfully, by means of guerrilla warfare, against a variety of enemies, including four major campaigns launched by Chiang Kai-shek beginning in 1930. The raising of effective guerrilla forces, dependent almost by definition on popular support, necessitated a flexible policy of social revolution to give the poorer peasants a sense of stake in the Communist regime. Mao experimented accordingly, and with considerable success, with various types of land redistribution, without employing undue violence against landlords. After 1931 he soon understood, more clearly than most of his colleagues, that the party's future depended on its success in associating with and manipulating to its own advantage the tide of anti-Japanese nationalism then rising in China.

By 1930 Mao was clearly the most prominent of the CPC's rural leaders. At the end of the year he consolidated his position in Kiangsi by rooting out forcibly a group of opponents who were allegedly loyal to Li Li-san, some of whom may have objected to Mao's willingness to carry the mobility implicit in guerrilla warfare to the point of abandoning friendly villages readily to the Nationalists, under the slogan of "luring the enemy in deep." In 1931 most of the Returned Students came from Shanghai to Kiangsi, and for the first time since the mid-1920s nearly all the party's leaders found themselves in the same place. In November 1931 a Central Soviet Government for all the Communist base areas was proclaimed at Juichin, in Kiangsi, in at least nominal rivalry with Chiang Kai-shek's government at Nanking, and Mao was elected its Chairman. During the next three years he evidently had some disagreements with the Returned Students over military strategy, policy toward the Japanes threat, and above all agrarian policy, and he probably suffered some erosion of his previously nearly complete ascendancy in Kiangsi, but he remained an active member of the leadership and in fact probably its most important single member.

By 1934 Chiang Kai-shek had eliminated the other major Communist base in Central China and was surrounding the Kiangsi soviet with an enormous army of close to a million men. Under these circumstances it is unlikely that the far smaller Communist forces could have survived no matter what strategy they adopted, and it is perhaps not surprising that in their desperation they shifted from guerrilla to positional warfare, with disastrous results. In mid-October, however, most of what was left of the Communist forces in Kiangsi and their civilian colleagues succeeded in bribing their way past some provincial units in the Nationalist blockading force and made their escape to the southwest. So began the famous Long March.

By the end of 1934 the marchers were in Southwest China, near the large and fertile province of Szechuan. There was a powerful Szechuanese group within the party leadership, and its members apparently argued for making the party's new base in that province. Mao opposed the idea, partly it would seem because he correctly judged that the warlords in Szechuan were too strong, partly because he did not want to see the party controlled by his Szechuanese colleagues, and partly because he preferred to be closer to the area of Japanese incursions in North China. Those who agreed with Mao accompanied him through incredible hardships to northern Shensi, where they arrived in October 1935. They were joined a year later by a dissident force under Mao's main rival at that time, Chang Kuo-t'ao; this army had been badly defeated by a Moslem force on its way to Shensi, and Chang's power had been accordingly weakened to the point where Mao had little trouble in ousting him from the party in 1938.

In 1932, as Chiang Kai-shek continued to temporize with Japan, the CPC launched an intensive anti-Japanese propaganda campaign designed to mobilize Chinese public support for itself and thereby weaken Nationalist pressures on the party if possible and even to start a political movement that might lead to the actual overthrow of Chiang Kai-shek. All Chinese, including dissident Kuomintang members, were invited to form a united front with the CPC against Chiang and his supporters, although on the few occasions when some other group attempted something of the sort the CPC displayed a marked lack of good faith. It wanted instruments, not allies. By 1936 Chiang Kai-shek had begun to show a more anti-Japanese attitude and greater effectiveness in coping with his domestic opponents, the Communists included. Accordingly, Stalin began secret negotiations with him for a pact, and the CPC moderated its line on Chiang and on social revolution, although in an inconsistent fashion that suggested disagreement within the leadership. Chiang, for his part, tried to continue his military campaigns against the Communists, but some of his troops, especially certain units that had been driven out of Manchuria by the Japanese, had become susceptible to the Communist appeal for some sort of anti-Japanese united front.

From these conflicting attitudes there erupted on December 12, 1936, the famous Sian Incident. Chiang Kai-shek was seized by the troops of his Manchurian commander, Chang Hsueh-liang, at the Northwest China city of Sian and held prisoner for two weeks in an effort to make him join the CPC in a national resistance to Japan. When the astonished CPC leadership, located not far to the north, heard the news, it had three possible lines of action open to it; each one seems to have had some supporters within the party.

It could denounce Chiang's kidnapping and his captors and even support a punitive expedition that was then being prepared by Nanking, which was the line that the Soviet press was taking. It could, at the other extreme, demand Chiang's liquidation, as some of his captors (but not Chang Hsueh-liang) were urging. Or it could send a delegation to negotiate some sort of settlement with Chiang, preferably along the lines being urged by Chang Hsueh-liang, and trust in Chiang's good faith for its implementation, which was the policy actually adopted, and probably favored by Mao Tse-tung. As it turned out, an agreement, but only a very general and informal one, for a cessation of civil war and a joint resistance to Japan was reached between Chiang and the CPC. Neither this agreement nor the idea of a Soviet pact with the Nanking government, however, took final form until the late summer of 1937, after Chiang's stout although unsuccessful resistance to the Japanese at Shanghai had given a seemingly convincing pledge of his good faith. At that time he got a nonaggression pact and a military aid program from Stalin and a pledge of military support and political cooperation from the CPC in exchange for a grant of civil liberties that would permit peaceful Communist activities within the Nationalist areas.

The Sino-Japanese War confronted the Chinese Communist leadership with some major decisions, on the outcome of which the future of the party was likely to depend. Some party leaders seem to have agreed with Stalin that the party should support Chiang Kai-shek loyally, at least until the defeat of Japan. Mao Tse-tung, however, insisted that the party should observe little more than the outward formalities of cooperation with the Kuomintang and fight the Japanese no harder than might prove safe and useful to do, but that it should use the techniques of guerrilla warfare and peasant organization developed in Kiangsi to expand Communist influence and power wherever accessible weak spots appeared in either the Kuomintang or the Japanese positions. However, in order to avoid the charge of treason in wartime, the party's activities should be carried out in the name of opposition to the Japanese alone. In short, revolutionary political and military struggle against the domestic opponent should be conducted in the shadow of the more popular struggle against the foreign invader. Any resulting strains on the nominal united front between the Communists and the Nationalists could be blamed on "reactionary" elements among the latter, who could be accused of seeking to come to terms with Japan. As he indicated in an interview with the American newspaperman Edgar Snow in 1936, Mao correctly expected Japan to bring on its own defeat by expanding its war in China into a general war in the Pacific. In the course of this titanic struggle the CPC could expand its power and quietly emancipate itself from what remained of Stalin's influence over its internal affairs and policies without having to break with him openly or even forfeit all of his approval and support.

In 1937 and 1938 Mao was able to carry a majority of his leading colleagues with him, and the strategy adopted was therefore his. The CPC expanded its military and political activities eastward from Northwest China into the North China Plain and in the process came into conflict not only with the Japanese but with the Nationalists. By the spring of 1939, armed clashes with Nationalist troops had begun and the Kuomintang had commenced to impose a partial blockade of the Communist areas. The blockade soon necessitated austerity measures and increased economic mobilization of the peasants in the Communist areas. Partly in order to prevent unrest from ensuing and partly to form as favorable a contrast as possible with the deteriorating political and economic conditions in the Kuomintang areas, the CPC also introduced some elective institutions, which while seemingly democratic were actually skillfully controlled by the party. Land reform and other manifestations of class struggle were kept at a level just low enough not to drive away the wealthier and more skilled elements of the rural population or make it appear that the CPC was breaking its promise to the Nationalists and yet just high enough to retain the support of the poorer peasants.

As the party's membership and the population of its expanding base areas grew, serious problems of indoctrination and control arose. Accordingly, Mao launched a "rectification" campaign about the middle of 1939 to cope with these problems, as well as, perhaps, to deal under cover of the larger campaign with the objections of party leaders who like Stalin were distressed that the adoption of Mao's strategic formula had led to open fighting with the Nationalists. An obscure but evidently serious crisis within the party leadership began after Stalin's armistice with Japan in mid-September 1939 and the proclamation of a Japanese-sponsored puppet government, claiming to be that of China, early in 1940. Mao's opponents may well have argued that Mao's strategy was no longer a feasible one; the Japanese could not be attacked, politically or militarily, as openly as before without fear of Stalin's wrath, and further attacks on the Kuomintang might drive it to reach an accommodation on an anti-Communist platform with the puppet government in Nanking. This debate, which seems to have seriously inconvenienced Mao, who was unwilling to modify his strategy beyond making flattering statements calculated to mollify Stalin, was probably the source of the CPC's decision to attempt its largest single military operation of the war. For some months it had been harassed by Japanese encirclement tactics in the North China plain; now (on August 20, 1940, the anniversary of the beginning of the final and successful Soviet offensive against the Japanese in Outer Mongolia in 1939) it launched the so-called Hundred Regiments Offensive, one of whose purposes was probably to disrupt Stalin's moves toward an accommodation with Japan. The political result was negligible; Stalin signed a neutrality pact with Japan in April 1941. The military result was a disastrous defeat for the Eighth Route Army, as the Chinese Communist forces in North China were then known.

The CPC was saved from excessive Soviet interference and Japanese pressures by events elsewhere. The German invasion of the Soviet Union in June 1941 gave the CPC, like other Communist parties, considerably greater autonomy with respect to Moscow. Japan's initiation of war in the Pacific in December 1941 tended to divert its attention increasingly to that area and away from China. American political support for and aid to the Kuomintang after Pearl Harbor made it increasingly improbable that Chiang Kai-shek would be pressured into an accommodation with Nanking by Communist or any other pressures. Conditions were once more relatively favorable for Mao's wartime strategy, for his efforts to cut down Stalin's influence on the party, and therefore for his own rise to unchallenged power within it.

By 1942 Japanese military pressures on the Communist areas in

North China began to ease, and after 1943 the Communist forces expanded in many parts of eastern China, usually at the expense of the Nanking puppet government's forces and with the aid of the intense anti-Japanese feelings created among the peasants by Japanese atrocities. By the end of 1944 the CPC controlled some twenty base areas containing between 60 and 100 million people and had an army of close to a million men. In the process, there were clashes with the Nationalists, who were so alarmed by the CPC's growth that they launched attacks on it at two seemingly favorable times: in early 1941, after the failure of the Hundred Regiments Offensive, and again in 1943, when Stalin had dissolved the Comintern and thereby seemingly indicated that he no longer cared much about the fate of the CPC.

Actually, Stalin meant no such thing, and his press quickly began to criticize the Kuomintang publicly, for the first time since 1937, in order to correct the impression. Nevertheless, the dissolution of the Comintern in May 1943 did have the effect of removing a check on Mao's rise to power. Up to that time, Mao had busied himself mainly with politico-military strategy and territorial administration and had thus built up an impressive base of power and support from which he became after about 1930 clearly the most important single leader in the party, but he had never put himself formally at the head of the party apparatus. The fact that he did so, although without publicity, in June 1943, the month after the dissolution of the Comintern, with the title of Chairman of the Central Committee, strongly suggests that up to that time he had been anxious not to put himself in a position so closely related to Stalin that he could not avoid choosing between defying Stalin and bowing to him, neither of which he wished to do. This dilemma having been eliminated and Mao having at last assumed a title corresponding to his real position in the party, he began to make the latter unassailable. Already, in early 1942, he had launched a major "rectification" campaign aimed mainly at intellectuals but also designed to provide a suitable cover for political pressures on his opponents. At the same time, there began a cult of Mao and his "thought" in Chinese Communist propaganda and schools that has continued at a rising pitch down to the present. At the end of 1943 a new, Maoist, version of party history began to be propounded, according to which Mao was not responsible for the military disasters in Kiangsi or on the early leg of the Long March, because most of his power had been taken away in some unexplained fashion by the Central Committee leaders who had come down from Shanghai. But then, in the same unexplained fashion, Mao had assumed the leadership of the party and the army at the beginning of 1935. Mao's position at the head of the party was legitimated, in a manner reminiscent of Stalin's after the Purges but far less bloody, at the CPC's Seventh Congress in the spring of 1945, where a new party constitution declaring his "thought," together of course with Marxism-Leninism, to be the CPC's ideological base.

Chinese Communist political strategy at the end of the war was dominated by two decisions: that of the United States not to invade China in the course of finishing off Japan and that of the Soviet Union to invade Manchuria and part of North China in order to insure itself a major role in the postwar settlement. Clearly, a major Soviet military presence in the vicinity of its main base areas would be a major factor for the CPC to reckon with. Since Stalin was anxious to avoid a military clash with the United States, such as might arise out of an open outbreak of civil war in China after the defeat of Japan, he wanted the CPC to seek a coalition with the Nationalists once more, rather than fighting them, and to work toward ultimate power by political means. For its part, the CPC saw certain attractions in an arrangement, if it could be worked out, that would leave them the substance of control over their base areas but would give them freedom of political activity in the Nationalist areas, where they could rely on the Kuomintang's incompetence and their own wartime popularity to benefit them. Such a situation would also render them less easily controllable by the Soviet Union. Accordingly, late in 1944 the CPC began to propose a coalition government along these lines. The United States, which was anxious to stave off civil war, which it correctly thought would increase the chances of the Kuomintang's collapse, also favored such a coalition as the best alternative and mediated unsuccessfully in an effort to bring one into being. On the other hand, the CPC was not overly optimistic about getting a coalition on its own terms and was prepared to fight if it could not. The Kuomintang, for its part, was under such political pressure that it had to agree to discuss a coalition, but it did so with obvious lack of enthusiasm and a clear preference for a military solution. Its leaders did not realize that their position had been so eroded by the war with Japan that theirs was soon to become the first major government to be overthrown by a Communist insurgency.

This outcome was due mainly to the impact of the Japanese invasion on Nationalist China, to the Kuomintang's failings, and to the CPC's own performance (including the leadership and strategy of Mao Tse-tung). The Soviet Union unquestionably played some role, partly by providing ideological inspiration and a degree of political guidance and partly by aiding the CPC in a variety of ways to establish itself in Manchuria in the months following the Japanese surrender in August 1945, but the Soviet role was certainly of far less importance in determining the outcome than were the three major factors just mentioned. The same can be said, even more strongly, of the United States, which was not always very wise or effective in its aid to the Nationalists or in its efforts at the end of the war to mediate between them and the Communists, but which can hardly be accused with any real justification of having contributed materially to the Communist victory.

This victory, and the circumstances of the final years in which it was won, exerted a major influence on the Chinese Communist outlook on foreign policy and foreign affairs. Mao's own belief, and the belief of most members of his party and of many non-Communist Chinese, in his wisdom and indeed infallibility seemed to find confirmation in the resounding Communist triumph. Fresh impetus was given to a favorite idea of Mao's—expressed for example in a message sent by the CPC to the so-called Calcutta Youth Conference of February 1948, a meeting at which plans were laid for Communist-led armed risings in various parts of Asia—the idea that the revolutionary experience of the Chinese Communist movement, at least as interpreted by Mao, constituted the best model for similar movements elsewhere in Asia and in fact in the whole developing world; the essence of the model was guerrilla warfare combined with anti-"imperialist" political appeals. Of more immediate importance was the fact that the CPC counted on receiving continued ideological and political support, military protection, and economic and military aid from the Soviet Union as the result of a close alliance. Finally, for a number of reasons, including an ideological belief in the existence of an "imperialist camp" led by the United States, a felt need for a political demon to facilitate domestic political control and mobilization, a desire to isolate the Chinese people from contacts with the United States, and a resentment of American intervention in the Chinese civil war, Mao had already decided by 1949 that the CPC must maintain a policy of hostility toward the United States and not establish diplomatic relations with it. These three attitudes, toward the developing world, the Soviet Union, and the United States, were to persist and to color the whole of Communist China's foreign policy.

SOME INHERITED ATTITUDES

Behind these basic external strategies lie some fundamental political emotions and attitudes acquired by modern Chinese elites, and the Chinese Communist leadership in particular, from their combined heritage of traditional China, modern China, and Marxism-Leninism. The summary of these attitudes that is attempted here owes much to Professor Lucian Pye's recent and stimulating book, *The Spirit of Chinese Politics.*

Chinese political thought and behavior have hardly been westernized at all. What modernization they have undergone has been largely of the type that might be called Leninization: the imposition of Communist ideology and organization, in this case on a vast country most of which was only in the early stages of modernization. Communism has reinforced and preserved the traditional Chinese tendency to distrust spontaneity in public life (until Mao Tse-tung attempted to revive it in the Cultural Revolution) and to exalt the principles of an authoritative ideology and a hierarchical and all-embracing organization, namely of course the "thought of Mao Tse-tung" and the Communist Party apparatus respectively.

Communism has also reinforced and preserved the traditional importance in Chinese politics of propaganda and terror, but with some important changes deriving from the modern period of China's history. Political emotions are organized, but for the purpose of expressing them, rather than as in traditional China for the purpose of suppressing them. Naturally Mao and his party work hard to ensure, through endless indoctrination, that the emotions expressed are the "correct" ones. So much stress is placed on the evocation and expression of political emotions through propaganda that the expression tends to be taken as being equivalent to the act envisaged, indeed to the completed act. This gap between word and deed helps to account for the otherwise puzzling lack of correspondence between the observer's initial expectations of violence, whether in domestic Chinese politics or in Chinese foreign policy, and the significantly lesser actual incidence of such violence. Violent language tends to be followed, but only to a rather limited extent, by violent deeds; the former's purpose is presumably mainly to produce a psychological effect, both on the source and on the object.

Now as for many centuries, the Chinese remain deeply convinced of their own superiority to other peoples. This superiority they consider to be based on racial quality, size and population, and culture, in descending order of importance. On the other hand, they are profoundly convinced that in modern times China has been deeply wronged by the "imperialist" powers by virtue of the latter's material strength and China's material weakness, which they intend shall be only transitory. China having thus been victimized in modern times, its leaders, notably the Communists, have tended to see the world as divided sharply into friends and foes, with little room for neutrals. In this respect, as in several but not all others, modern Chinese attitudes fit remarkably well with Marxism-Leninism.

At the same time, China's Communist leaders feel proud that since 1949 China has "stood up," in Mao Tse-tung's phrase. Above all, it has achieved unity for the first time in many decades. This unity, however, is precarious, because of the deep divisions carved by physical and human geography across the face of the country. It requires an overarching ideology and organization in order to survive, but there is some difficulty in making these fit, partly because both, Maoism and the Communist Party apparatus, are of foreign origin to a significant extent. Maoism in particular requires the acceptance of much absurdity, and the payment of a heavy price in the form of retarded development, in the name of psychological and political uniformity and unity. Most Chinese, it seems, have been willing to pay that price, because in their eyes, and on the basis of their reading of modern Chinese history, disunity breeds weakness and weakness invites foreign pressures or even domination. This cannot be allowed to happen again.

PART ONE

CHAPTER II

Stalinism and
Armed Struggle (1950-53)

MAO TSE-TUNG and his colleagues came to power in 1949 determined, in his phrase, to "lean to one side," or in other words, to Stalin's side in the Cold War. On the other hand, they had no desire to have diplomatic relations exclusively with Communist countries or to allow Stalin to determine the pattern of their diplomatic relations. Nor was there any need. By virtue of China's size and the circumstances of the CPC's attainment of power, the new Chinese People's Republic (CPR) was not a Soviet satellite in the usual sense. It had "stood up."

THE PATTERN OF DIPLOMATIC RELATIONSHIPS

In the autumn of 1949 the new Chinese regime in Peking announced its willingness to establish diplomatic relations with foreign governments that displayed a friendly attitude and did not have relations with the Chinese Nationalists, who by then were in the process of establishing themselves on Taiwan (Formosa).

The Soviet Union and the Communist states of Asia (North

Korea and Outer Mongolia) and Eastern Europe promptly extended recognition, and with two exceptions the CPR reciprocated immediately. One exception was Outer Mongolia, whose declaration of recognition Peking took ten days to acknowledge. Like earlier Chinese regimes, the CPC feels that it has some sort of claim to Outer Mongolia, and it undoubtedly realized that recognition would tend to weaken this claim. Nevertheless, Stalin was determined to maintain Outer Mongolia's status as a Soviet buffer and satellite, and there was no practicable alternative for Peking to recognition. The other exception was Yugoslavia, which was then involved in a feud with Stalin and was therefore not recognized by the CPR until five years later, when relations between Moscow and Belgrade had begun to improve. In mid-January 1950 the CPR took a significant diplomatic initiative by being the first state to recognize Ho Chi Minh's Democratic Republic of Vietnam. This action, which reflected a claim on Peking's part to a uniquely close relationship with the Vietnamese Communist movement by virtue of geography, culture, and comparable revolutionary traditions, compelled Moscow to follow suit and does not seem to have been very pleasing to Stalin.

A number of neutral, newly independent Asian states extended recognition to the CPR. The first (in December 1949) was Burma, a weak state then torn by Communist and ethnic insurgency and one that has long lived in fear of Chinese pressures. The second (in early January 1950) was India; Nehru admired China and the Chinese Communists and believed strongly that they must be brought into the international diplomatic community for the good of Asia and of world peace. Pakistan recognized the CPR the next day, so as not to let India steal a march on it. Indonesia recognized the CPR shortly afterward, but because of the complicated and controversial question of the large overseas Chinese community in Indonesia diplomatic relations were slow in being established. After the CPR began actively to woo the uncommitted Afro-Asian countries in the mid-1950s, there was another wave of recognitions from Asia and the Middle East, and sub-Saharan Africa began to yield some in the early 1960s.

Even if the CPC had been willing to establish relations with the United States, as it was not, the United States would not have felt itself in a position to do the same, at least at that time. Domestic politics and an unwillingness to sever relations with the Nationalists forbade it. A number of other Western countries suffered no such inhibitions, however. The British government was determined to recognize Peking, mainly because it feared that otherwise Nehru's indignation would lead him to take India out of the British Commonwealth and also because it wanted to safeguard Hong Kong and the substantial British investments on the mainland of China. The British hoped that the United States could be persuaded to take the same step jointly with them, but when President Truman made it clear, on January 5, 1950, that he would not do so, British recognition of Peking followed on the next day. Mainly for commercial reasons, a few other Western countries recognized the CPR at about the same time: the Scandinavian countries, the Netherlands, and Switzerland. The only other Western country to date to do the same was France, in January 1964.

At the present time (mid-1968), approximately forty-five countries have diplomatic relations with the CPR. The figure has fluctuated from time to time, and presumably will continue to fluctuate, not only because new recognitions are extended now and then but because occasionally governments that feel offended at China's behavior break relations formally or informally, as Burundi, Tunisia, Ghana, and Indonesia have done. There is no point, therefore, in attempting to be precise and detailed on this subject in the brief account that is offered here.

THE SINO-SOVIET ALLIANCE

The most important single step in the field of foreign policy taken by the new Communist Chinese regime in the first few months of its existence was the forming of an alliance with the Soviet Union. The motivations on the Chinese side have already been briefly discussed.

On his side, Stalin saw good reason to welcome the CPR as an ally. His general strategy was a thoroughly continental and geopolitical one; he had created a buffer in Eastern Europe at the end of World War II for the main purpose of enhancing Soviet security and to a limited extent had tried to do the same in the

Far East. The anti-Western revolts in southern Asia that he began to encourage in 1948 he seems to have visualized in a secondary role, perhaps as a form of compensation for the successful American intrusion (as he saw it) into the western half of the former vast British empire and sphere of influence, or in other words into the Mediterranean and the Middle East. China, as a continental state and an immediate neighbor of the Soviet Union, represented in his eyes a valuable accretion of security and power to his camp and one for whose revolutionization he had labored mightily although unsuccessfully a quarter of a century before. He was sufficiently impressed with its value, and with the resounding military victories that the CPC had been winning over the Nationalist forces since the spring of 1949, so that he was willing to accept it as a junior partner in lieu of the satellite status that he was mercilessly forcing on the Eastern European regimes, barring of course that of the defiant Tito. Stalin even went so far, in June 1949, as to indicate a measure of acceptance of Mao Tse-tung's revolutionary strategy as the best model for the rest of Asia. This concession, a major and unusual one for Stalin, implied a willingness to grant an independent and even leading role to the CPC in the guidance of Communist movements and revolts in Asia, and it must have been clear to him that the CPC would not be content to regard these as merely an adjunct to Stalin's struggle for the mastery of Europe. He also must have been aware that the CPC wanted aid, support, and protection from him, without being willing to pay the usual price of political subordination.

From mid-December 1949 to mid-February 1950, while Liu Shao-ch'i was left in charge in Peking, Mao Tse-tung and a high-ranking Chinese delegation negotiated with Stalin and his colleagues in Moscow. It was Mao's first trip outside China. Although most of the substance of these talks remains a secret, it is clear from a variety of circumstantial evidence that a number of questions relating to the fortunes of Asian communism were among the topics discussed. The Japanese party was sternly told to stop cooperating with the American occupation authorities and prepare for a revolutionary struggle against them, presumably for the purpose of obstructing the actual American intention to sign a peace treaty with Japan and restore its independence as well as the supposed American intention to rearm Japan, and also in order to make its contribution to Stalin's design for Korea. There can be little doubt that Stalin and Mao discussed the Korean situation in detail, with results that are dealt with in the next section. Mao probably informed Stalin of his plan, which was then under way, to launch an offensive against the Nationalists on Taiwan, a project to which Stalin can have had no serious objection since President Truman had stated on January 5, 1950, that the United States did not intend to defend the island. The Communist insurgency in Vietnam, to which the CPC was beginning to give increasing aid, was undoubtedly discussed, and there may have been a dispute over the CPR's prompt diplomatic recognition of Ho Chi Minh's regime. There can be little doubt that the other Communist revolts in Southeast Asia, those in the Philippines, Malaya, and Burma (an abortive one in Indonesia had been crushed in the autumn of 1948 by the nationalist Republic of Indonesia), were also on the agenda, but the nature of the conclusions is speculative; Stalin may well have told Mao that the prospect of war in Korea rendered the revolts in Southeast Asia more marginal than ever and that Mao was free to make out of them what he could. The Indian Communist Party, whose pro-Soviet leadership had been making rude remarks about Mao as a means of combatting the bumptiousness of a pro-Chinese rural-based faction then operating in the state of Andhra, was told through the Cominform press to mind its manners.

Rumors circulated at the time of extensive secret concessions by Mao to Stalin, to take effect in the event of a Soviet-American war in the Far East, but some of these rumors seem implausible and none can be confirmed. More to the point, on February 14, 1950, as one of his last acts in the Soviet Union, Mao took part in the signing of a thirty-year alliance between the two giant Communist states. It was directed against Japan or any ally of Japan's, meaning the United States, and probably reflected a genuine although unfounded fear on the part of both Mao and Stalin that the United States in fact intended to rearm Japan to compensate for the virtual loss of its position on the Asian mainland as a result of the Communist conquest of China. Since neither party seems fully to have trusted the other, another purpose may well have been so to commit both parties to a common cause as to preclude either from making a separate accommodation with an opponent of the other, as each had shown an occasional tendency to do in the past.

At the same time, the Soviet side agreed to make available a long-term development credit worth $300 million. It was to be used, and in fact was used, to buy industrial equipment, with repayment to begin in 1954. While in the Soviet Union, Mao had evidently been greatly impressed with the Stalinist model of industrialization, which was already obsolescent and controversial even then, although he probably felt that the Stalinist method of exploiting agriculture for the sake of extracting resources to be used for industrialization would not be suitable to China's poorer and more densely populated countryside. It was agreed that the Soviet Union should continue to enjoy the predominant position in the main Manchurian railways and ports (the latter being Dairen and Port Arthur, both near the tip of the Liaotung Peninsula) that it had been granted under a treaty with the Nationalist government in 1945, but only until the end of 1952 or until both parties signed a peace treaty with Japan, whichever came sooner; thereupon the railways and ports would revert to China. At the end of March 1950 a separate Sino-Soviet agreement provided for the establishment of four "joint" companies, for shipbuilding (at Dairen), for oil extraction and nonferrous minerals (both in Sinkiang), and for an airline (across Central Asia). Although these companies were evidently not so exploitative as the "joint stock" companies through which Stalin was then milking the resources of Eastern Europe, they were still run mainly for Soviet benefit and indeed seem to have given Stalin something resembling a temporary sphere of influence in western Sinkiang.

Mao could take satisfaction in the fact that he had dealt with Stalin more nearly on terms of equality than any foreign Communist had done for a quarter of a century, and from that day to this the Soviet Union has treated the CPR as occupying a unique place, the second most important, in the "socialist camp," or Communist bloc.

THE ORIGINS AND OUTBREAK OF THE KOREAN WAR

In 1948 South Korea had attained independence under a non-Communist government and United Nations auspices, and the United

States began to withdraw its occupation forces. Soviet troops were similarly withdrawn from North Korea and a Communist state, the "Democratic People's Republic of Korea," was proclaimed there, but the area remained under effective Soviet control. At about the same time, the United States began to make preparations for a peace treaty with Japan, a step for which Stalin was not ready and to which he objected strongly, since his image of the desirable future for Japan naturally differed greatly from the one entertained by the United States government. As George Kennan's memoirs show, he realized at the time that the American move toward a Japanese peace treaty, without Soviet participation, was likely to produce a strong Soviet response of some kind. In the case of Germany, a somewhat similar initiative, the unification of the currencies of the three Western occupation zones in 1948, brought on a Soviet blockade of Berlin. In the Far East, the result was the Korean War.

Stalin, and probably the Chinese Communists as well, feared that the United States intended not only to make a separate peace treaty with Japan but to rearm it, something at which General MacArthur seemed to hint in his New Year's Day message to the Japanese people on January 1, 1950. This was presumably the main contingency against which the Sino-Soviet alliance of February 14, 1950, was directed. Stalin's means for influencing the situation in Japan were limited, but he did what he could; in the spring of 1950, on Chinese Communist as well as Soviet insistence, the Japanese Communist Party launched an energetic but unsuccessful armed rising. Much as the prospect of the unification of the Western occupation zones in Germany provoked a Soviet effort to pinch off the exposed and seemingly vulnerable enclave of West Berlin, so the seeming prospect of an American-Japanese military partnership provoked a Soviet effort, by proxy, to pinch off the exposed and seemingly vulnerable enclave of South Korea.

The proxy chosen for this operation, so as to minimize the risks of a direct Soviet military confrontation with the United States at a time when the latter was still the only true nuclear power, was the obvious one, North Korea. The Soviet role was to be confined to political direction, military advice and equipment, the provision of technicians and pilots, and the deterrence by the least necessary means (such as hints of direct Soviet involvement and reminders of the real or supposed Soviet ability to overrun Western Europe) of any American escalation of the conflict beyond the borders of Korea or to the level of nuclear war. The North Korean regime led by Kim Il Sung, although essentially a Soviet satellite, was a highly militant and activist one and had already been trying to overthrow the South Korean government by methods stopping only just short of the formal invasion now contemplated. It must therefore have welcomed the green light flashed to it from Moscow early in 1950.

One of Stalin's purposes in organizing an invasion of South Korea was undoubtedly to compensate himself for recent setbacks in the West, such as the failure of the Berlin Blockade and the formation of NATO. The memory of the energetic American response that had produced these setbacks led him to wait for an apparently definite indication that there would be no similar response in Korea before reaching a firm decision to proceed with his invasion plans. He thought he saw such indications in an important speech by Secretary of State Dean Acheson, who was known to be close to President Truman, on January 12, 1950. In this speech Acheson made it clear that the United States, which still regarded general war with the Soviet Union as a real possibility, did not intend to defend Taiwan or any area on the mainland of Asia against possible Communist attack but hoped that the United Nations would be able to guarantee its security.

From that time on, political and military preparations for the invasion of South Korea proceeded steadily. On January 13 the Soviet delegate walked out of the United Nations Security Council, in protest against the presence of the Chinese Nationalist representative, probably in the hope of paralyzing its deliberations when the United States lay the Korean crisis before it, and perhaps also to help purchase Chinese Communist cooperation in Stalin's plan. The flow of Soviet arms to North Korea, mainly across Manchuria, was greatly accelerated.

There can be no doubt that the Chinese Communist leadership was aware of the impending invasion of South Korea, and it is highly probable that the operation was discussed in some detail by Stalin and Mao during their long talks in Moscow. The CPC could hardly have failed to be aware of the increased flow of Soviet military equipment across Manchuria to North Korea, and it played its own part in this buildup by turning over to North Korean control, at some time during the winter of 1949–50, a sizable force of Korean troops who had earlier fought under Chinese Communist command in Manchuria. Peking's feelings about the Korean operation, however, were probably mixed. The expected success of the invasion would of course deal a heavy blow to the American position in Northeast Asia. On the other hand, it would also increase Soviet influence there to an extent that might prove troublesome to the Chinese, even if they did not find themselves directly involved in the fighting. The CPC, like some other observers including American officials, may have regarded an invasion as unnecessary, since there was a distinct possibility of overthrowing the South Korean government through insurgency, a technique that the traditions of the Chinese Communists taught them to prefer to conventional military operations. A Korean crisis would help the CPC little if at all with its efforts to "liberate" Taiwan through a very difficult amphibious assault. Chinese Communist military units began to move away from the Taiwan Strait in a northerly direction in the spring of 1950, as though the CPC had given up hope of invading Taiwan before the outbreak of war in Korea and considered the balancing of the increasing Soviet presence in Manchuria to be a matter of higher priority. There can be little doubt, however, that in the interests of overall relations with the Soviet Union, which in turn made very substantial concessions to Chinese interests in early 1950, the CPC acquiesced in Stalin's grand design for Korea. It is quite possible that in effect Mao conceded Stalin the leading role in Northeast Asia and Stalin conceded Mao the leading role in Southeast Asia.

Immediately following the successful North Korean surprise invasion of South Korea that began on June 25, 1950, the United States reversed its stand and committed what forces it could to the defense of South Korea. This decision came as an unpleasant surprise to everyone on the Communist side, but there seemed to be no alternative but for the North Koreans to move ahead as rapidly as possible in the hope of "liberating" South Korea before American aid could become effective and presenting the United States with a *fait accompli* that it would have to accept. Of more immediate concern to the CPR was the fact that on June 27 President Truman announced that in the future the United States, meaning mainly its Seventh Fleet, would prevent military offensives in either direction across the Taiwan Strait. Since the Nationalists were in no condition to attack the mainland, this step in effect simply extended American protection to Taiwan. Peking was of course furious at this blow to its hopes for "liberating" the island, and after the visit of General MacArthur, who had been appointed to command the United Nations forces in Korea, to Taiwan in July, the Chinese began to fear that American plans might come to include support for a Nationalist move of some kind against the mainland.

Events in Korea soon raised it to first place on the list of Chinese priorities, in place of Taiwan. In mid-August, as the North Korean offensive was finally brought to a halt, American spokesmen began to proclaim an intent to reunite Korea rather than stop at the 38th parallel, the dividing line between North and South Korea. The first Chinese ambassador arrived in Pyongyang, the North Korean capital, on August 13, and Peking probably began to make contingency plans for intervention in Korea at about that time. In late September, as United Nations forces approached the 38th parallel, Peking warned through various channels that it would fight if American forces crossed the parallel, as they did in early October. General MacArthur was determined to turn North Korea over to his friend President Syngman Rhee of South Korea, and he believed that the Soviet Union would do nothing to prevent this. He also doubted that China would intervene and felt sure that if it did American airpower would destroy its forces before they could reach the front.

CHINESE INTERVENTION

Stalin was obviously angry at the failure of his plan to overrun South Korea and worried by the impending loss of North Korea, which would carry with it a threat to the rest of his territories and allies in the Far East. He was still unwilling to intervene directly, however, because a direct clash between Soviet and American forces would clearly have been likely to start a Third World War. There was only one available proxy, and that was the CPR. Stalin presumably relied on his leverage on the Chinese and on Kim Il Sung's impressive political skill to prevent them from transforming North Korea into a Chinese satellite in the process of saving it. Over and above any direct Chinese interest in intervention, Stalin was prepared to promise, and actually delivered during the next several months, substantial new military aid to Communist China of the kind that he had sent to North Korea before the beginning of the war. It is possible that Stalin hoped that in the process of intervening, even if successfully, in Korea the CPR would suffer such heavy losses that it would be more manageable than otherwise. Possible evidence of Chinese distrust of Stalin's motives is the acceleration in October 1950, as intervention in Korea was getting underway, of Peking's timetable for the "liberation" of Tibet. The least implausible explanation is fear of Soviet influence; it should be remembered that western Sinkiang, from which western Tibet is accessible, was something of a Soviet sphere of influence at that time.

There is reason to believe that Stalin's views on Korea weighed heavily, although not necessarily decisively, with Peking. On the other hand, Mao was prepared to take advantage of his indispensability to Stalin in the crisis to bargain vigorously with him for military aid and for deterrent protection against direct American threats to the mainland of China under the terms of the Sino-Soviet alliance, if it should be required.

Perhaps even more significant in Chinese eyes was the security of Manchuria, China's most important heavy industrial region, and the hydroelectric plants on the Yalu River, between Manchuria and Korea, which provided much of Manchuria's industry's need for power. The CPC probably feared that the "imperialist" United States, like Japan not long before, would use Korea as a springboard for an attack not only on Manchuria but on China Proper, this time in cooperation with the Chinese Nationalists and perhaps the rearmed Japanese. Peking may have calculated that the United States would regard the Sino-Soviet alliance as ineffective if the Chinese themselves gave the same impression through refraining from intervening in Korea.

In addition, the Chinese leadership undoubtedly hoped to gain prestige and influence for their young regime by fighting the

United States, although they would probably not have been willing to run such serious risks for this reason alone. As long as the United States did not carry the war to the mainland of China, there was a reasonable hope of enhancing political control and mobilization at home, acquiring increased economic and military aid from the Soviet Union, compelling the United States to withdraw from the Taiwan Strait as well as South Korea and to let the CPR into the United Nations, and enhancing Chinese influence on Asian communism and the revolts then in progress in Southeast Asia.

There are a number of indications that a desire to save North Korea for its own sake ranked at about the bottom of the list of Chinese motives for intervention. Among them is the fact that Peking defined the *casus belli* as an invasion of North Korea by American forces, the implication being that it might have tolerated the reunification of Korea by South Korean forces alone. Indeed, both Chinese pronouncements and Chinese actions suggested that Peking might actually have even tolerated an American intrusion that penetrated well into North Korea but left a rump state under Communist control as a buffer for China's Manchurian frontier.

General MacArthur, who appears not to have realized that Chinese troops had begun to cross the Yalu River into North Korea about ten days before and who certainly felt no interest in leaving China a buffer zone, ordered his American units on October 24 to move to the Yalu. On October 25 the "Chinese People's Volunteers," so called so as to give the United States an excuse for refraining from considering itself formally at war with China if it wished, were officially formed and went into action against American units, apparently with the aim of inducing them to respect the buffer, or better still to retire to the 38th parallel. Not only did MacArthur fail to heed this warning, but a month later he launched his famous "home by Christmas" offensive, aimed at completing the unification of Korea. Chinese troops promptly struck his badly disposed forces with devastating effect, in what he termed an "entirely new war." Since MacArthur had ignored the earlier warning, there seems to have been agreement on the Communist side that he must be pursued not only down to the 38th parallel but beyond and thrown out of Korea altogether if possible.

For his part MacArthur, as his troops in some cases were driven and in some cases fled to the 38th parallel and beyond, began to advocate expanding the war beyond the confines of Korea as the only way to salvage the situation. As he later explained, he favored aerial reconnaissance and probably bombardment of the "privileged sanctuary" in Manchuria and of China Proper, a naval blockade of the China coast, and support for Chinese Nationalist operations against the China coast. He also seems to have favored the use of radioactive waste as a defensive barrier in Korea and perhaps the actual use of nuclear weapons. Once General Ridgway began to stabilize the situation on the ground in Korea, these proposals seemed not only politically objectionable but militarily unnecessary in Washington and were accordingly rejected. In March 1951, however, MacArthur began to advocate his proposals again, this time in public, apparently because he foresaw that otherwise there would be an armistice that would leave Korea divided and so put the stamp of error and failure on his earlier march to the Yalu. For his public reopening of his rejected proposals he was relieved of his command by President Truman on April 11.

In mid-January, at the high watermark of the advance of its "volunteers" into South Korea, Peking proposed that a peace conference on the Korean question be held in China. At that time, its three main demands on the world were for the withdrawal of American troops from Korea and of American protection from Taiwan and its own admission to the United Nations. Far from agreeing to these demands, the United States maneuvered the condemnation of Communist China as an aggressor by the United Nations General Assembly on February 18 and subsequently, on May 1, a vote urging all United Nations members not to ship "strategic" materials to China. The United States, for its part, had already embargoed all trade with the mainland of China. About this time, the United States began to construct an imposing network of military bases, alliances, and economic and military aid programs in the Western Pacific and the Far East with the aim of "containing" any possible expansion of Communist China, whether through direct military action as in Korea or through support for local Communist insurgency. Although, as in the case of Western Europe, the military threat was probably never as great as the

United States officially perceived it to be, it does not follow that military "containment" was totally unnecessary in Asia any more than in Europe. It may in fact have been more necessary in Asia, so as to compensate for the extreme weakness and fragmentation of non-Communist Asia at that time. Whether militarily necessary or not, American "containment" at that time had a valuable psychological effect on the non-Communist countries and probably made Peking more cautious in its external behavior than it would otherwise have been.

In the second half of April Peking, whose "volunteers" had been pushed back approximately to the 38th parallel, seems to have felt both elated at the relief of MacArthur and concerned that opinion in the United States, the Soviet Union, and much of the rest of the world appeared to be in favor of an armistice on the basis approximately of the *status quo ante bellum*, with the important qualification that foreign (in other words, mainly American and Chinese) troops were to remain. Whatever the Chinese view of this idea on its merits was, Peking clearly wanted, at a minimum, to go into the negotiations in a stronger bargaining position than it would have then had. At a maximum, it still hoped it might be able to drive American troops out of Korea before the talks began. Twice, accordingly, in late April and again in mid-May, Chinese troops launched massive offensives aimed initially at taking Seoul, the South Korean capital, only to be driven back with appalling casualties by United Nations firepower.

In June, to make matters worse, two British diplomats, Guy Burgess and Donald Maclean, who had been passing information on American operations in Korea to the Soviet Union, which in turn had probably been passing it to Peking, fled to Moscow, apparently because they feared exposure now that MacArthur, who had realized that some one was transmitting secret information on his plans to the other side, had returned to the United States. It seems quite possible that with its antennae thus desensitized in part, although not entirely, since Kim Philby remained active, the Communist side decided that as it could no longer read the adversary's intentions clearly it would be wise to go to the conference table without further delay. On June 23, accordingly, the Soviet Union proposed talks on an armistice along the lines already indicated, and in July the commanders of the North Korean and Chinese forces endorsed the proposal in a message to the United Nations Commander, General Ridgway. Armistice negotiations began about a week later, with neither side clearly victorious in the field and with fighting still in progress. In reality, however, the Chinese and North Koreans had been severely hurt in April and May, and if it had not been for a political decision by the United States government to discontinue major offensive operations the Chinese could probably have been defeated and driven out of Korea without the adoption of MacArthur's recommendations, barring major new infusions of Chinese or conceivably Soviet troops. As it was, the Communist side had to try to compensate by political means at the conference table for its lack of a victory in the field.

CHINA AND "ARMED STRUGGLE" IN SOUTHERN ASIA

Like the invasion of South Korea, Communist revolt, or "armed struggle," in South and Southeast Asia owed more to Stalin than to Mao in its origins. Local Communist leaders were certainly eager to try to wrest power from their nationalist rivals, but there is much evidence suggesting that they required a sign from Moscow before they felt free to do so. This sign was first given in a general fashion in the summer of 1947, when to Stalin's mind the United States stepped into the gap left by the collapse of European power in Western Europe itself and in the Mediterranean and Middle East. Stalin was determined not to let what he regarded as a fraudulent "decolonization" process managed by the Western powers farther to the east deprive him of compensating gains in the region east of the Persian Gulf. At the time of the so-called Calcutta Youth Conference in February 1948, some sort of Soviet signal was passed to the key Communist parties of Southeast Asia, with the Indian party acting as a key transmission belt.

It is clear that the CPC was in favor of "armed struggle" from the beginning. It believed in the spuriousness of "decolonization" and of the independence and neutrality in the Cold War of the successor nationalist regimes. Like Stalin, it tended to overestimate the revolutionary opportunities presented by the virtual collapse of Western power in eastern Asia. It believed in principle in the spread of communism in the former Western colonies in Asia, preferably by means similar to those employed so successfully in China. Finally, it could hardly afford to let Stalin get ahead of it in this field and in a region so close to China, where there seemed to be a vast potential for Chinese influence and perhaps for an outright Chinese sphere. At the Calcutta Youth Conference, accordingly, the CPC was represented by an active and vocal delegation, and in its message of greeting to the conference the Chinese Communist radio spoke of "armed struggle" along Chinese lines as the wave of the future for Asian communism.

By far the most promising case of armed struggle in Southeast Asia was that of Vietnam, where since 1946 a vigorous Communist movement led by Ho Chi Minh had been fighting a guerrilla war against a powerful French expeditionary force. The ultimate victory of the former, in 1954, was to be due not only to its own strong points and the shortcomings of its adversary, but to some extent to Chinese aid and support. For whereas the Soviet Union was very halfhearted in its support of Ho Chi Minh's Viet Minh, as it was later to be in the case of the anti-French revolt in Algeria—on account of a desire not to alienate France, make the lot of the powerful French Communist Party unnecessarily difficult, or strengthen the Western alliance—Peking felt no such inhibitions.

The "liberation" of South China by the Communists in late 1949 soon transformed the character of the struggle in Vietnam. It gave hope to the Viet Minh even while diminishing their freedom of action; it worried the French but gave them a new and persuasive argument with which to extract increased American economic and military aid in connection with their effort in Indochina. The CPR recognized Ho Chi Minh's Democratic Republic of Vietnam in mid-January 1950, before any other state did so, and in the following spring began to make limited quantities of economic and military aid available to it. The volume of this aid remained low for several reasons: the modest capability of the CPR for providing it, the poor state of communications in the contiguous portions of both states, the overriding Chinese commitment in Korea and the inadvisability of provoking Western "imperialism" on two fronts at the same time, and probably also a genuine and general Chinese Communist tendency to want not to endanger the political autonomy of another Communist movement if the latter is vigorous and doing well. Sino-Vietnamese relations continued in essentially this state down to 1953. On the other hand, Chinese political advice seems to have played an important part in the Vietnamese Communist decision to form a new party, tighter than the Viet Minh, the Vietnam Dang Lao Dong (Workers' Party), in 1951, in the aftermath of some severe defeats at the hands of the French.

With regard to other areas of southern Asia, the Chinese Communist sense of political commitment was about equally great, but the opportunity for effective action was significantly less. Either the local Communist movement was ineffective, or the opponent (whether indigenous or Western) was effective, or the area was not contiguous to China, or there was some combination of these things. In Malaya there was a large Chinese population resentful of the Malays and the British colonial administration, as well as a hard core of Chinese Communist guerrilla fighters remaining from the days of the war against Japan, but the area was almost inaccessible from China and the British proved able at great cost to find effective countermethods, both political and military, to a Malayan Communist insurgency (largely Chinese from the ethnic viewpoint) that began in 1948 but was brought under substantial control by the mid-1950s. In Burma, the Communist movement was divided, and the indigenous government of U Nu made sufficient headway against it and against various ethnic minority revolts so that the Chinese had little incentive or opportunity to take a hand to any significant extent. The Philippines were too remote for the CPC to play more than a minor role in the insurgency of the so-called Huks, who fought for several years before being brought under control by a dynamic new Secretary of Defense, Ramon Magsaysay, in the early 1950s. Remoteness, as well as the vulnerability of the large Chinese community to Indonesian reprisals, also rendered almost minimal the Chinese involvement in the short-lived insurrection in 1948 of the Indonesian Communist Party against the independent Republic of Indonesia, which although then at war with the Netherlands crushed the Communists with dispatch. There was little Chinese involvement in the futile efforts of a rurally based section of the Indian Communist Party to fight the far superior independent government of Jawaharlal Nehru from 1948 to 1950, but the pro-Chinese views of this group irritated the Moscow-oriented central leadership of the party and drew from it some public criticisms of Mao Tse-tung as a peasant leader rather than a Marxist-Leninist. While in Moscow in January 1950, Mao saw to it that this rudeness was rebuked and silenced by the press of the Cominform (Communist Information Bureau), which Stalin controlled.

With respect to all these revolts, the Chinese gave propaganda support, denounced the leaders of the opposition whether Western or indigenous, and in some cases provided a necessarily limited and ineffective amount of concrete aid and support. But in every case, with the resounding exception of Vietnam, Communist insurrection was a failure. The new nationalist regimes succeeded in demonstrating, even in Communist eyes, their staying power and the genuineness of their independence from colonialism and (in most cases) of their neutrality in the Cold War. For China, an external agency, to try to keep armed revolt going against such heavy odds seemed increasingly unpromising, especially at a time when growing preoccupation with the dangerous situation in Korea indicated the wisdom of trying to mobilize the diplomatic support of the new Asian states on this overriding issue rather than antagonizing them in a hopeless revolutionary cause. In the spring of 1951, partly at least in order to please India, whose diplomatic support in the Korean crisis was needed and to a considerable degree forthcoming, Peking promised to respect the autonomy of the Dalai Lama's government in Tibet.

Much the same considerations influenced Stalin, who since about 1950, a year or more before the Chinese did the same, had begun to lose interest in the revolts in southern Asia. In addition, Stalin seems to have feared that even if they could be sustained they might lead to an undesirably great degree of Chinese influence on Asian communism. In late 1951 a leading Soviet Asian specialist stated publicly and significantly that the Chinese revolutionary model was not to be regarded as a "stereotype" for Asia. As long as Stalin lived and the Korean War continued, however, both Moscow and Peking were considerably inhibited in their search for a viable successor to the strategy of "armed struggle" for southern Asia, even though it was recognized as virtually bankrupt everywhere but in Vietnam.

During the two years (July 1951–July 1953) of intermittent armistice negotiations in Korea, the Chinese as the major belligerents played virtually a dominant role on the Communist side, although the North Koreans were allowed to do most of the talking. Peking was concerned to achieve a relaxation of hostile military pressure on its forces and if possible to improve its own military position, particularly with respect to the location of the front, which obviously would become the basis of the ceasefire line since the United Nations Command refused to accept the 38th parallel for that purpose. A *de facto* temporary ceasefire in December 1951 allowed the Communist side to strengthen its positions to such an extent that ground operations thereafter were confined to local actions aimed at gaining a better front line and therefore a better ceasefire line. Peking kept trying to achieve through political means objectives that it had failed to gain through military means, notably the withdrawal of foreign troops from Korea (it was not entirely clear whether the Chinese "volunteers" were to be considered troops). Since it knew that the United States was very anxious to have a ceasefire, it attempted to make a general political conference on Far Eastern problems, which it greatly desired, a condition for a ceasefire. (This conference was eventually held at Geneva in 1954, but it achieved nothing significant with respect to Korea.)

In January 1952, when the major issues seemed to be on the way to solution, the United Nations side began to insist that it would not repatriate against their will any of the prisoners it was holding. It later developed that about 70 percent of all Chinese prisoners, and a comparable percentage of the North Koreans, rejected repatriation for one reason or another. There were some weighty reasons for the United Nations stand, notably a vivid recollection of Stalin's brutal treatment of many of the Soviet defectors who had been returned to his control by the Western Allies in 1945. For the same reason, the Soviet Union gave strong support to the insistence of Peking and Pyongyang that they would not agree to an armistice that did not include the principle of compulsory repatriation of prisoners, one that they obviously considered to be of immense political importance to themselves. The idea that any substantial proportion of a group of former citizens as highly indoctrinated as Communist soldiers were refusing to return home would have serious domestic and international effects. Peking and Pyongyang could not admit, and have never admitted, that such a thing could happen except as a result of coercion. To enhance control over the prisoners and put political pressure on the United Nations Command, the highly effective Communist organization among the North Korean prisoners launched a series of major riots in the spring of 1952. At about the same time, the awesome propaganda apparatus of the Communist side began to accuse the United Nations of conducting "germ warfare," a lie whose main purpose was probably to focus world attention on the United Nations Command and inhibit any possible tendency on its part to resort to nuclear weapons.

Nuclear weapons were not used, but the United States did begin to bomb the Yalu dams for the first time on June 23, 1952. The sense of crisis in Korea added an extra and dangerous dimension to a series of important Sino-Soviet negotiations that took place in Moscow for several months beginning in August 1952. On July 1 the Soviet ambassador left Peking for Moscow, and the probability that his return was not merely a routine one connected with the negotiations is indicated by the fact that he did not go back to Peking and that his successor did not arrive there until December.

For several months beginning in August 1952 there was nearly always at least one high-level Chinese delegation in Moscow. Peking was scheduled to launch its First Five Year Plan at the beginning of 1953, and Stalin made important new commitments of economic aid in connection with the plan. In addition, he also agreed to a substantial increment of military aid, undoubtedly with an eye on Korea. In mid-September it was announced that the Soviet Union would withdraw from the major Manchurian railways as provided in the Sino-Soviet agreements of February 1950 but that it would stay on in Dairen and Port Arthur, the ports at the southern tip of the railway system, until the Communist states had concluded a peace treaty with Japan. This arrangement seems to have been of greater practical advantage to Peking than to Moscow. Control of the railways was important to the war effort in Korea, where the Chinese were heavily reinforcing their units, and a continued Soviet presence in the ports would tend to deter possible American escalation against Manchuria. The Chinese were careful to refer loudly to this presence as the tension over Korea mounted.

In November 1952 the Indian government, which had made several earlier attempts to mediate the Korean crisis and was now greatly concerned over the deadlock on the prisoner question, introduced a resolution on it into the United Nations General Assembly. Although nominally a compromise, it had been cleared in advance in Peking and actually favored the Communist position in the sense that it emphasized the right to be repatriated (rather than the right not to be repatriated against one's will) and envisaged final disposition of unwilling prisoners by the remote and hypothetical political conference that the Communists were demanding. Apparently in deference to American objections, however, the Indian proposal was soon modified so as to stress the right not to be repatriated against one's will and to provide for the reasonably prompt release of prisoners refusing repatriation.

The revision of the Indian proposal promptly injected a degree of tension into the Korean situation unknown since the early days. Moscow, Peking, and Pyongyang joined in denouncing the modified proposal. They may have believed that it would be better to face up to the crunch before the incoming Eisenhower administration, an unknown and somewhat perturbing quantity, had a chance to get its hands on the reins. It is quite clear that Stalin, who was probably not of sound mind at the time, was contemplating a vast domestic purge, and there is some evidence that he was planning to attack Yugoslavia, which had recently begun to receive substantial military aid from the United States. On February 17, 1953, in his last interview with a foreigner, he warned the United States through the Indian ambassador to the Soviet Union that if the United States acted on its recent "unleashing" of Chiang Kai-shek (one of the Eisenhower administration's first acts) he would retaliate forcibly. For its part, the CPR gave evidence of being willing to resume heavy ground fighting in Korea rather than give in on the prisoner question.

Late in February the Eisenhower administration, which was determined to have the armistice in Korea that it had promised the voters by whatever means were necessary, began covertly to threaten the CPR, through a variety of channels, with the extension of the war from Korea to the mainland of China and with the use of nuclear weapons if the CPR did not sign an armistice promptly and on the basis of voluntary repatriation. Peking immediately appealed to Moscow for support. From such evidence as the fact that the leading Chinese nuclear physicist arrived in Moscow on February 24, it seems probable that Peking asked for an immediate transfer of nuclear weapons and appropriate delivery systems, in addition probably to strong Soviet declarations of support and if necessary the use of Soviet forces under the terms of the Sino-Soviet alliance. It is impossible to determine Stalin's attitude toward the Chinese demands, which may have been the item highest on his agenda at that time. The seriousness of the crisis may have contributed to his final illness and death, which was officially announced as having occurred on March 5, although there is some reason to believe that it may actually have occurred somewhat earlier and not have been entirely due to natural causes. In view of this possibility, and in view of the change in Chinese policy on the Korean crisis after his death (see Chapter III), it is not impossible that Stalin was prepared to go rather far in support of the Chinese. If so, the world was spared what might have been the only case to date of the full implementation of the Sino-Soviet alliance, as well as a serious danger of general war.

CHAPTER III

The Road to
Bandung (1953-55)

WHATEVER THE EXACT circumstances of Stalin's death, it was an event of crucial importance to the world Communist movement, to the main international crisis in which the latter was then involved (the Korean War), and to the Communist Party with the greatest stake in that crisis (the Chinese). For a full generation this evil political genius had dominated his own party through police terror and his incredible organizational and manipulative gifts, including his success in monopolizing Lenin's mantle and having himself proclaimed the greatest man of the age by a propaganda apparatus without parallel in history, and through his own party had controlled to a high although not quite complete degree the other parties of the movement. The passing of such a giant was bound to leave a mark on his heirs, his subjects, and the world.

THE LIQUIDATION AND LESSONS OF THE KOREAN WAR

From the heavily military composition of the delegation that the CPR sent to Stalin's funeral (March 9, 1953), and from the continued issuing of bellicose statements from Peking, it is logical to infer that the CPC at first saw in Stalin's death no reason to abandon its increasingly risky stand on the Korean prisoner question and pressed Stalin's successors, as it had him, for active military support. But uncertain of their domestic position and determined to liquidate much although by no means all of their dead master's legacy at home and abroad, the heirs wanted no part of a military confrontation with the United States over Korea or anything else. At the end of March, Chou En-lai, who had led the Chinese delegation to Stalin's funeral, returned to Peking and began to issue relatively conciliatory statements on the prisoner question. The CPC, in other words, saw no alternative to giving in, but characteristically it managed to find ways of denying that it was doing so.

Negotiations on the prisoner question were soon resumed, and agreement was reached on an armistice that embodied voluntary repatriation and nonwithdrawal of foreign troops, both principles intrinsically obnoxious to Peking. An armistice on any basis at all was obnoxious to President Syngman Rhee of South Korea, since it would reduce his chances of reuniting his country. He therefore unilaterally released, in early July, all his North Korean prisoners who were refusing repatriation, without waiting for the screening procedures prescribed by the draft armistice agreement; his purpose was presumably to sabotage the signing of the agreement. The Chinese "volunteers" responded with their last offensive of the war; it fell only on the South Korean forces and carefully avoided American units. Rhee's opposition to the armistice collapsed, and it was signed on July 27. At that time the sixteen nations that had contributed troops to the United Nations forces fighting in Korea issued a warning that the armistice should not be used as an opportunity for Communist pressures elsewhere, meaning Indochina, and that any resumption of aggression in Korea would be met with a response that might not be confined to Korea, presumably meaning nuclear weapons to be used against China if necessary.

The outcome of the Korean War represented a clear-cut victory for neither side, mainly because political inhibitions and largely unnecessary fear of the Soviet Union had prevented the United States from employing all the conventional military power that it possessed. On the one hand, South Korea was saved, Communist momentum in Asia received a major setback, the Soviet Union was forced into an arms race with the United States that it could not afford, and the CPR after heavy losses saw most of its political demands rejected and decided to exercise greater caution in the future in military confrontations with the United States. On the other hand, the CPR gained greatly in prestige from its impressive military showing in Korea against a technically superior opponent, the Sino-Soviet alliance enjoyed what was probably its finest hour to date, the CPR received greatly increased military aid from the Soviet Union, North Korea was saved from MacArthur, a serious strain was thrown on the American political system, and a strong feeling was created in the Pentagon that "never again" must American ground forces be committed to the mainland of Asia. The Korean War vastly exacerbated Sino-American hostility, for many reasons which included the fact that Mao Tse-tung lost a son in Korea and saw Taiwan denied to him by the Seventh Fleet. In order to prevent a repetition of what it regarded, with some oversimplification, as unprovoked Chinese aggression in Korea, the United States began early in the conflict to try, with considerable success, to contain the CPR by military means, and with much less success to isolate it by diplomatic means from international contacts. As the Berlin Blockade drew the lines in the Cold War in Europe, so the Korean War drew the lines in the Cold War in Asia.

MAO TSE-TUNG AS SENIOR COMMUNIST

As a leader who had gained control without indispensable aid from Stalin of a party and a country that ranked second only to his in the Communist world, Mao not surprisingly considered that Stalin's death left him the senior figure in that world. By absenting himself from Stalin's funeral and sending a primarily governmental rather than party figure, Chou En-lai, to represent him, Mao demonstrated his feeling of superiority to Stalin's heirs.

What is surprising is that the latter almost seemed to agree with him. Perhaps because of the need to find a way of making it swallow the bitter pill of essential capitulation on the Korean prisoner issue, they treated the Chinese delegation and its absent superior with great deference. When Beria and Malenkov, who led the strongest single combination in post-Stalinist Moscow, set out promptly to confer on Malenkov the status of being "more equal" than the others, one of the means employed was to crop a photograph of the signing of the Sino-Soviet alliance on February 14, 1950, in such a way as to bring Malenkov next to Mao Tse-tung. This move was soon followed by some setbacks for Malenkov, in particular his being compelled to give up the First Secretaryship of the party while retaining the premiership. It is quite possible that Malenkov's effort to suggest Chinese support for his position brought protests from Peking and that these played some role in the partially successful effort of his colleagues to set a limit on his and Beria's evident ambitions.

Beria and Malenkov remained powerful in Moscow for a time, however. Beria was overthrown in July 1953 and executed on December 23. The main charge levied against him by his colleague-opponents, to the effect that he had tried to use his position as head of the police to set up a personal dictatorship on the Stalinist model, appears to be a considerable oversimplification of the truth. While in power he had made substantial concessions to Soviet public opinion, although to be sure these moves could be interpreted as efforts to curry popular favor at the expense of his colleagues. In reality, his fall seems to have been due mainly to the fact that he showed some signs of being willing to make concessions to the West on the crucial German question, at East German expense. When the East Berlin rising of June 17, 1953, drove home to the Soviet leadership the extreme precariousness of the Soviet political position in Germany, the Soviet Army probably joined hands with Beria's civilian colleagues to overthrow him, and his other past sins were then also raked up against him.

Beria had developed through his police connections powerful ties with a number of important Communists in other parties, and during the months following Stalin's death he was a man for all foreign Communists to reckon with. In the case of the Chinese party, the leader with the closest connnections with Stalin and Beria appears to have been Kao Kang. Kao was the dominant Chinese in Manchuria—China's key heavy industrial region and an area under extensive Soviet influence after 1945—down to at least the end of

1952, when he became Chairman of the State Planning Committee and was charged with drawing up the forthcoming First Five Year Plan. He seems to have tried to use his ties with Stalin, and after Stalin's death with Beria, to secure massive Soviet commitments to support the plan and to have been confident of success. But the commitments had not been put into final form by the time Beria fell; when they were, in mid-September, the reality sank below what Kao had probably encouraged his colleagues to expect. His position undoubtedly suffered; his personal arrogance, his political ambition, his Soviet connections, and his substantial residual position in Manchuria, which had irritated his colleagues for some time, now seemed too high a price to pay for his demonstrably limited influence on Beria's successors, among whom Khrushchev was coming to the fore. Still, it was not until December 24, 1953, the day on which Beria's execution was announced in Moscow, that the first known sign that Kao was in serious trouble appeared. On that day, it was later revealed, Mao Tse-tung criticized the ambitions of certain Chinese leaders at a closed meeting. Soon afterward Mao fell ill, and Kao allegedly took advantage of this opportunity to conspire with the most powerful leader in East China, Jao Shu-shih, in an effort to gain army support for Kao's elevation by means unknown to the party constitution to the position of Mao's heir. He failed, was purged, and allegedly committed suicide in the spring of 1954. His former colleagues withheld publication of their version of this episode, which naturally said nothing about the highly sensitive Soviet aspect, until the end of March 1955. It is probably not a coincidence that less than two months earlier Beria's erstwhile ally Malenkov had been forced to resign as premier in favor of Khrushchev's henchman Bulganin. In other words, Kao Kang's career seems to have been protected for a time by Beria's physical survival, and his posthumous reputation by Malenkov's political survival.

The converse also applied; the Chinese also exerted indirect political influence in Moscow. The post-Stalin and post-Beria Soviet leaders competed with each to flatter the Chinese and seek their support. Their desire for Chinese support is not easy to understand. It probably stemmed from such considerations as the competitive situation in Moscow and the CPR's impressive ability to make difficulties for the Soviet Union by starting trouble in Asia if it chose. As a later section of this chapter explains, Khrushchev proved to be the most adept at bidding for Chinese support, but others played the game as well. In February 1955, for example, the hard-nosed Stalinist Molotov became one of several Soviet leaders to refer to the "socialist camp [in other words, the Communist bloc] led by the Soviet Union and China," a concession unheard of before 1954. Although Mao was not recognized in Moscow as being first among Communists, his party was clearly conceded to be the second among Communist parties, almost, although definitely not quite, on a par with the Soviet party itself.

LIMITED VICTORY IN INDOCHINA

In the early spring of 1953, as soon as it had decided reluctantly to yield on the Korean prisoner question, Peking began to accelerate its deliveries of military equipment to the Viet Minh. The French in turn increased their political and military efforts under a plan designed not to achieve an impossible military victory but to create at last a viable non-Communist state capable of surviving a French withdrawal, which by that time all major sections of French opinion desired for one reason or another. In February 1954, at Berlin, the Foreign Ministers of the Big Four agreed that the war in Indochina and the region's international status should be placed on the agenda of the conference on Far Eastern affairs, notably Korea, that had been envisaged by the Korean armistice agreement of 1953.

Whatever slight chances of success the French plan for Indochina may have had were ruined by a famous military blunder. Late in 1953 the French command established a fortified post at Dienbienphu, in northwest Vietnam, in the hope of preventing further Viet Minh incursions into Laos. After careful preparations that included the positioning of artillery provided by the Chinese, the Viet Minh forces launched a devastating attack on the post in mid-March 1954 and took it on May 7, just as the Geneva Conference, having accomplished nothing in particular on Korea, took up the Indochina question.

In order to understand why this celebrated conference did not fully reflect what was by that time an undoubted military victory for the Viet Minh, supported by the Chinese, over the French, supported by the United States, it is necessary to understand the international climate in which the conference took place. The United States was in an angry mood. In April Secretary of State John Foster Dulles had tried unsuccessfully to engineer a joint (Anglo-French-American) military intervention, possibly supported by "tactical" nuclear weapons and followed by retaliation against the CPR if the latter intervened, both in order to save Dienbienphu and to create what he hoped would be a favorable atmosphere for the inauguration of a collective defense organization for Southeast Asia comparable to NATO in Europe. Dulles's military plan was dropped on account of strong opposition in all three of the countries involved, but it created an atmosphere that undoubtedly made the Soviet Union and the CPR nervous and anxious not to provoke the United States unnecessarily. Other American actions also contributed to this atmosphere, which Anthony Eden in his memoirs says was one of the most valuable assets that the non-Communist side at Geneva possessed. On January 12 Dulles made his famous "massive retaliation" speech, the main purpose of which was to prevent the same sort of miscalculation of American resoluteness that he felt had been engendered in the case of Korea by Secretary Acheson's speech exactly four years earlier. In March the United States conducted an awe-inspiring series of thermonuclear tests in the Pacific, and at about the same time it was announced that "tactical" nuclear weapons were now available for use by American forces in Europe if necessary.

The Soviet Union, as usual, was in no mood for a military confrontation with the United States. Khrushchev and Malenkov were involved in a power struggle one of whose manifestations was a debate over military strategy. In March 1954, as the American thermonuclear tests were in progress and the siege of Dienbienphu was about to begin, Malenkov stated publicly that another world war might mean the end of human civilization, the implication apparently being that the Soviet Union should reserve what deterrent capability it possessed to cover itself and its immediate allies, not faraway areas in Asia. Khrushchev insisted stoutly that another world war would destroy only "imperialism," not all human civilization, meaning apparently that the Soviet Union was strong enough and should be resolute enough to use its deterrent power actively to cover not only itself but the Viet Minh and if necessary the CPR, as well as other "socialist" regimes. As usual, the Soviet leadership was also paying close attention to Europe. It was concerned not to give so much support to the Viet Minh as to anger France and startle it into ratifying and bringing into existence, contrary to expectation, the European Defense Community (EDC), a proposed multilateral army to which West Germany would have provided troops and, in rotation, a commander. The Soviet desire not to press the United States too far, for military reasons, and not to press France too far, for political reasons, was instrumental in limiting Soviet support for the Viet Minh at the Geneva Conference and in leaving Ho Chi Minh with a decidedly limited victory.

Peking was much less concerned than Moscow with France and the European situation, and it felt a greater sense of political commitment to the cause of the Viet Minh and of Communist revolutionary warfare in general. On the other hand, it was nervous about American intentions, and it clearly remembered that it had been compelled to back down over Korea a year earlier in the face of a nuclear threat. It probably felt sure that it could no more rely on effective Soviet support and protection now than it had then, since there was no certainty that in a crunch Khrushchev's line would prevail over Malenkov's. As in the Korean case, the CPR was unwilling to risk the escalation of the war to the level of an attack on Chinese territory, but unlike Korea there was no need for an involvement of Chinese ground forces and therefore much less likelihood of such escalation. Chinese diplomatic support for the Viet Minh at Geneva was governed by these considerations and therefore proved to be less than total.

The conference, in which Molotov for the Soviet Union and Eden for the United Kingdom played the role of the major honest brokers between Dulles and Chou En-lai, the two major antagonists, and to a lesser extent between the two immediate but smaller antagonists, the French and the Viet Minh, soon deadlocked over the initial Viet Minh demands, which were sweeping and were at first supported by Molotov and Chou. Ho Chi Minh's delegation demanded what amounted to a package settlement for the whole of Indochina, so that the clear-cut Viet Minh victory in Vietnam would have exerted a "domino" effect on Laos and Cambodia as well. The result was the fall of the French government and the formation of a new one under Pierre Mendès-France, who was liked in Moscow because he opposed the EDC and yet was prepared to bargain energetically for the best possible settlement in Indochina. In addition, on June 11 Secretary Dulles implied publicly that even at this late date the United States might take military action in and over Indochina unless a reasonable settlement were forthcoming.

Peking evidently felt no interest in going to the brink with the United States on behalf of Ho Chi Minh. Over and above the obvious military risks, there were important political considerations as well. It had already shifted substantially away from the "armed struggle" strategy, with the single major exception of its support for the Viet Minh's struggle in Indochina, and it was now more interested in cultivating the good will of neutral countries and even of allies of the United States, especially in Asia, as a means of creating a political counterweight to American containment and to the continuous possibility, however remote in reality, of American attack. The CPR was enjoying at Geneva its first participation in a major international conference, with very beneficial effects on its prestige, and Chou En-lai was in the process of scoring both a personal and a diplomatic success. It was known that Chinese support for Viet Minh demands on Laos and Cambodia, areas that were generally regarded as quite distinct from Vietnam and as cultural daughters of India, would jeopardize the position that the CPR was trying to create for itself. This would be an especially serious matter, since the keystone of the new Chinese approach was cultivation of India.

In mid-June, accordingly, Chou and Molotov began to make concessions to the Western position, to the obvious outrage of the DRV (the Democratic Republic of Vietnam, or Ho Chi Minh's Communist state, often referred to as North Vietnam). In particular, Chou agreed to support the idea of a separate and differentiated settlement for each of the three Indochina countries, rather than a basically package deal as demanded by the DRV. The conference then picked up speed, and a series of agreements was concluded on July 21. The best known was a general declaration that is un-signed (and therefore of doubtful legal validity) because the United States would not sign a document that would also be signed by Peking and would allow some territory to be "lost" in the sense of passing under undisputed Communist control; the American government nevertheless declared that it would not "disturb" the operation of the agreements by force. The declaration provided that all three Indochina countries should contain no foreign military bases or forces (a point of the utmost importance to Peking, which feared possible American military pressures from bases in Indochina), except for a residual and temporary French presence. The effect of this declaration, plus separate agreements on the individual countries negotiated at the same time by the French and the governments concerned, was to exclude the Viet Minh from any formal role in Cambodia, allow it two provinces in Laos on the Chinese and North Vietnamese borders for "regrouping," and divide Viet· nam *de facto* into two supposedly temporary states by directing all Viet Minh forces to regroup north of the 17th parallel and all French forces to the south of it. Elections were to be held in all three countries, in the cases of Laos and Vietnam for the purpose of establishing new nationwide governments. Because of Soviet and Chinese unwillingness to support Viet Minh demands for a quick election, the one in Vietnam was to be held only after two years, but few observers supposed that a viable non-Communist state could be established in South Vietnam within that time. The implementation of the agreements was to be supervised by the three International Control Commissions (ICC), one for each country.

Peking viewed the exclusion of American bases and forces from Indochina by the agreements as a major gain, even though it had been unable to get the United States to commit itself formally by signing the declaration. This achievement, plus the gain in Chinese international prestige, was quite enough to offset the confining of the DRV to the territory above the 17th parallel, especially since that situation was expected to be temporary in view of the elections scheduled for 1956 and since to have insisted on more would have created a risk of a military clash with the United States. The DRV was consoled with substantial aid from both Moscow and Peking and with the prospect of taking control over South Vietnam through the anticipated election, in which there would be a huge majority for Ho Chi Minh in the Communist-controlled north and a very substantial vote for him in the south as well, so that he would have an overall majority in the country as a whole. If the South Vietnamese government tried to save itself by refusing to agree to the election, presumably it could be brought into line by international pressures. But the emergence in Saigon of a government strong and confident enough to be capable of refusing openly to bound by the Geneva agreements in this important question seemed most unlikely.

CRISIS IN THE TAIWAN STRAIT

Immediately after the signing of the Geneva agreements, Peking's propaganda apparatus began a campaign in favor of the "liberation" of Taiwan from American "imperialism," which was incorrectly asserted to have occupied it since June 27, 1950, when the Seventh Fleet had begun to give it protection. In early September Chinese Communist artillery began to shell Quemoy, a large offshore island held by the Nationalists and lying close to the port of Amoy. This sequence of events seems to suggest that Peking had merely waited for the tension over Indochina to be eased by the signing of the Geneva agreements before displaying again the kind of military aggressiveness that, according to one view, it had shown in Korea. In reality, the question is not quite so simple. American military aid to the Nationalists had been substantially increased since the "unleashing of Chiang Kai-shek" (in other words, the nominal removal of the American prohibition on Nationalist operations against the mainland) by the Eisenhower administration in February 1953. By 1954 the Communists thought they had reason to anticipate such operations on a significant scale. The crisis in the Taiwan Strait that they launched after the signing of the Geneva agreements, then, was to a large extent a preemptive or spoiling attack, and their dispositions remained essentially defensive throughout the early weeks. By early 1955, however, Communist air and naval activity in and near the Taiwan Strait had grown to the point where the Seventh Fleet evacuated the Nationalist garrison from the Tachens, the northernmost and most exposed of the offshore island groups held by the Nationalists.

In return for their agreement to evacuate the Tachens, the Nationalists evidently thought they had a commitment that the United States would defend the other Nationalist-held offshore islands, consisting mainly of Quemoy and the Matsus, near the port of Foochow. The actual formal American commitment was not quite so clear-cut, however, and remains somewhat ambiguous to this day. In December 1954 the United States and the Republic of China (Nationalist China) signed a mutual security treaty (or defensive alliance) binding the United States to defend against Communist attack Taiwan itself and such other areas under Nationalist control as both governments might agree to be covered. At the end of January 1955 the "Formosa Resolution" was passed by both houses of Congress to clarify the conditions under which American forces might be committed to the defense of the offshore islands; the requirement was that the President must judge that a Communist attack on them was part of an assault on Taiwan itself. At the same time, the CPR declined an invitation from the United Nations Security Council to send a delegation to the United Nations to discuss the situation in the Taiwan Strait, on the ground that the United Nations had failed so far to seat the CPR or take any action on its many charges of American aggression.

Air and sea actions in the Taiwan Strait continued during the early spring of 1955, and the atmosphere remained tense. During April, however, Peking began to ease its pressure on the Nationalists, apparently for three reasons that were analogous to the factors that had affected the Chinese stand at the Geneva Conference a year earlier. The United States seemed to determine to defend the offshore islands if necessary, and a statement by Secretary Dulles on March 5 seemed to threaten retaliation for an attack on them; on the other hand, the United States did not appear to consider itself bound to support any offensive action by the Nationalists and in late April tried unsuccessfully to persuade them to evacuate the offshore islands. Regard for neutral opinion continued to be an important consideration in Peking, especially since an important conference of Afro-Asian nations was to open at Bandung, in Java, on April 18, and tension in the Taiwan Strait did not improve the

CPR's standing in neutral circles. Finally, the Soviet Union was clearly nervous about the possibility that the crisis might escalate and could not be relied on to give effective support to the CPR if it brought on American retaliation by an act of its own.

ACCOMMODATION AND COMPETITION WITH KHRUSHCHEV

We have seen that in the aftermath of Stalin's death the competition among his successors, as well as the CPR's troublemaking capacity in a region in which they had no desire to become embroiled, conferred a considerable political leverage on Peking in its dealings with Moscow. We have also seen that Peking had reason to prefer the views of one contender, Khrushchev, on the crucial question of military strategy and the Soviet Union's foreign military commitments to those of his main opponent, Malenkov. In addition, Khrushchev seemed preferable by virtue of his emphasis on heavy industry, as opposed to Malenkov's on light industry.

It evidently appeared to the contending leaders in Moscow that whichever of them could gain Chinese support would substantially improve his chances of becoming decisively "more equal" than the others. In any case, the time was ripe for a comprehensive review of the state that Sino-Soviet relations had assumed since the death of Stalin. The Taiwan Strait crisis that erupted in the summer of 1954, when Moscow was mainly preoccupied with the approaching admission of West Germany to NATO and was trying to reinsure its Pacific flank by "normalizing" its relations with Japan, made the reaching of an understanding with Peking urgent. A convenient occasion was provided by the fifth anniversary of the establishment of the CPR (October 1, 1954), an occasion that clearly called for the presence in Peking of a high-level Soviet delegation. In some fashion or other Khrushchev succeeded in capturing the leadership of the delegation and excluding Malenkov and some of his other opponents, notably Molotov, from membership in it.

While in Peking, Khrushchev displayed only the necessary minimum of enthusiasm for the CPR's claim to Taiwan and in private no doubt cautioned the Chinese leadership not to go too far in the Taiwan Strait or count on Soviet support if it did so. According to

a later (July 10, 1964) statement by Mao Tse-tung, Khrushchev
was at that time confronted by some sort of Chinese claim to
Outer Mongolia that he refused to discuss; it is uncertain, however,
whether Mao's account is accurate.

On the other hand, in spite of differences such as these Khrushchev's talks in Peking ushered in a far-reaching understanding between himself and the Chinese which, although it survived for
only a short time, promised briefly to put Sino-Soviet relations on
a more stable footing and undoubtedly encouraged Khrushchev to
open his public campaign against Malenkov, which he did shortly
after returning to Peking. The first overt sign of this Sino-Soviet
understanding was an important joint communiqué issued on October
11, at the conclusion of Khrushchev's visit. This document announced that the Soviet Union would extend an industrial credit
of $130 million, as well as technical assistance including "peaceful"
nuclear aid that (although it was not so stated, since China's political
and military leadership was still arguing the comparative advantage
of "going nuclear" as against continuing to rely on the Soviet deterrent) would make it possible for the CPR ultimately to become
a military nuclear power if it chose; that the Soviet Union would
withdraw from Port Arthur and turn over its share in the joint
stock companies, for compensation, in the spring of 1955; that both
countries would build new rail connections between them across
Outer Mongolia and Sinkiang; that both parties intended to continue
their allegedly peaceful approach to international problems, notably
those of Asia; and that both parties wished to establish "normal"
relations with Japan (a practical impossibility for the CPR, since
Japan had diplomatic relations with the Republic of China, but not
for the Soviet Union, which shortly proceeded to exchange ambassadors with Japan even in the absence of a peace treaty),
Western-oriented though its government was.

Although the CPR had already softened its line toward the
neutral countries with Moscow's evident approval, it had retained a
worrisome and unpredictable tendency to take military action in its
own immediate vicinity (Korea, the Taiwan Strait, Indochina, and
the Himalayan region). In effect, the CPR promised Khrushchev
political cooperation in the form of restraint on its behavior toward
these regions, plus a continuation of its friendlier line toward the

neutral countries, in exchange for an increment of Soviet economic and military aid and technical assistance. February 1955, the same month in which Khrushchev seemingly completed his triumph over Malenkov by forcing him to resign as premier, also saw the CPR put its First Five Year Plan, which had officially gotten under way in 1953, into final shape, apparently on the assumption that only then was it safe to count on Khrushchev's being able to fulfill the commitments he had made in Peking the previous October, and soon afterward it announced the fall and death of Kao Kang, which as we have seen had a Soviet aspect.

Hardly had Khrushchev unseated Malenkov, however, than the seeds of the collapse of the former's accommodation with the Chinese began to be sown. The basic issues at this time were two: relations with the United States and policy toward the developing countries.

As for the first of these issues, the CPR has always been fundamentally opposed to détente, let alone positive cooperation, between the United States and the Soviet Union, on two main grounds: Leninist ideology if strictly interpreted calls for struggle, not compromise—except of a minimal and tactical kind—with "imperialism"; and improvements in Soviet-American relations tend to make Moscow even less willing than otherwise to take serious risks in a remote region of secondary interest to itself by actively supporting the CPR in its continuing confrontation with the United States over Taiwan and other issues. In 1955, mainly it appears on account of concern over the risks in Europe seemingly created by the admission of a supposedly "revanchist" West Germany to NATO, Khrushchev went rather far in conciliating the West. His measures for reducing tension in Europe culminated in the Geneva Summit Conference of July 1955, at which the chiefs of government of the Big Four sat down together for the first time in a decade without the presence of a government that regarded itself as rightfully a great power entitled to take part in such affairs or to prevent them if it chose—namely, the one in Peking. Although the CPR gave public approval to the Geneva Summit Conference, it probably felt some reservations as to how far Khrushchev might go in compromising with "imperialism." It was no doubt to stiffen his spine, among other reasons, that some Chinese leaders including

Mao began about this time to say that a world war would not be a total disaster, since mankind and "socialism" would survive.

The most that the CPR itself was able and willing to do in dealing with "imperialism" was to inaugurate, following some preliminary overtures at the summit conference, a series of informal talks with the United States at the ambassadorial level, beginning in August 1955 at Geneva. Apart from an agreement in principle to release all nationals of each party being held by the other, little was achieved. The United States demanded a "renunciation of force" by the CPR with respect to the Taiwan Strait, and the CPR countered with a demand for an ending of the American "occupation" of Taiwan. Seeing that it could make no headway on the Taiwan issue through direct discussions with the United States, the CPR in early 1956 began to make public, but unsuccessful, pleas to the Nationalists to come to an understanding on the "peaceful liberation" of Taiwan.

Even more serious, at that time, in disrupting Sino-Soviet harmony was the adoption by Khrushchev in 1955 of an unprecedently active Soviet policy in the developing world. The Soviet Union was undoubtedly annoyed at not being invited to the Bandung Conference and afraid that the CPR, which played a very prominent part at the conference, might gain an insuperable lead over itself in the Third World. The great increase in Soviet interest and activity that began almost immediately after the Bandung Conference must be interpreted to a large extent in the light of this nervousness. In this emerging competition for comparative influence in the Third World, the main weapon on the Chinese side apart from political ploys was cultural relations, and on the Soviet side (again apart from political ploys) economic and military aid. The Soviet effort was focused on Egypt, the sale of Soviet arms to which, through Czechoslovakia, in the late summer of 1955 did much to produce the Suez crisis of 1956, and on India, Premier Nehru being thoroughly in sympathy with Khrushchev's emphasis on minimizing the risk of general war through conciliation within limits of the West and of course delighted to accept Soviet aid.

Although greeted with approval in Peking at first, these developments were disruptive of Sino-Soviet relations in the long run because Khrushchev was, in effect, adopting a global strategy instead of the essentially continental strategy that had prevailed under Stalin and indeed down to 1955. Under the older strategy the emphasis had lain heavily on the Eurasian continent and on the territorial security of the Soviet Union. These preoccupations required, in Moscow's eyes, the greatest attention to the political reliability of Eastern Europe and China as buffers and as allies against any possible resurgence of a militant Germany or a militant Japan with American support. Eastern Europe, except for Yugoslavia, was held down forcibly, at least while Stalin lived and even to a degree after that. China's political reliability could not be assured in this way, since the Soviet Union was in no position to control it. Even Stalin had had to treat it with substantial consideration. In retrospect, Khrushchev's accommodation with the CPR in October 1954 and early 1955 can be viewed as the last major manifestation of the continental strategy in the field of Sino-Soviet relations. Under the global strategy Eastern Europe remained crucial because of Moscow's overwhelming concern with the German problem, but the bumptious Chinese now appeared not only less essential to Soviet interests but actually competitive in the Third World that Khrushchev was coming to regard as a safer arena than the Eurasian continent for his long-term struggle against the West. There also existed among the Soviet public, and perhaps to a degree among the Soviet elite, an elemental emotional fear of the CPR as the current incarnation of the traditional "yellow peril" that in various guises had threatened Russia over the centuries. Any indication of Chinese territorial designs in Inner Asia, such as Mao Tse-tung's claim to Outer Mongolia if he actually made it, would have been sufficient in these circumstances to set in motion in Moscow a trend toward thinking of the CPR as a potential enemy in Eurasia as well as a competitor in the Third World, instead of a loyal if occasionally assertive ally.

The fruition of these tendencies toward a serious worsening of Sino-Soviet relations was not to come for several years, but their origins can be discerned in 1955.

"PEACEFUL COEXISTENCE" WITH NEUTRAL ASIA

The "armed struggle" strategy favored by the CPC after 1948 for the Communist parties of Asia had failed, except in the special case of Vietnam. The Korean War and the ensuing crises in Indo-china and the Taiwan Strait, in the context of American containment of the CPR, had created military risks that Peking could not cope with by strictly military means but could hope to render manageable through the sympathy and political support of the neutrals. A number of international developments, such as the Geneva Conference, demonstrated to Peking that, its revolutionary objectives being largely unattainable in the short run, its national interest could best be served for the time being by maximizing its influence in Asia through the application of the carrot rather than the stick.

These considerations dictated a de-emphasis, although not a total and permanent abandonment on principle, of "armed struggle" and an emphasis on "peaceful coexistence." Peking began to cultivate neutral governments and to encourage Asian allies of the United States to shift to a neutral posture rather than inciting Asian Communist parties to revolt. Naturally, Peking had to concede and praise the highest goals of the leaderships of the countries being wooed rather than denying and denouncing them as it had done during the phase of "armed struggle": their independence (as against allegedly "neocolonial" control by the West), their neutrality in the Cold War (as against the myth that they were "running dogs" of Western "imperialism"), and their right to choose their own political and social systems rather than having these imposed on them by a concert of domestic and external Communist pressures exerted in the name of historic inevitability.

For a variety of reasons, the key country in the CPR's shift to a "peaceful coexistence" strategy was India. Its obvious assets were its influence in neutral and Western circles, its effort to mediate rather than merely shun the Cold War, and Prime Minister Nehru's friendly feelings for the CPR even though it was in no position to duplicate the Soviet Union's performance in extending massive economic aid. Nehru had persisted in demonstrating friendship for the CPR in spite of the latter's obvious dislike and suspicion of him in the early years after 1949. These hostile feelings were soon outweighed, although not eliminated, by a realization in Peking that India's active efforts to settle the Korean crisis, whatever their intent, had an objective effect favorable to the Communist side. Accordingly, positive Chinese efforts to cultivate Indian good will on the diplomatic plane began as early as January 1951, while Chinese propaganda was still denouncing Nehru and other neutral Asian statesmen as lackeys of Western "imperialism." These absurd accusations tapered off during 1951 and 1952 to the point of virtual disappearance except in occasional publications designed for domestic consumption. India's shift of position on the Korean prisoner question did not prevent an intensification of Chinese cultivation of Indian good will after the signing of the Korean armistice. Probably the most important technique employed was that of cultural relations and propaganda stressing a mythical "two thousand years of friendship" between the Chinese and Indian "peoples."

In the spring of 1951 Peking had promised autonomy to the Tibetans, to a great extent in order to please India, but the problem of Indian consular rights in Tibet inherited from British days and that of Indian recognition of the situation in Tibet remained unsettled. In addition, there were known to be some differences on the location of the Sino-Indian border, and Nehru and many other Asian leaders were worried that the Chinese might not really have abandoned "armed struggle" and might continue to foment it in neighboring countries through ethnic minorities, Overseas Chinese communities, or the local Communist parties. Being the most concrete of these questions, the status of Tibet was the first to become the object of Sino-Indian diplomatic discussions, in late 1953. The result was an agreement of April 1954 in which, in effect, India recognized the Chinese position in Tibet, terminated its own special rights there, and refrained from pressing for a clarification of the Sino-Indian border question in exchange for the "Five Principles of Peaceful Coexistence," a flowery set of platitudes amounting to a mutual pledge to maintain friendly relations and not interfere in one another's internal affairs. With the signing of this agreement, Peking's new policy of "peaceful coexistence" passed from the informal to the formal stage.

From the beginning, the shift away from "armed struggle" had been motivated to a high degree by the need for foreign political support against possible American military threats or pressures. In the spring of 1954, at the time of the Dienbienphu crisis, Secretary Dulles began to construct a Southeast Asia Collective Defense Organization (usually called SEATO, by analogy with NATO) so as to offer protection to the countries of the region, especially Thailand, against possible attack or subversion from China or the DRV. At that time, the countries of Southeast Asia were confronted in effect with a choice between two formulae for coping with this threat. These were Dulles's formula of a military alliance, which was adopted by Thailand and the Philippines (Pakistan also joined SEATO, but for different reasons), and Nehru's formula of friendship with the CPR, as embodied in the Five Principles, which was adopted by Burma, Ceylon (after a major political crisis), Cambodia, and Indonesia. Generally speaking, the choice was made on the basis of the pre-existing posture of the country in question with respect to the Cold War.

It should be obvious that the CPR vastly preferred Nehru's approach to Dulles's. The main Chinese objective was to ensure that southern Asia did not harbor American bases and forces of the kind that had been creating difficulties and insecurity for the CPR in the case of Northeast Asia and the Western Pacific. If a given country were willing to maintain friendly relations with the CPR and refrain from signing treaties with the United States or harboring American bases, it seemed a small price to pay to abstain, for the time being although not necessarily in perpetuity, from stirring up subversion and Communist insurrection.

Late in June 1954, while the Geneva Conference was in recess, Chou En-lai flew to New Delhi, where he and Nehru issued a statement reaffirming the Five Principles. From there he went to Burma, evidently at Nehru's suggestion, and issued a similar statement jointly with Premier Nu. Later in the year, Nehru and Nu paid separate visits to Peking. From all this diplomatic activity, Nehru believed, although with what justification it is hard to be sure, that he had extracted an informal but reliable pledge that the CPR would not only refrain from aggression and subversion against other Asian countries but would negotiate the troublesome question of the citizenship of the 12-odd million Overseas Chinese.

Lingering fears of Chinese troublemaking and concern over the tendency toward the polarization of southern Asia by the formation of SEATO were among the main problems that were placed on the agenda by a group of Asian countries that in late 1954 began to organize an Asian-African (or Afro-Asian) Conference for April 1955. There is no need or space here for a detailed description of this conference, which met at Bandung, in Java, on April 18, except to say that the diversity of the countries represented (anti-"colonialism" was virtually the only common bond) and the competitive vanities and ambitions of various leaders (notably Nehru, Chou En-lai, Sukarno, and Nasser) prevented anything very concrete from being achieved. Probably the most important role was played by Chou En-lai. With his usual charm and diplomatic skill, he relieved some of the anxieties even of the Thai and in general portrayed the CPR convincingly as wholly committed to "peaceful coexistence." At the end of the conference he created a sensation by offering to negotiate the status of Taiwan with the United States. He signed a treaty providing that Chinese in Indonesia with dual citizenship should opt for the exclusive citizenship of the CPR or of Indonesia, or in case of failure to opt should take the citizenship of the father (usually Chinese rather than Indonesian). Chou returned from Bandung evidently convinced that the policy of wooing neutral countries was a rewarding one and must be pursued with even greater vigor. Chinese propaganda and diplomacy began to indulge in the most excessive flattery of the neutral countries and their leaders, with considerable effect. Many Asian statesmen almost seemed to forget the essentially Communist, or at any rate Maoist, nature of the CPR's leadership and policies. They were to be reminded in due time.

The Challenge to Mao
and His Response (1956-58)

UP TO THIS point this account of Communist China's foreign policy has proceeded as though it, and the political system that formulated it, were a seamless web devoid of internal policy conflicts. This approach has been adopted solely for convenience; it does not correspond to the facts. After the definitive attainment of power within the party by Mao Tse-tung in the early 1940s, and still more after 1949, the Chinese Communist poltical system rested on two main foundations. The first of these was the leadership and cult of Mao himself, which were accepted and propagated by his colleagues because of his political ability and strategic insight and as a source and focus of national unity in a country pulled by centrifugal forces. The other was the Communist Party apparatus, or in other words, the inner core of the party, which tied the country together and provided it with organization and stability, whereas Mao and the "thought of Mao Tse-tung" provided it with ideology and dynamism. For the first few years after 1949 the combination of Mao and the apparatus functioned well and helped along with other factors to give the regime its period of greatest effectiveness at home.

But Mao had come to power in the party during the Stalin era, even though not because of Stalin's support, and with Stalin's death he was bound to seem increasingly archaic in the eyes of younger and often more pragmatically minded colleagues, some of whom controlled the party apparatus. Mao's increased ideological and international pretensions after Stalin's death were matched by increasing arbitrariness at home; in July 1955, for example, he forced through over the objections of most of his colleagues a marked acceleration in the pace of collectivization of agriculture. Mao's prestige was too great to allow of his being attacked openly without serious danger to national unity, but to some of his colleagues it may well have seemed that his position could profitably be reduced to more reasonable proportions if he had not seemed secure in Soviet favor and if the Soviet Union had not still appeared essentially reliable as an ally and provider of aid.

THE TWENTIETH CONGRESS

The historic Twentieth Congress of the Communist Party of the Soviet Union opened, not by accident, on the sixth anniversary of the signing of the Sino-Soviet Alliance, February 14, 1956. This was probably Khrushchev's way of saying to the CPC that although certain aspects of the congress would be profoundly disturbing to it, the alliance was still regarded, in Moscow at least, as intact.

In his formal report to the congress as First Secretary, Khrushchev laid down a number of propositions of profound significance to the CPC as well as to the rest of the world Communist movement. In particular, he said that "war," meaning general war, was not "fatally inevitable," the implication being that it alone could stop the onward advance of "socialism" (communism) and that therefore it must not be risked. This proposition could only confirm in Peking the already growing suspicion that the Soviet Union intended to place strict limits on the aid, support, and protection that it would accord the CPR in any crisis involving the United States. Khrushchev also indicated that the Soviet Union would expect local Communist parties seeking power to do so primarily by legal and parliamentary means; he added that in cases where this was impossible because of the reactionary character of the government, a "sharp" revolutionary struggle must then be launched, but he gave no sign that the Soviet Union would consider itself ob-, ligated to lend active support to such struggles. Although he did not say so, it seems clear that the major motivation for this mild line on local Communist revolutions was the same as that for the line on the noninevitability of war: reluctance to become militarily embroiled with the United States.

On the final day (February 25) of the congress Khrushchev threw his famous bombshell by unexpectedly denouncing Stalin, in the so-called Secret Speech, as a bloodthirsty tyrant in his behavior after 1934, the year of the beginning of the Great Purges, and particularly in his treatment of his own colleagues and the Soviet military. Khrushchev was clearly, and opportunistically, bidding for the support of these elements in his bid to consolidate his own personal power. Having repudiated much of Stalin's foreign policy, he had now attacked his reputation in an act bound to have profound effects on the domestic positions of other Communist leaders and parties.

CHINA AND THE EAST EUROPEAN CRISIS

Although no official text of the Secret Speech has been published to this day, news of its content spread rapidly in Communist and diplomatic circles by word of mouth or through unofficial and slightly edited texts circulating privately. It was one of the latter that was published by *The New York Times* in June. At that point, public discussion of the sensational speech spread rapidly in Eastern Europe, which to a considerable extent was still governed by "little Stalins" whose moral authority was now shaken by the assault on their dead master. There were ferment and demonstrations, notably in Poland, Hungary, and Czechoslovakia.

The CPC, which at that time was pursuing a relatively relaxed domestic policy, at first looked on these developments with a kindly eye. In principle, it did not believe in control over one "socialist" state by another, even by the Soviet Union, and particularly not when the Soviet leadership was one that had just made itself guilty of serious departures from what the CPC regarded as sound policy. In September 1956 the Polish delegation to the CPC's Eighth Congress were encouraged by the highest Chinese leaders, including Mao himself, to assert their independence of Soviet control in their own domestic affairs. The sense of having Chinese support played at least a marginal part in the decision of the Polish leadership in October to recall Gomulka to power and reduce Soviet influence in a variety of ways. For a time it appeared that Khrushchev was prepared to crush the Poles by force, but he did not. Seven years later the CPC was to claim the credit for this, on the ground that it had urged Khrushchev not to move against the Poles; although it seems unlikely that, if such a Chinese view was expressed, it exerted a decisive effect, the puzzling fact remains that the Soviet Union has never denied this assertion.

At the outset, the developments in Hungary seemed essentially no different from those in Poland, and the CPC's first public commentary on the East European ferment, a radio broadcast on November 1, gave cautious approval to both. A revised version broadcast three hours later showed reservations about Hungary; in the interval, Premier Nagy had rashly announced the dissolution of one-party Communist rule and an intention to withdraw from the Soviet-dominated Warsaw Pact. Seven years later, the CPC claimed to have been responsible for Soviet intervention in Hungary, and again there has been no Soviet denial. Whatever the truth about the causes, the Soviet Army units already in the country did begin to crush the Hungarian Freedom Fighters shortly after Nagy's announcement, which unquestionably was too much for Moscow as well as for Peking. Peking, of course, endorsed the Soviet intervention.

Presumably the CPC had not realized until November 1 how far the anti-Soviet trend in Eastern Europe was capable of going. It had no desire to see a disruption of the Warsaw Pact, if only because of the bad example that such a process would set for the Sino-Soviet alliance, although the latter to be sure was a far looser affair lacking a joint command. It did not wish to see an end to Soviet hegemony in Eastern Europe where matters of foreign policy were concerned, even though it would never have tolerated such a hegemony over itself; it merely wanted to see decline in Soviet influence on the strictly internal affairs of the East European countries.

On December 29 the CPC published a long editorial which, in addition to undertaking to define the essentials of Marxism-Leninism and passing a definitive and predominantly favorable judgment on Stalin, attempted to indicate in what way the developments in Eastern Europe had gone too far by explaining the Chinese view of the proper relationship between the Soviet party and state and the others. The Soviet party and state, it said, properly occupied a leading role mainly because of their greater experience. This rather theoretical argument was given some substance when Chou En-lai interrupted a tour of southern Asia to fly to Moscow, Prague, Budapest, and Warsaw, the four capitals most affected by the recent developments, early in January 1957. His main purpose was to bolster the position of Khrushchev and the Soviet Union in dealing with the centrifugal forces unleashed in 1956. He succeeded to a limited degree, but Khrushchev, who was in political difficulties at the time and somewhat troubled by the extent to which he had become beholden to Peking for help in Eastern Europe, showed little if any gratitude, a scarce commodity in politics.

MAO AND THE DE-STALINIZATION QUESTION

If 1956 was a year of political trouble for Khrushchev, it was hardly less so for Mao Tse-tung. The Secret Speech suggested the thought in a number of Communist capitals, including Peking, that if so colossal a figure as Stalin, even though dead, could be denounced, perhaps the positions of the heads of other parties need not be held sacred either. The CPC's delegation to the Twentieth Congress had apparently not been informed in advance of Khrushchev's intent to denounce Stalin and was therefore taken by surprise. After the congress, most of its members stayed in the Soviet Union for several weeks and were presumably carefully briefed. They returned to Peking on April 2. A Politburo meeting was promptly held, at which they evidently explained to their colleagues what they had learned and the implications of the Twentieth Congress were discussed. On April 5 the *People's Daily* published a rather cautious editorial on the Secret Speech, without referring to it, and on the de-Stalinization question. The verdict was that Stalin's merits outweighed his defects, but that the latter had left some marks on the Soviet system that his successors were right to eliminate, provided they did so in an orderly and moderate manner. Although the editorial did not go so far as to imply that China too was suffering from the effects of a "cult of personality," neither did it mention Mao or the "thought of Mao Tse-tung," a rather unusual omission. The document was rather cautious and bureaucratic in tone and reads as though it were more the work of Mao's colleagues than of Mao himself.

At the minimum, we can be sure that Mao felt himself under some political pressure to prove that he was not vulnerable to the criticism of having created a "cult of personality" and of being essentially obsolete. Later events were to suggest that the situation was even more serious and that Mao's colleagues were trying cautiously and probably politely to cut his image down to life size. That there may have been Soviet support for such a move is suggested by the fact, revealed later, that Wang Ming, who had been a rival of Mao's during the 1930s, fled to Moscow at some time in 1956. In any event, Mao responded with a major political initiative bearing his personal stamp and designed to show that he was not an obsolete despot, because in China, unlike the Soviet Union, the people were so solidly behind the regime that they could safely be encouraged to speak their minds. Beginning in the spring of 1956 a series of modest concessions was extended to the Chinese public, the best known of which, the so-called Hundred Flowers campaign, consisted of an invitation to non-Communist intellectuals and technicians to say what was on their minds. At first little was forthcoming except for some largely technical suggestions; the persons involved were uncertain how far they could safely go.

This absence of the kind of response anticipated by Mao tended to weaken his position and lend encouragement to the effort of his colleagues to limit his role. At the CPC's Eighth Congress (September 1956), some important innovations of an anti-Maoist character were introduced into the organization and functioning of the party. All references to the "thought of Mao Tse-tung" were deleted from the party constitution. The post of honorary chairman of the Central Committee was created, presumably in the hope, unfulfilled to this day, that Mao could be persuaded or even compelled to occupy it in the fairly near future and leave the actual direction of affairs to younger colleagues. To a degree at least, Mao lost control over the important administrative work carried on by the various departments under the Central Committee; the title of General Secretary, which had lapsed in the CPC about twenty years earlier, was revived and bestowed on Teng Hsiao-p'ing, a leading figure in the party apparatus. The major document of the congress, the report of the outgoing Central Committee, was delivered, not as at the Seventh Congress (1945) by Mao himself, but by Liu Shao-ch'i, the second ranking leader in the party and a man seemingly becoming more and more doubtful of Mao's cult and policies.

The East European crisis tended to rescue the Hundred Flowers campaign from the skepticism of Mao's colleagues. No longer did it seem merely a risky ploy designed to vindicate Mao's personal standing. It now appeared desirable and even necessary as a safety valve, or as a device for determining if in fact China had the potential for becoming another Hungary. In fact, news of the Hungarian revolution produced some strikes and demonstrations in China. On February 27, 1957, accordingly, Mao in a secret speech of his own renewed the invitation to the educated section of the public, non-Communists in particular, to speak out, and he implicitly promised them immunity if they should criticize the regime. Not until an unattributed paraphase of the speech was published in the *People's Daily* on April 13, however, was the promise of immunity taken seriously enough for public discussion to get under way. When it did, many very severe criticisms of the regime were expressed, not only by non-Communists, but even by some party members.

It would be hard to overstate the impact of this episode on Mao Tse-tung and the history of Chinese communism. Mao was surprised, disappointed, and made to look like a fool, since he had obviously lost touch with the true state of public opinion. He had no choice but to agree to the silencing, public denunciation, and punishment of the critics, an act that of course constituted an outrageous violation of the pledge of immunity that had been given them. The attempted solution to this problem was to publish his speech of February 27 in an edited version appearing on June 18, so as to make it appear that no such pledge had been given. The affair was all the more painful for Mao because it coincided approximately with a personal triumph for Khrushchev, his narrow victory over the powerful "antiparty group" led by Malenkov and Molotov that tried to unseat him in the summer of 1957. The victorious Khrushchev had already indicated that he had reservations about Mao's campaign for free discussion.

For all these reasons, the year 1957 is a major turning point in the career of Mao Tse-tung and in the political history of the CPR. Mao was embittered and further radicalized, an old man in a hurry. He still had to vindicate himself from the suspicion of being obsolete and creating a personality cult, and in addition, he had to overcome the effect on his position of the huge fiasco of the Hundred Flowers. His solution was to be a titanic effort to get China "moving again."

THE EAST WIND

The year 1957 was the last of the First Five Year Plan and the last in which any Soviet funds were made available under the development credit announced in October 1954. Soviet aid to and of course trade with China continued, but they were financed on a relatively current basis rather than out of the proceeds of long-term credits advanced by Moscow. Although the First Five Year Plan had achieved impressive successes in the industrial sector, it was fairly generally agreed among the Chinese leadership that centralized planning and administration of the Soviet type had proved too cumbersome for China and that the Second Five Year Plan, which was to begin in 1958, would have to be marked by greater adaptation to peculiar Chinese needs.

Beyond this point in the argument, disagreement developed. Liu Shao-ch'i and the administrators of the party apparatus tended to favor decentralization of control over the industrial sector down to the provincial level along the lines of a reform that Khrushchev introduced into the Soviet economy during that period. In practice, this would have vested control in the provincial party committees rather than in the provincial governments. Probably for this reason it appears that this plan, whose announced aim was to make it possible for the CPR to catch up with Great Britain in total output of major industrial commodities within fifteen years, was opposed by Premier Chou En-lai, who gave his support instead to the alternative approach espoused by Mao Tse-tung. Mao's past and temperament impelled him to give priority to the peasants rather than to industry. His idea, which he hammered out in debate with his colleagues during the last three months of 1957 and the first three of 1958, was to combine slogans, propaganda, and organizational pressures to be exerted by the party apparatus into the greatest mass campaign yet launched in the CPR, one designed to increase the labor output of the peasantry to an unprecedented level. In this way, Mao evidently expected, his reputation for creative statesmanship would be vindicated, the catastrophe of the Hundred Flowers obliterated, a march on the way to "communism" stolen on the Soviet Union and Khrushchev thus put down, and China raised suddenly to a new plateau of national unity and power.

For such a colossal effort, Mao evidently believed that a favorable international environment was needed; the Chinese people would respond more energetically to his call if it could be persuaded that it was not struggling along, but was riding a historic high tide of some kind. On October 4, 1957, following a successful test of an intercontinental ballistic missile in the previous summer, the Soviet Union successfully orbited Sputnik I, the first artificial earth satellite. The psychological effect of this impressive technological achievement on the world, and especially on the United States, where there was much talk about a "missile gap" and about the need to "catch up with the Russians," was enormous. Mao evidently reasoned that with the United States thus intimidated, the Soviet Union no longer had reason to fear American nuclear brinkmanship and could therefore play a more active role in support of the international Communist cause, that of China of course included. But even if it did not assume this role, the Chinese people could be told for a time that it was doing so and that the CPR must play its part in a worldwide effort that was led by the Soviet Union. Undeterred by the rather irresolute Soviet performance in a crisis over Syria that occured in the summer and autumn of 1957, Mao told an important international Communist conference meeting in Moscow in November that the principle of Soviet leadership must be respected; at the same time, he told a group of Chinese students in Moscow that "the East Wind has prevailed over the West Wind," meaning that as a result of Soviet technological achievements and political leadership, the overall balance of power was shifting in favor of "socialism" and against "imperialism."

Returning to China after his second and last visit to the Soviet Union, Mao pushed through a massive peasant labor campaign during the winter months, pronounced the results successful, and got the consent of a majority of his colleagues for a "Great Leap Forward" along the lines already indicated. In the late spring it developed that the main feature of the Great Leap Forward was to be the "people's commune," an organization lumping together about a dozen collective farms in such a way as to facilitate intensive, although not necessarily intelligent, utilization of whatever material and human resources were available.

This is not the place for a detailed analysis of the Great Leap-Forward; the emphasis must be on the external aspects of this extraordinary period in the history of the CPR, the crucial one in fact to date.

Apparently in the aftermath of the Twentieth Congress and as a result of a sense of the unreliability of Soviet protection, a consensus seems to have been reached within the Chinese leadership in 1956 that the CPR must have its own nuclear weapons. But they could be acquired only with Soviet aid, and this fact probably helped to restrain Chinese polemics against Khrushchev for a time. In April 1956, no doubt as part of the interchange following the Twentieth Congress, the Soviet Union agreed to provide a nuclear research reactor, as well as additional industrial aid (not covered by a credit, however); the reactor went into operation in the summer of 1958. This was obviously not an adequate basis for a nuclear weapons program, however.

In the summer of 1959 it was revealed from Peking, without either confirmation or denial from Moscow, that in mid-October 1957 the Soviet Union had committed itself to an extensive program of technical assistance to the CPR in the field of modern weapons, apparently including nuclear weapons. There is reason to believe that further agreements along these lines were reached in the following month and that the net result included substantial Soviet aid to a Chinese nuclear warhead program, including the furnishing of a gaseous diffusion plant, and aid in a Chinese surface-to-surface missile program. These were commitments of a kind that the Soviet Union is not known to have made to any of its other allies and which therefore require an extraordinary explanation. First, the arrangement can be regarded partly as an act of coalition diplomacy on the part of the Soviet Union, designed to keep the Chinese firm in their support of the principle of Soviet leadership of the "socialist camp" (the Communist bloc) and the international Communist movement. Second, Khrushchev was probably buying, and he did in fact receive, Chinese propaganda support for the idea of a nuclear test ban agreement even in the absence of an agreement on general nuclear disarmament, an idea that Khrushchev had first floated at the Twentieth Congress and probably thought of mainly as a device for creating a climate of confidence that would minimize the chances of West Germany's "going nuclear." Finally, Khrushchev seems to have had in mind trying to draw China into a military relationship with the Soviet Union similar to that enjoyed by the lesser powers in the Warsaw Pact: in other words, a "joint" command actually controlled from Moscow, and perhaps Soviet missiles stationed on Chinese soil. He may have hoped that Soviet aid to a Chinese nuclear weapons program would somehow make the idea of "joint" control acceptable sooner or later.

As has often happened in the history of the Sino-Soviet alliance, a sudden strain was thrown on this evolving Sino-Soviet nuclear relationship by an action of the United States. Late in January 1958 the United States, whose patience had been exhausted by repeated Communist violations of the Korean armistice's restrictions on modernization of armaments, announced that it was about to introduce delivery systems for "tactical" nuclear weapons into South Korea. As nearly as the rapid and obscure ensuing sequence of events can be reconstructed, it appears that the CPR confronted Moscow with a demand for a prompt transfer of operational nuclear weapons and delivery systems, something that, in contrast to the provision of technical assistance to a Chinese nuclear weapons program, the Soviet Union had not yet agreed to do. The Soviet Union apparently refused except on condition that the CPR agree to place the most modern forces at its disposal under "joint," or in other words, essentially Soviet, command. This Peking refused to do, and therefore no operational Soviet nuclear weapons were forthcoming. This was indicated in a number of Chinese statements issued in the spring of 1958, to the effect that the CPR would acquire nuclear weapons through its own efforts and that the time required might be considerable. The earlier agreement on Soviet technical assistance to the Chinese nuclear program remained in effect, for the time being at any rate. But the Korean problem remained. The CPR's answer, announced in February 1958, was to withdraw all its remaining "volunteers" from Korea by the end of the year, and in clear opposition to the wishes of the North Koreans, who did not want them to leave as long as American forces remained in South Korea.

Mao Tse-tung clearly regarded the spring of 1958 as a major turning point. In May the Great Leap Forward was formally announced at a secret extraordinary session of the Eighth Party Congress; by a Communist custom, the leader of the losing faction, Liu Shao-ch'i, acted as spokesman for the prevailing line. The same month also saw the CPC use the occasion of the 150th anniversary of the birth of Karl Marx (May 5) to launch a heated attack on Tito's revisionism. Tito was regarded as a bad example for China by virtue of his backsliding domestic program, and worse still, as a bad influence on Khrushchev by virtue of his neutralist tendencies in the Cold War and his deep distaste for the CPC's pronouncements on nuclear war. By attacking him, it was evidently hoped to stiffen the spine of Khrushchev, whom Mao apparently did not yet regard as entirely beyond hope.

PAPER TIGERS IN THE TAIWAN STRAIT

Khrushchev followed the Chinese lead to the point of a partial break with Tito, although one far less sweeping than the one of 1948 between Tito and Stalin. But he still failed, in his behavior toward the United States, to live up to the implications of Mao's pronouncement that "the East wind has prevailed over the West wind." When a sizable crisis erupted in Lebanon, Jordan, and Iraq on July 14, he disgusted the CPC by failing to face up to the West and by taking his case to the United Nations, where for a time he even indicated a willingness to discuss the issue within the framework of the Security Council, or in other words, with the participation of Nationalist but not Communist China. This of course had happened many other times in the history of the Security Council, but to Mao's militant mood of the moment, the idea seemed unusually obnoxious. Chinese propaganda to the effect that the Soviet Union should at least send "volunteers" to help the Arabs against the "imperialists" was to no avail.

From May 27 to July 22, 1958, a unique and highly important conference was convened in Peking by the Military Committee of the CPC's Central Committee. Most of the top party and military leaders were present at one time or another. The topics discussed were probably very close to the ones that have been dealt with in this chapter: the Great Leap Forward, military policy, relations with the Soviet Union, etc. The official, or Maoist, solution for these problems was no doubt explained. From the course of subsequent events, however, it appears that the nature of that answer changed somewhat by the end of the conference. For by that time it had become fairly clear that Khrushchev did not propose to take action on the Middle East in the spirit of "the East wind has prevailed over the West wind," a failure that seemed especially serious to Mao because the Great Leap Forward was then getting under way and a favorable international atmosphere was considered highly desirable, if not essential; the CPR's first major "people's commune" had already been named *Wei-hsing* (Satellite, or Sputnik). It was evident that the Soviet Union would not create such an atmosphere, and references in the Chinese press to Soviet achievements in space began to decline in the second half of 1958.

If there was to be a favorable, or seemingly favorable, external environment for the Great Leap Forward, it would have to be created by the CPR itself. The logical area was the Taiwan Strait, where the directness of the confrontation with the United States would be somewhat less than in Korea, where the Communist side of the operation would be entirely controllable from Peking, and where the political appeal to the people of the mainland would be maximal. Furthermore, it might be possible to smoke out the Soviet Union and the United States as to their real views of their respective commitments regarding the Taiwan Strait and the offshore islands and to create dissension between the Americans and the Nationalists and thus increase the chances of a favorable accommodation with the latter. In addition, an operation in the Taiwan Strait might have some value as a spoiling or preemptive attack; the Nationalists had been pressing the United States successfully for more advanced military equipment and seemed to be contemplating some offensive operations against the mainland.

No sooner had the military conference adjourned, than the CPC press began a propaganda campaign for the "liberation" of Taiwan. Air fields long since constructed opposite Taiwan but previously left empty were occupied in late July. These alarming developments brought a Soviet delegation led by Khrushchev and his Defense Minister, Marshal Malinovsky, from Moscow at the end of July. Malinovsky evidently tried to persuade the CPC not to provoke the United States and explained that the Soviet Union was in reality inferior to it in strategic weapons. Khrushchev indicated the political limits on Soviet support and tried to win Chinese cooperation by agreeing not to discuss the Middle Eastern crisis in the Security Council. But the Russians clearly had no success in persuading Mao to cease and desist in the Taiwan Strait. The most the Russians could do at that time was to circulate, via Warsaw, a rumor that the Soviet Union had turned over nuclear weapons to the CPR, the desired result presumably being to render the United States more cautious in confronting Peking.

On August 23, the anniversary of the Hitler-Stalin pact and a day probably selected in order to remind Moscow of the dangers of compromising with "imperialism," Communist artillery began to shell Quemoy. Although the Communist press indicated that a landing would be attempted, no assault forces or landing craft were ever moved into the area; it was to be entirely an effort to blockade Quemoy into surrender by air and sea action. In view of the ineptness of the Nationalist Navy, there seemed to be a reasonable prospect of success until it became clear after a few days that the

Seventh Fleet would escort Nationalist supply ships as close to Quemoy as the three-mile limit. Thereupon the CPR announced that it was claiming a twelve-mile limit on its territorial waters, only to be warned on September 4 by Secretary Dulles that the United States would not recognize this claim and might retaliate against any Communist effort to interfere with American ships between the three- and twelve-mile limits.

On September 5 the Supreme State Conference, a sort of forum for the Chairman of the CPR (Mao Tse-tung), convened in Peking, and the following day Chou En-lai in addressing it said that the CPR had no desire for war with the United States and proposed a resumption of the Sino-American ambassadorial talks, which had been in recess for several weeks. On September 6 the United States accepted Chou's offer, and the talks resumed on September 15 in Warsaw where they have been held at somewhat irregular intervals ever since. On September 7 Khrushchev, who had kept quiet up to that time until he saw that the period of greatest danger was over, issued a mighty propaganda blast against the United States for its behavior in the Taiwan Strait, to the effect that "an attack on the CPR . . . is an attack on the Soviet Union." It was a ludicrous performance, and one for which the CPR later ridiculed him in public. Twelve days later he sent an even more abusive message to Washington, which was returned unacknowledged on the ground that it violated diplomatic usage. Khrushchev, impressed no doubt with the fact that the United States was sending nuclear-capable howitzers to Quemoy, then subsided into comparative silence.

On September 22 it was announced that a high Nationalist official, obviously exasperated by the continued Communist shelling of Quemoy, had warned that unless the shelling eased within two weeks, the Nationalists would take action against the mainland gun positions, presumably by air attack. On October 5, the day before the deadline, the Soviet news agency, Tass, obviously speaking for Khrushchev, stated that the Soviet Union did not propose to interfere in the Chinese civil war; in other words, the Soviet Union did not propose to act if the Nationalists attacked the mainland without direct American support. The following day the CPR announced a one-week ceasefire, an arrangement that was changed within a few weeks into the present unique one whereby the CPR reserves the right to shell Quemoy on odd-numbered days, as a means of keeping its claim to the island alive.

By early or mid-October, then, the crisis was over as far as the Communists were concerned. An analogous development on the Nationalist side occurred on October 23, when President Chiang and Secretary Dulles, at the conclusion of a visit by the latter to Taiwan, issued a joint statement in which the Nationalists pledged themselves not to use force, or in other words, invasion, as the primary means of recovering the mainland, something they were in no position to do in any case.

Since Mao's unsuccessful ploy in 1958 in the Taiwan Strait, the CPR has been more cautious about getting involved in military confrontations with the United States, and it is reasonable to suppose that a decision in favor of greater caution was taken at that time. But Mao's unwritten rules seem to require that the trumpet that sounds retreat must be made to appear to the uninitiated as though it sounds the call to advance. At the end of October, accordingly, a collection of his earlier statements on the United States was issued under the imposing title, "Imperialists and all Reactionaries are Paper Tigers." On the surface, the message conveyed was that the United States, although well armed and militarily dangerous, was a political "paper tiger" and could eventually be done in by the aroused "revolutionary people of the world." Beneath the surface, the point was that since it was risky for the CPR to confront the "paper tiger" directly, it would not do so; instead, the task would be largely delegated to revolutionary movements in the Third World, where the risks to the CPR would be far less even if the results were difficult to predict.

As time was to show, there is a risk inherent in this strategy. In order to make it convincing, and in order to excuse itself from putting its own shoulder directly to the revolutionary wheel by confronting the United States "eyeball to eyeball," the CPR must be able to claim credibly that the "revolutionary people of the world" are in fact making significant progress in their alleged struggle against American "imperialism," and there is a strong natural temptation for the CPR to do what it can, within reason, to make sure that such progress occurs. But in dealing with third countries, it is easy to overplay one's hand, and the CPR has repeatedly tried to go too far too fast in inducing revolutionary situations in the Third World by the usually rather limited means available to it. The result has occasionally been a serious Chinese setback.

MAO AND HIS SKEPTICAL COLLEAGUES

By the end of 1958, if there was a paper tiger in the picture, it was Mao Tse-tung. The Hundred Flowers campaign had been a spectacular failure. Although the same could not be said quite so flatly of the Great Leap Forward, by the autumn of 1958 it too had run into sufficiently serious difficulties so that major adjustments were clearly necessary. Over and above Khrushchev's own transgressions against the CPR, Sino-Soviet relations had been seriously worsened by Mao's aura of unpredictability, by the claim implicit in the Great Leap Forward to have found a method for advancing toward "communism" at a pace faster than Moscow's, and by the strains placed on the Sino-Soviet alliance by Mao's performance in the Taiwan Strait. If there was any hope of restoring the Sino-Soviet alliance to effectiveness and getting Khrushchev to resume industrial credits to the CPR, it clearly did not lie in a continuation of these policies.

Developments at that time and later evidence both suggest that a number of Mao's most influential colleagues, including Liu Shao-ch'i, were thinking roughly along these lines. Even Mao himself may have been in a somewhat contrite mood as the Sixth Plenary Session of the CPC's Central Committee met in early December. It is probable that he had already decided that he must put more effort into his party and theoretical roles. At the end of the meeting, two important statements were issued. One announced a significant de-escalation of the Great Leap Forward, the details of which need not be discussed here; by implication the sweeping theoretical claims for it were abandoned. The other announced that Mao would not be a candidate to succeed himself as Chairman of the CPR, or chief of state, the reason given being that he wished to devote more time to "theoretical work." In fact, at the next meeting of the National People's Congress, in April 1959, Liu Shao-ch'i was "elected" to this prestigious, if largely ceremonial, post.

These proceedings seem to have reflected, barely under the surface, a compromise between Mao and his critics, led by Liu Shaoch'i, a compromise symbolized and effectuated by the creation of a dual leadership of sorts with the election of Liu as Chairman of the CPR. The critics were to have the predominant although not exclusive voice in determining domestic economic policy, the economy being in serious difficulties by the end of 1958. A fresh increment of industrial aid was to be sought from the Soviet Union and was actually promised in March 1959, although without an accompanying credit. Mao was to retain his personality cult and his predominant role in foreign policy, although it was understood that relations with the Soviet Union must be conducted in a somewhat more polite way. When Chou En-lai attended the Twenty-first Congress of the CPSU in January 1959 as the CPC's chief representative, his tone was distinctly conciliatory, and Khrushchev reciprocated by renouncing any claim to a first place on the way to "communism" through his admission that all "socialist" countries would achieve it "more or less simultaneously." It was on approximately this basis that the Chinese leadership turned to face the problems of 1959, which were to prove formidable.

CHAPTER V

The Struggle Against Khrushchev (1959-64)

IN THE HISTORY of Communist Chinese foreign policy, the period from 1959 through 1964 is one with several themes, but there is a theme that stands out above the others: the increasingly tense and vigorous struggle, a political one with military overtones, against Khrushchev and his policies. The three major Sino-Soviet issues already mentioned—differences over policy toward the United States, differences over strategy for the Third World, and Mao's resentment at the implications for his own position of Khrushchev's attack on Stalin—grew in seriousness, and two more were added to them: Mao's objections to Khrushchev's domestic program—to his universalist pretensions for it and its possible effects on China—and a somewhat spurious but emotionally charged dispute over territory.

THE FRACTURING OF THE SINO-SOVIET ALLIANCE

In 1963 the CPC denounced a Tass statement of September 9, 1959, obviously reflecting Khrushchev's views, as having been the first occasion on which one "socialist" state had publicly criticized the foreign policy of another. The background to this charge seems an appropriate place at which to begin a consideration of the fracturing of the Sino-Soviet alliance, especially since the origins go back to roughly the beginning of the period covered in this chapter.

In 1958 an anti-Chinese revolt by the unruly Khamba tribesmen of eastern Tibet assumed serious proportions, and Nehru, who was already concerned at the unrest that the CPR's heavy-handed policies in Tibet were arousing, was compelled by Peking to cancel a scheduled visit to Lhasa. Nehru was also concerned by the publication of a Chinese map showing as Chinese territory two major areas claimed by India: the area in the east known in India as the North East Frontier Agency, which lies between the Himalayan ridgeline and the plains of Assam; and the area in the west regarded by India as the northeast corner of Kashmir, which is known as Aksai Chin.

There is no space here to go into the complex background of this dispute. India was claiming a border established by the British, one whose basis in law and history was far from unchallengeable. The CPR was challenging it on the dubious ground, and one that was anathema to Moscow in view of its implications for the Sino-Soviet border, that a frontier originally established by "imperialism" was invalid.

The 1958 map showed a highway as having recently been built across Aksai Chin, presumably to connect western Tibet with western Sinkiang for military purposes. Clearly this road would be rendered very important to the CPR by the Khamba insurgency farther to the east if it actually existed, and investigation by India soon showed that it did. Indian protests at the building of the road soon brought the border dispute into the open. In early 1959 Chou En-lai, the main Chinese spokesman in the controversy, hinted that the CPR would be willing to waive its claim to NEFA, as the disputed eastern sector is often called, at least *de facto,* in return for *de facto* Indian recognition of Chinese possession of Aksai Chin, which from the Chinese point of view was by far the more important and accessible of the two areas. The offer, which was rather ambiguously phrased, was officially ignored in New Delhi.

In March 1959 fighting broke out in Lhasa itself and the Dalai

Lama fled to India, where he was not only granted asylum, but was given a rousing reception by nearly all sections of Indian public opinion but the extreme left. This show of sympathy for the Tibetan cause infuriated the CPR, which had long objected to Nehru's interest in Tibet, his sympathy to many of Khrushchev's views, his receptiveness to Soviet aid, his hard line toward the Indian Communist Party, and his unwillingness to adopt the stance of an adversary toward the United States. Chinese propaganda accordingly began to denounce Nehru publicly in May 1959, for the first time since the early 1950s. As Khambas fled across the frontier to India and Nepal, where many of them seemed to find arms somehow, Chinese troops began to move forward toward the CPR's version of the frontier except in the east, where Indian border police occupied the territory up to the Himalayan ridgeline, along which runs the famous McMahon Line claimed by India as the boundary. In the process there were a few fire fights, with the better-armed Chinese having the advantage. There was one near the western end of the McMahon Line, just east of Bhutan, in August. On September 9, as Nehru and Chou were corresponding over this issue and over the border question in general, came the Soviet statement already mentioned. It took an attitude of pained neutrality and therefore implicitly supported India, which was clearly on the defensive at that time. In early October there was another fire fight, this time in the vicinity of Aksai Chin.

Meanwhile, a major watershed had been reached in Soviet-American relations. In the spring of 1959 the formidable John Foster Dulles had resigned as Secretary of State on account of ill health and had died shortly thereafter. Now that President Eisenhower had lost his good right arm, Khrushchev evidently decided to see what could be gained by a tactic of seeming sweetness and light. He eased his pressure on Berlin and took a number of steps to improve his relations with the United States, the culmination being his American visit in the late summer. It was as part of this tactic, the CPR was to allege four years later without contradiction from Moscow, that on June 20 he canceled his military nuclear aid agreement with the CPR. It is entirely possible that Khrushchev did this in order to help disentangle himself from an ally who was growing increasingly troublesome and unruly at a time when he was trying to ingratiate himself with his major opponent, but the case is probably not so simple as the Chinese claimed; the United States was left unaware of the cancellation, and indeed it was unaware of the original agreement. Khrushchev may have taken this drastic step in order to strengthen the hand of Chinese Defense Minister P'eng Te-huai, who was then beginning a fight for his political life; if so, Khrushchev's action probably had the opposite effect to the one intended.

P'eng had been arguing for some years for a rational, long-term approach to industrial development, against a Chinese nuclear weapons program for the time being, in favor of close relations with the Soviet Union for the sake of military aid and protection, and in favor of technical modernization and comparative de-ideologization of the "People's Liberation Army." He found himself thoroughly out of sympathy with the whole Maoist approach of 1958, and above all, with the Great Leap Forward and the heavy demands that it made on the PLA in the form of inputs of manual labor and increased political indoctrination. He objected to the effect of Mao's erratic policies on the relationship with the Soviet Union. While in the Soviet Union in the late spring of 1959, he evidently aired his views to some senior Soviet generals, and perhaps to Khrushchev himself, and found them decidedly sympathetic. But if P'eng was to try to reverse Mao's policies by winning over a majority of the CPC leadership, few things could have been of less benefit to him than the suspicion or knowledge that he had been communicating privately with the Russians. In July, Khrushchev evidently tried, unconvincingly and unavailingly, to improve his reliability in Chinese eyes by telling Averell Harriman in a published interview that he would support the CPR actively whenever it chose to try to take Taiwan and that he had sent the CPR missiles, though of what kind he did not say.

In August, P'eng took his case against Mao to the Eighth Plenary Session of the CPC's Central Committee. As a military man without much political sophistication, and furthermore as someone who had been abroad during much of the last crucial months, P'eng probably did not realize that in effect he was attacking not only Mao's policies but the more moderate consensus between Mao and his principal colleagues that had been worked out at the end of 1958 and during the early months of 1959. Virtually the whole party leadership closed ranks against this raucous voice from outside the inner circle, for P'eng was a blunt man with few friends among the top leaders, and he was removed as Defense Minister and reduced to inactive status as a Politburo member. He was succeeded as Defense Minister by Lin Piao, the CPR's most famous field commander, a man who had long been a personal rival of P'eng's and unlike him had been careful to display strong public devotion, whether sincere or not it would be hard to say, to the "thought of Mao Tsetung." In either case, he was for all practical purposes Mao's man, and his appointment as Defense Minister was a major triumph for Mao, since it meant that the armed forces were his and some day might be used, really for the first time since 1949, for domestic and partisan political ends. P'eng Te-huai's ideal of a thoroughly professional army closely related to the Soviet military establishment, an ideal already undercut by Khrushchev through his withdrawal of military nuclear aid, appeared to be dead.

The CPC, which always takes a dim view of Soviet-American détente, was greatly angered by Khrushchev's visit to the United States, where he hobnobbed with Eisenhower, praised him as a "man of peace," and in a speech before the United Nations General Assembly, advocated "general and complete disarmament" within four years. From this (to the Chinese) revolting performance, he came almost directly to Peking, where he was coolly and even rudely received by his hosts, to attend the celebration of the tenth anniversary of the foundation of the CPR (October 1, 1959). While in Peking, he evidently lectured his hosts severely on their adventurous domestic and foreign policies. According to a later, plausible, Chinese account, he advised the CPC to tolerate indefinitely the existence of a separate Taiwan. In public, he urged his hosts not to "test by force the stability of the capitalist system."

Hardly had he left Peking when he was confronted, on October 7, by a speech by United States Under Secretary of State Douglas Dillon, in which it was stated that the United States would hold the Soviet Union "partially responsible" for the deeds, or misdeeds, of the CPR. In other words, if Khrushchev really wanted good relations with the United States, he would have to do something effective to restrain the CPR, not merely lecture it. The

CPR, for its part, had been insisting for some time that the Soviet Union was the "leader of the socialist camp" and that this role required it to seek politico-military confrontations with the United States short of actual war, on behalf of general Communist, including Chinese, interests. Khrushchev's answer to this dilemma came in a speech delivered at the end of October. The "socialist camp" neither had nor needed a "leader"; in other words, the Soviet Union should not be held accountable for acts of the CPR, because it could not and would not try to control the CPR. Khrushchev was therefore rejecting the role the CPR was urging on him, which in effect was one of maximal responsibility combined with minimal authority.

Khrushchev's disarmament ploys deeply worried the Chinese leadership, especially since he was engaged in negotiations with the United States under which the two superpowers would have undertaken to fix a limit on the size of the Chinese conventional forces as well as their own. The abolition of all nuclear weapons would relieve the CPR of the greatest threat to its existence and one of the main barriers to the expansion of its power and influence, but the elimination or major reduction of all conventional forces would deprive it of a valuable instrument of domestic control and a major source of security and influence. In other words, the CPR, at least at that time, had a very big stake in conventional forces, but very little in nuclear weapons. Khrushchev, on the other hand, was anxious, with or without nuclear disarmament, to save money for domestic development by reducing his swollen and expensive conventional forces, and in January 1960 he accordingly announced that they would be cut by one-third, a move later reversed on account of the Soviet Army's objections. The CPR was obviously concerned that he might try to bind it to reduce its own conventional forces correspondingly. On January 20 a resolution of the Standing Committee of the National People's Congress, chaired by Marshal Chu Teh, stated that the CPR would not consider itself bound by any disarmament agreement in whose negotiation and signing it had not taken part.

By this time, very little was left of the Sino-Soviet alliance in relation to any but the most extreme and therefore improbable contingencies. The tenth anniversary of its signing (February 14,

1960) was spent by Khrushchev, not at some celebration in Moscow, but in New Delhi, the capital of a country whose relations with the CPR were basically bad.

By the end of 1959 Khrushchev's heavy-footed trampling on Chinese interests and sensibilities, unjustifiable though some of the latter clearly were, had gone far to alienate the most powerful leaders of of the CPC. It was not only Mao and his most fanatical disciples who were becoming convinced that one could not do business with Khrushchev. More and more, Mao seems to have been given his head for an open political campaign to discredit Khrushchev, force a change of attitude and policy upon him, or if necessary and possible, bring about his overthrow by his own colleagues. In the process of rallying support against Khrushchev, Mao, still acting within the terms of the political agreement that we have inferred as having been concluded at the end of 1958, was beginning to win back at least some of the political capital that he had squandered by his ill-considered initiatives of 1956–58.

THE LAUNCHING OF THE SINO-SOVIET POLEMIC

Deeply distrustful by now of Khrushchev's liking for negotiations with the West and of his occasional tendency to make compromises with it, Peking viewed with strong distaste the approach of the Paris Summit Conference, which was scheduled by the Big Four for May 1960 and in which the CPR was of course not to participate. It took the occasion of the ninetieth anniversary of Lenin's birth (April 22) to publish a long and militant statement of the Maoist view on the questions under dispute with Khrushchev, notably that of policy toward the West, under the title "Long Live Leninism!" Even though Khrushchev was not named and the Soviet Union was not explicitly referred to, there was no mistaking the intended target of the lecture, and this document can reasonably be regarded as the opening gun of a Sino-Soviet polemic at a level stopping just short of complete openness. The essential argument of "Long Live Leninism!" is that "imperialism" is a deadly enemy to be struggled against, not something to be compromised with. When necessary, it must be confronted militarily and the risks of escalation to the level of general war accepted; with blood-curdling fundamentalism it is stated that in a world war "imperialism" would be destroyed and mankind would build a better, and of course socialist, future on its ruins.

There seems to be little doubt that Chinese pressure, of which this editorial was the most conspicuous manifestation, had its effect on Khrushchev, who in any case sensed that the Western powers proposed to stand firm at the Summit Conference on the main issue, Germany. He therefore welcomed the providential downing of an American U-2 reconnaissance aircraft over the Soviet Union on May 1 as a pretext for torpedoing the Summit Conference once President Eisenhower, whom he had praised earlier as a man of peace, accepted personal responsibility for the U-2 flight. The CPC undoubtedly considered that its estimate of "imperialism" had been triumphantly vindicated.

Khrushchev could not afford to admit publicly that the CPC had been right, and his dispute with it escalated rapidly. Early in June the CPC took the important step of beginning to criticize the CPSU in meetings of international front organizations, in the first instance a meeting of the World Federation of Trade Unions in Peking. Khrushchev promptly retaliated by denouncing the CPC at a congress of the Rumanian Communist Party. At that meeting the CPC developed considerable support, mainly from several of the Asian parties and from the Albanians. The Communist world was soon electrified by news of the fact, which up to that time had not been widely grasped, that the two giants among Communist parties were seriously at odds.

In July, Khrushchev, who was obviously enraged, played what was almost the highest card in his hand by abruptly terminating Soviet economic aid to the CPR and recalling the 1,390 Soviet scientists and technicians then playing an indispensable role in the Chinese industrialization program. Soviet military aid was apparently terminated at about the same time. The effect was to leave unfinished many of the plants then being constructed under the terms of earlier aid agreements and to set Chinese industrialization back by five or ten years. The effect was all the worse because the CPR had entered 1960 with the expectation of importing more Soviet capital goods than ever before and because the harvest of

1960, following the mediocre one of 1959, was poor. By the early autumn it was clear to all in Peking that the economy was in a very serious state and that energetic measures must be taken. In brief, the steps taken in late 1960 and early 1961, mainly under Liu Shao-ch'i and other leaders more pragmatic than Mao Tse-tung, were to begin importing grain from non-Communist countries (other than the United States, of course, although President Kennedy offered to sell grain to the CPR), to shift what industrial purchases could still be made to Japan and Western countries (again apart from the United States), and above all, to modify the Great Leap Forward drastically in the direction of giving the peasants significantly increased incentives to produce.

Khrushchev presumably thought his body blow would bring the CPR to its knees, or at least extract major concessions from it. If so, he was wrong. His irreconcilable anti-Chinese attitude tended to unite with Mao Tse-tung, on at least the issue of the dispute with the Soviet Union, even those Chinese leaders who opposed many of Mao's other policies. It was Liu Shao-ch'i who led the Chinese delegation to an important conference of eighty-one Communist parties that met in Moscow in November and December 1960, mainly in order to discuss the issues raised by the Sino-Soviet dispute, and to a lesser extent the growing Soviet quarrel with Albania.

The debate at the conference was often heated, especially between the Chinese and Soviet delegates. The main issues were two. The first revolved around the question of "imperialism" and the related problems of war, peace, and disarmament, the two positions being as already stated, with Khrushchev repeating his renunciation of Soviet leadership of the "socialist camp." The second major issue was an organizational one. The Russians demanded decision by majority vote ("democratic centralism"), whereas the Chinese insisted on "unanimity through consultation" and won on this issue because many other parties feared Soviet domination in the event of majority rule. The Chinese had the full support on substantive issues only of the Albanians and a majority of the Asian parties, a significant exception being the party of Outer Mongolia, which fears the CPR and is thus kept firmly in line by the Soviet Union through a variety of pressures and benefits. The final statement issued by the conference was necessarily vague and inconclusive on the main issues, since the Chinese had won on the organizational question and the statement therefore had to be acceptable to all the parties. The CPC's performance had been impressive; it had won a hearing for its views and had avoided being steamrollered by a pro-Soviet majority.

ALBANIA AND ALL THAT

It is superficially paradoxical that at a time when the CPC was beginning to retreat from the Great Leap Forward in the direction of moderation, it should embrace the most Stalinist of all the parties in power in the "socialist camp," that of Albania. In reality, there were reasons of principle as well as expediency for this odd relationship. Over and above their Stalinist domestic policy and their unreconstructedly Leninist view of international relations, the Albanians were alarmed by Khrushchev's growing closeness to Tito, whom they hated and suspected of wanting to annex Albania, as the bad blood left by the limited Soviet-Yugoslav break of 1958 wore off. They resented Khrushchev's effort to control their economic development through increasing integration of the economies of the East European countries under Soviet leadership. Albanian criticism of the Soviet Union grew loud in 1960 and became virulent at the Moscow Conference. In the spring of 1961 Khrushchev broke off economic and military aid to Albania, much as he had done to the CPR the year before, and went even farther in the Albanian case in that he severed diplomatic relations. The Albanians turned to the CPR for economic and political support, which Peking was glad to provide. The CPR for its part welcomed Albanian political cooperation in its quarrel with Khrushchev and sympathized with Albanian dislike of the "revisionist" Tito. Albania provided a potentially valuable springboard in Eastern Europe for contact with the Mediterranean world, including North Africa. Its value as a trading partner was also far from negligible, since it is the world's sixth largest exporter of chrome ore, which in finished form is used in high-grade alloys employed in a number of modern processes, including the production of nuclear weapons.

Growing Chinese support for Albania interrupted the brief lull in the Sino-Soviet dispute that had followed the Moscow Conference. Another serious issue that arose between Moscow and Peking in 1961 was Khrushchev's domestic policies. Up to that time, the CPC had made clear its basic disapproval of his experimental and "revisionist" tendencies, much as Khrushchev had made clear his objections to the Great Leap Forward, but this question had not yet become a major issue in the public polemic between the two parties. Apparently this was because Khrushchev had so far kept his policies within his own borders and had not attempted to hold them up publicly as a model for other "socialist" countries, beyond urging a degree of de-Stalinization on them. But in mid-1961, in preparation for the CPSU's Twenty-second Congress to be held in October, Khrushchev published a long and pretentious program for his party. The second part of this document, which departed so far from such orthodox Stalinist principles as the priority of heavy industry over light industry that it was later modified at the insistence of Khrushchev's opponents and in fact was largely ignored, was clearly addressed to the rest of the Communist world and constituted a plea to it to follow Khrushchev's domestic policies. Since the program did not really catch on even in Moscow, it did not become a major issue in the Sino-Soviet dispute, but it nevertheless foreshadowed a time not long afterward when Mao's objections to "Khrushchev revisionism" were to become a major feature of his anti-Soviet polemics and even of his domestic policy.

For his own political reasons, Khrushchev came to the Twenty-second Congress determined to resume his struggle against the conveniently unresisting Stalin and against the residual influence of the "antiparty group" that he had overthrown in 1957. He was also determined to denounce the defiant Albanians. As in 1956, the CPC may not have been aware of his intentions in advance. After Khrushchev had attacked the Albanians by name in a speech to the congress, Chou En-lai in his address criticized Khrushchev's action and soon afterward left the congress and the country, but not before placing a wreath on Stalin's tomb. Although Khrushchev had little success in his campaign against the "antiparty group" at the congress, he did persuade the congress to authorize the removal of Stalin's body from its place alongside Lenin's and its reburial in a less conspicuous place. When workmen came that same night to remove the body and blast Stalin's name from the front of the mausoleum, they presumably found Chou En-lai's wreath.

The CPC clearly regarded Khrushchev's behavior at the congress as beyond the pale and was evidently impressed by the apparent strength of the opposition to Khrushchev within his own party. It probably hoped that Kozlov, the leading hardliner, who had seen Chou En-lai off at the airport and who received relatively favorable treatment in the Chinese press as compared with Khrushchev, might be able to put together a coalition that would oust ·him. A campaign of public attacks began in the meetings against Khrushchev by name, although not yet in the official press after the Twenty-second Congress, a fact that suggests that his performance had convinced some previous doubters that criticism of him would be useful as well as justified as a means of uniting Chinese public opinion against him and behind the CPC.

THE LAOTIAN CRISIS

The CPC had long believed that its higher estimate of the aggressiveness of "imperialism," as compared with Khrushchev's estimate, was being validated not only by Lenin's theories but by experience. Only a little more than a year after the Geneva Summit Conference had come the Suez crisis and the proclamation of the Eisenhower Doctrine for the Middle East. In East Asia, which of course was of much greater concern to Peking, there had been a series of events including alleged American involvement in the anti-Sukarno risings in Indonesia in 1958 and growing American aid and support for the Diem government of South Vietnam. Into this pattern of rising aggressiveness on the part of American "imperialism," as viewed from Peking, developments in Laos fitted neatly and therefore alarmingly.

Acting under the terms of the Geneva agreements of 1954, the neutralist Premier of Laos, Prince Souvanna Phouma, had worked out in 1956–57 an arrangement for integrating the essentially Hanoi-controlled Pathet Lao, its territory (the two border provinces already referred to in connection with the Geneva settlement), and its armed forces into the general political life of the country. Under this arrangement an election was held in the spring of 1958, with the result that the Pathet Lao and its allies secured a substantial bloc of votes in the National Assembly. The United States, which viewed Souvanna Phouma and his arrangement with disfavor, now put successful pressure on him to resign. The next Premier, Phoui Sananikone, enjoyed American support and took a strongly anti-Communist, if not overtly pro-Western, line. The American idea at that time seemed to be to make Laos into an anti-Communist bastion, something that the Geneva agreements had not intended and something that Laos is geopolitically incapable of becoming. The Pathet Lao, the DRV, and the CPR were naturally alarmed by this trend. The result was a crisis of sorts in 1959, in which low-level military pressures by the Pathet Lao and the DRV, combined with political and propaganda activities by them and the CPR, demonstrated to the Laotian government the limits to which it could safely go.

The Laotian government remained anti-Communist and essentially pro-Western, however, and this fact was a source of worry to a number of Laotians, including a brave and patriotic, although not very astute, paratroop captain named Kong Le. In August 1960 he and his troops seized control of Vientiane, the capital, and invited Souvanna Phouma to resume the Premiership. This he did, but a right-wing coalition with American support drove him into temporary exile in Cambodia and Kong Le into the hills and the arms of the Pathet Lao in December. It was at this point that the Laotian crisis assumed major proportions.

Souvanna Phouma appealed for Soviet aid, and the response was prompt. Soviet cargo aircraft began to airlift military equipment to the area via Southwest China and North Vietnam, nominally in support of Kong Le's forces, but in fact most of it found its way into the hands of the Pathet Lao forces and of the North Vietnamese who were infiltrating the highlands of eastern Laos in increasing numbers during this period, not only to influence the situation in Laos itself but to secure a supply route that could support the growing insurgency in South Vietnam. On January 6, 1961, in the course of a speech reporting on the Moscow Conference, Khrushchev definitively repudiated Soviet leadership of the "socialist camp" but promised active Soviet support for anti-"imperialist" "wars of national liberation." Presumably the airlift to Laos, which constituted probably the most overt act of Soviet intervention in Southeast Asia up to that time, was the sort of thing he had in mind.

This speech and the Laotian crisis itself weighed heavily on the Kennedy administration as it took office in January 1961. It quickly decided not to interfere with the Soviet airlift, presumably on the theory that to do so would produce a serious confrontation with Moscow. In view of the intrinsic difficulties of the situation, the presence of several thousand North Vietnamese troops in eastern Laos, and the availability to these forces of considerable equipment by virtue of the Soviet airlift, the decision was also reached not to commit American ground forces to combat in Laos, even though it was realized that the situation there held serious implications for South Vietnam and Thailand, as well, of course, as for Laos itself. The American decision, confirmed in conference with Khrushchev at Vienna in June 1961, was to "neutralize" Laos, as indeed the spirit of the Geneva agreements of 1954 demanded.

Accordingly, a major international conference met intermittently at Geneva from May 1961 to July 1962 in order to deal with the Laotian crisis. The CPR was represented by a delegation led by Foreign Minister Chen Yi, who had replaced Chou En-lai in that position in February 1958. The Chinese delegation took a rather intransigent stand and tried to gain consideration of two demands of peculiar interest to Peking: the complete abolition of SEATO, rather than a mere prohibition against its extending protection to Laos as desired by the other Communist participants; and the expulsion from Laos of any remaining "KMT irregulars," a Burmese term for a force of National Chinese troops that had been present in various areas along the Southwest China frontier since 1949. On neither of these issues did the CPR achieve anything significant.

The final outcome most closely resembled the somewhat less demanding Soviet desiderata for Laos. There was to be a ceasefire and all foreign troops were to be withdrawn; those few American troops who were in Laos did indeed withdraw, but the North Vietnamese, who had never been admitted publicly by Hanoi to be there, did not. Under a separate agreement, whose exact terms were worked out by the major Laotian political factions, the neutral Prince Souvanna Phouma was to resume the Premiership and there were to be two Vice Premiers, one pro-Communist and one anti-Communist; any one of the three could veto a major act of this government. The implementation of the military aspects of the agreement was to be supervised by a revived International Control Commission, whose actual powers, however, were severely limited at Communist insistence, since the leftist forces were the stronger on the ground and stood to benefit by not having their activities watched too closely by an external agency.

The CPR evidently considered that this arrangement met its own minimum security needs with respect to Laos and has since engaged in no major intervention in support of the Pathet Lao. The latter, and the North Vietnamese forces that are their senior partners, still control most of the Laotian highlands, although the increasingly anti-Communist Souvanna Phouma has not only remained in control of the Mekong Valley but has occasionally shown surprising political and military strength in contests for limited areas in the highlands. In general, Hanoi has chosen to subordinate its interests in Laos to those in South Vietnam, and therefore to content itself for the most part in using the highlands as a supply route rather than giving full support to a Pathet Lao drive into the Mekong Valley.

BRIGHT HOPES FOR THE DARK CONTINENT

Prior to 1960, Chinese Communist interest and involvement in sub-Saharan Africa was almost negligible. The wave of decolonization that began about 1960 rapidly changed that attitude, however. The effect on Peking was analogous to that of the wave of decolonization in South and Southeast Asia beginning about 1947. In each case, the CPC proceeded to overestimate the revolutionary potential of the situation and to overcommit its prestige, and to a lesser extent its resources, to the revolutionary cause. In particular, the CPC was actually aware of the central importance, in view of its location and resources, of the former Belgian Congo, in which the situation did indeed appear revolutionary in 1960. Published

Chinese statements of the period and some classified Chinese military journals dating from 1961, copies of which fell into foreign hands and were later published in the United States in English translation, both make it clear that at that time the CPC regarded, or claimed to regard, sub-Saharan Africa as the region of maximum revolutionary potential. One of the major considerations was almost certainly the fact that Chinese support for revolutionary activity in Africa, although it would have to be at a fairly modest level, would be less risky to Chinese security than a comparable level of activity in Asia, where American containment and the possibility of retaliation were always present. Furthermore, Maoist ideology insisted that American "imperialism" would try to suppress anti-"imperialist" revolution by armed force wherever it appeared, and a wave of revolutions in Africa might therefore have the effect of dispersing the United States' strength and distracting it from the Far East.

From about 1962 it became clear that the leftist cause in the Congo had little immediate future, however, and the emphasis of Chinese subversion and revolutionary activity shifted to a number of the neighboring countries, notably Congo Brazzaville (the former French Congo), Burundi, and the Central African Republic, where it was hoped to create bases from which the adjoining provinces of the Congo could be infiltrated and revolutionized at a later date.

At the end of 1963 and the beginning of 1964 Chou En-lai paid a long visit to North Africa and sub-Saharan Africa, mainly in order to mend fences with the governments in the aftermath of the Sino-Indian border war of 1962 and to survey the prospects for revolution south of the Sahara, which he publicly pronounced excellent. He apparently concluded that the revolutionary outlook was brighter in East Africa than in Central or West Africa, although the supreme importance of the Congo was apparently never lost sight of in Peking. In particular, Chou and his colleagues were impressed with the leftist and anti-Arab revolution in Zanzibar in January 1964 and the subsequent political union of Zanzibar and Tanganyika, under the name of Tanzania. Here was a large area strategically located on the shore of the Indian Ocean and in proximity to the "white redoubt" (the Portuguese territories of Angola and Mozambique, plus Rhodesia and South Africa). Leftist tendencies in Tanzania seemed to offer promise if cultivated, and Zanzibar already contained satellite tracking facilities and might be useful if the CPR should ever wish to test intercontinental ballistic missiles over the Indian Ocean rather than over the Pacific.

THE HUMBLING OF INDIA

Khrushchev's visit to India and Indonesia, with both of which the CPR was then on bad terms, in January and February 1960 startled Peking and called up the spectre of an anti-Chinese combination supported by Soviet economic and (in the case of Indonesia) military aid. In both cases, the CPR moved promptly to mend its fences, but the results were sharply different.

When Chou En-lai came to New Delhi in April 1960 at Nehru's invitation to discuss the border dispute, he privately made explicit his implicit proposal of 1959: that the CPR give up its claim to NEFA in return for Indian recognition of China's control over Aksai Chin. Nehru showed some interest, but the proposal was firmly vetoed by the powerful and conservative Home Minister, Pandit Pant. The divergent positions of the two sides as to the proper location of the border were then referred to committees of lower-ranking officials, who met at Rangoon later in 1960 but without positive result.

The CPR had already begun to move to prevent its border disputes with other Asian countries from becoming a source of political advantage to India and the Soviet Union and to bring additional pressure on them to show what Peking would regard as a reasonable attitude on border questions. Agreements in which the CPR, generally speaking, compromised its original demands and fixed on a boundary also acceptable to the other side were reached with Burma (January 1960), Nepal (March 1960), Pakistan (December 1962), Outer Mongolia (December 1962), and Afghanistan (November 1963). The agreement with Pakistan was nominally provisional, since it related to the border between Sinkiang and the Pakistani-held portion of Kashmir, a region whose political status both Pakistan and the CPR claim has not yet been definitively determined. In addition, the CPR probably made a similar agreement with the small Himalayan state of Bhutan, but if so it was never announced, since India has the treaty right to conduct Bhutan's foreign relations. By the time this series of agreements was concluded, the CPR had formal boundary disputes with only two countries: the one with India, and a less-publicized one with the Soviet Union.

To a large extent for domestic political reasons and because of its dispute with Pakistan over Kashmir as a whole, India was unwilling to leave the CPR in undisputed possession of Aksai Chin. In 1961, therefore, with the help of special equipment purchased from the United States and the Soviet Union, it began to move its own military outposts farther forward in the contested area, until by the autumn of 1962 it had established a total of forty-three in territory claimed by the CPR, although none was actually on the plateau of Aksai Chin. These moves reinforced the dislike with which the CPR viewed Nehru's attitude on Tibet and on world affairs in general and led to a series of protests from Peking. These were rejected, and Nehru made it clear that he expected to eject Chinese troops from Aksai Chin simply by moving Indian troops forward. It does not seem to have occurred to Nehru, Defense Minister Krishna Menon, or to the Indian Army that the Chinese might actually fight to retain possession of Aksai Chin.

But from Peking's viewpoint, not to have contested control of Aksai Chin would have involved an unacceptable loss to Chinese prestige in the Himalayan region and the Third World in general. Furthermore, the Indian Army might then have gotten itself into a position and a mood to intervene actively in Tibet. Conversely, to expel the Indian Army from territory claimed by the CPR in the Aksai Chin area would enhance both Chinese security and Chinese prestige, at least in Peking's opinion, and in addition would deal a major if indirect blow at Khrushchev, whom the Chinese seem to have suspected of egging the Indians on and whom they certainly suspected of being basically sympathetic to India as against China on the whole range of political issues between them.

In the spring of 1962 the CPR saw the Indian advance toward Aksai Chin as only one of a series of threats to which its security was exposed. In Sinkiang, dissident Kazakhs and others were beginning to demonstrate and in some cases flee to the Soviet Union, evidently with Soviet encouragement and support. In mid-May the United States sent troops for a few weeks into Thailand, in order to exert pressure on the Communist side for a settlement in Laos and to calm Thai fears about the Laotian situation. Worst of all, the Chinese Nationalists were giving indications of a serious intent to launch some sort of military operation in the Taiwan Strait. The CPR promptly doubled its troop strength opposite Taiwan to about 600,000, a figure roughly equal to the size of the Nationalist armed forces, and on June 23 secured from the United States at Warsaw a pledge not to support a Nationalist attack if one were attempted. The crisis in the Taiwan Strait eased, and Peking was free to turn its attention to the Sino-Indian border.

This it did promptly. In July Chinese troops began to apply military pressure to Indian outposts in the western sector (the Aksai Chin region), and in September there was a military clash near the western end of the McMahon Line in the eastern sector (the NEFA region). The CPR publicly warned Nehru to "rein in on the brink of the precipice" by ceasing what Peking labeled his aggressive military activities in both sectors, and Khrushchev privately begged him to reach an accommodation with the CPR on the border dispute on virtually any terms.

Far from heeding these warnings, Nehru and Menon announced in mid-October that the Indian Army would soon expel all Chinese troops from territory claimed from India. On October 20 Chinese troops launched successful offensive operations against the poorly prepared and poorly led Indian forces at several points in both sectors. Four days later, Peking proposed a ceasefire and a mutual withdrawal to a depth of twenty kilometers from the existing "line of actual control" pending negotiations between the premiers of the two countries. On October 27 the *People's Daily* published a long editorial denouncing Nehru and demanding unequivocal support from the Indian Communists and the Soviet Union.

In reality, Moscow had already endorsed the Chinese proposal of October 24 as a reasonable basis for a settlement. Khrushchev's reason was apparently the same as for his earlier plea to India to accommodate the CPR: his preoccupation with Cuba and his unwillingness to see, or at any rate to become involved in, another major politico-military crisis at the same time. The main reason for which Khrushchev had decided to emplace offensive nuclear-capable missiles in Cuba in mid-1962 was to acquire additional leverage on the United States for the purpose of a German settlement on his terms; the CPR was apparently aware of his intention and approved of it on this basis. It also approved of, and may have contributed to, a breaking off by Moscow of talks with the West on a nuclear test ban agreement in the summer of 1962. In essence, Peking gave initial support to Moscow's Cuban policy, and Moscow gave initial support to Peking's policy toward the Sino-Indian border. Mao's dislike of Khrushchev and his distrust of Khrushchev's tendencies in foreign policy, however, were too great to enable this tacit understanding to survive the strains of the two simultaneous crises for long. Early in November, when it had become clear that Khrushchev proposed to ignore Castro's strenuous objections to his agreement with President Kennedy to withdraw Soviet offensive missiles and bombers from Cuba, Peking began to curry favor with Castro and score points against Khrushchev by accusing the latter exaggeratedly of having engineered "another Munich." Khrushchev promptly reverted to a stance of pro-Indian, rather than pro-Chinese, neutrality on the Sino-Indian border dispute and went on to make the equally exaggerated countercharge that the CPR had been trying to incite thermonuclear war between the United States and the Soviet Union over the Cuban issue. There were a number of other occasions during these years when Khrushchev took advantage of the militant Chinese stand on East-West relations and of foolish Chinese statements on nuclear war to brand the Chinese as the "war party," mainly for the consumption of other Communist parties.

Far from being stunned by its initial defeats into acceptance of the Chinese proposal of October 24, India had been galvanized into a state of national unity such as it had never known. Clearly it was in no mood whatever to accept the Chinese proposal, at least while its military record in the conflict remained one of unrelieved defeat. So careful was Chinese management of the crisis, however, that Peking waited until the formal Indian diplomatic note rejecting the offer of October 24 had been received on November 15 before ordering its forces to resume their advance. This time there were rapid and major Chinese gains against disorganized Indian opposition in the eastern sector, and to a lesser extent in the western. Then on November 21 the CPR announced that its forces would cease fire unilaterally and in a few days would withdraw twenty kilometers behind the "line of actual control" as of November 7, 1959, a line whose true location is open to dispute and has indeed been disputed between the two sides.

The reasons for this surprising, and yet typically Maoist, way of terminating the conflict appear to be several. To date, the fighting had taken place entirely on territory claimed, with whatever degree of justification, by the CPR; for Chinese forces to have continued their advance much farther would have brought them onto territory admitted in Peking to be Indian and into areas where Indian military weakness would be balanced by difficult Chinese lines of supply. It would also have created an almost impossible logistical problem to keep the Chinese forces involved in the operation south of the Himalayan ridgeline during the coming winter. The CPR had achieved its main goals of safeguarding what it regarded as the security of its frontier and of enhancing its own prestige by damaging that of India, yet world opinion was taking a predominantly pro-Indian line and to have pursued the conflict would have cost the CPR dearly in this respect. India had appealed for military aid from the United States on November 18, and two days later the United States had announced the lifting of its "quarantine" on Cuba, the implication being that it now proposed to give its main attention to the crisis in the Himalayas. It is also possible that some sort of Soviet pressures or even threats behind the scenes were a factor in the Chinese decision to stop fighting and to return to roughly the *status quo ante*.

Since that time, the Sino-Indian border dispute has enjoyed a vigorous diplomatic life, and there have been occasional minor frontier clashes. The most important trend has been an impressive strengthening of the Indian Army's position in the Himalayas down to 1965 with the help of shipments of American military equipment. It is unlikely that the balance of political and military power has actually tipped in India's favor in the Himalayas, but it appears to be in a far more favorable position than in 1962. This increase of Indian strength has affected not only the CPR, which since 1962 Indians have generally claimed to be their main opponent, but Pakistan, which to a disinterested observer is likely to appear as India's main adversary, and has pushed it and the CPR into a sort of informal alliance.

THE REVOLUTIONARY TIDE IN SOUTHEAST ASIA

In 1959 a serious diplomatic dispute had arisen between Peking and Djakarta as a result of the efforts by chauvinistic local Indonesian military commanders to drive Chinese merchants out of their retail businesses in the rural areas. The situation was complicated by the fact that, as a result of numerous disputes over implementation, the Sino-Indonesian agreement of 1955 on the citizenship question had still not gone into effect. At the end of 1959, at about the time that Khrushchev's forthcoming visit to Indonesia was announced and quite possibly for that reason, Peking suddenly dropped its abusive line toward Djakarta for a conciliatory one. Sukarno reciprocated by using his enormous influence to bring about an easing of the pressures on the Indonesian Chinese and the reaching of an agreement on the implementation of the citizenship agreement. There was a radical improvement in Sino-Indonesian relations, while Moscow allowed Djakarta to use its dubious credit to buy large amounts of often highly sophisticated military equipment. Early in 1961 Chen Yi visited Djakarta and signed a treaty of friendship.

Although Mao Tse-tung would probably have preferred to support the large and influential Communist Party of Indonesia (PKI) in a struggle for power against Sukarno, this view did not prevail in Peking, partly no doubt because the PKI and Sukarno were on excellent terms, each benefiting from the other's support as each became increasingly distrustful of the basically anti-Communist army. In other words, by supporting Sukarno, Peking could at the same time, and at least for the time being, support the PKI. Although not a Communist, Sukarno was decidedly leftist and militantly anti-"imperialist," and he had modeled his increasingly authoritarian political order on that of the CPR to some extent after a visit to Peking in 1956. Active Sino-Indonesian cooperation might serve to advance the strategic and political interests of both partners, for example by forcing the United States to divide its attention between the Taiwan Strait and the Southwest Pacific.

Accordingly, the CPR gave active political support to Sukarno's long-standing struggle against the Netherlands over West Irian (Dutch New Guinea), a struggle that had the additional advantage of directing much of the army's attention outward, increasing the flow of weapons from the Soviet Union, and giving the army a vested interest in continuing to tolerate Sukarno and the PKI rather than moving against them. A Dutch agreement in August 1962 to turn West Irian over to Indonesia after a brief period of United Nations administration deprived this issue of utility, but another was not hard to find.

Since 1961, with the support of moderate elements in each component, the United Kingdom had been working out a plan to create a Federation of Malaysia out of Malaya, Singapore, and the Borneo Territories (North Borneo or Sabah, the small protectorate of Brunei, and Sarawak). The main single purpose was to check and contain a threatened growth of leftist political influence, notably in Singapore. For this precise reason, and also because Indonesia viewed Malaysia as a rival and even something of a threat, the PKI, Sukarno, and the CPR launched a violent propaganda campaign against the plan. The management of this campaign was one of the main subjects discussed by Chairman Liu Shao-ch'i during a state visit to Indonesia that he made in the spring of 1963.

In September 1963 Malaysia was formally inaugurated minus Brunei and to the outrage of Sukarno, who promptly proclaimed a "Confrontation" with Malaysia and vowed to "crush" it. The CPR lent him active support verbally and otherwise, for example by stirring up leftist Chinese guerrilla activity in various parts of Malaysia, mainly Sarawak. By this time, both Peking and Djakarta evidently felt confident that the "Confrontation" would succeed in spite of British toughness. One major probable reason for this confidence was an expectation of an imminent revolutionary victory in Vietnam, which would tend to trap Malaysia between two hostile leftist powers, led respectively by Ho Chi Minh and Sukarno, to the north and south.

Although the CPR was angered by the nonmaterialization of the promised elections in Vietnam in 1956, it contented itself for the time being with registering a protest, continuing its economic and military aid to the DRV, and advising Hanoi to keep its hands off the growing insurgency against the authoritarian Diem government of South Vietnam, an insurgency which although Communist in nature was led by Communists who were South Vietnamese rather than North Vietnamese. Peking's restraint was probably motivated by lack of desire for another crunch with the United States like the one of 1954, by the Laotian crisis for a time, and after about 1960 by a feeling that safer revolutionary opportunities existed elsewhere, notably in Africa. In addition, the CPC tends to feel that revolutions should be as self-reliant as possible. Partly at least in deference to Peking's wishes, Hanoi gave little support to the militant Communists in the south and even on occasion publicly denounced their liking for armed struggle. Any other reservations on Hanoi's part were progressively overcome, but the Chinese attitude remained a prohibitive bar until 1960. The near-collapse of the Chinese economy in that year forced the CPR to reduce its aid to the DRV drastically, and the latter now felt free to increase its support for and its leadership of the growing insurgency in South Vietnam.

By the spring of 1963 Peking's attitude had changed. It was anxious to ensure the support of the militant Asian parties in its contest with Khrushchev. It was at that time that the publication of a volume entitled *Selected Military Writings of Mao Tse-tung* occurred, Peking apparently being anxious to appear less abstract in its support of Communist armed struggle in Asia than its theoretical polemics with Moscow had tended to make it appear. The CPC began to give greater propaganda support to the armed struggle in South Vietnam and apparently gave permission for weapons that it had shipped to the DRV to be used in the south. In return for this real, if limited, support, Hanoi began to give substantial support to the Chinese position in the Sino-Soviet dispute, but without going so far as to burn its bridges with Moscow. This bargain was probably concluded in final form at the time of a visit by Liu Shao-ch'i to Hanoi in the spring of 1963. Peking's superior anti-"imperialist" militancy, particularly now that Khrushchev was in a chastened mood after overplaying his hand in Cuba, also lined up most of the other Asian Communist parties on its side in the Sino-Soviet dispute at this same time, always with the notable exception of the Outer Mongolian party.

The year following the overthrow of Diem by his own army commanders in November 1963 was a trying one for Peking, because although it saw impressive military gains for the Viet Cong (a term widely used for Vietnamese Communists), it also witnessed some threatening behavior on the part of the United States. In February 1964, when in reply to a menacing statement by President Johnson the DRV said editorially that if the United States attacked the DRV it would have to cope with China and the rest of the "socialist" countries, Peking when reprinting the editorial deleted this passage. The appointment of General Maxwell D. Taylor as American Ambassador to Saigon in June worried the CPR and evoked a higher level of tension in its propaganda comments on the Vietnamese situation, presumably because General Taylor had led an important mission to Vietnam in 1961 and was known to be a major proponent of the strategy of "flexible response," which Peking interpreted as mainly one for suppressing "national liberation movements." The American air strike of August 5, in retaliation for alleged probes by North Vietnamese torpedo boats against American destroyers in the Gulf of Tonkin, naturally appeared alarming. But it was not repeated, and during the American election campaign President Johnson took a relatively soft line on Vietnam as compared with his opponent. The prevailing opinion in Peking apparently was that there would be no major American military involvement, not enough at least to stop what looked like the onward march of the Viet Cong with growing support from North Vietnam; such was the burden of some remarks by Mao Tse-tung on Vietnam to the American journalist Edgar Snow in January 1965. As usual, however, the CPR was concerned for its own security. On August 1, 1964, in an unattributed interview with the Austrian journalist Hugo Portisch, Chen Yi said that the CPR would intervene militarily in the Vietnamese crisis if, and only if, the United States invaded North Vietnam or northern Laos.

THE LAST ROUND WITH KHRUSHCHEV

At the beginning of 1963, mainly as a result of the serious differences that had developed over the major crises in the Caribbean and the Himalayas, the Sino-Soviet dispute, much of which was carried on in the form of published polemics, escalated sharply. The CPC generally held the initiative, at the verbal level in particular, and on the whole it also had the better of the engagement. Khrushchev was a rather impulsive antagonist who tended to move rapidly in the direction of playing his high cards when it would have been advisable to play more cautiously.

A few new concepts were introduced into the polemic in early 1963. Early in March the CPC described the countries lying politically between the "imperialist" and "socialist" camps as a "vast intermediate zone" and implied that it would feel free to maneuver against the Soviet Union in this zone as vigorously as against the United States. It was of course only the formula, not the idea or the fact, that was new. A year later, the CPC refined the formula somewhat by dividing the "vast intermediate zone" into two parts, the first consisting of the developing countries and the second of the developed countries (including Japan but excluding the "imperialist" United States). Different strategies were clearly appropriate in dealing with each category, and the main purpose of the distinction was apparently to rationalize Peking's policy of trade and friendly relations with advanced capitalist countries (other than the United States, of course), notably France at that time.

Also in early March 1963, the CPC introduced an element of far greater practical importance into its polemic against Khrushchev. In reply to an unkind query from him as to why the CPR was so reluctant to eliminate the "imperialist" vestiges represented by (British) Hong Kong and (Portuguese) Macao when it was so heavy-handed with neutral India, the CPC threatened to review a number of old treaties fixing its borders with other countries, including the Soviet Union. This was truly a Parthian shot from the polemical standpoint, but in other respects it was countereffective. Theoretical and political arguments are certainly of some interest to the Soviet civilian leadership, but hardly to the army, whereas questions of territory and security are of overwhelming interest to both. The Soviet Union did not fight to preserve its European territories from Nazi Germany in order to tolerate the loss or erosion of others to another adversary, even one calling itself Communist. The Sino-Soviet dispute took on a new and potentially deadly dimension.

Another issue very much to the fore in the Sino-Soviet dispute at that time was that of an international Communist conference comparable to the Moscow Conference of 1960. In 1962 the CPC had been pushing for such a conference and the CPSU had been resisting the idea. In 1963 the positions were reversed, and a complicated series of letters was exchanged between the two Central Committees on this and related subjects. In Khrushchev's mind, the conference would have a distinctly anti-Chinese purpose, and the CPC bitterly contrasted his hostility toward itself with his friendship with the "revisionist" Tito, which had been growing warm since 1961. It was on the question of Yugoslavia that Khrushchev apparently won a major triumph over his hardline opponent Kozlov, on whom the CPC had been pinning its hopes, in the spring of 1963. Khrushchev, who had been in political retreat from his domestic opponents for several months following his humiliation over Cuba, insisted successfully that Yugoslavia be treated in official Soviet statements as a fully "socialist" state, and shortly thereafter Kozlov, who disagreed, went into political decline and suffered an attack of ill health that took him out of the picture until his death in 1965. After this episode the CPC, which had hoped for Khrushchev's overthrow when it was unrealistic to do so, gave up hope and apparently continued in this mood until after his overthrow had become a real possibility.

In July 1963 delegations representing the two Central Committees met in Moscow to discuss the issues between them, but to no avail. Neither was willing to make the sweeping concessions that would have been necessary for an accommodation, and Khrushchev, who did not attend the talks, had already decided on a move that he must have known would probably outrage the CPC more than anything he had done to date: the signature of a nuclear test ban agreement with the United States and Britain.

To be sure, this was to be a partial ban (not applicable to underground testing) and not subject to inspection, but it was still anathema to the CPC for several weighty reasons. In the first place, it constituted the outstanding example to date of détente between the Soviet Union and the United States, which, as we have seen, has always been highly objectionable to Peking on both theoretical and practical grounds. It appeared as not only a violation but a virtual repudiation of the spirit of the Sino-Soviet alliance and as a device to make it more embarrassing, although not necessarily more difficult, for the CPR as well as West Germany to acquire nuclear weapons, which Peking had come to regard as essential both to its security and its influence.

The Chinese response was prompt and vigorous. Peking loudly demanded complete nuclear disarmament through a summit conference of all nations in the world, failing the acceptance of which impractical demand it implicitly vowed to continue with its own nuclear weapons program. It took the unusual step of sending two diplomatic protests to the Soviet government, in the course of which it revealed some obviously sensitive information on earlier military relations between the two countries. Moscow replied rather weakly that the CPR had no need for its own nuclear weapons, since the Soviet strategic umbrella still covered it as long as it refrained from aggression, and threatened to withhold military information from it in the future. Early in September the CPC inaugurated a series of long editorials, attributed jointly to the *People's Daily* and the theoretical journal *Red Flag*, against Khrushchev and all his works. In these editorials, of which there were nine altogether, Khrushchev was mentioned by name for the first time in published Chinese statements, and the history of the dispute as seen from Peking was told in considerable detail. The last editorial, published on July 14, 1964, denounced Khrushchev's domestic program as "phoney communism" and indicated that it might spread to China unless its beginnings there were resolutely rooted out.

The CPC also launched at about this time a drive to win over the leaderships of hitherto uncommitted or hostile Communist parties, or where this was impossible, to split them and bring about the creation of new "Marxist-Leninist" parties that would support its line and follow its leadership. This campaign achieved only very limited success, except in the case of the majority of Asian parties, since elements in other parties so extreme as to be willing to support the CPC in its struggle with Moscow were usually also so extreme as to be of little effectiveness within their own political environments. Chinese success with the international front organizations was somewhat greater, and the CPC succeeded in creating to a degree a series of Afro-Asian organizations responsive to its lead on the anti-"imperialist" issue and scornful of the CPSU as soft on "imperialism" and in any case non-Afro-Asian.

There was a Soviet aspect to the CPR's greatest diplomatic triumph during this period, its exchange of diplomatic recognitions with France on January 27, 1964, in the course which it maneuvered President de Gaulle into abandoning his initial effort to retain his relations with the Republic of China as well. The CPR, which was largely passive in the negotiations that led to recognition, felt an interest in the transaction that was limited if real. It was happy to be recognized by a third permanent member of the United Nations Security Council and a power with considerable influence in Indochina, its policies toward which were nearly as anti-American as those of the CPR itself. The CPR felt some interest in trade and technological relations with France, but not much. It was certainly unwilling to make any significant concessions, such as toleration of continued French representation in Taipei, for the sake of de Gaulle's recognition, nor did it have to make any. For his part, de Gaulle was suffering from an acute "Yalta complex" in the aftermath of the test ban treaty and was anxious to establish rapport with another major government that objected to the treaty and intended not to sign it. By giving China a window on the west at a time when it was embroiled with the Soviet Union as well as with the United States, he hoped to give France a window on the east that would not only facilitate a settlement in Indochina, Chinese cooperation in which he considered essential, but might give France a unique influence in Peking and improve France's trade with China. That none of these calculations was borne out to any significant extent, and that de Gaulle should have known this from the beginning, weakens but does not entirely dispose of the rationale for French recognition of the CPR, for de Gaulle had one additional motive that was essentially irrelevant to the CPR, in addition to the familiar argument that realism required recognition of the government in Peking even if Communist. De Gaulle was irritated by Soviet objections to his dealings with West Germany, and he wanted to repay the Russians by establishing closer relations with their other major adversary (other than the United States, of course).

The spectacle of at least superficially friendly relations between the CPR and a France that was at least temporarily on good terms with West Germany seems to have roused in Khrushchev's mind the old Russian bogey, which had never quite materialized during

World War II, of a two-front involvement in East and West. He deeply distrusted the independent nuclear policies of France and the CPR and suspected West Germany, largely without justification, of aspiring to get ultimately independent access to nuclear weapons through the proposed Multilateral Nuclear Force, which was under active discussion at that time. He was probably concerned over the ties between Senator Goldwater, the Republican presidential candidate, and the West German right wing.

It was while in this mood that he learned of an extraordinary interview that Mao Tse-tung had given to a delegation of visiting Japanese socialists on July 10, 1964. At one point Mao remarked with seeming casualness that the Soviet Union had taken entirely too much territory from its neighbors, especially since 1945. He specified, in addition to the CPR and its claim in 1954 to Outer Mongolia, Japan, Finland, East Germany, Poland, and Rumania. He could be taken as suggesting political cooperation among these countries for the purpose of effecting a revision of the territorial situation achieved at the end of World War II. Whatever Mao's actual intentions in raising this issue may have been, in the eyes of the Soviet leadership there could be no more serious one short of a threat of thermonuclear annihilation. For one thing, the uneasy truce between the Soviet regime and its people rests in part on the former's pledge that never again will Soviet territory be invaded, ravaged, or amputated as it was for a time by Hitler's Germany. The Soviet comment on Mao's statement was delivered on V-J Day (September 2, 1964), in the form of a sober warning that if the CPR really intended to threaten Soviet Asian territory it risked the fate of the Japanese empire.

On top of these tensions, which were probably responsible for the fact that in mid-1964 Soviet forces in the Far East conducted extensive maneuvers based on the assumption of an invasion by a powerful Chinese army from Manchuria, came the prospect of an imminent nuclear test by the CPR. Given Khrushchev's estimate of the nature of Chinese policy, it seems certain that this prospect filled him with apprehension. It should be remembered that he had soon repented of the nuclear aid he had agreed to extend the CPR in 1957 and had canceled it in 1959. Chinese pretensions and arrogance, already insufferable to him, would probably be enhanced, and the

CPR might become downright aggressive in its behavior in Asia and its support for "national liberation movements" there and elsewhere. Khrushchev was in the process of disengaging himself to a degree from Asia, partly on the ground that he could not compete there effectively with the CPR; it was one thing to contemplate the filling of that vacuum by a nonnuclear China, another thing to contemplate its being filled by a nuclear China.

Probably with these considerations in mind, Khrushchev moved in early September to improve his relations with West Germany, presumably in order to free his hands to deal with the CPR. This step unquestionably upset some of his colleagues, with whom fear and hatred of Germany is a stock in trade. There is some evidence to suggest that Khrushchev was seriously contemplating military pressures on the CPR, perhaps an invasion of Sinkiang, as is fairly widely believed in Europe, or else a strike at Peking's nuclear weapons installations in the wake of the first Chinese nuclear test. There is also some evidence suggesting that Peking was aware of his project, whatever its exact nature may have been, and was threatening to invade Outer Mongolia if he carried it out. He never did so. He was overthrown by his own colleagues, in his absence and with great secrecy and haste, on October 12–13, and it seems highly probable that his increasingly bellicose and inept China policy was a major if not the decisive count in the indictment against him. On October 16, the day after his fall was officially announced in Moscow, the CPR conducted its first nuclear test.

CHAPTER VI

The Foreign Policy of the
Cultural Revolution (1965-68)

THE OVERTHROW of Khrushchev coincided with and contributed to a period of high hopes in Peking for success in foreign policy. Most if not all of the Chinese leadership seem to have believed that Khrushchev's successors had confessed, by the fact of ousting him, the bankruptcy of his domestic and external policies and would therefore make radical alterations in them in a direction acceptable to Peking. The wind appeared to be blowing strongly in China's favor in the Third World, and major successes there were anticipated in 1965. These great external expectations must have been all the more pleasing to Mao Tse-tung because he was feeling rather discouraged about the domestic situation and was convinced that not only were some of his leading colleagues infected by "revisionist" ideas of the Soviet variety, but, as he told the American journalist Edgar Snow in January 1965, that the youth of China was insufficiently revolutionary and needed to be shaken up. As Mao began to move, early in 1965, to remedy this deplorable domestic situation, his hopes for easy successes abroad began to go up in smoke. The first place in which signs of serious external trouble appeared was Moscow.

THE CAMPAIGN AGAINST KHRUSHCHEV'S SUCCESSORS

For a few weeks after Khrushchev's fall there was an easing of tension and published polemics in the Sino-Soviet dispute while each side, the Soviet in particular, contemplated the alternatives now open to it. A high ranking Chinese delegation led by Chou En-lai visited Moscow for the annual celebration of the anniversary (November 7) of the October Revolution of 1917. On November 6, the day of its arrival, Soviet First Secretary Brezhnev delivered a speech that must have shaken the Chinese.

Although he took a hard line on the United States, he implicitly endorsed most major planks of Khrushchev's foreign policy without explicitly denouncing the Chinese. To them he appealed for a reconciliation of the differences on the state level, each side to agree to disagree amicably on the party and theoretical plane. He went so far as to endorse the idea, espoused by Khrushchev but anathema in Peking, of another conference of Communist parties. This was not a speech likely to be pleasing to Mao Tse-tung.

It is highly probable that during Chou's stay in Moscow his Soviet hosts elaborated considerably, but unacceptably, on what they had in mind. In terms somewhat reminiscent of what Khrushchev had proposed in Peking in October 1954, they evidently indicated that they intended to improve their state relations with China within the framework of an Asian policy much more active than Khrushchev's had been in his last years. They were willing to resume economic and perhaps military aid to Peking, and they also intended to increase their aid to North Korea and North Vietnam. In the latter case, they probably hoped to climb on the bandwagon of an expected Communist victory in South Vietnam and unquestionably proposed to provide Hanoi with antiaircraft defenses against anticipated American air attacks, such as began to be discussed publicly in the United States in that same month (November 1964). The general Communist belief apparently was that American air power would not be sufficient any more than it had been in Korea and that the memory of Korea would prevent the United States from taking the necessary further step of committing ground forces; such an estimate was certainly in accord with the tone of President Johnson's statements on Vietnam during the presidential election campaign. In return for a resumption of Soviet aid, the Chinese were expected to cooperate at least passively in Moscow's policy for Asia, to avoid public polemics against Khrushchev's successors, and to stop trying to form pro-Chinese splinter parties within or alongside the international Communist movement.

The Soviet proposals were unquestionably the subject of major discussions in Peking when Chou brought them back. It is entirely possible that some of Mao's colleagues, presumably those who tended to oppose other aspects of his policy, favored their acceptance at least in part, but it is clear that Mao objected to them in their entirety. He could not bring himself to accept the proposition that the party and theoretical aspects of his quarrel with Khrushchev were so minor that they could now be swept under the rug in the name of pragmatic collaboration between the Soviet and Chinese states. Although it is difficult to imagine a realistic Soviet program that would have satisfied Mao, the fact remains that he appears to have been genuinely disturbed that "Khrushchev revisionism" had not been fundamentally changed but had been succeeded in Moscow by what his propagandists were soon to begin calling "Khrushchev revisionism without Khrushchev." The reasons for his concern were probably at least as much domestic as external. The first public indication of his attitude was an emphatic editorial entitled "Why Khrushchev Fell," published in *Red Flag* on November 21; Khrushchev's domestic and foreign policies, at least as viewed by Mao, were excoriated, and a resumption of political warfare was implicitly threatened unless they were reversed.

They were not. The Soviet leadership had no intention of allowing themselved to be bullied in this way, and they probably believed with some justification that, although the Chinese leadership had been almost united in opposition to the irreconcilably anti-Chinese Khrushchev, they themselves had made a sufficiently reasonable overture to Peking so that they had struck a sympathetic response among at least some of Mao's colleagues. Perhaps the latter could be galvanized into effective action of some kind if Moscow made clear its objections to Mao's attitude and proceeded with the remainder of its program while postponing further efforts to improve Sino-Soviet relations at the state level. On November 24 Moscow resumed its moves toward an international Communist conference with a call for a twenty-six-party drafting committee to meet in Moscow on March 1, 1965, to prepare the way for a full-fledged international conference at a later date. At the end of January 1965 it was announced that Premier Kosygin would shortly visit North Vietnam; his party turned out to contain a number of Air Force and Air Defense generals.

Having received a purely routine welcome when he stopped at Peking on his way to Hanoi, Kosygin returned to Peking on February 11, with Soviet policy seemingly justified to the extent that American air attacks on North Vietnam had begun on February 7. This time he was received by Mao and appears to have held serious discussions with him. In addition to repeating the substance of the earlier Soviet proposal, Kosygin seems to have urged that under cover of Soviet air defenses for North Vietnam the Communist states involved open negotiations with the United States for a settlement of the Vietnamese crisis without further dangerous escalation. Mao presumably clung to his earlier position that the state aspects of the Sino-Soviet dispute could not be settled on Soviet terms, which he undoubtedly feared would tend to enhance Soviet influence in Asia substantially, without a settlement on terms acceptable to him of the party and theoretical issues inherited from the Khrushchev period.

In this situation, the obvious and logical Soviet course was to proceed with the existing program and ignore the Chinese as much as possible. But it was not possible to ignore the Chinese entirely. For one thing, the greatly increased shipments of Soviet military equipment, notably air defense equipment, to North Vietnam that were envisaged in Moscow would have to move at least in part across China, by rail, since the sea route was long and slow and furthermore could be interfered with by the United States Seventh Fleet if Washington should choose to risk the consequences that such interference might entail. Accordingly, a Soviet request was made in private to China on February 25 for the necessary rail transit facilities. The outlook for a favorable response was not encouraging. On March 4, in protest against Soviet policy in general and against Soviet policy toward the United States and Vietnam, as well as toward the question of another international Communist conference in particular, Chinese and some North Vietnamese students rioted outside the American Embassy in Moscow.

When the preparatory conference, which had been postponed to March 5 and downgraded from a drafting to a consultative conference, opened in Moscow, seven of the twenty-six invited parties were absent in protest. Among them, of course, was the Chinese party, as well as the Rumanian and several of the Asian parties including the North Vietnamese, which evidently was unwilling to antagonize Peking completely over an issue of little practical importance to Hanoi at a time when the vital question of rail transit across China for Soviet military aid was still unsettled. The conference was a fiasco, because although there was little support for the Chinese position among the parties that did attend, there were numerous objections to allowing the Soviet party to use conferences as a way of increasing its authority over the others by exploiting such issues as Peking's obstructionism. Accordingly, the Soviet party wisely abandoned for the time being any idea of trying to summon an international Communist conference, became more tolerant (more than it had been under Khrushchev and far more than Peking has been since his fall) of a neutral attitude toward the Sino-Soviet dispute on the part of other parties, and shifted increasingly to the far more profitable ground of advocating "united action" (the term is also often translated as "joint action") by the Communist world, implicitly under Soviet leadership, on Vietnam.

The appeal for "united action" was a difficult one to fault in principle, and for a time it appeared that even the Chinese might be willing to fall in with it. On March 30 Peking agreed secretly to provide rail transit facilities, to an uncertain extent, for Soviet military equipment bound for North Vietnam. It promptly became clear, however, that this was not the end of Soviet demands. On April 3 Moscow privately proposed a high-level conference among the Soviet, Chinese, and North Vietnamese regimes and requested air transit rights across China for military equipment bound for North Vietnam as well as permission to establish one or two air bases in Southwest China, presumably for logistical rather than combat purposes. Peking flatly refused both halves of this demand. The first carried unacceptable implications of Soviet management of the Vietnamese crisis. The nature of Chinese objections to the second is more difficult to infer, especially since China had cooperated in the Soviet airlift to Laos from 1960 to 1962. There were probably two main reasons for the Chinese attitude: a fear of possible American air action against the proposed bases and against Chinese territory and a belief that agreement would lead to an undesirable degree of Soviet political influence not only on North Vietnam but on China itself, more so than would the comparatively inconspicuous and innocuous procedure of shipping equipment by rail.

In the late spring of 1965 the focus of the Sino-Soviet dispute shifted to the Third World, and in particular to the forthcoming Afro-Asian Conference to be held at Algiers in succession to the one ten years earlier at Bandung. The Chinese clearly counted heavily on this conference as a means of increasing their influence in the Third World, to the point of outright leadership if possible, and intended to use such methods as utilizing their political alliance with an increasingly revolutionary Indonesia and excluding the "revisionist" Soviet Union. A speech delivered in Indonesia in May 1965 by P'eng Chen, the municipal boss of Peking and perhaps the most outspokenly anti-Soviet of all high Chinese leaders, in which he used anti-Soviet language that was strong even by Chinese standards, can easily be understood in this context. Enraged, the Soviet leadership in early June reversed Khrushchev's stand on this question by indicating publicly that it would like to attend the Algiers conference, Chinese objections notwithstanding. An editorial published jointly by the *People's Daily* and *Red Flag* on June 13 reiterated P'eng Chen's argument, in some ways in even stronger language, as though to show that he had not spoken for himself alone. The editorial displayed great sensitivity to the Soviet charge that China was obstructing "united action" against "imperialism" in the case of Vietnam. The issue of Soviet attendance at the Algiers conference was shortly resolved by the failure of the conference to meet at all.

The arrival of American Army units in South Vietnam in the summer of 1965 was an important watershed not only militarily but politically, far more so than the sending of Marine units the previous spring to guard certain ports. For the army units had clearly come to stay and to fight mobile warfare in the interior. The United States had now completed in slow motion roughly the same cycle that it had gone through with respect to Korea between June 27 and June 30, 1950, a cycle that the Communist side had evidently not expected to see repeated. Superficially at least, this development could only increase the already impressive plausibility of the Soviet call for "united action." But Mao's objections to this line remained unchanged, and indeed were if anything stronger than ever, since his campaign against Soviet "revisionism" abroad was by now inseparably entwined with his campaign against what he regarded as its manifestations at home. In early 1966 he personally blocked an effort by the Japanese Communist Party to strengthen the Communist position in Vietnam by improving Sino-Soviet relations.

Moscow watched with growing concern the development of both Mao's domestic and foreign programs. Presumably it was disturbed by the purging, about the beginning of 1966, of Chief of Staff Lo Jui-ch'ing, who had advocated using an active Chinese military policy toward Vietnam as a means of re-establishing working relations with the Soviet Union at least in the military sphere, even though Lo was purged much less for his objections to Mao's foreign policy than for his objections to Mao's domestic policy. Moscow was also evidently disturbed by the fact that in the autumn of 1965 the supervision of Mao's program for a Cultural Revolution in China was entrusted to the virulently anti-Soviet P'eng Chen. The ensuing sequence of events is far from being entirely clear, but it appears that the Soviet Union began to contemplate some sort of military intervention in support of Mao's opponents, if they could bring themselves together into an effective coalition and into a state of willingness to cooperate with Moscow, and that it even exerted some threats and pressures to this effect. There were reports of Sino-Soviet border tension at the end of 1965, and again in the spring of 1966. Moscow was remarkably ostentatious about renewing its defensive alliance with Outer Mongolia at the beginning of 1966, and there were plausible reports at about that time of a substantial movement of Soviet troops into eastern Outer Mongolia where they would be as close as possible to Peking. From the Chinese side, there have been vague and conflicting reports, denied from time to time in high places, of a "February plot" aimed at overthrowing Mao with some sort of Soviet support. It is quite clear that at some time during the next few months each side withdrew its ambassador to the other, without publicity. Late in March, after some delay and probably some debate, the Chinese refused a Soviet invitation to send a delegation to the Soviet party's Twenty-third Congress. The decision was explained on the ground of a Soviet letter circulated secretly earlier in the year, in which China was denounced and its behavior attributed mainly to rampant nationalism.

At about the same time, the beginning of senatorial hearings on China policy in the United States seems to have awakened fears in Moscow, fantastic though the idea may appear, of some sort of Sino-American reconciliation at Soviet expense. The idea appears a little less fantastic if one recalls that the notoriously anti-Soviet P'eng Chen still seemed to be in high favor and that he had given some indications of favoring a limited easing of Sino-American tension. In April, however, it became clear that P'eng Chen was in disfavor with Mao and not likely to survive for long. The cause, to be sure, was not his detestation of the Soviet Union but his objections to Mao's domestic policy, but the effect on Moscow seems to have been a calming one, and in any case there was no sign of an effective anti-Maoist coalition in China with which the Soviet Union could cooperate. Any idea of direct Soviet intervention in the internal Chinese scene appears to have evaporated in the late spring of 1966 or shortly thereafter. Moscow probably began to hope instead that the Chinese party apparatus, led by Liu Shao-ch'i and General Secretary Teng Hsiao-p'ing, would block Mao's domestic program and in time swing Chinese foreign policy around to a more reasonable if not more friendly attitude toward the Soviet Union.

If there was such a hope, it was doomed to disappointment. Liu and Teng proved in the summer of 1966 their inability to stop Mao, and in the ensuing autumn they became the main targets of his wrath to the point where their personal political effectiveness was reduced almost to zero. Even before moving against them, Mao's Red Guards had begun to demonstrate riotously against the Soviet Union and the Soviet Embassy in Peking, in addition to other manifestations of what they considered undesirable foreign influence.

At about the same time, Red Guards and other militant followers of Mao began to create incidents along the Sino-Soviet border, mainly the Manchurian rather than the Central Asian sector, not necessarily on direct orders from Peking but rather to demonstrate beyond doubt their personal devotion to the struggle against "revisionism." In some cases, Chinese peasants were herded across the border by Maoist students and soldiers and onto Soviet territory. In spite of its extreme sensitivity to the territorial issue, Moscow reacted rather calmly to these incidents, as though to indicate an awareness that they did not indicate a considered policy in Peking to start a border war or something of the sort. In September 1966 authority to deal with these incidents was delegated to local Soviet commanders, and they seem to have done a competent job of coping with them without allowing them to develop into a serious issue.

A problem of evidently greater practical concern to Moscow was that of delays in the forwarding of Soviet equipment to North Vietnam by rail. Public Soviet charges that such delays were occurring and were due to official Chinese obstruction began in a small way in the spring of 1966, and in a much bigger way toward the end of the year. The Chinese reacted by indignantly denying the charges and asserting that the Soviet Union was shipping obsolete equipment. It seems probable that there was some foundation for the Soviet charge, but it also seems likely that late in 1966 the Cultural Revolution began to produce such disorder in the provinces of South China, through which China's only two rail links with North Vietnam pass, that rail shipments were delayed whether Peking wanted them to be or not. Moscow seems to have considered and shelved once more the idea of military intervention, since it could find no cooperation in China.

In late January 1967, in a frenzy of militancy, Red Guards and others laid siege to the Soviet Embassy in Peking. As Moscow pointed out in its strongly worded protests, one of the effects of this action was to hinder the work of Soviet personnel engaged in supervising the forwarding of military equipment to North Vietnam. The problem was particularly acute because it was already known that the United States intended shortly to station B-52 heavy bombers in Thailand, from where they could easily bomb North Vietnam and also hit western China in the event of a Sino-American war. The siege was lifted after a little less than three weeks, for exactly what reasons is not clear. In any case, during the following several weeks the Chinese evidently agreed in private, under pressure from Moscow and Hanoi, to be more cooperative in forwarding military shipments to North Vietnam. In return, possibly, Hanoi publicly rejected President Johnson's invitation to negotiate and took the unusual step of publishing (on March 21) the letter in which it had been conveyed.

From about this time on, the Sino-Soviet dispute seems to have taken on less of an air of direct confrontation and to have remained rather at the level of propaganda and political harassment. On March 1, 1967, for example, Moscow launched a new radio station, known as Radio Peace and Progress, one of whose main missions was to make anti-Chinese propaganda, such as trying to incite revolt among non-Chinese minorities by broadcasting interviews with members of such groups who had fled from China to the Soviet Union. By and large, Moscow seemed to be waiting out the confusing Cultural Revolution, a course more tolerable than might appear because the Cultural Revolution was drastically reducing China's effectiveness in nearly every department of its foreign policy.

For their part, the Chinese harassed the Soviet Union, for example by occasionally seizing a Soviet ship on the ground that its crew had shown disrespect for Mao while in a Chinese port. The issue of obstruction of Soviet aid bound for North Vietnam reappeared from time to time, but usually in a context that suggested simple disorder as the main cause and a basic willingness in Peking, at least on the part of relatively moderate elements such as Premier Chou En-lai, to be reasonably cooperative. Peking was enraged by what it regarded as Moscow's insufficiently pro-Arab line during the Middle Eastern crisis of mid-1967, and above all by Premier Kosygin's trip to the United States to discuss the crisis at the United Nations and at Glassboro with the "imperialist" President Johnson. A Chinese thermonuclear test, the first test to be held of this kind, was conducted on June 17, almost at the instant when Kosygin set foot on American soil, as though to dramatize Peking's preference for militant confrontation rather than compromise with "imperialism." Chinese leverage on the Soviet Union and North Vietnam was presumably somewhat increased by the fact that the Suez

Canal remained blocked after the crisis, so that the route across China to North Vietnam became more important than ever.

THE LAUNCHING OF THE CULTURAL REVOLUTION

It has already been suggested that in the mid-1950s serious differences began to appear between the two main pillars of the Chinese Communist political system, Mao Tse-tung and the party apparatus, and in particular between Mao and Liu Shao-ch'i. These differences were to some extent ideological and personal or temperamental, but they also concerned such genuine issues as economic development, the nature and role of the armed forces, and to some extent Sino-Soviet relations. Mao tended to take the radical, romantic side of each debate, Liu the pragmatic. This cleavage between Mao and the leaders of the party apparatus, who did not constitute an organized faction trying to overthrow him but whom he came increasingly to regard as "bureaucratic" and even "revisionist," was the first and perhaps the most important cause of Mao's Cultural Revolution.

Mao's differences with the apparatus began to become acute in 1962, when the onset of recovery from the economic effects of the Great Leap Forward raised the issue of future economic policy. Mao evidently feared that recovery would solidify and perpetuate the pragmatic, "revisionist" economic policies that had made recovery possible, whereas he was apparently anxious to return to a more radical policy at the earliest practicable time. At that point, his suspicions of the party apparatus leaders began to be artificially fanned. A visit to China in late September 1962 by Mme. Hartini Sukarno, the beautiful and politically active wife of President Sukarno of Indonesia, led to the first recorded public appearances by a number of wives of high Chinese leaders, among them Chiang Ching (Mme. Mao Tse-tung) and Wang Kuang-mei (Mme. Liu Shao-ch'i). Mme. Liu, as the wife of the chief of state, accompanied her husband on an official visit to Southeast Asia in the spring of 1963 and clearly aroused the jealousy of Mme. Mao in the process. Chiang Ching also wished to become politically active, but the party apparatus had imposed, as a condition of her becoming the fourth

Mme. Mao in 1939, the condition that she must not. Since the apparatus seems to have maintained its attitude nearly a quarter of a century later, Chiang Ching's personal interest in fanning her husband's suspicions of Liu, his wife, and the other apparatus leaders is obvious. In this she evidently had the collaboration of a rival of Liu's within the apparatus, a rather shadowy figure named K'ang Sheng, who comes from the same province (Shantung) as Chiang Ching and seems to have formed a political alliance with her some time ago. K'ang may have hoped to displace Liu as the leader of the party apparatus, if not as the next wearer of Mao's mantle after his death, and Chiang Ching clearly wanted to oust Wang Kuang-mei from the limelight and become China's First Lady.

Another major source of the Cultural Revolution, and one of a much more ideological kind, was Mao's hatred of "Khrushchev revisionism," by which he apparently means rule by a party apparatus plus "goulash communism," or a stress on the improvement of living standards. By the time of Khrushchev's fall, he had already become worried that "Khrushchev revisionism" might spread to China, if not during his lifetime then after his death, not only because of the "bureaucratism" of the party apparatus but because of what he considered to be the insufficiently revolutionary quality of China's youth. This fear seems to have been greatly heightened by the survival of the essentials of "Khrushchev revisionism" in the Soviet Union after the fall of its alleged author and probably by a tendency on the part of the party apparatus leaders to show some interest in dealing with the post-Khrushchev leadership. Mao now became obsessed with the fear that what his propagandists sometimes called "Khrushchev revisionism without Khrushchev" might indeed spread to China and rob it of its revolutionary élan.

Although some observers have concluded that developments outside China, notably American escalation in Vietnam, induced the Cultural Revolution, external developments do not in fact seem to have been decisive apart from the factor of "Khrushchev revisionism" just mentioned. On the other hand, it is very likely that Mao expected his domestic program of 1965 to proceed against a favorable backdrop of external developments that would lend it an air of appropriateness and inevitability. Of these anticipated developments, the major ones were a Communist victory in South Vietnam, a political triumph for China and its partner Indonesia at the forthcoming Afro-Asian Conference at Algiers, a success for the Sino-Indonesian "Confrontation" with Britain and Malaysia, and probably a flourishing "people's war" in Thailand. Chinese nuclear tests were expected to act in some way as an encouragement to these and other lesser efforts by the "revolutionary people of the world." The outcome of these great expectations will be described later. The point here is that none of them, nor any frustration of them that may have occurred, played a major causal role in the Cultural Revolution.

Mao's purposes in launching the Cultural Revolution were apparently to humiliate and punish his various critics, from writers who had criticized him for policies such as the Great Leap Forward to his opponents within the party apparatus; to vindicate himself, his cult, and his various policy initiatives; to preclude the emergence of "Khrushchev revisionism" in China even after his death; and to inject his own vaguely defined concept of "uninterrupted revolution" ineradicably into the Chinese political system, mainly by giving the youth a synthetic revolutionary experience analogous to the genuine one undergone by himself and his colleagues before 1949.

At first, Mao apparently hoped that his virtually complete control over China's vast propaganda apparatus would enable him to create a political climate such that his party colleagues would agree to at least the first part of his program, the purging of the intellectual community. But in case this proved impossible, he wanted to be in a position to go outside the apparatus and use the army and revolutionary elements among the youth to promote the Cultural Revolution and bring pressure on the apparatus itself. Accordingly, with the climate of opinion, sometimes referred to as a "siege mentality," created by American escalation in Vietnam as a backdrop, a major step in the guerrillaization of the armed forces was taken in late May 1965 with the abolition of ranks and insignia. These vestiges of the era of P'eng Te-huai and military collaboration with the Soviet Union seemed inappropriate to an era when the army was intended to serve Mao's political aims.

Still trying to take advantage of the climate created by the Vietnamese crisis as well as by a long programmatic statement on "people's war" by Defense Minister Lin Piao published on September 3, Mao went before the Central Committee later in September and demanded a Cultural Revolution directed against China's intellectuals. He seems to have argued that only such a program would put China's house in order to meet the possible challenge of American escalation of the war in Vietnam to the level of an attack on China. The opposition, which appears to have contended that the dangerous situation in Vietnam dictated minimal disruption of the domestic scene, was strong enough so that Mao had to accept a much diluted version of his program under the supervision of P'eng Chen, the municipal boss of Peking.

Dissatisfied, Mao retreated from Peking for about six months to the Yangtze Valley, where he laid plans for a major political offensive. He had the support of Lin Piao and took advantage of it to tighten his grip on the army, which was made ready for a crucial role in the mobilization of the youth and in the Cultural Revolution as a whole. Chief of Staff Lo Jui-ch'ing, who objected to this program, was quietly purged early in 1966. In May, with the support of the army, Mao returned to Peking and purged P'eng Chen, who had proven unwilling to escalate the Cultural Revolution to the level desired by Mao. It was at this time that units of Red Guards, fanatically pro-Mao high school and college students, began to be formed under the auspices of the army. Early in June, Mao again retreated to the Yangtze Valley, leaving Liu Shao-ch'i and Teng Hsiao-p'ing to cope with the Red Guards. As he probably anticipated, they proceeded to do so in a normal bureaucratic fashion (by Chinese Communist standards), which had the effect of antagonizing the Red Guards.

Late in July, Mao again returned to Peking, this time to try conclusions with the party apparatus leaders at a plenary session (the eleventh) of the party Central Committee. Here Mao seems to have been in a minority, but with the help of his known appeal to the populace, the support of Lin Piao, and the packing of the galleries with Red Guard units and soldiers in a most irregular fashion, he succeeded in manipulating an authorization to himself to proceed with his version of the Cultural Revolution. In mid-August there began a series of eight giant rallies, at which some 11 million Red Guards saw Mao, a new party rank order reflecting Mao's current preferences was revealed, and a new body known as the Cultural Revolution Group and charged with the mission of supervising the implementation of Mao's program was unveiled. It was necessary for the Red Guards to see Mao so that they would agree to leave Peking. This in turn was necessary because they were overcrowding the city badly and because, the central party apparatus centering in Teng Hsiao-p'ing's Secretariat having already been rendered virtually inoperative by some means or other, the next major target was the party apparatus at the provincial level.

However, demonstrations and attacks by Red Guards and other Maoist militants were resisted by the provincial party apparatus, often with considerable success, and by the end of 1966 chaos threatened. In January 1967, accordingly, Mao and Lin Piao ordered the army to intervene, with the mutually imcompatible missions of restoring or maintaining order and promoting the Cultural Revolution. After that, the army tried to implement these two missions and, with the reluctant consent of the center in Peking, tended to give increasing priority to the first. The center itself was divided into two main factions, a radical one seemingly led by Chiang Mao and Lin Piao trying without much apparent success to keep some sort of direction over the course of events. The Cultural Revolution, by Maoist standards or any others, seemed increasingly a failure.

CHINA AND THE CRISIS IN VIETNAM

In his important interview with Edgar Snow in January 1965, Mao indicated full confidence in the ultimate victory of the "people's war" in South Vietnam but no awareness that North Vietnam intended to inject its own regular forces into the struggle as it soon did (probably at least in part in order to retain control over the Viet Cong and the National Liberation Front in their hour of triumph). Mao specifically said that he did not expect the United States to escalate the war either by committing its own forces to South Vietnam or by attacking China, and he predicted that it would withdraw entirely from the struggle in a year or two.

The beginning of the American bombing of North Vietnam on February 7 must therefore have come as a shock to Mao and his colleagues. Although he had been issuing a series of personal statements on certain foreign policy questions with anti-American implications since August 1963, beginning with one on the Diem government's attack on some Buddhist pagodas, he did not issue such a statement now, nor has he done so on Vietnam since then. It may be that he does not wish to associate his name with an issue whose outcome is so doubtful and potentially dangerous from the Chinese standpoint.

Although there was no public statement by Mao, apart from one on May 12 on the risk-free question of the Dominican Republic, a major strategic debate was touched off in Peking by the beginning of the American escalation in Vietnam. The essential issues can be disengaged, although not easily, from the public statements of the major participants, and it can be safely assumed that much more was said in private. The first issue was that of the objectives that China should hope to see achieved, or conceivably itself achieve, in the present stage of the war. Should the war be fought mainly to eliminate the American military presence, which constituted a threat to China, from the area? Should it rather be fought for political purposes, to provide an example and a catalyst for "people's wars" elsewhere and an appropriate backdrop for the Maoist domestic political program? The second issue, the question of strategy, followed naturally. Should China approve and support the sending of regular North Vietnamese army units into South Vietnam to fight the Americans? Should it rather urge on Hanoi a strategy of intervening in the south only enough to keep alive there a "protracted" and "self-reliant" (both favorite Maoist phrases) "people's war?" The third issue dealt with what the Chinese role should be. To what extent and under what circumstances should China intervene? The fourth took up the Soviet role. Should China cooperate in forwarding Soviet military equipment to North Vietnam? Should it perhaps go so far as to reach a broad political accommodation with Moscow for the purpose of prosecuting the struggle in Vietnam and for other longer-range purposes as well? The final issue concerned the chances of the United States attacking China, and if it should do so, the form the attack would take.

Were China's nuclear installations in danger of being "taken out" by an American air strike?

There is no need to go into the debate in full; some of it was highly esoteric. But all students of it agree, although they differ as to interpretation, on the importance of a "hawkish," essentially professional and military viewpoint expressed by Chief of Staff Lo Jui-ch'ing in an article published on May 10 in commemoration of the twentieth anniversary of the German surrender at the end of World War II. Lo seemed to say, with a good deal of arcane language, that if the war in Vietnam were allowed to drag on there was a good chance of a strategic air attack on China by the United States. The best preventive was a quick victory in Vietnam, and to this end he urged giving full support to the sending by North Vietnam of its regular army units into the south, under the rubric of "active defense." China should be prepared to intervene with its own forces if in its judgment the objective situation in Vietnam, as distinct from Hanoi's attitude, so required. At home, Lo advocated an extensive program of pre-attack mobilization, or in other words, technological preparations of a kind that would enhance the influence of economic planners and military professionals and require an improvement of relations with the Soviet Union, for the sake of both aid and protection. Lo did not shrink from drawing this conclusion; he carefully refrained from denouncing the post-Khrushchev leadership (referred to in Maoist statements as the "Khrushchev revisionists"), and it was during the period of his relative ascendancy that the agreement with the Soviet Union on shipment of weapons to North Vietnam was signed. His ascendancy was brief, however, and the article, which implicitly compared his opponents with Chamberlain and Daladier at Munich, may have contributed to its demise by being too outspoken. The abolition of military ranks later in May can be viewed as, among other things, a blow at the military professionals, of whom Lo during this period made himself the chief spokesman.

Although a document with other purposes as well, Lin Piao's famous tract, "Long Live the Victory of People's War," published on September 3, 1965 (the twentieth anniversary of China's V-J Day), can be regarded as a rebuttal to Lo Jui-ch'ing and as the major statement of the Maoist point of view. In practically every respect, he disagrees diametrically with Lo. He argues that the war in Vietnam must be kept "protracted" and "self-reliant," like the one that the Chinese Communists fought prior to 1949. Thus by clear implication, he deprecates the sending of North Vietnamese troops to South Vietnam and of Soviet equipment to North Vietnam, as well as the likelihood of direct Chinese involvement in the war. He denounces the Soviet leadership and insists that no accommodation with it is possible. If the United States attacks China, it will invade as the Japanese did and be similarly crushed in a "people's war" led by the Communist Party. There is every likelihood that the "people's war" in Vietnam will prove to be only one of a series throughout the developing world (or "world countryside," as Lin put it in a phrase borrowed from the Indonesian Communist leader D. N. Aidit), the effect of which will be to sweep American "imperialism" from the stage of history.

Although Lin did not mention the domestic Chinese scene, it seems probable that his tentative and fantastic forecast of an American invasion of China was designed to provide a backdrop for a "siege mentality" that would downgrade economic and military professionalism, exalt the role of the guerrillaized armed forces that he was in the process of creating, and promote the Maoist political program. But in spite of Lin's denunciations of the Soviet Union, his image of an American invasion, however absurd in reality, logically suggested the desirability of a reconciliation with Moscow. Such a conclusion was of course unacceptable to the Maoists on political grounds and had to be quashed. In a press conference held on September 29, Foreign Minister Chen Yi alleged that not only the United States but the Soviet Union (he threw in Britain, Japan, and India for good measure) were planning to invade China and that his hair had grown gray waiting for the day. He laughed as he said this, and the correspondents present took it as a joke, but the humor was missing from the Chinese releases and the correspondents' dispatches on the interview. Logically, the point was clear: it would make no sense to seek an accommodation with the Soviet Union for the purpose of warding off an American invasion if Moscow was planning a similar invasion. The close connection between this determination to maintain an adversary relationship with the Soviet Union and the Maoist domestic program was dramatized by the appearance a few weeks later on successive days (November 10 and 11) of the first major editorial announcing the launching of the Cultural Revolution against the intellectual community and the first major editorial denouncing the principle of "united action" with the Soviet Union.

By the summer or autumn of 1965 the strategic debate centering on Vietnam had been almost concluded, and even more than in the domestic debate the victory had gone to the Maoists. Since that time, accordingly, with some variations to be indicated shortly, China has officially regarded the war in Vietnam in a highly politicized light, as a source of "people's wars" elsewhere and as a backdrop for the Cultural Revolution at home. Hanoi has been urged to keep its role in the south down to the level consistent with the concept of "self-reliance" and to fight on, rather than negotiate, until the Americans are forced out by military defeat and political humiliation. The Chinese role has consisted mainly of shipping rice and infantry weapons to Hanoi and the Viet Cong, stationing some fifty thousand military engineer troops in North Vietnam to keep the lines to China open, and maintaining at a modest level a defensive military posture near the Vietnamese border and air defense preparations at various key points. In addition, the Chinese press has continued to utter occasional threats of intervention, but with decreasing frequency, precision, and credibility.

Although Peking has tended to become less apprehensive of American attack, it has continued to observe what it regarded as necessary caution. Its second nuclear test (May 14, 1965) occurred during a brief pause in the American bombing of North Vietnam. When the longer bombing pause at the end of 1965 was broken without substantial American escalation, Chinese fears seem to have been eased considerably. In the spring of 1966 some sort of tacit understanding seems to have been reached between China and the United States to the effect that as long as Chinese troops did not intervene in the war the United States would not attack China, and vice versa. Chinese blood pressure rose when American aircraft began bombing close to the Chinese frontier in the summer of 1967, but apparently only for the time being.

In addition to the trend toward diminishing military concern on

Peking's part, there has been a tendency toward increasing logistical support, or at least an increasing commitment to provide such support. American bombing of the Hanoi area in July 1966 produced a pledge that China would increase its aid and would become the "vast rear area" for the struggle. As already indicated, an agreement was apparently reached with Moscow and Hanoi early in 1967 for more active cooperation in forwarding shipments of Soviet military equipment to North Vietnam.

Given the Maoist preference for a "protracted war" as against negotiations, it is not surprising that Peking did not trouble to conceal its disapproval of the talks between the United States and North Vietnam that got under way in Paris on May 13, 1968. But although China had some means of putting pressure on Hanoi, for example by threatening covertly to send aid via Cambodia to bitter-enders among the Viet Cong if a truce should be agreed on, and although Hanoi had to take some account of Chinese pressures, it continued to manage its end of the crisis and the talks essentially as it saw fit. In the last analysis, China seemed to be inhibited both by military risks and by its own doctrine of "self-reliance" from trying to assume a dominant role.

SETBACKS IN THE THIRD WORLD

There have been two main strands in Chinese policy toward the Third World. One is the Maoist strand of revolution, including "armed struggle" or "people's war." The other is the diplomatic strand, which it seems reasonable to associate with Liu Shao-ch'i. Both approaches sustained setbacks in 1965 and 1966, but the diplomatic approach was the worse sufferer. This fact may have facilitated the discrediting of its patron by the Maoists, during the Cultural Revolution, as the "Khrushchev of China" and as a man who had preached the "three unities and the one diminution" (uniting with "imperialism, modern revisionism, and reaction," and reducing aid to "national liberation movements").

Since the early 1960s China had been concerned over the emergence of a series of conferences of nonaligned nations, from which it was of course excluded but in which its foe Tito, who has done much to discredit the Chinese in the Third World by his criticisms of them, has played a prominent part. As a countermeasure, China cooperated actively with Sukarno in an effort to hold a second Afro-Asian Conference, at which China would of course be represented, in succession to the one held at Bandung in 1955. One of the main purposes of an extended tour of Africa that Chou En-lai made at the end of 1963 was to arouse support for such a conference. He succeeded, and the conference was fixed for June 1965 at Algiers.

By that time, however, China and Indonesia, which hoped jointly to dominate and exploit the conference, had aroused the resentment of many of the Afro-Asian states. India, which had been humiliated in 1962, could be counted on to be hostile. The liking of the Afro-Asian countries for the United Nations, as an organization where they could exert disproportionate political influence and through which they could get aid, had been outraged when Indonesia walked out of the United Nations in January 1965 in protest over the seating of Malaysia on the Security Council. China had promptly endorsed the Indonesian exit and had proposed a rival, "revolutionary" United Nations, to replace the old one. As the Algiers Conference approached, Peking insisted on the exclusion of the Soviet Union, which most Afro-Asian countries regard as a valuable source of aid, and Malaysia, with which the overwhelming majority of them had no quarrel. It insisted that no observer from the United Nations could be admitted. It demanded that the conference condemn the United States for its policy toward Vietnam and repudiate the acceptance of aid by Afro-Asian countries from non-Afro-Asian ones.

These overbearing demands had so irritated many of the prospective participants that, when a revolution occurred in Algeria a few days before the conference was scheduled to open, a move got under way to postpone the conference on the pretext that political conditions were too unsettled. To counter this trend, Peking promptly and opportunistically recognized the new Algerian government of Boumédienne, even though it had been on very good terms with the preceding Ben Bella government, and insisted that the conference go on as scheduled. But China's insistence had no effect, and in October, after the coup in Indonesia had weakened

Sukarno and made it clear that even if the conference were held it could not be the kind of conference desired, Peking announced its agreement to the indefinite "postponement" (in reality, cancellation) of the conference.

By the spring of 1965 China's relations with Indonesia were probably closer than with any other country. Peking was supporting Sukarno's foreign policy and had agreed to furnish some weapons, mainly small arms, in connection with the "Confrontation" with Britain and Malaysia. Peking was encouraging Sukarno to accelerate the leftward movement of his domestic policy, and in particular, to use the "Confrontation" as a cover for distributing arms to a "Fifth Force," to be composed largely of Communist-led mass organizations, as a means of balancing and ultimately combatting the army. Peking had excellent relations with the Indonesian Air Force, which was under leftist leadership, and there is even some reason to think that it may have dangled the offer of some sort of nuclear aid in front of the latter as an inducement to friendship. The Indonesian Communist Party was heavily, although not quite totally, committed to the Chinese side in the Sino-Soviet dispute.

This was a difficult and dangerous situation for all concerned, but it did not begin to turn into a disaster until August 1965, when Sukarno was taken ill, seriously it appeared. It was mainly his influence and popularity that had been preventing the army from moving against the Communists for the past several years. The panic-stricken Communists brought a team of Chinese doctors from China to care for Sukarno, who proceeded to recover within a few weeks. But by that time, it was too late. The Communist leadership and Sukarno were already planning a coup against the army; whether for fear that their plans had been discovered or for fear that the army was planning to move against them for some other reason, they saw no choice but to go ahead. There is reason to believe that Peking knew of and supported the plans for a coup; it invited a very large number of Indonesian Army leaders, some of whom declined, to Peking for the National Day celebrations on October 1, presumably to weaken the army's response to the coup. On the other hand, Peking did not necessarily approve of the PKI (Indonesian Communist Party) plans, which as on two previous occasions (in 1926 and 1948) when it had risen only to be slaughtered, smacked of the sin of "adventurism." Sukarno was more positive; he knew of the plot and approved of it, although he apparently did not realize the lengths to which it would go.

The coup, which occurred on the night of September 30–October 1, succeeded in killing enough generals to give the army an excellent pretext for striking at the PKI, but not enough to weaken the army's response, which was devastating. Within a few months, troops and aroused mobs had killed many thousands of Communists and driven the remnants underground. Although Peking made it clear from the beginning that it objected to the army's behavior, it did not begin to make a serious issue of its objections until mid-October, when the army began to accuse it of complicity in the plot, to connive with students in raids on its embassy and consulates, and to maltreat Indonesian Chinese to some extent on charges that they had supported the PKI. The resulting controversy led to an almost complete diplomatic break between China and Indonesia in the spring of 1966. Whatever the exact degree of its participation in the coup, China had shown itself powerless to protect the PKI, the Indonesian Chinese, and Sukarno, who lost virtually all his power in March. The "Confrontation" was terminated in the spring of 1966. The best Peking could do was to give asylum and encouragement to an exiled group of Indonesian Communists claiming now to be the legitimate leadership of the PKI, to wait hopefully for the new, essentially military, government of Indonesia to fail in its domestic programs, and to sow the seeds of another, more successful, effort to move the country to the left.

Both China and North Vietnam had been involved since the early 1960s in trying to stir up a "people's war" in Thailand, with emphasis on the backward and impoverished northeastern section of the country. In late 1964, perhaps in anticipation of a Communist victory in South Vietnam and in an effort to create a counterweight under its own control, Peking began to create on Chinese soil what it hoped would be a counterpart to the National Liberation Front in South Vietnam. The presidency of this body, known as the Thailand Patriotic Front, seems to have been offered in October 1965 to a distinguished Thai leftist exile living in China, but if so he evidently refused. One of Peking and Hanoi's main purposes in fomenting "people's war" in Thailand, which they did with only indifferent success, was to punish the Thai government for its pro-American orientation and if possible deter it from supporting the American effort in Vietnam. In the latter respect, the policy was certainly a failure. Thailand agreed to send some combat troops to Vietnam, and at the beginning of 1967 it took the extraordinary step of allowing the United States to base B-52 bombers on Thai territory, the first time since World War II that American strategic weapons systems had been stationed on the mainland of Asia.

The emergence of close Sino-Pakistani relations, on the basis of common detestation of India, had begun in the very early 1960s and had been greatly accelerated with the rapid buildup of Indian military power following the great humiliation of 1962. Although aimed nominally at China, this buildup had far more practical effect on Pakistan, which saw the threat to its security increased and its claim to Kashmir rendered even more difficult of realization than before. Pakistan's major ally, the United States, was of doubtful use in this situation; in fact, American military aid to Pakistan had always been conditional on the requirement that it not be used against India.

In the spring of 1965, probably as part of its program for sweeping successes in the Third World, China began to prod a receptive Pakistan into stronger action. Some heavy but localized Indo-Pakistani fighting in the spring and early summer, shortly after a visit by President Ayub to Peking and in an area remote from Kashmir known as the Rann of Cutch, led as Peking had probably predicted to a partial suspension of American military aid to Pakistan. Meanwhile, Peking had invited Sheikh Abdullah, the champion of Kashmiri autonomy, to visit China, but he was arrested in India as he was about to do so. In August Pakistani irregulars began to raid across the ceasefire line in Kashmir, presumably in the hope of generating a "people's war" in the Indian portion. This hope was not fulfilled, and instead the Indian Army invaded Pakistan-held Kashmir in late August. Early in September other Indian units invaded Pakistan proper, an act that brought not only American, Soviet, and Chinese protests but also a suspension of all "lethal" American military aid to both belligerents.

By mid-September Pakistan was getting the worse of the conflict and President Ayub suggested American mediation. Peking promptly took steps that it hoped would strengthen the Pakistani "hawks," led by Foreign Minister Bhutto, and keep Pakistan fighting until some sort of concessions could be extracted from India. On September 16 China served an ultimatum of sorts on India, giving it three days within which to cease certain violations of the border between Tibet and Sikkim of which it was alleged to be guilty. India returned a conciliatory answer falling short of acceptance, and China extended the deadline for three more days. By September 22, however, both India and Pakistan had accepted a ceasefire order from the United Nations and a proposal of Soviet mediation. Peking then allowed its "ultimatum" to evaporate and made no serious effort to obstruct the Indo-Pakistani talks that were held under Soviet auspices at Tashkent in January 1966, even though the talks produced no Indian concessions on Kashmir. Not only had Pakistan failed to press either its guerrilla or its regular military operations against India as China had evidently hoped, but Bhutto was discreetly eased out of the Foreign Ministry later in 1966, probably as the price for a limited resumption of American military aid. China had scored one success, however: it appeared in the eyes of the Pakistani public as the only power that had supported Pakistan, and it was credited with having deterred an Indian invasion of East Pakistan that in fact was probably never contemplated.

By 1965 China's policy toward sub-Saharan Africa was involved in two main enterprises. One was an effort to create revolutionary bases aimed at the Congo in neighboring countries, an effort whose prospects appeared to be dimmed by the virtual crushing of such leftist revolutionary forces as existed in the Congo itself in 1964, by "white mercenaries." The second was an effort to establish close relations with the strategically located state of Tanzania, on the east coast. The latter effort went ahead relatively well; Tanzania signed a treaty of friendship with China in 1965, and the Chinese began to take part in training African revolutionaries for action against the target countries of the "white redoubt" (Angola, Mozambique, Rhodesia, and South Africa) in Tanzania as well as in China itself. In the more conservative French-speaking states bordering the Congo, however, the Chinese proved to have overplayed their hand. Burundi, where Peking had not only tried to create a revolutionary base for use against the Congo but had intervened outrageously in local tribal feuds, broke diplomatic relations in the spring of 1965 on the ground of Chinese involvement in the murder of the premier. Early in 1966 two military coups, in Dahomey and the Central African Republic, brought to power new governments which broke diplomatic relations with Peking on the grounds of subversion. Worse still, in February 1966 President Nkrumah of Ghana, with whom both Moscow and Peking had had very close relations and whom they were using as a conduit into leftist states and movements in Africa, was overthrown while on his way to Peking. His military successors severed diplomatic relations with China later in the year.

Direct Chinese influence on the Latin American left being rather slight, Peking had made considerable efforts to woo Castro after his seizure of power in 1959, but he like Nasser always insisted on clinging to Moscow's economic coattails even though he approved in principle of Peking's anti-American militancy. In 1965 China began to try to counter this attitude by distributing its anti-Soviet statements in Cuba, to army officers among others. Castro strongly resented this behavior as an act of interference in Cuba's internal affairs, and Peking retaliated by cutting down its purchases of sugar from Cuba and its shipments of rice to Cuba, on the pretext that it would be better for Cuba if it were self-sufficient in rice. In January 1966 Castro began to criticize and denounce the Chinese publicly, accusing them among other things of "making a laughing stock of socialism." This nearly complete break with Castro appeared likely to cost Peking whatever slight hope it might reasonably have had for exerting significant influence on the Latin American left.

Castro's attack was all the more embarrassing because it came on the eve of the first Tricontinental Afro-Asian-Latin American People's Solidarity Organization, which met at Havana in January 1966. Although the Chinese delegation did achieve some tactical triumphs, notably by preventing the complete absorption by this body of the Afro-Asian People's Solidarity Organization, where Chinese influence was greater, Peking also encountered some setbacks. It was unable to prevent Soviet participation and the adoption of some resolutions that tended to favor the Soviet line on international questions over the Chinese.

Although Peking has never conceded that it suffered setbacks in the Third World during this period, there can be little doubt that it is fully aware of the fact. During March 1966 the Chinese press began to carry a series of articles to the effect that the world was undergoing a "major upheaval, major division and major re-organization." Revolution was described as a "wavelike process," and although it was not admitted that the process was in a trough, it was at least conceded that troughs existed. Cryptic statements of this kind are the closest expressions to Maoist admissions of set-backs or defeats in the Third World that one can normally expect to see.

In the spring of 1966 Liu Shao-ch'i made a number of state visits to countries of South and Southeast Asia, notably Pakistan and Burma. Although his Maoist colleagues may well have wanted him out of the way while they pushed ahead with preparations for the Cultural Revolution, Liu's own purpose was probably to see what results of his policy of cultivating friendly states, with little regard for their revolutionary utility, survived. Whatever his con-clusions, his trip was the last to be made by a high Chinese official, apart from a visit by Chou En-lai to Rumania and Albania in June 1966, until after the Cultural Revolution.

THE RISE AND FALL OF RED GUARD DIPLOMACY

The Cultural Revolution being an essentially domestic phenome-non tending to rivet the attention of the elite and people of China more and more on internal as against external affairs, it is not sur-prising that Chinese foreign relations for a time were subordinated to it and received a strong imprint from it.

At about the end of 1966, large numbers of Chinese diplomats, including nearly all the ambassadors, began to be recalled to China. They were clearly considered likely to have been corrupted by con-tact with the outside world, to be unsympathetic to the Cultural Rev-olution, and to require intensive reindoctrination in the "thought of Mao Tse-tung." Until 1969 no successors were named to their posts. At about the same time, Red Guard posters began to de-nounce Foreign Minister Chen Yi for being allegedly nonrevolu-tionary, too lax in defending the interests of overseas Chinese such as those being harassed in Indonesia, etc. He responded by a series of radical statements designed to disprove the charges, but his influence declined and Red Guard pressures of various kinds on the Foreign Ministry tended to increase. The result of these pressures, and of independent action by Maoist militants in the field of foreign relations, was an extraordinary phenomenon that may be called Red Guard diplomacy. It becomes at least partly understandable if we remember that the extreme Maoists, including Red Guards, were refusing to draw any ideological distinction between Chinese and foreigners; all should conform to the "thought of Mao Tse-tung," and the Cultural Revolution could and should be exported throughout the world. Indeed, Chinese propaganda was trying to give the impression that the Cultural Revolution was spreading among the "revolutionary people," as distinct from their "reactionary" governments, nearly everywhere in the world.

Attacks on foreigners and demonstrations against foreign embassies in Peking by Red Guards began in August 1966 and were greatly intensified in 1967, following the siege of the Soviet embassy in late January and early February. All foreign students were expelled from the country in September 1966.

Slightly farther afield, Red Guards and other Maoist militants staged an impressive series of what may be termed border incidents. Those along the Sino-Soviet border have already been mentioned briefly. As a decadent and vulnerable vestige of "imperialism" on China's immediate periphery, the Portuguese colonial government of Macao felt the weight of massive Red Guard demonstrations from November 1966 to January 1967 and made a virtual surrender, so that China has been granted what looks like a veto on any major act of the colonial government. Hong Kong logically began to receive similar treatment in May 1967, but being far larger, stronger, more stable, and better administered, it came through largely unscathed. Neither incursions across the border nor demonstrations within the colony accomplished much against the judicious combination of firmness and restraint that the British displayed. The outcome would of course have been different if Chinese troops had crossed the border and joined in, but it was clearly no part of Peking's policy to take over Hong Kong, an act that would have cost it several hundred million dollars of hard foreign currency acquired each year mainly by selling food and water to Hong Kong, or even Macao. Insofar as the Red Guards who took action against Macao and Hong Kong had any encouragement from Peking, it probably came from Chiang Ching's Cultural Revolution Group rather than from Mao Tse-tung, Lin Piao, or Chou En-lai.

Abroad, Chinese diplomats, students, seamen, residents, and other militants created a number of incidents to dramatize their devotion to the Cultural Revolution or their opposition to some policy of the local government. The most serious of these occurred in Burma, where Chinese students defied a ban on the wearing of Mao badges and created a major riot in which the Burmese populace supported its own government in drastic action against Chinese diplomats, students, and residents. This episode in turn led to a series of vitriolic propaganda outbursts by Peking against the Ne Win government, with which it had previously maintained relations ranging from polite to friendly.

By the summer of 1967 some thirty countries had been affected to varying degrees by one or more varieties of Red Guard diplomacy. Among the moving spirits was a former diplomat named Yao Tengshan, who had served with the Chinese embassy in Djakarta, been expelled, and returned full of enthusiasm for Red Guard diplomacy. On August 19 he and his supporters seized control of the Foreign Ministry and on August 22, in reprisal for the suppression of some leftist newspapers in Hong Kong, sacked and burned the British diplomatic compound in Peking. This act, which was followed a few days later by an outrageous demonstration by Chinese diplomatic personnel in London, was evidently too much for nearly everyone in Peking. By August 23 the militants were ousted from the Foreign Ministry, and Chen Yi and Chou En-lai resumed effective control over foreign relations. On September 1 the Red Guards were told by two of their heroes, Chiang Ching and K'ang Sheng, to leave the Foreign Ministry and foreign embassies alone. Chou En-lai managed to avoid a diplomatic break with Cambodia by disavowing some Chinese-supported revolutionary activity in its border provinces that had come to Prince Sihanouk's attention, although without lulling his suspicions completely or putting a full stop to the objectionable activity. A minor fire fight at the

Tibet-Sikkim border in early September was not made the pretext by either side for a major controversy. By the end of 1967 abuse of Ne Win had greatly declined, and it appeared that at least a limited reconciliation might be in the making.

It is important to realize that, just as Red Guard diplomacy owed its origins to the domestic phenomenon of the Cultural Revolution, so its virtual termination in the late summer of 1967 owed much to the comparable swing to the right that occurred in domestic policy at about the same time, following the Wuhan Incident. Its end was followed by more correct and even polite Chinese diplomatic behavior, including for a time toward the United States at Warsaw, and by efforts to mend fences selectively with countries of the Third World.

CHINESE FOREIGN POLICY IN 1968

If, as seems probable, Mao Tse-tung's main single objective is to struggle against what he regards as manifestations of Soviet "revisionism" at home and abroad, he could be excused for feeling somewhat discouraged. Despite his strenuous efforts, the domestic manifestations of the despised phenomenon did not appear to have been scotched, and the foreign manifestations certainly had not. The Soviet Union was becoming increasingly active and influential in the Third World, for example, and its difficulties in Eastern Europe must have struck Peking as poor consolation.

Worse still, largely because of the Cultural Revolution China's international position had by 1968 become one of isolation and ineffectiveness. The major Communist parties of Asia, those of Japan, Korea, and Vietnam, were seriously alienated. As a series of major events during 1968 further demonstrated the weakness of Chinese influence on international politics, Peking began to move rather clumsily in the direction of a new policy, or at least a new stance, that might improve its effectiveness without sacrifices of principle.

The seizure of the U.S.S. *Pueblo* by North Korea in January dramatized the tension in that country that had been on the increase since 1965. The growth in North Korean bellicosity was a trend over which Peking had no control and seems to have tried to exert none. In view of the risks to China connected with any major crisis in Korea, it must have been with relief that Peking saw the year pass without such a crisis and the crew of the *Pueblo* released. But the fundamental problem still exists; Korea is a source of potential serious trouble, and China's means of influencing developments there are rather slight unless, as in 1950, it chooses again to take the extremely risky step of sending in combat forces of its own.

At the end of January 1968 the North Vietnamese and the Viet Cong launched the famous Tet offensive, apparently as a result of a calculation in Hanoi that the war was gradually being lost and that the situation could only be restored by an all-out attack. There is no reason to think that Peking influenced the decision to launch the Tet offensive. On the contrary, the strategy it employed was a definitely non-Maoist one, in the sense that it was used to avoid defeat rather than in the last stage of a successful guerrilla stuggle. Although the Tet offensive failed at heavy cost, in conjunction with an ensuing request by General Westmoreland for 206,000 more troops it precipitated a crisis of decision in the United States. The Johnson administration's answer was to deny Westmoreland his additional troops and once more invite Hanoi to negotiate, the invitation being sweetened by a partial cessation of bombing of North Vietnam. For a number of reasons, of which the effect of the Vietnamese situation on his political fortunes was certainly one, President Johnson stated at the same time, on March 31, that he would not seek renomination. A few days later, Hanoi announced an acceptance of the Johnson invitation that, even though it was conditional, still constituted a departure from the previous position that negotiations could begin only after a complete bombing halt. The entire proceedings, which led to talks in Paris beginning in May and a complete bombing halt in early November, were anathema to Peking, whose pleasure at the prospect of a reduction of the American military presence in Asia was more than offset by the certainty that such a reduction would not occur as the result of a dramatic politico-military defeat and humiliation, which Mao Tse-tung seems to regard as more desirable, because of its presumed favorable effect on his revolutionary strategy around the world, than a Communist takeover of South Vietnam per se. Chinese displeasure at Hanoi was expressed in a number of ways, by Red Guard demonstrations among other things, and relations between Peking and Hanoi grew still cooler as a result. But some at least of the Chinese leaders apparently did not want to lose all influence on Hanoi and on the Vietnamese situation in general. Of all the Red Guard violence in the summer of 1968, one of the most distressing features to Peking was an interruption of the flow of goods and military equipment to North Vietnam by disorders along the crucial railway running through the South China province of Kwangsi. This particular episode was probably one of the main factors that decided Peking, apparently in late July, to permit and even encourage local military authorities to take much stronger action than before to curb Red Guard disorders and even break up their units outright. At the same time, the process of forming provincial Revolutionary Committees, which were essentially under military control in most cases, was resumed and completed, the last two (for Tibet and Sinkiang) being announced on September 5. After the complete bombing halt in early November, most if not all of the Chinese railway troops who had been helping to maintain the major North Vietnamese railways (which in effect form the southern loop of the South Chinese rail net) were withdrawn. The Soviet Union, which far from opposing Hanoi's decision to open talks with the United States seems to have favored and probably encouraged it, maintained the rather high level of its aid to North Vietnam, with the emphasis now on industrial rather than military equipment; most of it went by sea, rather than by rail across China. As the situation in Vietnam moved a little closer to normality, and in spite of the absence of obvious progress at Paris toward a settlement, Peking found it advisable to reduce greatly its verbal attacks on the talks and on Hanoi for participation in them; for one thing, if the talks broadened into a major conference like the one on Laos in 1961–62, Peking did not want to be in the position of having excluded itself in advance.

Perhaps even more important to China than the decrease of tension in Vietnam was the increase of tension in Eastern Europe. To Peking, Alexander Dubcek and his reformist colleagues in Czechoslovakia were objectionable as revisionists, but their harassing effect on the Soviet Union was applauded. The Chinese also appear to have felt some interest in a tentative move on the part of some members of the Czechoslovak leadership to seek some kind of Chinese support in the face of Soviet pressures. Anything of this sort was of course precluded by the Soviet invasion of Czechoslovakia on August 20. The Chinese denunciation of this action, which can be explained only in terms of the exaggeratedly "defensive conservatism" (Michel Tatu's phrase) of the current Soviet leadership, was one of the strongest issued by any Communist Party. While Peking excoriates almost everything the Soviet Union does, more was involved in this case. The Soviet occupation of Czechoslovakia appears to have coincided with an increase of tension along the Sino-Soviet frontier, beyond the small-scale armed clashes that have been the norm since about 1966. Like all developments in that mysterious region, this one is hard to interpret, but in this case it appears that the Soviet Union may have been afraid that the Chinese might retaliate for, or take advantage of, the invasion of Czechoslovakia by some sort of military action. At first, the feeling in Peking after the invasion was probably one of some alarm at the possibility of a similar Soviet action against China, much as the beginning of American escalation in Vietnam had created a climate of tension. The enunciation soon afterward of the so-called Brezhnev Doctrine, which claims for the Soviet Union the right in principle to intervene in another Communist country whenever it considers that the cause of "socialism" is in danger, as Moscow clearly holds it to be in China, must have reinforced this sense of insecurity. In reality, however, the doctrine seems to have been promulgated mainly to provide the embarrassed Kremlin with an excuse for the invasion when it found that it could not manufacture the credible semblance of an invitation from its Czechoslovak friends, and as in the case of Vietnam, Peking's fears appear to have eased with the passage of time.

A more serious problem was possible Soviet action against Rumania, Yugoslavia, or Albania, all of whose relations with Moscow were bad to one degree or another. Albania, of course, had long been an informal ally, and almost a dependency, of China. Peking loudly announced its support for Rumania and Albania in the event of Soviet attack, and like Tirana ceased its denunciation of

Tito. Agreements for an increase of Chinese economic and military aid to Albania were apparently concluded when an Albanian military delegation visited China at the end of September and a similar Chinese delegation reciprocated soon afterward, but in view of the closure of the Suez Canal since June 1967 it appeared that Peking would find it difficult to do much that would be really effective for its Balkan partner in the event of a serious crisis. There was some speculation that the Chinese might actually emplace missiles of their own in Albania to cover the Ukraine and counterbalance the medium-range Soviet missiles that undoubtedly cover targets in China, but any such attempt would expose Peking to the risk of a crisis and setback of the Cuban variety. Probably more to the point, Peking increased its direct control over Sinkiang, which is dangerously vulnerable to Soviet pressures, in the last months of the year by paring down the political position of Wang En-mao, the strong man of the region up to that time, and on December 27 conducted its second thermonuclear test (the first had been held on June 17, 1967) over the eastern part of the region.

In spite of Czechoslovakia, there were signs during 1968 pointing to the possibility that Peking's nightmare of a détente and even collaboration between its two main opponents, with probable results that it could only expect to be adverse to its interests, might materialize. The critical issue was the nuclear one. Both Washington and Moscow were anxious to check the spread of nuclear weapons to presently nonnuclear countries, and on both sides there was serious concern, except within the ranks of the "military-industrial complex," at the imminent prospect of a huge escalation of military expenditures as a result of technological innovations like antiballistic missile defenses and missiles with multiple warheads. On the first score, Washington and Moscow had agreed by the beginning of 1968 on the draft of a nonproliferation treaty, although the United States withheld its actual signature. On the second score, there were indications on both sides of an interest in reaching an agreement on a freeze or reduction in the field of offensive strategic weapons; if anything, the interest appeared greater on the Soviet side, perhaps because President Nixon had said before his election that he was determined if necessary to maintain a substantial American lead in offensive weapons. At a time when developments of such importance were in progress, it was obviously undesirable from Peking's point of view to be an isolated bystander. With the minimum objective of re-establishing communication with the United States and taking the pulse of the new administration, Peking proposed on November 26 that the Sino-American ambassadorial talks at Warsaw, which had been suspended since early in the year, be resumed on February 20, 1969.

These various developments in Chinese foreign policy, all of which bore the character of national interest rather than revolutionary ideology, were probably intrinsically distasteful to Mao Tse-tung, although he must be assumed to have agreed to them even if he did not initiate them. In foreign as in domestic policy, even at a time of fundamental withdrawal and consolidation, some scope must be given to Maoist policies as long as Mao lives and his " thought" remains China's official ideology in more than name. In the foreign field, this means mainly that the sacred flag of a "people's war" must continue to be waved wherever possible. To the extent practicable without an open break with Hanoi, Peking appears to be encouraging the National Liberation Front to look to it for guidance and to obstruct any settlement at Paris. Since the failure of the Tet offensive, Hanoi itself under the influence of the supposedly pro-Chinese (but apparently non-Maoist) Truong Chinh has adopted a more Mao-like strategy of protracted guerrilla warfare combined with a variety of political ploys, but this trend does not seem to indicate an actual increase of Chinese influence in Hanoi. To the extent compatible with some improvement of relations with Rangoon at the state level, Peking continues to incite and support in various ways tribal and leftist insurgency in northern Burma, as well as in the adjacent region of Assam. A similar program is under way for northern Thailand, and there are signs that Peking may be contemplating the same thing for northern Laos. To date, these efforts have achieved few visible results and are confined to remote areas and for the most part to tribal populations. In the intrinsically more important island of Java, Peking suffered another major vicarious setback when the Indonesian Army carried out some devastating raids in the summer of 1968 against emerging Communist guerrilla bases in the central part of the island.

All in all, its resounding propaganda declarations notwithstanding, the Peking regime did not seem to have much basis for optimism with respect to its foreign policy as it entered its twentieth year. Considerable successful effort would be required before the damage to Chinese influence inflicted by the Cultural Revolution could be undone, and much more before China could seriously hope to attain the status of a superpower comparable to the United States and the Soviet Union, if indeed this were possible at all. In the process of trying, however, China clearly had it in its power to cause a great deal of trouble and worry to its neighbors and even to the superpowers.

PART TWO

CHAPTER VII

The Making of
Foreign Policy

No more in China than in any other important country do the making and execution of foreign policy emerge simply in reaction to external situations and stimuli. The interests and objectives of China itself, or those of its leaders at any rate, are always significant and sometimes decisive in this connection. Obviously neither element should be exaggerated or considered in isolation, but a good deal has already been said about situations, and not very much about interests and objectives of a general and enduring kind as seen from Peking. It is time to try to strike a balance.

CONCERNS AND GOALS

Clearly the primary interest of any state is to survive, politically as well as physically, or in other words, to attain at least a minimum acceptable level of security. To the leaders of a country as large, poorly developed, and at times assertive as China, the attainment of security almost necessarily presents a problem of special difficulty. Peking retains, even while exaggerating it for propaganda purposes, a lively memory of the injuries, humiliations, and "semi-colonial" status inflicted on China in the nineteenth century by the "imperialist" powers of that era, tsarist Russia included. When viewed, as it is in China, from a Leninist perspective, this process seems to acquire a degree of inevitability, organization, and durability that conduces to visualizing current security problems in similar terms. Nor did "imperialist" pressures on China end with the nineteenth century. The worst of all was the Japanese invasion of 1937–45, which exerts an analogous although probably somewhat less powerful influence on the thinking of the Chinese elite to that exerted on the Soviet leadership by the war with Hitler. The boastful tone of its propaganda on this subject notwithstanding, Peking appears to take account in its more honest and sober moments of the truth that China, including its Communist Party, was quite unable to cope unaided with the Japanese; that the Soviet role, including the invasion of Manchuria, was not decisive and offers little encouragement to the idea that Moscow would be of much use in any future anti-"imperialist" war in which Cuba might become involved; and that what was decisive were the defeats inflicted on the Japanese by the United States in the Pacific. It is interesting that in the original version of his *On Coalition Government*, which was composed in the spring of 1945 before the deterioration of American relations with Moscow and Yenan, Mao Tse-tung awarded high marks to the military operations of the United States in the Pacific. This praise has of course been deleted from the official version published since 1949.

Leninism holds that "imperialism" tends to be organized into a "camp," at least when it is a case of opposing "socialism," and that the "camp" will have a leader or leaders. Since 1945 the Chinese like other Communists have of course held that the leader of the "imperialist camp" is the United States. But the Chinese party, more than most others, has reasons over and above this ideological one for hating and fearing the United States. Leaving aside the plausible but controversial proposition that the Chinese political "style" includes a cult of hatred, vociferously expressed even when, or especially when, it is not acted on, we must concede that after 1945 the United States occupied Japan and within a few years began to build it up in lieu of continuing to punish it. In

Peking's eyes, this means that the United States has succeeded Japan as the main external threat to China's security and may at any time begin actively to encourage and support Japanese rearmament or even attack China itself, as Japan once did. As for the possible motivation for such an attack, for a time after 1949 Peking feared or claimed to fear that, just as "imperialism" intervened militarily in Russia from 1918 to 1922 to strangle Bolshevism in its cradle, in Winston Churchill's phrase, so American "imperialism" might now intervene in the same way and for the same purpose against Chinese communism. This fear was intensified, initially at least, when the United States began to protect the Chinese Nationalists on Taiwan (or "occupy" Taiwan, as Peking would put it) in mid-1950 and to give them substantial economic and military aid. Not only did this policy prevent the unification of China through the "liberation" of Taiwan by Peking, but it created the spectre of a Chinese Nationalist military attack on the mainland with American support, probably at a time of trouble on the mainland. Peking seems to have been afraid in the spring of 1962 that such a situation might be about to materialize.

The United States is regarded in Peking as a strategic threat, not only by virtue of its connections with Japan and Taiwan but in its own right. This fear tends to increase at times of crisis, notably in 1965 following American escalation in Vietnam, at which time there was apparently some concern in Peking that the United States might "take out" China's nuclear installations, even if it did nothing more. There is a clearly understood need on both sides for a sort of political strategic warning system for occasions such as this. Public warnings and indirect contacts having proved insufficient in 1950 to achieve a state of mutual deterrence and prevent a Sino-American war over Korea, a more direct and effective method is obviously necessary, and this is one of the main functions served by the Sino-American ambassadorial talks that have been in progress intermittently, first in Geneva and then in Warsaw, since 1955.

Chinese nervousness over the threat of American nuclear attack, the existence of the questionably effective Sino-Soviet alliance notwithstanding, was sufficient in early 1953 to compel a reluctant decision to sign an armistice in Korea. It rose again a year later with the enunciation, at a time of great tension over Indochina, of John Foster Dulles's doctrine of Massive Retaliation. It seems to have declined somewhat since Dulles's death in 1959, except for a period of about a year following the escalation of early 1965. There is of course an alternate form that the American strategic threat to China could conceivably take, that of an invasion. In 1954 Secretary Dulles spoke vaguely of a possible "three-pronged" attack on China from Korea, Taiwan, and Indochina, and during the period of greatest concern over American escalation in Vietnam some of the more Maoist-minded members of the Chinese leadership claimed to believe that an American invasion was more or less imminent. On September 29, 1965, Foreign Minister Chen Yi went so far as to state at a press conference—he laughed as he said it, but the humor is lost in the published reports—that not only the United States but the Soviet Union and some other countries were planning to invade China; one of his purposes in making this extraordinary statement may have been to anticipate the argument that if there was an American threat China should reconcile itself with the Soviet Union. The myth of likely American invasion, which was at its height in 1965–66, is probably not seriously believed by many of the top Chinese leaders, but it served the Maoist purpose of domestic political mobilization fairly well at that time, through helping to create what has been called a siege mentality. One of Mao's favorite strategies for fighting a "people's war," although a very controversial one in the eyes of some of his colleagues, has long been to "lure the enemy in deep," and no matter how impractical it may now appear, he seems reluctant to stop talking about it.

Even if Peking does not consider an American attack by air or land to be as likely as it sometimes asserts, it probably still believes that the problem may grow more serious as it builds up its nuclear forces and the United States correspondingly shields itself behind its own "thin" or "anti-Chinese" antiballistic missile system. In any case, the Chinese leadership must take the American threat into account, and it understandably would very much like to see the existing American military presence in the Far East, and in Japan and Okinawa in particular, eliminated or at least greatly reduced. As it is, the United States could launch a nuclear attack against China with regionally based forces, without involving forces based in the United States itself, and Peking seems to have come by about 1958 to doubt that in such a situation it could rely on Soviet protection. If, on the other hand, the United States were forced to rely on strategic forces, intercontinental ballistic missiles in particular, based in the United States to deter or attack China, it would be unable to do so without creating a greater risk of general war with the Soviet Union and would therefore probably be less able to exert effective restraint on China.

Increasingly since about 1960, China has been forced to think of the Soviet Union not only as an ideological backslider and an unreliable ally but as an actual threat. The origins of this problem are complex and obscure but appear to lie in the general deterioration of political relations between the two regimes after 1958–59. At about that time, not only Khrushchev but the Soviet leadership as a whole seems to have begun to regard their bumptious and increasingly unpredictable "ally" as in fact a threat, not only in the long run when it should acquire a substantial nuclear stockpile and might decide to attack the Soviet Union, but also in the short run through some step that might start a crisis in the Far East into which the Soviet Union would be drawn. Especially after early 1964, when Peking and Bonn held secret, unsuccessful talks on the possibility of establishing consular relations, Moscow was seized with vague fears of seeing its ultimate horror, a two-front threat, emerge in the form of some sort of combination between China and West Germany. It seems likely that the Soviet Union increased its military strength and preparedness in the Far East at that time to the point perhaps of emplacing medium-range missiles (MRBMs) in Outer Mongolia, where they could cover many important targets including the entire complex of Chinese nuclear installations, and that these moves were a major source of the Sino-Soviet tension, in which Outer Mongolia was also involved, at the time of Khrushchev's fall. There is little doubt that Soviet qualms about China's antics as it entered the Cultural Revolution led not only to an ostentatious renewal of the Soviet-Outer Mongolian defense treaty in January 1966 but to a further strengthening of Soviet forces in Asia. These moves, combined with apparent Soviet incitement of tribal unrest in Sinkiang, are a more serious matter than the very vague Chinese claims to Soviet Asian territory, although the latter are a source of some alarm in Moscow, and it is not surprising that in recent years Peking has evidently regarded the Soviet Union as in some ways a more serious threat to its security than the United States. Mao is reported by Japanese Communist sources to have predicted in early 1966 that if the United States invaded China as an outgrowth of the Vietnam crisis—something that Mao seems to have expected for a time—the Soviet Union would similarly invade from the other direction. In a characteristic Maoist gesture of probing and defiance, Red Guards began to demonstrate along the Sino-Soviet border in 1966, and Chinese soldiers even began to go so far as to herd peasants across onto the Soviet side and themselves engage in small-scale fire fights, which still occur, with Soviet border guards.

China feels a fairly acute nervousness about the security of its entire border. With few exceptions, its border regions are thinly populated, poorly developed, and impossible to garrison in strength for logistical reasons. The loyalties of the minority populations that traditionally inhabit many of the border regions are none too secure. Peking remembers, almost too clearly, that in the nineteenth century various foreign powers, including tsarist Russia, detached tributary dependencies of the Manchu empire and in some cases also carved out spheres of influence in China Proper. Any sort of presumed hostile military presence near a frontier, especially if it actually conducts some sort of a border probe, creates an acute nervousness in Peking and may seem to call for a military response; the classic examples are Korea in 1950 and the Indo-Tibetan border in 1962. By the same token, China dislikes intensely overflights, intentional or accidental, by foreign military aircraft (notably Nationalist reconnaissance aircraft), intrusions within the twelve-mile limit by ships of the U.S. Seventh Fleet, and the like. Clearly Peking would like to see formally or informally neutral buffer zones, free of troops defined as hostile, established on the other side of its entire frontier. Since there is obviously no chance of this happening on the Soviet side, it is mainly to the south of China that this desire assumes some practical importance. The question, a debated one among foreign China specialists, is whether neutrality and preferably weakness represent the maximum demand that China intends to make on its southern neighbors. The writer's own answer to this question, to be developed later, is no.

Another of Peking's major objectives is modernization, after its own fashion. All important Chinese leaders of the twentieth century have understood that some sort of modernization was essential if China was to enjoy security, prestige, and influence in the world. Few, however, have grasped the extent to which the West had to modify its own tradition in order to modernize or the extent, therefore, to which China would have to do the same. Mao Tsetung, whose "thought" is a highly personal and Chinese reading of an imperfectly understood and intrinsically defective philosophy, Marxism-Leninism, cannot be said to have understood how modernization could be achieved in China. The damage that he has inflicted on Chinese education in the course of the Cultural Revolution alone is enough to prove the point.

For a few years, however, until Mao began to radicalize and assert his ideas in the mid- and late 1950s, the Chinese leadership carried out a modernization program that represented a seemingly viable blend of Soviet theory and organization with adaptations based on Chinese conditions. Ultimate freedom and prosperity were to be achieved through transitory sacrifice and bureaucratic dictatorship, epitomized in a series of Five Year Plans. There was to be jam, not tomorrow but by about the end of the twentieth century, when it was hoped China would have completed "all-round socialist industrialization" and be in a position to provide its population with a reasonable standard of living. In the meantime it would be difficult, because of the unfavorable ratio between population and resources, to offer much in the way of material incentives. Mao himself came increasingly to hold that it was not only difficult but undesirable, because the zeal for revolution would tend to be lost in the push for modernization. Better to preserve revolutionary zeal by offering ideological incentives than material ones, even if this meant slowing down the process of modernization.

Leaving aside the important ideological differences between Mao and some of his colleagues we can see that, given the overriding goal of a planned model of development, the basic strategy adopted has been the obvious one. Efforts have been made, not always successfully, to ensure enough agricultural output to maintain the growing population at least at a subsistence level and to allow something for export and other state requirements. Mainly by selling a large part of its output, notably processed consumer goods, back to the public at higher prices, the state has derived sufficient resources to undertake an ambitious program of heavy industrialization. Foreign aid in various forms, especially Soviet aid during the period 1950–60, has been important, but mainly as a source of technology rather than as a source of capital; all long-term debts incurred to the Soviet Union have been repaid, and China's current international credit rating is good. The heart of the industrialization program, to judge by the apparent fact that it is the last to be cut in time of difficulty, is the modern weapons program, especially its nuclear aspect. Clearly this is regarded as an indispensable source of security and bargaining power, and cost is a secondary consideration.

Another major goal of the Chinese leadership is of course unification of the country through the "liberation" of Taiwan. Unlike the obscure and ambiguous case of Outer Mongolia, Taiwan is regarded in Peking (and, for that matter, in Taipei) as an integral part of China, along with such other outlying regions as Manchuria (referred to in China as the Northeast), Inner Mongolia, Sinkiang, and Tibet. This was not always so. In 1936 Mao Tse-tung told Edgar Snow that after the defeat of Japan, which he predicted, Taiwan should become independent. But at the Cairo Conference in 1943 the British and American governments promised Taiwan to Nationalist China—a promise that the United States now officially regards as not binding—and the Nationalists were allowed to occupy it in 1945. Since 1949 the island has been the Nationalists' main base, and since 1950 it has been under American protection and the recipient of American military aid. These facts are quite enough to explain the fact that Mao's offhand remark of 1936 has long since been dropped down the memory hole and replaced by an apparently burning determination that Taiwan must be "liberated." Although this determination is genuine enough, and almost certainly sufficient to prevent an accommodation with the United States at least as long as it protects Taiwan and Mao Tse-tung and his "thought" hold sway on the mainland, two important qualifications should be noted. The issue is a useful one for purposes of domestic political mobilization, and there is an obvious incentive not to risk committing suicide by seriously attempting a military "liberation" of the island in the teeth of American opposition.

To Peking and to many Chinese, it is a genuine source of intense humiliation and frustration that China is a divided country, that it is in some danger of being split more or less permanently into "two Chinas," and all the more so because the division is so unequal and unification, except for the interposition of the United States, so close. The Nationalist-held offshore islands, Quemoy in particular, play an important role in the struggle over Taiwan, although a political more than a military one. They link the two contestants together, inhibit the emergence of a clear-cut "two Chinas" situation, and give the Nationalists at least some basis for claiming that they are not confined entirely to Taiwan. That being so, Peking apparently feels no interest in taking the offshore islands unless it can "liberate" Taiwan at the same time. The islands can be used as a means of leverage on the Nationalists and the United States, as they were during the crisis of 1954–55 and again in 1958, but with doubtful effectiveness. The main result of the first of these crises was a defensive alliance between the United States and Nationalist China, and the main result of the second was probably a further deterioration of Sino-Soviet relations. For it became obvious at that time that, although Soviet power was needed to counterbalance American power if Taiwan were to be "liberated," Moscow was the reverse of interested in exposing itself to serious risks on behalf of its increasingly troublesome ally. Meanwhile, Peking had tried with no visible results to achieve "liberation," or at least to hasten it, first by means of negotiations with the United States (in 1955) and then by means of propaganda appeals to the Nationalists (in 1956).

Peking has consistently maintained that the Nationalists can avoid the alternatives of ultimate conquest or unconditional surrender through a negotiated settlement, one that would presumably leave Taiwan a degree of autonomy. There seems to be no chance of such a settlement while either Mao or Chiang lives, and even after that there would be serious problems. Even if the United States could somehow be ignored or bypassed, the indigenous Taiwanese would object strenuously to being bargained away. The island's prosperity, as compared with the mainland, could not be jeopardized without serious consequences. Furthermore, the political position of the Nationalists is far from desperate. They have the island under excessively good control, if anything, enjoy fairly widespread diplomatic ties, and have important relations with the United States and Japan. Indeed, if the United States loses its bases in Okinawa, Taiwan is likely to assume an enhanced military importance in American military eyes. It may be that Peking will have to continue to tolerate what it regards as an intolerable situation.

We come now to the most complex category of Peking's external objectives—Peking's quest for status and influence. A number of factors are involved here. Among them are a pride in China's size, population, potential power, and traditional cultural brilliance and a desire to capitalize on them to restore China to a pre-eminent place in the world. China's humiliation in modern times at the hands of other countries must be wiped out, politically if not militarily. There is an immense felt need for prestige, for universal acceptance of Peking's self-image of a uniquely valid and effective "model" of revolution and a true world power having a voice in the deciding of all major international questions. There is an effort to generate, in support of this quest for prestige, a feeling, notably in Asia, that China in some sense represents the "wave of the future." The effect presumably hoped for is that smaller Asian countries will accommodate their foreign and even their domestic policies to Peking's wishes in the interest of purchasing exemption from direct Chinese pressures such as large-scale support for a "people's war" waged by the local Communist movement. In reality, both logic and Chinese behavior in certain cases, such as Burma since about 1963, suggest that the final result of such a policy would more probably be a facilitation rather than an avoidance of a Chinese-supported "people's war."

For it is reasonably clear that Peking aspires to some sort of sphere of influence in Asia, to the exclusion of external powers such as the United States and—if possible—the Soviet Union. Certainly the possession of a sphere of influence in its own vicinity could be thought of as a logical attribute of a great power, and recent Soviet behavior toward Czechoslovakia shows that the idea is far from dead. But the Soviet Union dominates its sphere in Eastern Europe not only by virtue of its power but with the assent, however reluctantly given, of its allies in the Second World War. China enjoys no such situation, apart from the assertion of some Western political scientists that China has traditionally dominated Asia, a very misleading proposition. No contemporary government, Asian or other, would concede the truth of such a proposition, and at least two, the American and the Soviet, seem prepared to oppose any attempt by Peking to make it good.

Even if it wished to do so, as it probably does not, China is in no position to assert a sphere of influence in Asia through overt force and outright domination. The threat of American retaliation is only the most obvious, and perhaps the most important, of a number of reasons why this is so. For one thing, China enjoys no such geographic highroad into adjacent territory, except to some extent in the case of Soviet Asia, as the Soviet Union enjoys into Eastern Europe; it is hemmed in to a great degree by seas, mountain, and jungle. Not only its destructive power but its strategic mobility would have to be increased to a level not now in prospect to bring about any significant change in this situation. And regardless of physical obstacles, the political costs of overt military action by China against any of its neighbors would be very great. One has only to think of the political hornet's nest that Moscow brought down on its head by invading a country more or less admittedly within its sphere of influence, Czechoslovakia.

Furthermore, Mao Tse-tung and his colleagues have traditionally tended to prefer less direct, and less dangerous, methods of promoting both Communist revolution and Chinese influence in nearby countries. These methods are more appropriate than overt military coercion to the apparent objective, which is something significantly less crude than a chain of Chinese colonies or satellites. Peking's desired outcome seems to be a series of Communist-controlled states, in which the local Communist parties have come to power by a Chinese-style "people's war," with just enough Chinese aid, support, and advice to ensure success and a significant degree of Chinese influence (but probably not amounting to control). On the other hand, the extent of Chinese involvement must not be great enough to render the Maoist shibboleth of "self-reliance" obviously inapplicable or to expose Peking to undue risks or costs. To a considerable degree, such an approach represents an effort to eat one's cake and have it too, and like most such efforts it has not been notable to date for its success. It is also clear that, assuming this line of analysis to be at least approximately correct, China feels no serious interest in the rest of Asia as a "rice bowl" from which to feel its own surplus population or as a dumping ground for the latter. Economic, political, and military realities all dictate that if China's effort to feed its population is to succeed, the victory must be won on Chinese, not foreign soil; food imports can be of no more than marginal significance, except perhaps in exceptional circumstances analogous to the transitional period in its development during which Japan imported a large fraction of its food.

Peking's aims with regard to the rest of the Third World, beyond Asia, do not seem qualitatively different from those with regard to Asia itself. The main difference is that realities of distance, geography, and culture all necessitate a lesser degree of Chinese involvement and influence, on the average at any rate, than can be hoped for in Asia. Here again Peking is trying to eat its cake and have it too. It is trying to exclude major competitive influences, notably American and Soviet, and promote its own by stressing its own affinity to, and the unique relevance of its "model" of "socialist revolution" and "socialist construction" for, the peoples involved without going to the extent of appearing to wall itself off from the chance to seem relevant to and effective in the higher realms of power and influence where the great powers operate. In other words, China wants to be accepted as the only authentic Third World great power without cutting itself off in any way from the affairs, and in particular what Mao calls the "revolutionary people," of the developed countries. And again, China has not been notably successful to date. The undoubted unrest in both the underdeveloped and developed worlds, some of it of potentially revolutionary proportions, owes little to China or Mao for its inspiration. Nor is Mao especially accurate in his diagnosis of the cause of this phenomenon, which to his mind is the oppressive and exploitative behavior of the "ruling class" of the "imperialist" and "neocolonialist" countries. The secrets both of progress and unrest in developed and underdeveloped countries alike, a subject too complicated to be grappled with here, seem largely to have escaped Mao.

Nevertheless, Peking appears to think, and to a degree to be correct in thinking, of the Third World as a vast arena in which, without much risk or expense, it can compete with the United States, the Soviet Union, and lesser rivals like India and distract their unwelcome attention from China's immediate vicinity. In fact, Mao's obvious and sensible reluctance to challenge the United States or the Soviet Union to a direct trial of strength around his borders can be tacitly rationalized as a perception that such a step is unnecessary in any event, since with Chinese guidance, the "revolutionary people of the world" will in time dispose of the Maoist demons of "imperialism, reaction, and modern revisionism." But in order for this rationalization to have any chance of seeming convincing, in Peking or elsewhere, Mao must be able to point with some credibility to revolutionary progress in the Third World; if he admitted that there were none, it might then seem incumbent on him to do something directly against the United States or the Soviet Union by way of compensation. As it is, there is a natural tendency for Mao to overestimate the revolutionary potential of the Third World. This was notably true of Sub-Saharan Africa in the early 1960s, in the wake of decolonization. Chinese setbacks, both direct and by proxy, in that region probably contributed along with other setbacks such as that in Indonesia to fixating Mao on Vietnam as the main area where, although at great risk and cost, a major if proxy victory could be won against "imperialism" and the mystique and momentum of the Maoist revolutionary strategy regenerated.

It is clear that since the death of Stalin Mao, apparently with some opposition from certain of his colleagues, has made a Sino-Soviet dispute inevitable by rejecting Moscow's self-imposed and largely reasonable limits on its commitments to China and by asserting a leading role for his own party in the international Communist movement. The fact that no other major Communist Party has felt able and willing to follow the Chinese lead and example, except in a few cases for a short time, suggests that, by Marxist-Leninist if not by Maoist standards, the Soviet position is essentially the more reasonable of the two.

As we have seen, the Sino-Soviet dispute grew serious as a result of a Chinese tendency, after 1955, first to combat and then to exploit Khrushchev's tendency to conciliate the United States (where Chinese interests were concerned, at any rate) and adopt a domestic policy more or less reminiscent of Tito's "revisionist" one as well as compete actively with China in the Third World. By about 1958 Mao was offering the world models of "socialist revolution" and "socialist construction" that he claimed were both more truly Marxist-Leninist and better adapted to actual current conditions in the Third World and even in the developed countries.

Unquestionably Mao accepts as inevitable, and may even regard as desirable, the marked decline in organizational solidarity among Communist parties since the death of Stalin, a process to which he has massively contributed. Certainly he has opposed organizational solidarity since he decided, about 1960, that its most likely beneficiary, the Soviet Union, was irretrievably "revisionist," at least for the foreseeable future. Until the day comes, if it ever does, when "revisionism" has been substantially displaced by general acceptance of correct—in other words, Maoist—thinking, Mao apparently has no desire to see general organizational solidarity restored. In the meantime, he advocates solidarity based on ideology—again, his—among non-"revisionist" parties and splinter groups. There are about thirty of the latter in various countries, claiming in varying degree to offer a correct (Maoist) alternative to an established pro-Moscow Communist Party. Although Peking possesses and exploits various means of influence, including subsidies, over these groups, its essential hold is the ideological one: Maoism is really thought to hold the answers. Conversely, Mao and his supporters, foreign as well as Chinese, hold in effect that the Soviet Union can do nothing right, at least pending its predicted ultimate conversion to the correct, or Maoist, brand of Marxist-Leninism. This attitude provides one of the main explanations why the Soviet invasion of Czechoslovakia, an action of a decidedly non-"revisionist" kind and one that might be expected to evoke Mao's reluctant admiration, evoked instead nothing but abuse. To concede anything to Moscow, at least until it experiences an improbable ideological conversion, would be to lend aid and comfort to "revisionism."

It has already been suggested that Peking aspires to become a great, or super, power. At any rate, as long as Mao and his "thought" are influential, this means a power different from that of other great powers in a supposedly significant way. China is to acquire and exploit political, economic, and military influence appropriate to great-power status, but it is not to do so in a merely conventional way. In other words, it will seek to enhance not only its own national interests but the cause of world revolution, which it asserts that Moscow no longer seeks to promote. The Maoist mythology holds, in effect, that what is good for China is good for "progressive mankind." It insists that its two main opponents, the United States and the Soviet Union, are "colluding" against it with the aim of dividing the world between them. In reality, this charge is probably in large part propaganda, for if Peking really believed it, there would be occasion for more serious alarm than seems actually to exist. In reality, what is involved is a kind of tripolar Cold War, in which each party has an essentially adversary relationship with each of the other two (although this fact is not always recognized in the United States) and fears that the other two may combine against it, or at least reconcile their differences with adverse objective results for itself. The facts of the situation seem to militate strongly against full cooperation between any two of the three parties, at least for the so-called foreseeable future. There is at least one obvious and significant asymmetry in this conflict: China is not a true superpower and, even if the Maoist albatross could be cut from around its neck, is not likely to become one for a long time, if ever. Mao's attempted answer to this problem is a characteristically Asian one: to compensate for the opponent's superior brute strength by superior, or allegedly superior, skill.

POLICY DIFFERENCES

The subject of policy differences within the authoritarian leadership of an essentially closed society is obviously a difficult one to discuss with any degree of confidence. Even after we take account of what seems valid in recent Red Guard charges against Liu Shaoch'i, it remains even harder to analyze policy differences in Peking than in Moscow. Nevertheless, there are enough reasons to believe in the existence and importance of the subject so that even an imperfect attempt is probably better than no attempt at all.

As might be expected, it appears that the differences are somewhat less serious with respect to foreign policy than with respect to domestic policy. There seems to be, or to have been, a substantial measure of agreement between the Maoists and the non-Maoists, of whom Liu Shao-ch'i was almost certainly the leading figure until his downfall in 1966–67—although this group seems still to exist under different management—as to basic objectives, or in other words, as to the considerations of security and influence discussed in the preceding section. The main probable exception is with regard to the Soviet Union, which, as we have seen, Mao has come to regard for all practical purposes as an enemy and one in some ways more dangerous and despicable than the United States at that. It is probably not entirely without reason that the Soviet press refers hopefully to the existence of "healthy forces" within the CPC favoring the restoration of orderly bureaucratic rule and reasonably cooperative relations with the Soviet Union. It is, in short, both plausible and in accord with at least some evidence to hold that Liu Shao-ch'i and some other Chinese leaders, including probably some who are still active even if they must keep their true opinions to themselves, believe that the relationship with the Soviet Union is not, or should not be, fundamentally an adversary one. Ideological disagreements ought to be kept within bounds so that a viable relationship can be maintained under which China can benefit from Soviet aid, and if possible, protection. This school probably holds that the relationship with the United States is fundamentally an adversary one, at least for so long as the United States behaves as an "imperialist" power by Marxist-Leninist standards and continues to protect Taiwan.

It is in the field of method, or strategy, that the differences between the two schools seem to be most significant. As already suggested, the differences are probably greatest with respect to the Soviet Union. Mao's pretensions to personal leadership of world communism, and consequently some of his objections to Khrushchev's attack on Stalin, which tended to depreciate the idea of such leadership, are probably not taken very seriously by the other school and may even be objected to because they have worsened

Sino-Soviet relations to no very useful purpose. Somewhat similarly, Mao's vehement objections to the Soviet proposal for "united action," implicitly under Soviet leadership, on behalf of North Vietnam and the Viet Cong seem not to have been echoed by the other school, although Mao prevailed by virtue of his superior political strength.

As for the problem of coping with the United States, it seems probable that the non-Maoists do not regard Mao's technique of constantly expressing virulent hostility to be very effective, at least as long as it must be counterbalanced by a minimum of direct action to give effect to that hostility. Chinese behavior at the Warsaw ambassadorial talks with the United States has occasionally seemed to reflect such a difference of opinion, notably in February 1969, when Peking, after proposing such talks for February 20, canceled them two days ahead of time on the trivial pretext that a Chinese diplomat had defected from The Hague to the United States the month before. In all probability the resumption of talks had been controversial from the beginning, and the defection had merely provided the extreme Maoists with a handle for breaking off the talks, for the time being at least. It can be plausibly argued that from the American point of view the non-Maoist approach is more dangerous because more "rational." In other words, by devoting attention and energy to programs calculated to increasing China's real power rather than wasting resources on largely demonstrative actions, the non-Maoists if they had their way—as they may sooner or later—would pose a more serious ultimate threat. Even though the two approaches have been brought into better balance recently (see Chapter VI), it appears that the Maoist one tends to prevail in the event of a direct clash.

The differences regarding Asia and the rest of the Third World seem relatively clear-cut. Mao understandably prefers and stresses the approach "from below": Chinese-style Communist revolution, allegedly against "imperialism" but actually against any unacceptable regime, as the opportunity appears or can be created. The non-Maoists appear to regard this approach as not very effective, at least at the present stage when most governments in the Third World have not failed—if they ever do—to solve their pressing domestic problems. They tend to prefer an approach "from above," stressing the cultivation of governments some of which are distasteful to the Maoists, by such means as state visits, economic aid, and cultural relations. The idea presumably is to enhance China's national influence pending the day, if it ever comes, when the situation in the Third World becomes truly ripe for Communist revolution. A conjunction of events, probably not accidental, in the spring of 1963 illustrates the point. Liu Shao-ch'i, in his capacity of Chairman of the Chinese People's Republic or chief of state, paid formal visits to Burma, Indonesia, Cambodia, and North Vietnam, the first occasion on which he had visited a non-Communist country (Mao never has). At the same time, the Foreign Languages Press in Peking published what may be regarded as a handbook for foreign revolutionaries, a volume entitled *Selected Military Writings of Mao Tse-tung*.

MILITARY CONSIDERATIONS AND STRATEGY

It may be helpful to begin this discussion of the military aspects of foreign policymaking in China by outlining roughly the nature of actual Chinese military dispositions. The bulk of China's large (approximately 2.5 million-man) ground forces and of its less impressive air force is stationed in Manchuria and the eastern provinces of China Proper. This certainly suggests that the United States, and to a lesser extent Nationalist China, are regarded as the main threat, but other considerations are probably also involved. These dispositions parallel rather closely both population distribution and industrial development. In other words, in this way the armed forces, and the ground forces in particular, can more readily serve as instruments of politcal control to the extent that may prove necessary—as it generally did not until 1967, but has since then—and can more easily be supplied. Surprisingly little strength is disposed along the Sino-Soviet frontier, apart from its Manchurian sector, or along the Sino-Indian frontier. The reasons are mainly logistical, it appears, and since similar considerations operate on the other side the military situation in these regions was approximately balanced until the Soviet Union increased its forces along the Sino-Soviet frontier in 1969 and 1970 to about forty divisions. Two other obviously security-related measures, apart from the actual stationing of troops, may be mentioned with respect to Sinkiang. Since about the mid-1950s Peking has actively promoted a program of Chinese immigration and colonization, as it has in other border areas as well, and it has conspicuously failed to complete its leg of a major railway that was to have linked China with Soviet Central Asia via Sinkiang, although the Soviet Union has completed its relatively short leg long since.

Barring an unlikely breakup of the country into separate or even warring regional factions, China is in a strong defensive position when it comes to resisting conventional attack, notably invasion. Although not especially large in relation to China's size and population, its conventional forces are big enough and sufficiently modernized so that, in spite of their political "guerrillaization" after about 1963 and their heavy involvement in political activities since 1967, they render any major invasion of China, as distinct from a mere local penetration, virtually out of the question. In addition, the population seems likely to support the regime, in spite of the latter's loss of popularity in recent years, rather than a foreign invader, or at any rate the chances that this is true are great enough to serve as a significant additional deterrent to invasion. The discussion appears rather academic, since it is difficult to see any valid political incentives for an American or Soviet invasion. If there are any, they probably exist in Moscow, where a military operation to assist "healthy forces" to return to power may hold some hypothetical attractions. But the United States' difficulties in Vietnam have been great enough, even though there have been achievements as well, to discourage any idea that a comparable operation in a vastly bigger country like China would be worthwhile, unless it was certain of popular support. Against the idea is the example of Japan's invasion of China; Japan was not defeated in China, but neither was it victorious, and the costs of its operations there were immense in several respects.

If China is in a strong position to avoid or resist conventional attack, the same cannot really be said with respect to nuclear attack. It is true that Mao and some of his colleagues—Lin Piao in 1965, for example—have occasionally insisted that China, by virtue of its huge population, could survive a thermonuclear attack and that, in fact, the main result of a general war would be the collapse of "imperialism" and the triumph of "socialism" (the Chinese rather than the Russian brand, presumably). But it is very doubtful that anyone in Peking seriously believes this to be true, however useful such statements may be thought to be as propaganda. It is even more doubtful that in fact they have any validity. China's ability to function at all as a modern state depends, not on the size of its population, but on the modern sector of its economy and on its armed forces. Even the population lives densely crowded for the most part into the eastern third of the country, in flimsy structures that offer no shelter against nuclear blast and with its fields totally exposed to fallout. The vulnerability of the modern sector—cities, industries, command and control centers, etc.—is even more obvious. Neither an ignorance of this situation nor a willingness, in spite of the knowledge, to risk all in a nuclear war seems credible. There is not even any rational incentive for Peking to try to incite a thermonuclear exchange between the United States and the Soviet Union, if only because in such an event China could be reasonably certain that it would not be left untouched.

As already indicated, China possesses little strategic "reach." It has little in the way of airborne and amphibious forces, offensive naval units, and the like, and its nuclear forces are likely to remain almost negligible as compared with those of the United States or the Soviet Union, so that they will have direct military utility only if both the latter allow them to do so. Difficulties of terrain and logistics, the risks of retaliation, and the political consequences of military action on foreign soil combine to limit further China's actual and probable future capabilities for aggressive military action.

If China has virtually no hope of overcoming the American and Soviet leads in the field of strategic weapons and extracting offensive advantages in this way, it can nevertheless hope seriously to create an effective minimum deterrent against the possibility, however remote, of American or Soviet nuclear attack without provocation, by means of the ability to strike with nuclear weapons targets not only in Asia but in the United States and Soviet Europe as well. It can therefore hope to employ a sort of hostage, or "blackmail," strategy, but for defensive rather than offensive purposes. In other words, it may be possible to discourage, if not to deter altogether, any possible American or Soviet intent to threaten or carry out nuclear attack on China, at least aggressively and conceivably even in retaliation for some Chinese initiative of a subnuclear nature. This might be achieved by holding hostage to Chinese nuclear weapons, implicitly if not explicitly, American and Soviet home territory and still more American and Soviet bases, forces, and allies in the Far East. What may be termed a conventional hostage strategy is already in effect, at the verbal level at least, with respect to mainland Asia. In 1965 and 1966 in particular, Chinese sources, notably Foreign Minister Chen Yi, whose unenviable task was to give expression to both the Maoist and non-Maoist views in shifting proportions, threatened a "war without boundaries" in Southeast Asia in the event of an American attack on China. Although the effectiveness of such threats tends to diminish as time passes without their being implemented, countries on the Asian mainland are in no position to discount such threats entirely, especially in time of crisis such as existed for about three years after the American escalation in Vietnam.

China has entered into two formal military alliances, one with the Soviet Union (1950) and one with North Korea (1961). It has been reported to have offered another to North Vietnam in 1961 but to have been rejected, presumably because of a desire on Hanoi's part to preserve its freedom of action to the maximum, avoid antagonizing the Soviet Union, and avoid committing an open breach of the Geneva agreements of 1954. The alliance with North Korea was apparently signed mainly because the Soviet Union had done the same a week before, in the aftermath of the military power seizure in South Korea. Neither Moscow nor Peking has much control over North Korean behavior, and each certainly hopes that Pyongyang will do nothing to bring the alliance into effect. As for the Sino-Soviet alliance, it has been reasonably clear since about 1960 that the Soviet Union was most unlikely to give China any effective support or protection except perhaps in some emergency that seemed to involve a direct threat to Soviet security, such as a highly improbable American invasion of Manchuria.

Another category of China's external military relations is that of aid programs to governments and revolutionary movements considered sympathetic. This is a method much favored by major powers for acquiring influence at little risk and cost, as well as for disposing on occasion of surplus military equipment. The major governmental recipients of Chinese military aid have been North Vietnam (since 1950) and Pakistan (since 1966). In the former case, the aid has consisted largely of light equipment suitable for guerrilla warfare, which is what Peking has basically wanted Hanoi to wage; in the latter case, in view of the conventional nature of the Indo-Pakistani confrontation the aid has included heavy tanks and jet fighters. Other governmental recipients of Chinese military aid have been Indonesia (prior to the coup of 1965), Cambodia, and some states elsewhere in the Third World, such as Somalia. Revolutionary recipients have included the Viet Cong and assorted movements in other parts of Southeast Asia and in the Middle East and Africa, such as the Fatah. The Chinese have proved imaginative and adept at devising and making available equipment and weapons, as well as training, appropriate to the needs of revolutionary warfare; an example is the excellent AK47 rifle. Like other providers of military aid, however, the Chinese must live with the fact that arming someone else does not generally convey the power to influence his political motivations and behavior decisively.

Chinese statements to date on the subject of arms control and disarmament have almost entirely ignored the fields of covert military aid and conventional forces, where China has a relatively strong position and is reluctant to impair it, in favor of the nuclear aspect, where China is weak as compared with its major adversaries. Since at least as long ago as the nuclear test ban treaty of 1963, the Chinese public position has been that there must be complete nuclear disarmament, to be achieved preferably by means of a "summit meeting" of the chiefs of government of all countries, nuclear and nonnuclear alike. This proposal, which if realized would amount to trading China's embryonic nuclear stockpile for the much larger ones of its two major adversaries, has been rejected by the United States as not serious, at any rate in the absence of arrangements for other forms of disarmament as well, although the Soviet Union has expressed some nominal interest in it. As an interim measure, Peking has proposed to the United States a mutual no-first-use pledge, which again would have the effect of trading China's nuclear stockpile off against that of the United States, which understandably has declined the offer. In reality, of course, Peking almost certainly has no serious expectation that these proposals will be accepted and is fully determined to press ahead as rapidly as possible with the development of its own nuclear weapons and delivery systems.

Peking has taken the position in principle that the spread of nuclear weapons, at any rate to "peace-loving" and "anti-imperialist" states, is a good thing, because it enables the recipients to resist American or Soviet "nuclear blackmail" and further erodes the American and Soviet quasi-duopoly in this field. In reality, it is unlikely that China would welcome the acquisition of nuclear weapons on a large scale by any state, except perhaps West Germany (for its effect, in this case, on the Soviet Union). Soviet sources have hinted that China may be making use of West German nuclear scientists and rocket experts and perhaps even preparing to help West Germany test nuclear weapons on its soil, but although there is unlikely to be any truth in these charges, they say something about Moscow's state of mind and still more about its propaganda techniques. China would have reason to be concerned if India or Japan "went nuclear," and it knows that the thing most likely to produce such a result would be bellicose behavior on its own part. China opposes the Nuclear Nonproliferation Treaty on essentially the same political grounds as those on which it opposes the test ban: it represents an attempt by the United States and the Soviet Union to maximize their political influence by inhibiting the development of nuclear weapons by other states. Although this argument is questionable as to motivation and has obvious flaws, it is not entirely wrong.

As for the interesting question of whether Peking itself might transfer military nuclear technology or actual nuclear weapons to other states not now possessing them, the Chinese position has been rather ambiguous, whether by design or as a reflection of a disagreement in Peking. When Chen Yi was questioned on this point, in September 1965, he said, according to the contemporary version published in the Japanese Communist newspaper *Akahata*, that China had not yet been asked to do so. Actually this statement may not be strictly true; there are some tantalizing indications that in 1964 or 1965 Peking may have made some vague promises of a nuclear nature to the Indonesian Air Force, which was then under leftist leadership. When the official Chinese version of Chen Yi's statement was released a week after the interview, it said that the question was not "realistic." It seems fair to conclude, from this and other evidence, that Peking has sought to give the impression that it will not transfer nuclear weapons or military nuclear technology but has avoided giving a pledge to this effect that could be interpreted as binding. In short, it appears to be "keeping its options open."

FORMULATION OF POLICY

Like the subject of policy differences, that of the actual formulation of policy is difficult to study because of the shortage of relevant information. It is obvious that ideology plays a role, but since it needs to be interpreted and applied in each case, it is hard to say anything of general applicability about it that has much importance or interest.

There is no doubt that the Chinese leadership has available to it, if it chooses to avail itself of it, a great deal of information on the outside world. Its embassies, newsgathering agencies, and intelligence services funnel a great deal of information, overtly and covertly acquired, to it, and we know that largely unslanted summaries of foreign developments circulate—or at any rate circulated until the Cultural Revolution—in Peking for elite consumption.

By whom are major decisions relating to foreign policy made? The answer is the same for foreign policy as for domestic policy, but it is an answer that has changed over time. The Central Committee elected at the Eighth Party Congress (September 1956) in turn elected a Politburo (Political Bureau) and a Standing Committe of the latter. Without much doubt, this Politburo Standing Committee was intended to serve, and did serve, as the highest policymaking body in both the domestic and foreign fields. It consisted initially of six men: Mao Tse-tung (Chairman), Liu Shao-ch'i, Chou En-lai, Chu Teh, Chen Yun, and Secretary General Teng Hsiao-p'ing (apparently ex officio). In May 1958, perhaps partly to eliminate the possibility of tie votes on questions relating to the Great Leap Forward, Marshal Lin Piao, whose political stock had been rising for the past few years and who was to become Defense

Minister the following year, was not only added to the group but was ranked ahead of Teng Hsiao-p'ing. In spite of Mao's enormous prestige and influence, it appears that the principle of majority rule was observed in the Standing Committee, even after the difficulties encountered by the Great Leap Forward led Mao to step down, probably willingly and not reluctantly, as Chairman of the Chinese People's Republic in the spring of 1959 in favor of Liu Shao-ch'i. In other words, it is improbable either that Mao was able to set policy before that time without the support of a majority of the Standing Committee or that after that time the retreat from the thoroughly Maoist policies of the Great Leap Forward could have been executed except at the initiative of a majority. It seems likely that when Mao attempted a sort of political comeback after 1962 he had little success at first precisely because he could not command a majority in the Standing Committee and was forced to rely mainly on the propaganda apparatus and the armed forces, to both of which he had direct personal access. It does appear, however, that all during this period, down to the fall of Khrushchev, Mao was able to secure majority support for the cornerstone of his foreign policy, his campaign against "Khrushchev revisionism."

During the crucial spring of 1966, when Mao was trying to launch the Cultural Revolution, he evidently could count on the support of Chou En-lai and Lin Piao, and it is unlikely to be coincidental that they continued as China's Big Three throughout the Cultural Revolution. They needed one more vote for a majority but were probably faced with consistent opposition on the part of Liu Shao-ch'i, Chu Teh, and Chen Yun. Teng Hsiao-p'ing's was the critical vote, and it appears that he was in fact won over by some means or other; among the pieces of evidence that could be cited is an obviously important photograph published in May 1966, in which Mao, Teng, Chou, and Lin are shown together in that order of precedence. Presumably uncomfortable with such a narrow margin, Mao got the Eleventh Plenary Session of the Central Committee (August 1966), which he dominated through a variety of pressures, to enlarge the Standing Committee; he either did not try to purge it or was unable to do so. T'ao Chu, Ch'en Po-ta, K'ang Sheng, and Li Fu-ch'un, all of them apparently regarded as reliably pro-Maoist, were added. During the next few months, however, presumably under the impact of the realization of what Mao had decided to do to the party apparatus at both the central and regional levels, Teng Hsiao-p'ing and T'ao Chu evidently went over to the opposition. The crucial vote then became that of the economic planner Li Fu-ch'un, who appears to have vacillated for a time but to have been won over by certain measures taken in February 1967 to ensure that the army would protect the economy against the Red Guards and by an effort to reopen the schools, which had been closed since the spring of 1966.

Shortly afterward, probably in late March 1967, the new majority of six in the Standing Committee voted through a number of radical measures, notably the launching of a public propaganda campaign against Liu Shao-ch'i, "China's Khrushchev," and the unhorsing of the most strongly entrenched of the regional party bosses, Li Ching-ch'uan in the southwest, an area that since early 1965 had possessed an additional importance in Peking's eyes by virtue of the conflict in Vietnam. At about this time, and perhaps by this action, the Standing Committee seems to have more or less abolished itself; the last reference to it that the writer has detected dates from April 24, 1967. The full Politburo, which had also been somewhat enlarged at the Eleventh Plenary Session, continued at least a nominal existence.

In reality, however, the spring of 1967 witnessed the death of "democratic centralism," or majority rule, within the upper ranks of the party. Mao and his personal following, headed by the so-called Cultural Revolution, one of whose most prominent members was his wife, Chiang Ching, and the Red Guards dominated the scene. This was the period of maximum Red Guard activity in both domestic and foreign affairs. Late in the summer, when the dangers of such activity had become apparent to Mao, Lin Piao and Chou En-lai evidently secured his consent for sterner measures by the army to restore order. By the early spring of 1968 the radicals, Chiang Ching being the most conspicuous, were protesting loudly against this trend and doing their best to reverse it. Apparently because orthodox "democratic centralist" means of resolving the dispute were no longer available, a new, informal leading body attempting to represent all major interests other than those of the old, discredited leadership of the party apparatus made its appearance. This body, whose membership finally settled down at fourteen with the dropping in the autumn of the vacillating Li Fu-ch'un, was headed by the hard core of the old Politburo Standing Committee as enlarged at the Eleventh Plenary Session: Mao, Lin Piao (who had clearly been Mao's designated heir since the Eleventh Plenary Session), Chou En-lai, Ch'en Po-ta, and K'ang Sheng. In deference no doubt to Mao's still pre-eminent position, Chiang Ching ranked next, and there was a significant sprinkling of Maoist enthusiasts among the rest of the membership. The other major interests represented were the military and the security services. Presumably it was within this group, whose position appears to have been left untouched by the Central Committee's Twelfth Plenary Session (October 1968), that the major issues of domestic and foreign policy were decided during this period. The heterogeneous nature of the group, together with Mao's essentially unchanged ideas and still important role, probably helps to explain the rather hesitant character of the measures taken in 1968 to improve China's international position (see Chapter VI).

AVAILABLE STRATEGIES AND TACTICS

More for purposes of convenience than for any other reason, this discussion classifies the strategies and tactics available to the Chinese Communist leadership in the field of foreign policy under ten headings: propaganda, diplomacy, "people's diplomacy," aid programs, dealings with local Communist parties, fostering of subversion and "people's war," exploitation of disputes between other countries, manipulation of the overseas Chinese, border pressures, and military movements and actions. Since it will be obvious from what has already been said that some of these are of greater interest to the Maoists, and others to the non-Maoists, the point will not be belabored in the course of the discussion.

Propaganda is put first because it is probably the most important, or at least the most extensively used, of all. The discussion of it here will be kept as short as possible for the best and most obvious reason: to keep it from becoming as long as it could. In recent years the most pervasive category of Chinese foreign propaganda has been the "plugging" *ad nauseam* of Mao Tse-tung, his "thought," and his Cultural Revolution in particular. Since 1963, he has issued a series of personal statements on various issues capable of being exploited to the disadvantage of the United States, although curiously enough excluding Vietnam since the American escalation. One such, in April 1968, was a very halfhearted tribute to Martin Luther King and a much more enthusiastic incitement to black violence in the United States; Mao objected to King's devotion to nonviolence and was apparently only persuaded with difficulty to issue the statement. There have of course been a number of loud Chinese calls to "people's war" in the Third World, most notably Lin Piao's famous tract of September 1965. Each of China's seven successful nuclear or thermonuclear tests held until late 1968 was followed by an exultant statement portraying it as a triumph for the "thought of Mao Tse-tung" and a "great encouragement to the revolutionary people of the world." Most of these tests, furthermore, seem to have been timed to dramatize Chinese reaction to some external event. To take only the most obvious examples, the test of October 16, 1964 (the first), was clearly timed to dramatize the fall of Khrushchev; that of October 27, 1966, President Johnson's visit to the mainland of Asia (South Vietnam and Thailand); and that of June 17, 1967, Premier Kosygin's visit to the United Nations and the United States following the Middle Eastern war. There have of course been countless Chinese statements in opposition to "revisionism" in its various alleged manifestations. Less often now than formerly, there have been many declarations of "Afro-Asian solidarity" and "traditional friendship" between China and numerous Afro-Asian countries. Especially since 1965, there have been statements asserting in exaggerated form the existence of a threat to China's security from the United States, the Soviet Union, and sometimes other countries as well, presumably in the hope of gaining political support for the Chinese leadership at home and abroad. Conversely, there have been vague but dire threats against the sources of these alleged dangers if they dared to lay a violent hand on China. Finally, there have been various policy declarations, such as the sweeping nuclear disarmament proposals in the wake of the test ban treaty, with such an obviously low chance of acceptance (and probably such a low level of desire in Peking for acceptance) that they must be considered primarily as propaganda.

China's version of conventional diplomacy takes a number of forms. State visits have already been mentioned. Mao has been abroad twice (1949–50 and 1957), both times to the Soviet Union. Liu Shao-ch'i, in his capacity of chief of state, paid official visits to various countries of southern Asia in 1963 and 1966, as well as to North Korea in 1963. Because of the Cultural Revolution, there have been no important state visits by Chinese, even those inveterate travelers Chou En-lai and Chen Yi, since mid-1966, unless one counts the visit of Chief of Staff Huang Yung-sheng to Rumania and Albania late in 1968. Visits by high foreign officials to China have been an important adjunct to Chinese diplomacy, although these too have greatly declined since the beginning of the Cultural Revolution. Perhaps more important than the visits themselves has been outrageous Chinese flattery of foreign leaders, such as Prince Sihanouk, whom it has been desired to woo and impress. The subject of military alliances has already been discussed and may be omitted here. China has signed treaties of friendship (or, in the case of some nearby countries, treaties of friendship and non-aggression) with eleven Afro-Asian countries: Burma, Nepal, Cambodia, Indonesia, Afghanistan, Yemen, Ghana, Guinea, Mali, Congo Brazzaville, and Tanzania. Except for the one with Yemen, which was originally signed in 1958 with the government of the Imam and then signed again with the republican government in 1964, all these treaties occurred between 1960 and 1965. Their practical effect is doubtful, but their purpose is not; all were signed with governments that could plausibly be considered anti-"imperialist" (this fact explains in all probability the otherwise puzzling omission of Pakistan)and that offered a fair field for Soviet diplomatic activity. Probably the most brilliant Chinese diplomatic performances were at the Geneva Conference on Indochina (1954) and the Asian-African Conference at Bandung (1955), Chou En-lai as Foreign Minister being the main spokesman; Chen Yi's performance at the Geneva Conference on Laos (1961–62) was also impressive. The projected Afro-Asian Conference at Algiers (1965) might have turned into another success had not Peking, presumably at Mao

Tse-tung's insistence, made demands, for the exclusion of the Soviet Union for example, that were bound to disrupt rather than promote "Afro-Asian solidarity."

It seems necessary to mention two of the various aspects of "people's diplomacy," or informal diplomacy. One is cultural relations. At least until the glorification of Mao began to blot out every other theme shortly before the Cultural Revolution, Chinese drama troupes and the like were often spectacularly successful in impressing both foreign visitors to China and foreign audiences on their own ground, including some developed as well as many developing countries. The second aspect is Chinese efforts to exploit various leftist international front organizations. Of these probably the most important in this context has been the Afro-Asian People's Solidarity Organization; the Chinese have never had much success in older, traditionally Soviet-dominated, organizations such as the World Federation of Trade Unions. China's status as an indubitably Afro-Asian power and its eagerness for involvement soon gave it an influential position in the secretariat of AAPSO after that body was formed in 1957, with headquarters in Cairo. With the development of the Sino-Soviet dispute, however, Chinese activity within the organization gave such a heavy priority to anti-Soviet activity over anti-"imperialist" activity that Peking's prestige and influence declined, although it was still able in 1966 to prevent AAPSO from being swallowed up in an Afro-Asian-Latin American People's Solidarity Organization, where the solidly pro-Soviet Latin American Communist parties would have given the advantage to Moscow. Since its setbacks of 1965 and early 1966 in the Third World, China has placed greater stress on smaller and more specialized organizations of Afro-Asian writers, journalists, etc., which it can easily dominate, rather than on the larger AAPSO.

The subject of military aid programs has already been covered; the discussion here will deal entirely with economic aid programs. China is highly selective and political in choice of recipients. Its main object seems to be to compete with the Soviet Union, and secondarily with the United States. Like the Soviet Union's, China's program usually avoids grants; Peking is nominally the more generous of the two in that its interest rates are lower (usually 1 percent) or sometimes nonexistent. Unlike the Soviet Union, China has confined its heavy industrial aid to a few Communist countries, and in its programs in the non-Communist Third World it stresses highways and light industries. It claims that it has its technicians abroad live according to local standards, which is reasonable, and that it charges world prices for its goods, which is not, since they are generally below at least the best world standards. China entered the foreign aid business after the Korean War in the smaller Communist countries of Asia, where there was an obvious element of competition with the Soviet Union in its activities. In 1956; in the spirit of the Bandung Conference, it inaugurated a series of aid programs in non-Communist Afro-Asian countries, beginning with Cambodia; after 1960 the emphasis tended to shift from Asia to Africa. At the present time, the two major recipients of Chinese aid among non-Communist countries are probably Pakistan, which gets economic as well as military aid, and Tanzania, which is an important Chinese springboard in Sub-Saharan Africa and has happily authorized China to undertake surveys for a major railway to connect it with Zambia. Albania, a special case, has been a substantial recipient of Chinese aid since 1961.

Even Albania, however, is not entirely under Chinese control; this can be said only of a few small Asian parties, which probably receive their funds as well as directives from Peking. It is naturally easier for the CPC to find support from other parties for the negative purpose of obstructing Soviet aims, the main relevant one in this connection being what has been "collective mobilization" of the international Communist movement. The Chinese is by no means the only major party to object to such a procedure, which typically takes the form of a Soviet call to a conference on some major issue, such as disciplining the Chinese. To name only one obvious example, the Rumanian party is opposed to "collective mobilization" against the Chinese or for any other purpose. As might be expected, for some years the main Chinese demand on other parties, apart from the related one of acceptance of the "thought of Mao Tsetung," has been repudiation of Soviet "revisionism." Although few parties have been willing to accept the first of these, a larger number have been willing to come close to repudiating the second.

Maoist theory on "people's war," as propounded for example by Lin Piao in 1965, holds that this is essentially an anti-"imperialist" phenomenon. The Chinese case, which of course is held up as the prototype, strongly suggests that the point may be as much a practical as a theoretical one; without the Japanese invasion of China, the CPC would probably never have come to power. It is also true that in the other countries where an essentially guerrilla Communist movement has succeeded in seizing power—Yugoslavia, Albania, and North Vietnam—it did so by acquiring the leadership of a national movement of resistance against foreign fascism or colonialism, to a very large extent at any rate. This fact raises the intriguing possibility that the converse may also be true—in other words, that a guerrilla Communist movement cannot succeed in the absence of such a situation. Yet if the presence of some form of active foreign, allegedly "imperialist," influence is a necessary condition for a guerrilla Communist victory, the case of South Vietnam suggests that it is not a sufficient condition. In many cases it is difficult for the Maoists to make it appear that this condition, whether necessary or sufficient, exists at all, and the best that can be done is to assert that a given government whose overthrow is desired (like that of Ne Win in Burma, in 1967) is a lackey of "imperialism," but the charge may not be convincing. In any case, when China wants to start or intensify a "people's war" in a particular country it generally provides training to local militants (in China, in the country in question, or in some third country) and furnishes arms, funds, propaganda support, and political advice (frequently including the recommendation to avoid coups or military adventurism and to form the "broadest possible united front" with other dissatisfied elements). It preaches the imitation, sooner or later, of the Maoist revolutionary model, including the establishment of rural base areas and a guerrilla army. Where this is admittedly premature, Peking frequently supports other forms of violence, such as tribal revolts, communal disorders, student demonstrations, strikes, and simple riots. From its long observation of the Third World it has come to feel a deep distrust of local military elites; the memories of China in 1927 and Indonesia in 1965 are especially painful.

It is not difficult to predict which side China will take when it chooses, as it often does, to involve itself in some fashion in a dispute between two other countries. The key is Peking's desire to score political points for itself and against its three main foreign adversaries, the United States, the Soviet Union, and India. Thus it will back an actually or potentially anti-Western state against a Western or pro-Western one; it has supported North Vietnam against the United States, Cambodia against Thailand and South Vietnam, Indonesia against the Netherlands and Malaysia backed by Britain, the black African states against the states of the "white redoubt" (Portuguese Africa, Rhodesia, and South Africa), various Latin American countries against the United States, and various Western European countries when they were considered to have quarrels with the United States. Somewhat similarly, China will generally back any other Communist state in a quarrel with the Soviet Union; the obvious examples are Albania since about 1961 and Czechoslovakia, Rumania, and Yugoslavia since the summer of 1968. The interesting case of a quarrel between the Soviet Union and a non-Communist state obviously presents itself; it is perhaps a tribute to Soviet diplomacy that it has only two such quarrels of an overt and serious kind, those with the United States and West Germany. As for the confrontation between its own two major adversaries, China takes as we have seen essentially a plague-on-both-your-houses attitude, while behaving in a way that suggests that Mao at least regards the Soviet Union as really the more despicable of the two. The West German case is a very interesting one for a number of reasons. Peking is somewhat embarrassed and inhibited by the "bourgeois" and pro-American character of the Bonn government, but this consideration seems to be overridden by the latter's commendable dislike of the Soviet Union and its attractiveness as a trading partner. China accordingly has usually refrained in recent years from denouncing the Bonn government, has expanded its trade with it, and may some day consider an active political relationship with it, but has so far stopped short of explicitly endorsing Bonn's side of its bitter dispute with Moscow. Another interesting case is the one in which a Western-oriented party opposes an anti-Western and pro-Soviet one. The obvious example is the Arab-Israeli dispute, in which Peking has sided from the beginning with the Arabs; since China's choice was made at a time when the Sino-Soviet relationship was relatively close, few inferences of contemporary interest can be drawn from it. As for India, it is clearly with the main purpose of combatting it that China has supported Pakistan, as well as siding with the Himalayan states (notably Nepal) in their less spectacular differences with India. The nature of China's support varies considerably with the geography and other circumstances of the dispute; it may amount to little more than propaganda and may be given for devious motives that have little in common with the objectives of the party receiving it.

There can be little doubt that China would like to, and on occasion has tried to, exploit the overseas Chinese of Southeast Asia for political advantage. The main specific uses that suggest themselves are manipulation as a source and transmission belt for funds destined for local Communist parties, and organization for purposes of terrorism and insurgency. More vaguely, the overseas Chinese might serve to perpetuate Chinese culture in the region and help to generate a wave-of-the-future psychology. In reality, however, Peking has not gotten much value out of the overseas Chinese, even from the long-standing but rather small terrorist movement that it has succeeded in keeping going in Malaya (now Malaysia) since shortly after Pearl Harbor. The problem is essentially that the overseas Chinese communities, which have aroused considerable local resentment by their wealth and cultural exclusiveness, have little political influence and are highly vulnerable to pressures and reprisals from the governments, armies, and mobs of the host countries. The antagonism is much greater in the predominantly Malay and/or Moslem countries (Indonesia, Malaysia, and the Philippines) than in the predominantly Buddhist countries (Burma, Thailand, Cambodia, Laos, and Vietnam). Singapore is a special case, being populated largely by ethnic Chinese, but their majority is much less helpful to Peking than might be expected since the Singapore government, although left wing, is firmly anti-Communist. In none of these countries is Peking really in a position to extend effective protection to the Chinese community if the latter becomes the object of pressures or reprisals for some reason. Peking came to realize this fact following the failure of its efforts to use the overseas Chinese, most of whom are basically apolitical, effectively in conjunction with the wave of unsuccessful Communist risings in Southeast Asia after 1948. Accordingly, in 1954–55 it offered to renounce its claim to the citizenship of persons of Chinese descent born in Southeast Asia and actually signed a treaty with Indonesia to that effect. Indonesia delayed ratification, however, and no other Southeast Asian government followed its example, largely because it would obviously be easier to continue discriminating against overseas Chinese if they were not full local citizens than if they were. Regardless of citizenship technicalities, Peking was helpless to protect Chinese who got into difficulties of various kinds during crises in Indonesia in 1959 and 1965 and in Burma in 1967. In the last analysis, the overseas Chinese are not so much instruments in the hands of Peking as hostages for its good behavior, as well as their own, in the hands of the host countries.

The subject of Chinese border pressures on neighboring countries, or what is sometimes called "aggression by seepage," is an obscure and controversial one. There is no doubt that Peking has built roads in its own border territories and in some cases (as in Nepal, Laos, and perhaps Burma) has extended them onto foreign soil. This of course is not sinister in itself, but it does make sinister things possible. Roadbuilding, to be sure, has helped to make possible the maintenance of sizable, although as we have seen not enormous, Chinese forces along the inland borders. This process has been accompanied on occasion by serious border incidents of various kinds, whose purpose usually seems to be to assert the formal Chinese claim to the boundary in question or the informal claim to a sort of buffer zone on the other side of it or to humiliate the government of the other state in some way. A good example is the shelling of Indian by Chinese forces at the Tibeto-Sikkimese border in September 1967, probably because the ruler of Sikkim was then on a visit to India. China tries in a variety of ways to extract advantage from the minority peoples near its borders, most of whom have kindred on the other side. Elaborate claims are made about conditions in China, and especially in the "autonomous" areas that Peking has created for many of its minorities since the early 1950s. In some cases this propaganda has been frustrated by China's own behavior along the border—this is notably true of the Kachin sector of the Sino-Burmese border—and in other cases by the flight of minority peoples from China across the border to escape some such convulsion as the Great Leap Forward or the Cultural Revolution. Furthermore, there are serious geographic and cultural limitations on the effectiveness of Chinese border pressures. Movements among minority peoples in border areas, even "people's wars" such as allegedly exist in Nagaland, northern Burma, and various parts of Thailand, do not necessarily have much effect on the far more important lowland regions where the majority communities live; the Communist presence in the jungles and highlands of South Vietnam would probably not have been very serious if all or most of the Communists had been non-Vietnamese.

Greater possible gains, but also higher risks, seem to attend the next and last category of Chinese foreign policy instrumentalities to be discussed here, that of military movements and actions. First under this heading may be mentioned overt threats of military action. Chinese pronouncements over the years teem with statements to the effect that various neighboring countries are as the lips to its teeth, that Peking will not stand idly by if some friendly country or China itself is attacked, that some real or alleged act of provocation or aggression will bring dire consequences, and so on. The case of Korea in 1950 certainly makes it impossible to dismiss such warnings and threats out of hand. At the other extreme, the case of Vietnam since 1965 makes it unnecessary to take them altogether literally. Each case must be judged on its own merits. The same can be said of Chinese troop redeployments, which may indicate an actual intent to begin combat or merely a desire to deter some possibly imaginary threat. The movement into North Korea was obviously a case of the former type; the movement into the Taiwan Strait area in the late spring of 1962 was an example of the latter. In at least one case (Burma from 1952 to 1956) Chinese troops have quietly encroached on and in fact occupied, some territory belonging to a neighbor, presumably for devious political reasons relating to the situation in that area. There have been occasional skirmishes, notably along the Sino-Indian frontier at various times and along the Sino-Soviet frontier since about 1966. On two major occasions (in 1950 in Korea and in 1962 along the Sino-Indian frontier), Chinese troops have conducted major offensive operations that Peking apparently regarded as necessary spoiling or preemptive attacks designed to cope with a serious threat to its security. In all cases to date in which it has employed overt force, Peking has surrounded its actions with some sort of ambiguity, such as the claim that its troops in Korea were volunteers, presumably in order to minimize military risks and political liabilities.

Major decisions or initiatives in foreign policy are usually, although not always, announced in some fashion. If the matter is mainly of a state character, the method may be a governmental statement, such as the two that rationalized China's objections to the nuclear test ban treaty of 1963. If the matter is of a more party or ideological character, the method will probably be an editorial in the *People's Daily, Red Flag*, both jointly, or (as has often been the case since the start of the Cultural Revolution) jointly in the two of them plus the *Liberation Army Daily*. Such a statement is likely to be a complex document, since it attempts to communicate simultaneously with more than one audience (the Chinese elite, the Chinese people, foreign friends, and foreign adversaries, primarily), and it may well be difficult to interpret. In fact, students of the subject are by no means agreed today as to the exact significance of such major pronouncements of the past as the two Chinese statements of 1956 on the Stalin question and related matters. Subsequent Chinese behavior, of course, often helps retroactively to elucidate the document that presumably announced it, but not always.

The making and announcement of a major decision is accompanied by a selection of the strategies and tactics considered appropriate; the general nature of these has already been discussed. A political system of the size and complexity of the Chinese then has available a sizable array of organizational means for implementing its policy. Before the Cultural Revolution at any rate, the party Secretariat was a large bureaucracy concerned partly with foreign affairs: its United Front Work Department dealt with overseas Chinese as well as with non-Communist persons in China, and its International Liaison Department handled relations with foreign Communist parties. Another important means of policy implementation is the State Council (cabinet) under Premier Chou En-lai. Even since turning over the Foreign Ministry to Chen Yi in February

1958, Chou has continued to play a major role both as a formulator and as an executor of foreign policy. If anything, his importance in this respect has grown since Chen Yi came under severe political pressure after the onset of the Cultural Revolution. For Chen Yi and the Foreign Ministry then served as the most obvious lightning rod for Maoist, and in particular Red Guard, dissatisfaction with what was regarded as the tendency of pre-Cultural Revolution foreign policy to be too considerate of the attitudes and interests of foreigners. Although Mao Tse-tung and Chou En-lai consistently refused to dump him, Chen was repeatedly under strong criticism, not only from Red Guards but from more Maoist officials within his ministry, for such things as not being aggressive enough, in word if not necessarily in deed, toward the United States and the Soviet Union and for not being active enough in support of Maoist elements among the overseas Chinese when subjected to pressures from the governments of the host countries. The tendency of the Foreign Ministry to act as a focus for conflicting Maoist and non-Maoist pressures antedates the Cultural Revolution and can be seen, for example, in Chen Yi's remarkable press conference of September 29, 1965, in which he said things that, regardless of the degree of seriousness with which they were expressed, sound most extraordinary in the mouth of a foreign minister, even in China. Other organizations under the State Council with foreign affairs functions include the Ministry of Public Security, which has intelligence and counterintelligence responsibilities; and the New China News Agency, which maintains a substantial network of facilities abroad both for the collection and the dissemination of news, meaning in many cases propaganda. The People's Liberation Army, apart from its obvious role as the source of China's military power, has other functions relating to foreign affairs as well. It maintains liaison with foreign military establishments regarded as friendly, stations military attachés in some foreign capitals, and gives training to selected foreign revolutionaries. China's mass organizations play an important role in its "people's diplomacy." A coordinating function is vested in the Chinese People's Association for Cultural Relations with Foreign Countries. Specific, although less important, tasks are performed by the Friendship Associations that have been established to promote unofficial relations with a variety of foreign countries. Of these only one, Japan, is a country with which China does not maintain diplomatic relations, a fact that testifies to the importance of Sino-Japanese relations in general and of Japanese public opinion in particular in Peking's calculations.

Like anything else with dynamic properties, a Chinese foreign policy program requires and receives review and readjustment from time to time, although many outsiders would say not often or thoroughly enough. There appear to be three principal conditions under which such a process is likely to take place on a substantial scale. One is a major change in the existing power relationship between the Maoist and non-Maoist elements in the Chinese leadership, as when the destruction of "democratic centralism" at the top in March 1967 led not only to an open offensive against Liu Shao-ch'i but to the full-scale unleashing of "Red Guard diplomacy," such as the riotous demonstrations in Rangoon. A second condition is a belief in Peking that existing policy is not faring well and requires modification; an excellent example is the gradual introduction of the "Bandung" line after about 1952. Third, the Chinese leadership may decide, rightly or wrongly, that a major change has occurred in the external environment, independently of Chinese policy, that requires a shift in that policy; a good example is Mao's decision in 1957 that the overall balance of power between "socialism" and "imperialism" had begun to change decisively in favor of the former.

Since the need first arose in 1950 over Korea, the Chinese leadership has developed some rather effective techniques of crisis managment. In the first place, crises are usually discussed and if possible manipulated in such a way as to extract domestic political advantage, usually in the form of popular support, from them. More significant, probably, is a careful calculation, at successive stages, of risks and advantages. With a few exceptions during the Korean War, which served as the first major laboratory for these techniques, Peking tries to avoid genuine and serious risks when it considers its opponent capable of inflicting serious harm on it. Chinese crisis behavior therefore usually contains a prominent element of ambiguity designed to puzzle the opponent, minimize the effectiveness of his responses, and in particular refrain from provoking him to truly dangerous lengths. The pretense that Chinese troops fighting in Korea were volunteers is only one of the most obvious of many such devices to promote ambiguity. On the other hand, Peking often makes threats in crisis situations which, although not necessarily pure bluff, seem to have as their main purpose the smoking out of the adversary's intentions. The Chinese leadership appears to believe that aggressive behavior on its own part is always capable of bringing into being a superior hostile coalition of forces, and it therefore tends to "quit when it is ahead" in particular confrontations, even if the opponent of the moment is incapable of escalating the conflict by himself; a good example is China's calling off of its border war with India in November 1962. Conversely, since the Korean War Peking has generally preferred to cut its losses rather than escalate its involvement in a losing or unviable situation. Its behavior toward the conflict in Vietnam since early 1968 seems to fit this pattern.

Peking and
World Communism

THERE ARE MANY reasons why Peking's relations with other Communist parties and states can logically be considered the most important aspect of the spectrum of problems to which its foreign policy must address itself. Among these are the historic ties with Soviet communism and the fact that it is the communist international system, and no other, that Peking wishes to see expand to worldwide proportions, even if in the process it should ideally become something rather different from—in other words, more Maoist than—what it is now.

Since the Sino-Soviet dispute is obviously the main subject that needs to be considered under this heading, it seems desirable to emphasize at the outset that this is not a total adversary relationship and that there was a time when Sino-Soviet cooperation was substantial and significant. Indeed, it seemed to most observers in the early 1950s that the Sino-Soviet partnership was virtually unshakable. China gladly accepted Soviet seniority and aid, and the Soviet Union treated China as definitely the second state in the Communist bloc, *proximus sed longo intervallo*. But the strains imposed by the Korean War, and still more the changes in Soviet and Chinese attitudes and policies that began after Stalin's death, soon transformed the Sino-Soviet relationship until it was more a dispute than an alliance.

There can be no doubt that the Soviet and Chinese peoples are as xenophobic as most, that each includes the other among the major objects of its dislike, and that this feeling has been getting stronger rather than weaker. On the Soviet side, there is a Yellow Peril mentality that has come to embrace the Chinese since 1949. As early as the early 1950s, on the basis of extensive contacts with Soviet officials imprisoned in Stalin's concentration camps, a German physician, Dr. Wilhelm Starlinger, concluded that a fear of China and an apprehension of possible Chinese demographic pressures on Soviet territory were widespread in the Soviet Union. On the Chinese side, both tsarist and Communist Russia have been seen as an appropriator of Inner Asian territories that once belonged in some vague fashion to China and as a power historically ready to take advantage of any weakness in China to make further depredations. It was essentially to compensate for the embarrassing fact that it was a power with such an unfavorable image upon which the Chinese Communist regime was making itself dependent for support that Peking launched a pro-Soviet propaganda campaign of enormous proportions in 1950. It is very likely that the disengagement from Soviet influence after 1958 and the emergence of the Sino-Soviet dispute into the open shortly afterward were greeted with approval by the Chinese public and tended to increase Peking's popular support.

Possibly more important than popular attitudes is the fact that China, because of its size and peculiar history, is the only Communist state to have, or feel that it has, major unsatisfied claims for status and so on, over and above its urge toward territorial unification. In addition, it is the only Communist state or party outside the Soviet Union to have a leader who, since Stalin's death at any rate, has fancied himself as the leading figure in the international Communist movement. The Soviet party has produced no one who could claim, or who wanted to claim, comparable status, but it has been determined to retain as much as possible of its preeminent influence on the international Communist movement by other, less personal, means. The result has been that the parties to the Sino-Soviet dispute have often seemed to be talking not only in different terms but about different things.

Over and above the profound cultural differences between them, the Soviet Union and China are at different stages of development, the Soviet Union being at least a generation ahead, more of a satiated power, and more defensive and less revolutionary in its nationalism. To a large extent as the result of Mao Tse-tung's preponderant political influence in China, the two political systems have been moving in divergent directions. Even the trend in the Soviet Union, since Khrushchev's fall, away from his erratic liberalizing tendencies toward partial re-Stalinization, in the shape of more stringent police and bureaucratic controls and less freedom of expression, has not tended to bring Moscow into political alignment with Peking. For the trend in China in recent years has been first away from bureaucratic controls and toward "spontaneity," a state of affairs detested by Lenin and his Soviet successors, and more recently toward a high degree of military influence on power and policymaking, another state of affairs uncongenial to the Soviet tradition. An important series of articles in the Soviet theoretical journal *Kommunist* during 1968 denounced Mao Tse-tung's career and political influence as a disastrous deformation of Marxism-Leninism, while maintaining rather vaguely that "healthy forces" still exist in China and may in time bring it back to the Marxist-Leninist path.

On both sides of the Sino-Soviet dispute there is resentment and a measure of fear, on the Soviet side in the latter case more in the long than the short run. In addition, Moscow appears to feel a great sense of puzzlement as to how to handle China. Traditional Russian Asian policy has included a tendency to support China whenever it was threatened by another power that Russia regarded as a threat to itself as well and to encroach on China when Russia perceived no threat to itself in the Far East, but there is no tradition of China itself as the major source of the threat from the East. In strong and striking contrast to the case of Czechoslovakia, the Soviet Union has neither the necessary margin of power to impose its will on China nor a political rationale for doing so comparable to the arrangements of 1943–44 whereby the Soviet Union's wartime allies consigned Czechoslovakia to the Soviet sphere of influence.

THE QUARREL BETWEEN THE CHINESE
AND SOVIET PARTIES

Under Mao Tse-tung's influence, China in effect has sinicized Marxism-Leninism after importing it and has then turned against the country of origin and the form in which the doctrine exists there. This is a process by no means without parallels both in earlier Chinese history and in other countries, but its lack of uniqueness has not made it any less traumatic for Sino-Soviet relations.

Apart from doctrinal incompatibility, there have been serious Sino-Soviet tensions in the party organizational field. Since Stalin's death, each side has tried on occasion to influence not only the policies but the composition of the other's leadership. To date, the Chinese have been somewhat the more successful, or less unsuccessful, at this, because in the aftermath of Stalin's death there were serious differences on power and policy within the Soviet leadership that rendered Chinese support a temporarily useful asset. No split of comparable importance emerged within the Chinese leadership until the Cultural Revolution, and even then the power and speed of Mao's assault on his opponents or chosen targets left no time or opportunity for the Soviet Union to play a significant role in the struggle. Indeed, Mao may have moved as vigorously as he did precisely in order to preclude the possibility of Soviet action in support of the other side.

In retrospect, it appears that Chinese initiatives in 1956 played a large role in the deterioration of Sino-Soviet relations, even though Peking helped to rescue Khrushchev from a difficult position and even though recent Soviet editorials have praised the Chinese party's Eighth Congress, held in September 1956, as an example of "healthy forces" at work. Perturbed by the effects of Khrushchev's attack on Stalin, Peking undertook to pronounce authoritatively on two important subjects that the attack seemed to have thrown into confusion, namely the nature of Marxism-Leninism and the proper relationship between the Soviet Union and the other states of the Communist bloc. It was obviously humiliating, not only for Khrushchev but for the rest of the Soviet leadership, to be put in a position of being second in any significant respect to the Chinese, and the conference of November 1957 in Moscow was presumably called in part to rectify this situation by reasserting Soviet creativity and leadership.

The quarrel between Mao Tse-tung and Khrushchev seems to have begun in 1955, when each began to depart in the eyes of the other from the spirit of the bargain that they had concluded in Peking the previous October. Alone among major Communist leaders, Mao progressively rejected, not only vocally but with considerable political effect, the basic structure of Khrushchev's domestic and foreign policies: a degree of reform and liberalization at home, which in Mao's eyes rendered the Soviet Union less attractive as a Communist model and less dependable as a source of aid to China, and a degree of relaxation in the struggle against American "imperialism." After the crucial year 1959, in which each side made quite clear to the other its objections to its policies, the dispute came into the open. Especially after 1962, Khrushchev began to attempt "collective mobilization" of the international Communist movement with the purpose of disciplining or possibly expelling the Chinese. The latter responded not only with an effort, successful for the time being, to block "collective mobilization" but with a campaign, after 1963, to produce new, pro-Maoist, parties or splinter groups where an existing Communist Party was firmly pro-Soviet.

Probably the most traumatic development to date in the field of Sino-Soviet party relations has been Mao Tse-tung's assault on his own party apparatus during the Cultural Revolution, partly at least as an expression of his distaste for Soviet-style communism. From the Soviet point of view, this development represents a threat to orthodox "democratic centralism" roughly equal in seriousness, although approximately opposite in nature, to the threat posed by the movement toward liberalization in Czechoslovakia during 1968.

To the outsider, and probably to the Chinese leadership as well, it is an impressive fact that the repercussions of the Soviet invasion of Czechoslovakia slowed down but did not stop Moscow's effort to convene (in June 1969, according to the eventual timetable), another international conference of Communist parties like the one of 1960. Although this conference was not to have an overtly anti-Chinese purpose, it was still rigged in a manner calculated to ensure a Chinese boycott and therefore to promote the result that Moscow, with considerable help from Mao's policies, has been trying to achieve for the past few years: the self-isolation of the Chinese party from the international Communist movement as a whole.

THE CONFRONTATION BETWEEN THE CHINESE AND SOVIET STATES

The earliest source of serious friction between the Chinese and Soviet states was probably the increasingly evident reluctance of the Soviet Union, after Stalin's death, to live up to what Peking interpreted as its obligations under at least the spirit of the Sino-Soviet alliance. The Soviet Union not only showed no real enthusiasm for helping Peking to make good its claim to Taiwan but was obviously anxious to avoid the emergence of situations in which it might be called on to give or at least threaten protection for China against American pressures and possible American attack. It was reasonably clear by about 1958, and Peking made it explicit in 1964, that the Chinese view of the nature of Soviet obligations under the alliance and Soviet "leadership" of the Communist bloc and the international Communist movement combined maximum responsibility with minimum authority, a view understandably unacceptable in Moscow.

For a variety of political as well as economic reasons, including its ventures elsewhere in the Third World, the Soviet Union tended after the mid-1950s to reduce its commitments to extend developmental aid to China. The flow of Soviet industrial credits stopped in 1957, and Soviet technical assistance and the provision of industrial equipment came to a halt in 1960. Although this process was quite compatible with the increasing Maoist emphasis on economic "self-reliance," Peking can hardly be blamed for concluding that Moscow had decided to hinder rather than promote the industrial development of China.

Parallel with the general growth of the Sino-Soviet dispute and the emergence of a sense of mutual threat, there developed in the early 1960s a border dispute of a sort, in which Outer Mongolia was involved. Regardless of the logistical and other reasons why a major Sino-Soviet border war would be difficult and disadvantageous for both sides, it is a contingency for which the political and military leaderships in Moscow and Peking must and presumably do plan, with whatever sense of urgency.

As the Soviet and Chinese states have come to sense that they had a competitive and even adversary relationship with each other, each has tended to search for counterweights if not actual allies in the strange contest. Each has been hampered by the fact that the other's size and power, actual or potential, are so great that there is really only one adequate possible counterweight, the United States, a country which tends to have an adversary relationship with both and which presents serious ideological problems for any Communist power in search of support. Short of the United States, the Soviet Union has India and Japan potentially available as counterweights of a sort, and Soviet policy toward India since about 1955 and toward Japan since about 1961 suggests at the least a desire to promote pro-Soviet and anti-Chinese attitudes in these countries. China has a different, and in some ways simpler, problem. Short again of the United States, only West Germany would have much value as a counterweight. In a sense, it already is one, since it has an adversary relationship with the Soviet Union that helps powerfully to distract Moscow from focusing too much attention on China. It could be maintained that Peking really needs to go no farther than it already has in cultivating West Germany and that in the future, in view of the weakening of NATO and the setback to the German *Ostpolitik* from the Soviet invasion of Czechoslovakia, it is Bonn that is likely to cultivate Peking. Nervousness over this possibility has already reached seemingly significant levels in Moscow.

Another source of Soviet nervousness has of course been the Chinese nuclear weapons program. This has several potential drawbacks from the Soviet point of view. It tends to promote the unwelcome cause of nuclear proliferation, virtually the ultimate horror in Moscow's eyes being an acquisition of nuclear weapons by West Germany. It is clearly a source of tension in Asia, an area in which the Soviet Union has no desire to become militarily involved. It obviously poses a direct threat to the Soviet Union. It might even become the occasion of general thermonuclear war, slight though the probability appears. From the Chinese point of view, Moscow's obvious objections to Peking's nuclear weapons program, as expressed for example in the nuclear test ban treaty, represent a Soviet effort to keep China weak and manipulable and to preserve the possibility, if not the fact, of collaboration between the Soviet Union and the United States to control the fate of the world.

In somewhat more realistic terms, the Soviet Union clearly continues to regard Europe—Germany in particular—as the area where its most serious problems lie and the one from which it is least anxious to be distracted by commotion elsewhere. This is perhaps the main single reason why Moscow finds the bumptiousness of the Chinese state so distasteful. Both its present adversary relationship with China and China's perennial state of confrontation with the United States not only pose some direct risks to the Soviet Union but threaten to distract it from its main focus of attention in Europe. So too, would a thorough-going Sino-Soviet reconciliation that would involve the Soviet Union in substantial commitments of aid and support to China, or a rapprochement between China and the United States that Moscow would regard as directed against itself, in effect if not necessarily in purpose—each a rather hypothetical situation. The Chinese leadership, on the other hand, or the Maoists at any rate, feel no such sense of secondary priority in contemplating their Soviet adversary. For them, the Soviet Union is not a weaker opponent to be isolated and if possible ignored, but a stronger opponent to be combatted by all reasonably useful and safe means.

PEKING AND EASTERN EUROPE

During Stalin's reign, China could hardly be said to have had a significant policy toward Eastern Europe, since the region was almost totally dominated from Moscow and China was heavily preoccupied elsewhere, especially in Korea. After Stalin's death and the end of the Korean War in 1953, China began to develop an

East European policy. It rested at first on Peking's desire at that time for a tight Communist bloc under Soviet hegemony, subject to a few qualifications. China apparently wished to see the United States and the Soviet Union embroiled over the Berlin and German questions, so that both would be distracted from the Far East and China would be able to determine the nature of the Sino-Soviet relationship to the greatest possible extent. Peking seems to have visualized Eastern Europe as ideally held under effective Soviet control by a rough balance between fear of West Germany (or a reunited Germany whether Communist or not) and direct Soviet pressures, these being in the last analysis the only two means by which Soviet control of Eastern Europe can be effectively ensured. The weakening of the earlier fear of West Germany in Czechoslovakia by 1968 had much to do with the need, in Moscow's eyes, for the application of crude, direct force. After Stalin's death, the Chinese leadership considered at first that Soviet pressure on Eastern Europe had been maintained at an excessive level and could and should be reduced, at least as long as fear of West Germany remained intact. Bonn's admission to NATO in the spring of 1955 ensured the fulfillment of this condition. China accordingly began to improve its relations with Yugoslavia in late 1954, even before the Soviet Union began to do the same. In mid-1956, although seriously perturbed over the de-Stalinization campaign in the Soviet Union, Peking indicated its cautious approval for a lessening of Soviet influence in Eastern Europe.

The Chinese attitude changed sharply and abruptly when, on November 1, the Nagy regime in Hungary, under strong popular pressure, announced the dissolution of the Communist Party dictatorship and withdrawal from the Warsaw Pact. In combination with the impression of drift in Moscow, this development seemed to threaten the collapse of the Communist bloc and the international Communist movement, both of which Peking cherished for a variety of general ideological reasons and specific selfish ones. According to its own later account published in 1963, the Chinese party actually prodded Khrushchev into using force to crush the Hungarian revolution, and it is certainly true that the Chinese press gave this momentous step full support. Chinese policy now began to uphold the principle of unquestioned Soviet leadership in Eastern Europe, and Peking's insistence on this point grew much stronger after Mao Tse-tung decided, in the autumn of 1957, that Soviet feats in missilery and space technology had created a new, more favorable international climate. If the Soviet Union was to make gains against "imperialism" on the basis of the advantages that Mao attributed to it, on behalf of communism in general and China in particular, other Communist parties and states would have to accept it as their leader to a greater extent than ever before. Mao applied this conclusion even to China, or at least pretended to do so, and he certainly applied it to Eastern Europe. Even before unveiling his new formulation, he had begun to be obsessed with the problem of "modern revisionism," a moderate and allegedly degenerate trend within communism that he claimed to see at work in various places, including Eastern Europe and China itself. Tito, who was pursuing a "revisionist" domestic policy and refusing to accept Soviet leadership over his foreign policy, was the most conspicuous offender. In May 1958, accordingly, the Chinese party press launched a violent propaganda campaign against Tito's "modern revisionism," and Khrushchev, who apparently did not want to arouse Chinese anger any more than he already had through his lack of enthusiasm for Mao's formula that "the East wind has prevailed over the West wind," followed suit with apparent reluctance.

By 1959, however, it was becoming clear that Khrushchev was most unlikely to allow himself to be pressured or cajoled into confronting the United States, over Berlin and Germany for example, in the way that Mao wished. Soviet softness toward the United States in 1959 was probably all the more surprising and regrettable to Mao because opportunities for a contrary policy seemed to have been opened by the death of the formidable John Foster Dulles. In this new situation, Peking ceased to regard close Soviet control over Eastern Europe as necessary or even desirable, and in fact in about 1960 Peking began to bid in various ways for East European support in its own growing dispute with the Soviet Union. There were some reasons for hope on this score, especially in the direction of the more rigid states like East Germany, which had shown some admiration for the Great Leap Forward, even though it was anathema in Moscow. In general, however, Chinese attractiveness and Soviet repulsiveness proved insufficient, and Soviet influence too great, to produce significant results.

There was of course one exception, Albania, but its open quarrel with the Soviet Union beginning in 1960 and 1961 was the result not of Chinese policy but of Albanian hatred of Tito and fear of the results of a possible rapprochement between him and Khrushchev, which in fact occurred after late 1961. Albania urgently needed Chinese economic aid and political support, and in turn it was attractive to Peking for its rigidly Stalinist domestic policy, its value as an irritant to Moscow and a possible stimulus to further defections, its relative security from direct Soviet attack, its naval base at Vlore and its potential value as a Chinese springboard on the Mediterranean, and its possession of valuable supplies of copper and chrome. China and Albania became the only countries in the Communist bloc to give each other undeviating support in their respective quarrels with the Soviet Union.

In the early 1960s Peking gave a much more cautious welcome to Rumania's increasingly nationalist and independent policies. There was no real ideological affinity in this case, but Rumania was useful in Chinese eyes because it objected to Khrushchev's efforts to exploit the Chinese issue, or any other, so as to enhance Soviet influence through a process of "collective mobilization."

The replacement of Khrushchev with a more nearly Stalinist leadership in October 1964 did not help the cause of Chinese influence with the less rigid East European leaderships, which found its ideological posture too repellent; and the potential for Chinese influence in the more rigidly governed states, with the almost complete exception of Albania, tended to be undercut. The seemingly unreasonable Chinese objections to the idea of "united action" on behalf of Hanoi and the Viet Cong probably did Peking more harm in East European eyes than Moscow suffered from its transparent efforts to exploit the slogan for its own advantage. Even the Sino-Albanian partnership showed some signs of strain, or at least fatigue. It was soon revived, however, apparently by the Soviet thrust into the Mediterranean that began about 1966, and alarmed not only Albania but Yugoslavia, Israel, and of course NATO. Whatever the reason, Albania became the only Communist state, and almost the only Communist Party, to give loud approval to Mao Tse-tung's Cultural Revolution. Since, although not very impressive, this support was so close to being unique, it was correspondingly valued in Peking.

After the brutal Soviet self-assertion in Hungary in late 1956, it was nevertheless possible for direct Soviet influence in Eastern Europe to remain at a more moderate level that tolerated some interesting deviations from its own policies both to the right and to the left. This relative, although by no means complete, tolerance was possible at least partly because the West German menace still seemed to possess a significant degree of reality. Down to 1963 the Bonn government was led by the hostile, or seemingly hostile, Adenauer, and not long after his retirement the sensitive issue of the proposed Multilateral Nuclear Force (MLF), under which West Germany would have had access of a sort to nuclear weapons, emerged to keep the menacing image alive. Khrushchev's apparent willingness to seek an accommodation with Bonn was almost certainly one of the erratic initiatives that led to his overthrow.

Late in 1966 the newly installed Grand Coalition of Chancellor Kurt Kiesinger inaugurated its celebrated *Ostpolitik* with the intention of improving its relations with the Soviet Union and the East European countries and contributing in this way to the eventual reunification of Germany, as well as to the realization of certain other objectives. Results were achieved first with Rumania and Yugoslavia, where Soviet influence was relatively slight and fear of West Germany hardly existed. Much more significant was the appearance of signs of similar progress, in the direction of large economic credits and diplomatic relations, with respect to Czechoslovakia, which has a powerful tradition of Germanophobia and is central to the defenses against a possible German resurgence that Moscow has constructed in Central and Eastern Europe since the Second World War. This consideration, plus obvious Soviet objections to the liberalizing domestic course on which Czechoslovakia embarked in January 1968, seems to account for the Soviet invasion of August 20. Growing Soviet pressures during the preceding weeks led some liberal Czechoslovak leaders to consider appealing to China for whatever support it might be able and willing to give. They were compelled at the famous Cierna Conference of early August to renounce any such idea, but it is not clear whether they regarded this as a minor concession that they could easily afford to make in the hope of keeping their relations with the Soviet Union workable or whether the Russians regarded the matter as an important one and took the initiative in demanding such a pledge. In any case, actual Chinese influence on the confrontation was minimal, and judging from its virtually total silence on the subject Peking was apparently having difficulty in deciding whether the unquestionably "revisionist" Czechoslovak leadership deserved support. As soon as the question became largely academic as a result of the Soviet invasion, Peking began to issue loud declarations of support, not for the Dubcek leadership, but for the "Czechoslovak people," who were urged to fight. Peking had applied the sovereign rule that in the last analysis the Soviet Union can do nothing right. In addition, it evidently felt a genuine concern at first over the implications of the invasion for the security of Rumania, Yugoslavia, Albania, and even China. The so-called Brezhnev Doctrine, which was announced shortly after the invasion, claimed on the face of it that other "socialist" states had the right to interfere in the domestic affairs of another one whenever they judged the cause of "socialism" to be in danger there. In retrospect, it appears that in reality the Brezhnev Doctrine was promulgated to compensate for the embarrassing fact that it had proved impossible to put together a collaborationist regime in Prague that would claim to have invited the Russians in, but at first the doctrine seemed to be genuinely sinister.

In addition to denouncing the Soviet action, Peking stopped criticizing Tito and even began to take some small but positive steps to improve its relations with him, inaugurated a substantial but not very effective radio propaganda campaign aimed at Eastern Europe, and accused the Soviet Union of having made repeated overflights over an area in western Manchuria during the period of the invasion of Czechoslovakia. Apart from the obvious purpose of domestic political mobilization, Peking appears to have hoped by publicizing Sino-Soviet tension in this way to exert some genuine diversionary pressure on the Soviet Union without going so far as actually to create a serious risk of war, and to get credit in Eastern Europe for distracting the Soviet Union somewhat while reminding the East European countries implicitly that China could do little for them directly if only because of its problems along the Sino-Soviet border. China's reluctance to overcommit itself in Eastern Europe was displayed fairly clearly at the time of Chief of Staff Huang Yung-sheng's visit to Albania and Rumania at the end of November

1968. While probably promising further economic and military aid to Albania, Huang displayed caution in several respects, notably by refraining from echoing Albanian references to Chinese nuclear weapons as a guarantee of peace in Eastern Europe. Both in Tirana and Bucharest, Huang appears to have indicated that there were serious limitations on the practical lengths to which China could and would go in its support for them.

In February 1969 the Soviet Union joined in creating what looked for a time like a serious crisis over and around West Berlin. The nominal occasion for it was the forthcoming election of the President of the Federal Republic of Germany in West Berlin. A more important actual cause, in all probability, was the inauguration of a new American President, Richard M. Nixon, and his visit to Western Europe. As with President Kennedy in 1961, the idea seems to have been to teach him a lesson and give him at least a hint of the Soviet Union's capacity for causing trouble in Central Europe if provoked. This kind of exercise obviously creates certain risks, and some strange goings on in Moscow during this period suggest that the fact was far from lost on some members of the Soviet leadership. It was probably the latter who seized on a serious Sino-Soviet border clash of March 2 along the Ussuri River, between Manchuria and the Soviet Maritime Province, as a way out. Moscow anticipated Peking by two hours in taking the unprecedented step of giving prompt and loud publicity to a border incident of this kind. It must have been known that the publicity would alarm the Soviet public, as it did, and the purpose probably was partly to provide a distraction and a cover for a de-escalation of the Berlin crisis, which began almost immediately.

Although the two sides gave diametrically opposite accounts of the responsibility for the origin of the incident, and it is impossible to choose between them with any certainty of being right, it seems likely that the initiative rested on the Chinese side and was timed so that Peking could feel reasonably certain that it would not be embarrassed by a genuine and serious crisis over Berlin. Apart from that, Chinese motivations seem to have been very similar to those that have been attributed to Peking in connection with the publicity given to alleged Soviet overflights at the time of the invasion of Czechoslovakia. This time, judging by the nationwide anti-Soviet rallies that were promptly held and the expected imminence of the long-awaited Ninth Party Congress, the Chinese purpose probably had a higher domestic content than before. Another difference is that whereas on the earlier occasion the intended beneficiaries, if any, of Chinese behavior must have been mainly Rumania, Yugoslavia, and Albania, this time they must have included West Germany.

It has already been suggested that there are reasons why it would be difficult and in some respects not very attractive for China to attempt a dramatic improvement of its relations, such as they are, with West Germany. Among the problems is of course East Germany, no matter how objectionably pro-Soviet it may appear in Chinese eyes. To play fast and loose with a divided Germany might encourage others to do the same with a divided China. Or perhaps the cat is out of the bag. Victor Louis, a Soviet journalist, paid an unprecedented visit to Taiwan in October 1968; the Chinese Communist press began to cite this episode as proof that Moscow was promoting "two Chinas." It is conceivable that in retaliation Peking might overcome its reservations about tampering with the status quo in Germany as officially formulated in the Communist bloc—in other words, the existence of "two Germanies"—whether in a given case the Communist state in question maintains diplomatic relations with Bonn or not. For China to follow the lead of the Soviet Union, Rumania, and Yugoslavia in establishing such relations with West Germany might turn out to be the most important initiative that China had yet taken toward Europe, East or West. For that reason, it is a step that would have to be very carefully weighed before being taken.

PEKING AND THE ASIAN PARTIES

This discussion of Chinese policy toward the other Communist parties of Asia can logically begin with the parties in power and with the one that has been in power the longest, that of Outer Mongolia. Both the Soviet Union and China seem determined to keep this large but sparsely populated state within its present borders, or in other words, to frustrate pan-Mongol sentiment by retaining control over the Mongolian populations living in Soviet Asia and China. Of the two Communist great powers between which Outer Mongolia is sandwiched, it is of course the Soviet Union that since the mid-1920s has succeeded in dominating it and treating it as a buffer and in most respects as a satellite. Since 1966 if not earlier, there have been substantial Soviet forces in Outer Mongolia. In addition, the Mongolian leadership has inherited a traditional fear and distrust of China and a tendency to lean on Russia, white or red, for protection.

Since at least as long ago as the early 1950s, Peking has set out to woo or pry Outer Mongolia out of the Soviet embrace as much as possible, by such means as making Inner Mongolia a major center of Mongolian economic development, although of course under Chinese control in an ethnic as well as a political sense. It is not clear whether Peking seriously wants to go farther than to increase its influence in Outer Mongolia at Soviet expense and to incorporate the area into China. Mao Tse-tung said in 1964 that he had raised some such idea with Khrushchev ten years earlier, but that Khrushchev had been predictably uncooperative. There would be serious objections to any such step not only from Moscow but from Ulan Bator, and there is the further complication, which may not mean much to Mao but must to at least some of his colleagues, that since 1949 Peking has recognized Outer Mongolia as an independent "socialist" state. In any event, there was obvious jockeying for position by China and the Soviet Union in Outer Mongolia from the early 1950s, and Ulan Bator tried to enlarge its highly limited freedom of maneuver somewhat by playing them against each other. This game grew virtually impossible after 1960, however, because the eruption of an open Sino-Soviet dispute forced the Mongols to take sides, and they unavoidably chose the Soviet side. As a result of this choice, they are very much on the firing line in the Sino-Soviet border dispute. Because of terrain, Outer Mongolia is probably somewhat more vulnerable to possible Chinese military pressures. It must be realized, however, that any move on either side to translate the roles of these areas as hostages or targets from potentiality into actuality would probably bring on the large-scale Sino-Soviet border war that each seems anxious, and with good reason, to avoid.

North Korea, although it became a Communist state by virtue of Soviet military intervention as did Outer Mongolia, is situated very differently from the latter in several respects. Although it borders on both of the two Communist great powers, it is not sandwiched between them and therefore enjoys somewhat greater freedom of maneuver. On the other hand, it represents only one-half of a divided country whose other half is under American protection. North Korea is in a state of continual confrontation, and has of course fought a war, not only with South Korea but with the United States. It has an able and ruthless leader, Kim Il Sung, who has proved quite capable of taking advantage of external circumstances, playing China and the Soviet Union against each other, and enlarging the autonomy of his regime and his own control over it in the process.

Because of the circumstances of its birth, North Korea began its career as a Soviet satellite; any loss of Soviet influence resulting from the withdrawal of Soviet troops late in 1948 seems to have been at least compensated for by the indispensability of Soviet aid for purposes of economic development and military pressures on South Korea. Soviet influence was reduced during the Korean War, however, by a number of factors, among which Chinese intervention was of course one, and energetic elimination of the pro-Soviet and pro-Chinese factions in his own party by Kim Il Sung another. For reasons that are not entirely clear, China does not seem to have tried seriously to take advantage of the presence of a large Chinese army in Korea during the war to make North Korea a satellite of its own. The reasons may have been a consideration of principle, a reluctance to challenge the Soviet Union in this way, or a desire to avoid alarming and antagonizing Japanese opinion, or some combination of these.

The unilateral withdrawal of the remaining Chinese troops from North Korea in 1958 seems to have been more compensated for in Pyongyang's eyes by the impression made at first by the Great Leap Forward and by Peking's superior anti-American militancy as compared with Moscow's, as expressed for example in the treaties of alliance that they signed with North Korea in mid-1961 following the military seizure of power in South Korea. In proportion as North Korea inclined to the Chinese side of the Sino-Soviet dispute,

Khrushchev reduced his economic and military aid to Pyongyang. His successors promptly reversed this trend and benefited from a corresponding tendency toward a pro-Soviet stand by Kim Il Sung. As the Vietnamese crisis escalated and South Korean troops went to South Vietnam in 1965, North Korea increased its military pressures on the south, short of invasion, as a means of making a contribution to the Communist side in the Vietnamese crisis and improving the prospects for Korean reunification Communist style. At the same time, the influence of the North Korean Army on politics in Pyongyang appeared to increase greately. These trends, as well as the tension created by the *Pueblo* crisis, were unfortunate from the Chinese point of view, since they tended to produce at least indirect risks for China in an area over which it had no effective control. On the other hand, Pyongyang refrained from one unnecessary and offensive challenge to Peking by boycotting Moscow's preparations for a general conference of Communist parties.

The North Vietnamese party was of course not installed in power through Soviet intervention, or for that matter through Chinese intervention. During its rise to power and subsequently, the Chinese attitude has been essentially one of general political support and economic and military aid, with however some important qualifications. The most important of these is probably an obvious desire not to run serious risks to Chinese security, such as seemed for a time to exist in 1954. There has been some Sino-Vietnamese friction over Hanoi's desire to dominate Laos and Cambodia, as well as the whole of Vietnam. For his part, Ho Chi Minh is largely precluded by the realities of geography from trying to become an Asian Tito in his relationship with China. On the other hand, he has attempted successfully to keep Chinese influence within manageable bounds by such means as invoking a Soviet presence in his country and endorsing enthusiastically China's reluctance to send combat troops of its own to "help" Hanoi.

Following an apparent period of Chinese reserve toward the re-newal of Communist insurgency in South Vietnam under Hanoi's sponsorship, the two reached a meeting of the minds in the spring of 1963. Hanoi was annoyed at Khrushchev for his efforts, in line with the Geneva agreements of 1962 on Laos, to curb North

Vietnamese military infiltration and exploitation of the Laotian high-lands. Accordingly, Hanoi began to give noticeable although by no means total support to the Chinese side of the Sino-Soviet dispute, in exchange apparently for Chinese political support for the struggle in South Vietnam and permission for weapons of Chinese origin to be used in that struggle. Khrushchev ignored this development, but his successors promptly tried to reverse it through a policy of more active political support and greater economic and military aid for Hanoi, combined with tactful efforts to persuade it to seek victory through negotiations and political struggle rather than on the battlefield.

This new Soviet policy was just getting under way when the United States escalated the conflict, in February 1965. This development seems to have startled and alarmed the Chinese leadership. Its Vietnamese policy in the new situation was determined largely by the victory of the Maoists in the strategic debate and power struggle of 1965–66. In part, this policy was acceptable to Hanoi: an increase of economic and military aid, the sending of military railway units to help keep the two Sino-Vietnamese rail links in operation, and the avoidance of direct military intervention under the doctrine of "self-reliance." One element of the Maoist policy, the one that increasingly with the escalation of the struggle in Vietnam and the virtual evaporation of revolutionary prospects elsewhere, notably in Africa and Indonesia, insisted that the struggle must be conducted vigorously and in a "protracted" manner as a model and stimulus for "people's wars" elsewhere in the Third World, probably seemed ambivalent in Hanoi's eyes. On the one hand, this Chinese line tended to enhance North Vietnamese prestige abroad; on the other hand, it tended to deprive Hanoi of some flexibility in dealing with the situation in Vietnam itself. In part, the Maoist policy was clearly distasteful to North Vietnam: Peking's apparent objections to the sending of regular North Vietnamese units into South Vietnam from late 1964 on, Chinese rejection of the Soviet principle of "united action," occasional Chinese interference with the flow of Soviet aid and the occasional disruption of Chinese aid shipments by the Cultural Revolution, and vociferous Chinese objections to any sort of negotiations unless and until the United States had been handed a political and military defeat. In addition, Hanoi felt and displayed a notable lack of enthusiasm for the escalating cult of Mao and for the Cultural Revolution.

In keeping with its partial return to a more conventional foreign policy at that time, China stopped its public criticism of North Vietnam over its talks with the United States during the second half of 1968, but without giving the talks its endorsement or even being willing to mention them in its press. Behind the scenes Peking seems to have continued to put pressure on Hanoi not to agree to any settlement short of victory. On the Vietnamese side, the failure of the Tet offensive to achieve the political and military objectives set for it was followed by a rise in the political fortunes of the pro-Chinese (although apparently non-Maoist) Truong Chinh and the adoption of a more Chinese-style "fight-talk" strategy, but without any perceptible increase of willingness to accept Chinese leadership, let alone Chinese control.

Among the nonruling Asian Communist parties, the Indonesian (PKI) was at one time the most important. In view of the close relations between it and President Sukarno, Peking was in the happy position after 1960 of being able to cultivate them both without difficulty. Chinese anti-"imperialism" and lack of Soviet enthusiasm for Indonesia's "confrontation" with Britain and Malaysia brought the PKI clearly onto the Chinese side of the Sino-Soviet dispute in 1963. Peking then began to support the PKI's effort to use the atmosphere created by the "confrontation" to get Sukarno's consent to measures calculated to move Indonesian politics still further to the left and to enhance the influence of the PKI, by creating an armed "Fifth Force" composed of Communist-led unions and mass organizations, for example, presumably in preparation for an eventual trial of strength with the army. By 1965 these efforts had achieved considerable success. In August of that year, however, the PKI leadership panicked when Sukarno fell ill, seriously as it then appeared, and it seemed that the confrontation with the army could not be postponed much longer. With Peking's knowledge and not necessarily enthusiastic agreement, the PKI then prepared a coup against the army leadership. After its disastrous failure, in October 1965, the PKI split into a number of fragments, of which one of the most important was located in Peking and apparently maintained contact with and gave guidance to cadres trying to build up guerrilla bases in Central Java. Although the degree of Chinese involvement in this effort is uncertain, there is no doubt that Peking's hopes for Communist revolution and Chinese influence in Indonesia suffered another heavy blow in the summer of 1968, when the army launched a series of damaging attacks on the incipient guerrilla bases.

After 1965 the most important nonruling Communist Party in Asia was unquestionably the Japanese. For many years this party, or at least its so-called mainstream, was basically pro-Chinese, rather than pro-Soviet, on a common platform of political struggle to disrupt the Japanese government's ties with the United States and Nationalist China and get American bases out of the area. Beginning in 1965, however, the Japanese party became the object of increasing Soviet wooing and grew increasingly alienated from Peking. The Japanese were shocked by the results of what was not entirely accurately taken to be Chinese incitement of the PKI, by Chinese objections to "united action" on Vietnam, and by Mao Tse-tung's insistence that the Japanese Communists should seek power by armed struggle rather than parliamentary methods. An open controversy broke out in 1966 between the Chinese and Japanese Communist leaderships. The latter stopped short, however, of shifting to Moscow's side in the Sino-Soviet dispute. It boycotted the preparations for Moscow's international conference and criticized the Soviet Union severely for the invasion of Czechoslovakia. The Japanese position, then, was essentially one of independence and neutrality. In September 1968, evidently in an effort to recoup some of the lost ground, Peking published a statement by Mao Tse-tung allegedly composed six years earlier and urging the Japanese to be flexible rather than rigid in seeking power; the context suggested that the Chinese were retracting Mao's earlier advice to take up arms.

The Indian Communist Party is a fairly important party and would be more so if it did not share the general Indian tendency toward factionalism, including geographical balkanization. Since India is something of a rival of China's in Asia and the Third World, Peking would apparently like to see it break up into its component cultural units. If it did, the chances of the coming to power on a local scale of the strongest state machines among the Indian Communists, which happen to be also relatively pro-Chinese, would be greatly enhanced. The four states in which the local Communists tend to be both the most effective and the most pro-Chinese are

West Bengal, Punjab, Andhra, and Kerala. On the other hand, the central party machinery, the affiliated trade unions, and some of the state machines have tended to be pro-Soviet. The party as a whole has been greatly embarrassed and weakened by the Sino-Indian border dispute, which has cast China along with Pakistan as India's major enemy. As a result of the Sino-Indian and Sino-Soviet disputes, the Indian Communist Party split in 1964 into two distinct parties, one pro-Soviet and the other pro-Chinese. Due mainly to more effective Soviet policies in the subcontinent and the greater factionalism of the pro-Chinese party, the pro-Soviet party has tended to do somewhat better in most respects. It is true that the more or less pro-Chinese Communists have been in office in Kerala since 1965 and that in the general election of 1967 other sections of the pro-Chinese party did well in some states. The best known, although by no means atypical, of the odd situations into which it then got itself is the one in West Bengal. There young hotheads in the pro-Chinese party had prepared a rural rising in the expectation of a Congress victory in the election. When power passed instead to a multiparty coalition in which the pro-Chinese Communist Party was included, its senior leaders tried to get the rising called off, but without success, and they found themselves in the anomalous position of helping to suppress a peasant revolt led by some of their own colleagues and supported loudly from Peking. It is conceivable that the pro-Chinese party will split formally into two new parties, one loyal to the more radical and the other to the more moderate version of Maoist policy and strategy.

There are several countries in Asia (South Korea, Taiwan, Pakistan, Afghanistan, and the small Himalayan states) where there appears to be no Communist Party or movement worth mentioning. In one country, Ceylon, it is hopelessly split. In another, Laos, it exists and is effective but is largely under North Vietnamese influence. There are two cases, Cambodia and Nepal, where Communist parties exist and are oriented toward Peking but, with some qualifications, either are basically not in a state of revolt (Nepal) or enjoy little consistent support from China (Cambodia), clearly because Peking fundamentally prefers to cultivate, at least for the time being, the existing rulers.

There are several Asian Communist parties or movements that are pro-Chinese, supported from Peking, and basically in a state of revolt. One is the Burmese, which has always been poorly led, was scarcely supported from China until 1964, and was therefore not very effective; in 1967 it launched into a Cultural Revolution of its own that resulted in the violent deaths of several of its leaders, including its principal figure Than Tun. The Communist Party of Thailand is small and largely confined to outlying areas of hills and jungle; it is under some North Vietnamese as well as Chinese influence, and efforts by Peking to form a Thai Patriotic Front as the counterpart of the National Liberation Front of South Vietnam have not been notably successful. A small but militant Malaysian Communist Party, consisting largely of several hundred guerrillas based in the border region between Malaya and Thailand and of some similar units in Sarawak, exists and is under strong Chinese influence, if only because it is overwhelmingly Chinese by race. In Singapore, guidance of the local Communists seems to be shared by China and the PKI, but for several years it has been impossible to disrupt effectively the programs of the vigorous government of Prime Minister Lee Kuan Yew. After being nearly suppressed in the early 1950s, the Communist movement in the Philippines, usually known as the Huks, has again become a problem in recent years, mainly because of the ineffectiveness and corruption of the Philippine political system, but the current version of the Huks does not appear to be well organized or even to be a true Communist movement or front.

In general, since about 1965 there has tended to be an inverse relationship between the strength and effectiveness of a given Asian Communist Party or movement and the degree of Chinese influence on it. The stronger and more effective ones have not really adhered to Moscow, however; in essence, they have successfully asserted a growing independence.

PEKING, THE OTHER PARTIES, AND THE WORLD MOVEMENT

Elsewhere in the Third World, most parties are too weak or too immature, or both, to be able to assert much independence. Generally speaking, they tend to side with the Soviets against the

Chinese, formally if not always emotionally, because they see no practical alternative. The weak orthodox Communist parties of Latin America have always been dominated by Moscow. Castro's regime, which represents a much more authentically Latin American development, dislikes what it regards as Soviet reluctance to support Cuban-style revolutions elsewhere in the region, but this feeling has nearly always been outweighed by massive Soviet economic and military aid to Cuba itself and by Castro's distrust of the Chinese as potential rivals. In 1965 he took offense at Chinese efforts to propagandize their case against Moscow in Cuba, in the army among other places. In retaliation, Peking cut down its imports of sugar from Cuba and its exports of rice to Cuba, and an open quarrel erupted at the beginning of 1966. The Arab parties resemble the Latin American, minus Castro, whose analogue would be Nasser; they are weak, ineffectual, and Soviet-dominated. In Africa south of the Sahara there are few formal Communist parties, and Chinese influence in this region must be considered more as a factor in the revolutionization of Africa than as one in the conduct of the Sino-Soviet dispute.

Although badly shaken by the invasion of Czechoslovakia, the Western Communist parties, which with a few exceptions like the parties of France and Italy are weak, in nearly all cases prefer the Soviet to the Chinese side of the Sino-Soviet dispute. Of the limited number of pro-Chinese splinter parties that have emerged since about 1963 but are not recognized as part of the world movement by the orthodox parties, only one has much importance. This is the one in Belgium, which draws on a strong radical tradition among the workers and intellectuals and has had the leadership of a strong figure, Jacques Grippa. His movement suffered, however, when he fell out with the Maoist mainstream in China during the Cultural Revolution because he was considered sympathetic to Liu Shao-ch'i, or at any rate, to the views and interests represented by Liu.

Apart from orthodox Communist parties and more or less organized splinter groups, there are of course loosely structured radical elements in the Western countries, especially among students, who feel some admiration for the "thought of Mao Tse-tung," or for what they take it, often erroneously, to be. These groups play no role in the Sino-Soviet dispute within the international Communist movement, and apart from presenting Peking with occasional propaganda triumphs they have little utility to Chinese interests unless one assumes that they represent some sort of wave of the future in their respective countries.

At the end of 1964 the Soviet leadership revived the idea of holding another international conference of Communist parties like the one of 1960. The main purpose seems to have been to hold the world movement together and increase Soviet influence over it, for the movement had been shaken by Khrushchev's erratic policies and by the unceremonious manner of his overthrow. It was hoped to make the idea acceptable to the Chinese, to whom it had become anathema, by emptying it of any overtly anti-Chinese purpose. But the knowledge that the conference was intended to enhance Soviet prestige and influence was still sufficient to render the project unacceptable not only to the Chinese and most of the other Asian parties but to some non-Asian parties as well, notably the Rumanian. It was clear that the conference would be used as a forum for generating and expressing support, among other things, for Soviet policy toward Vietnam and the Middle East.

This opposition notwithstanding, Moscow succeeded during the four-year period from March 1965 to March 1969 in convening a series of preparatory meetings that were reasonably well attended. At one held in April 1968, it was decided to convene the plenary conference in Moscow on November 25 of the same year. The shock of the invasion of Czechoslovakia of course made it impossible to adhere to this schedule, and for a time it appeared that it might be impossible to hold the conference at all. But Soviet influence and diplomacy prevailed, and a preparatory meeting in mid-November fixed the new date for the conference at May 1969.

The Soviet method for handling China's objections to the conference and its intention to stage a boycott had been to allow the Chinese in effect to isolate themselves, while striking some telling blows against them in a series of major theoretical articles. In these Mao Tse-tung was accused, with a good deal of justification, of never having understood Marxism-Leninism and of having departed outrageously from it in theory and practice. He had, said the Russians, embarked on a "personality cult" and military dictatorship at home—after having discarded "democratic centralism" and destroying the Communist Party apparatus—and on a policy of expansionism abroad. In spite of, or perhaps because of, the element of polemical exaggeration in these articles, they not only constitute an impressive indictment of their target but help somewhat to distract the attention of the reader from the imposing series of blunders and excesses that the current Soviet leadership itself has committed at home and abroad.

CHAPTER IX

Peking and Asia

It is obvious that any government of a united China would be almost bound to play a major role in Asia. This is true by virtue of China's size and other geopolitical characteristics, the splendor of its tradition, and the widespread sympathy in Asia regardless of ideology for China's sufferings in modern times and the dramatic nature of the revolution that it has undergone. But it does not necessarily follow that a given Chinese government will come close to taking full advantage of its opportunities for playing a major role, constructive or destructive, in Asia. Communist China's performance in this respect is the subject of this chapter.

CHINA AS AN ASIAN POWER

It has already been suggested, although it would be impossible to prove conclusively, that Peking's intermediate objective with respect to Asia is to exclude or minimize the influence of extraregional powers, curb or at least manage the regional states, and promote some form of neutrality on their part as the minimum acceptable concession to Chinese wishes. Beyond that, the ultimate objective, at least as envisaged by the Maoists in the Chinese leadership, seems to be to create or promote a Chinese sphere of influence in Asia consisting of Communist states whose ruling parties had come to power more or less in the Chinese manner and with a degree of Chinese support, but without direct Chinese intervention and therefore without the need to be subject to direct Chinese control. The "thought of Mao Tse-tung" would presumably be the major tie that bound them. These objectives, and the strategies envisaged to pursue them, could of course change, presumably after Mao's death more than before, in the direction of either greater moderation or greater assertiveness.

The Chinese Communist leadership has never been willing to confine its active external role to Asia, or even to the Third World, but has insisted on acting as a world power in at least the political sense. It seems to believe that its Asian and extra-Asian policies reinforce each other. If so, the proposition is at best a debatable one, for Peking's extensive activities outside Asia have required a very significant diversion of attention and various kinds of resources to other areas. It is probably no coincidence that China's influence in Asia, relative to the opportunities offered by the conditions of the time, was almost certainly at its highest during the heyday of the Bandung era (1954–56), when Peking had stopped being overtly involved in wars and subversion in Asia and had not yet been led by external circumstances and its own inclinations to begin escalating its activities outside Asia. Peking's propaganda about Asian solidarity and its own status as a leading champion of that concept was at its most persuasive and effective during that period.

Immediately afterward, a series of events, notably it would seem the crisis in the Communist world beginning with the Twentieth Soviet Party Congress, Mao's failure to generate external revolutionary momentum for his regime by his ploy of 1958 in the Taiwan Strait, and the surfacing of the Sino-Indian ideological and border dispute in 1959, led to increasingly strenuous efforts on Peking's part to promote its interests by activity outside Asia as well as within it. China's tendency to pursue its vendettas with the United States, the Soviet Union, and India by often assertive and abrasive means, including loud demands for support and pressures of various kinds, had the effect of alienating governments and sectors of public opinion that previously had been relatively sympathetic.

Until the shifts of 1969 in Chinese and American policy, Asian states, almost regardless of their ideological orientation, found ways of going about their external business while ignoring or bypassing China to the extent necessary. This tendency was often found in combination with a natural hope that some day China will want to join existing international undertakings in Asia without trying to subvert or dominate them, and with a belief that the United States might contribute to hastening that day by relaxing its pressures on China. In reality, it seems improbable that as long as Mao and his "thought" retain a genuine, and not merely nominal, ascendancy in China Peking will want to live up to these hopeful expectations. And there is of course no way of knowing how long the era of Mao Tse-tung will last.

THE EASTERN FLANK

As it looks to the east, Peking sees a chain of territories (South Korea, Taiwan, and the Philippines, and beyond them Japan) and an ocean (the Western Pacific) where American air and sea power reigns almost supreme, or is capable of doing so when it chooses. Politically, too, anticommunism and an American orientation are the dominant feature, in a formal sense at least: the United States has bilateral alliances with Japan, South Korea, Nationalist China, and the Philippines. From the military point of view, which is the one of most urgent and immediate concern to Peking, the American military position in the Western Pacific, on which the "containment" strategy rests to a high degree, centers on the massive base complex on Okinawa. It is obviously in the Chinese interest to cultivate anti-American political tendencies in these countries, Japan in particular. It is also obvious, however, that the political climate in the two nearest of these areas, South Korea and Taiwan, is such that Peking has almost no means of direct access or influence and must rely mainly on external forces, such as possible American blunders and the simple passage of time, to bring about the desired withdrawal of the United States. In the case of the Philippines, China has no diplomatic relations but is trying to exploit through propaganda the significant reservoir of anti-American feeling among intellectuals and some sections of the political community.

The country of China's eastern-flank region where the stakes and opportunities for Peking are the highest is obviously Japan. The Chinese leadership appears to feel a mixture of resentment and respect for Japan as a country whose armies withdrew unbeaten (by the Chinese) from China in 1945 and has staged a phenomenal political and economic recovery from the depths of that period. Japan is highly useful to China as its leading trading partner, a status it has attained since the mid-1960s. It would probably be welcome to Peking as a junior political partner if it came under a government sufficiently anti-American and far to the left, although not necessarily outright Communist. Peking regards Japan as a potential threat under present conditions, however.

The Chinese image in Japan is basically a favorable one, far more so than the Soviet, as long as Peking does not create problems for itself by obtrusive behavior. The collective Japanese attitude toward China, which of course varies a good deal among different individuals and groups, is a complex compound of cultural empathy, shame for past Japanese aggression, respect for revolutionary modernization, desire for still more trade, and a certain nervousness over current Chinese unpredictability and over a future in which China will presumably be a major nuclear power. In Japan, more than nearly any other country, China serves as a utopia that alienated students and intellectuals are fond of comparing favorably with the order presided over by their own Establishment.

China has the disadvantage, in its dealings with Japan, of having no diplomatic relations. Japan maintains diplomatic relations with Nationalist China and trades with both Chinas. Since it would lose not only its diplomatic relations but also its sizable trade with Taiwan if it should recognize Peking, the Japanese government hesitates to take this step, which the United States would of course oppose. Peking has tried from time to time, with some success, to bypass this dilemma and obtain a kind of creeping recognition by a variety of informal or semiformal dealings with important Japanese individuals and groups, including members of the governing Liberal Democratic Party. These dealings have involved a variety of propaganda gestures and commercial agreements, usually with the explicit or implicit suggestion that a more leftist government in Tokyo would find Peking easier to deal with. At times, notably in 1958, when it repudiated all existing Sino-Japanese trade agreements in an unsuccessful effort to discredit and weaken the pro-American government of Premier Kishi, China has resorted to rather crude pressures on Japan. In general, however, it has had the sense to cultivate existing issues rather than create new ones. Probably the outstanding example to date is the crisis attending the renegotiation of the Japanese-American security treaty in 1960, which coming as it did shortly after the fall of the strongly anti-Communist Rhee government in South Korea seems to have convinced Peking for a time that things were moving its way in Northeast Asia. But although Kishi resigned after a major series of demonstrations, the latter were not staged essentially against the United States or even against the treaty as such, and certainly not in favor of China, but rather against the Japanese Establishment as a whole. The demonstrations subsided and the treaty was ratified.

There followed a period of several years during which China's image and influence in Japan suffered rather severely, mainly because of Peking's own behavior. Japanese opinion, with the main exception of the extreme leftist student organization Zengakuren, was affected adversely by such developments as the realization that China was beginning to produce nuclear weapons, Chinese opposition to the nuclear test ban treaty, Peking's rather strange performance with respect to Vietnam, the actual or supposed role of China in egging the PKI on to its virtual destruction, and the convulsions of the Cultural Revolution and the attendant difficulties for Sino-Japanese trade. In the Japanese mind, however, the crude Chinese performance was probably outweighed by objections to the American role in Vietnam and (on the left) to the way in which the Japanese Establishment was enriching itself from the Vietnamese war, and by growing discontent with the presence of American bases and forces and American administrative control over Okinawa. The year 1970, the first in which it would be possible for either party to denounce the Japanese-American security treaty ratified in 1960, appeared to offer interesting possibilities for a weakening of ties between the two parties and conceivably, therefore, for opportunities for Chinese foreign policy.

But to some extent this discussion, like much public discussion of these issues, misses the main point. If the United States should lose its base in Okinawa and Japan proper, it does not follow that Japan will feel compelled to come to some arrangement with China. Nor does it follow that the United States will no longer be able to exercise military containment of China. There will be an added role for other existing American bases, such as those in Guam and the Philippines, and there may be an interest in acquiring new bases, for example in Taiwan or the South Korean island of Cheju Do. But basically, the advance of military technology is likely to render local bases less important to the United States. It will be increasingly possible, from a strictly military point of view, to exercise military containment of China, to whatever extent it may prove necessary, by means of ICBMs emplaced in the continental United States and Polaris submarines. The ability to commit American conventional forces to local conflicts in Asia can probably be maintained to the extent necessary by means of developments in air transport now in prospect.

Still more to the point, the most important trend now at work in the region described here as that of China's eastern flank is without much doubt the rise of Japan. Its economy is now third in size in the world and may come virtually to dominate the international economics of Asia within the next few decades. Japan's passivity in international politics since 1945 is not likely to last much longer. But as Japan tries to play a more active international role, it is likely to find that mere economic strength, however great, does not confer the influence it desires. In other words, there are likely to be pressures toward a degree of rearmament, especially if the tie with the United States has been weakened and if China appears to be a threat. It is even conceivable, although it is not the policy of the present government, that Japan might decide to acquire nuclear weapons. The effect of all this on Asian international politics, including Chinese foreign policy, is of course hard to predict, but it is likely to be considerable.

THE SOFT UNDERBELLY

The vast region to the south of China differs significantly from its eastern flank. If China's own southern border regions are poorly developed and rather unstable, the countries beyond the border tend to be still more unstable. With the obviously important exception of the eastern corner, in Vietnam and Thailand, there are as yet no major American bases or forces in the region. There is likely to be an increase of American military activity in the Indian Ocean, however, by way of compensation for the British withdrawal. The long-term reduction of British commitments "east of Suez" that has been going on since World War II has been accelerated by a recent decision to complete the process by 1971, except for Hong Kong. The last major obstacle, the need for British military support for Malaysia in connection with its "confrontation" with Indonesia, disappeared with the Indonesian revolution of 1965 and the end of the "confrontation" the following year.

The American-sponsored Southeast Asia Collective Defense Organization (SEATO), although the target of violent Communist propaganda and not much more popular with the neutral states, has never amounted to much more than an American commitment to the defense of Thailand. Of the seven members other than the United States, Australia and New Zealand are increasing their interest and involvement in Southeast Asia, but not because of their commitment to SEATO. Britain and France have never been very enthusiastic about SEATO and are for all practical purposes inactive in it. All three of the Asian members have serious reservations about it. Pakistan joined it in the hope of obtaining a guarantee against possible Indian aggression, which in fact SEATO does not provide, and Pakistan is therefore essentially uninterested and inactive in its affairs. The Philippines is trying to play the role of an Asian power, and one of the requirements of such a status, especially for a country that has been an American dependency and has acquired the reputation since independence of being an American satellite, is to prove itself by periodic anti-American behavior; the Philippines' role in SEATO is therefore at best a marginal one. Thailand seems to be reappraising its commitment to SEATO and the probable value of American guarantees to itself in the expectation that the United States will withdraw from Vietnam sooner or later and will be reluctant to intervene militarily in Southeast Asia again. In short, SEATO is not a very serious threat or obstacle to Chinese policies.

Of greater probable concern to Peking at present is the growing role of the Soviet Union in the region. Since the mid-1950s, when it evidently became concerned over the Chinese role in the region and anxious to play a role of its own, Moscow has been heavily involved in aid to India. After 1960 it launched a similar program, but with much greater emphasis on military aid, in Indonesia. Immediately after Khrushchev's fall his successors increased their military aid to North Vietnam and acquired a significant, although far from decisive, influence on its behavior in this way. Soviet support for the neutral and leftist forces in Laos after 1960 and Soviet diplomacy played a crucial role in the settlement worked out for that country. Recently, perhaps to compete with Chinese influence and prepare for new developments following a possible settlement on Vietnam, Moscow has appointed one of its most experienced diplomats, S. M. Kudryavtsev, as ambassador to Cambodia. The Soviet Union has begun to extend economic and even military aid to Pakistan, much to India's distress. Soviet trade and naval activity throughout the Indian Ocean and Southeast Asia are increasing. Whatever the exact significance of the growing Soviet involvement in the affairs of southern Asia may turn out to be, it is obviously a development unfavorable to China's aspirations for primary influence in the region.

On ideological grounds, Peking undoubtedly believes that in the long run "reactionary" governments, in southern Asia and elsewhere, are digging their own graves. Regardless of the validity of this proposition, it is true, on the other hand, that in this region as well as others military regimes have stepped in to compensate for, or take advantage of, the weakness of civil government and at least in the short run have created a relative political stability that is unfavorable to Communist interests. This is not to say, of course, that military regimes are a satisfactory substitute in the long run for the development of stable civil polities. In southern Asia, military regimes have appeared (in chronological order) in Thailand, Pakistan, Burma, South Vietnam, and Indonesia. In the last two of these, the military power seizure occurred in direct response to a serious Communist threat or challenge, and it is entirely possible that similar military power seizures would occur if similar threats materialized in other countries.

Probably the most important determinant of future Communist and/or Chinese influence in southern Asia will be the political stability or instability of the states and governments of the region, of which it must be remembered that only one, that of North Vietnam, is Communist at present. Because of the great political differences among the states of southern Asia, it is difficult to generalize about them with any validity. Laos is probably the most obviously unstable and vulnerable state in the region and would be in serious difficulties if North Vietnam or China, or both, should shift primary attention from South Vietnam to it. If Laos should come under Communist control, its geographical position would make it a serious threat to Cambodia, South Vietnam (if it were still not Communist at that point), and Burma. In general, however, the level of political stability seems to be improving, slowly and unevenly. A sense of national identity appears to be emerging gradually that regards the possibility of a Communist seizure of power as an unwelcome threat, partly because it might lead to Chinese domination. In most countries of the region the threat is a remote one at present, because the local Communist Party is fairly weak. The main asset these parties have is probably the formidably effective Leninist model of organization, reinforced by proven methods of political struggle including propaganda. If anything, the surprising factor is that the local Communist parties in southern Asia, with a few exceptions, notably in South Vietnam and Laos, have generally not succeeded in achieving and expanding, or at least retaining, a high level of political influence. China's main asset in southern Asia is probably whatever image it possesses as the wave of the future. In retrospect, it may appear that the turning point for both China and the local Communist parties were the events of 1965: the American intervention to save South Vietnam, China's failure to get its Afro-Asian Conference and to help Pakistan with its struggle for Kashmir, and the disaster that the PKI brought down on itself.

In dealing with the countries of Indochina, China must take and usually has taken account of the policies of the United States, the Soviet Union, North Vietnam, and Thailand, none of which coincide with its own, at the minimum. There is a long-standing Sino-Vietnamese rivalry for preeminent influence over Laos and Cambodia. In the latter case, Peking has shielded the government of

Prince Sihanouk to a degree from Hanoi's pressures since at least as long ago as 1956, as well as against those of Thailand, South Vietnam, and to a degree the United States, even while occasionally applying pressures of its own calculated among other things to prevent Sihanouk from taking Chinese support for granted. In the case of Laos, China's influence has been limited in spite of its proximity by a number of constraints, such as the Laotian government's tendency to lean on the United States or the Soviet Union for support and the fact that the Laotian Communist movement is largely controlled, and was in fact virtually created, by its Vietnamese counterpart. Apart from its embassy in Vientiane, China confines its overt presence in Laos largely to the adjacent provinces, where it has built some roads connecting with its own road net. Both Peking and Hanoi are fully aware that a major incursion by either into the lowlands along the Mekong River, as distinct from the remote highlands along the Vietnamese and Chinese borders, would alarm Thailand and the United States and create a serious risk of war. A unilateral Chinese move of this kind would probably, among other things, drive the Thai farther into the arms of the United States—at a time when the possibility of a settlement on Vietnam seems to open opportunities for a loosening of the relationship between the two—and North Vietnam farther into the arms of the Soviet Union. Apart from these external restraints, however, Laos remains of course weak, vulnerable, and to that extent inviting.

Probably the most important single feature of Sino-Thai relations is the abiding Thai fear of China, which includes an apprehension that an increase of Chinese influence in Southeast Asia might lead to serious trouble among Thailand's large Chinese minority, which for the time being is in a state of comparative calm. Mainly out of fear of Chinese aggression and subversion, Thailand joined SEATO in 1954, but because of the shift in Chinese foreign policy at that time was rewarded with more blandishments than denunciations. China tried to woo Thailand away from SEATO and toward a neutral posture and achieved some success not only with Thai intellectuals but with the Thai government itself. But this trend stopped abruptly when the firmly anti-Communist Marshal Sarit seized power in late 1958. Chinese efforts to sponsor a "people's war" in the remote and impoverished area of northeast Thailand became noticeable in the early 1960s, at about the same time that Hanoi began to escalate its involvement in the insurgency in South Vietnam to serious proportions. Peking probably hoped to ensure among other things that the expected increase of Communist influence in Indochina did not lead to exclusive leadership for Hanoi over whatever potential for revolution existed in Thailand. In 1964–65, as the major escalation of the Vietnamese war got under way, Peking began to try, with little success, to put together under its own control a Thai equivalent of the National Liberation Front for South Vietnam. Growing Chinese involvement in insurgency in northeastern, northern, and southern Thailand, in the first two of which Hanoi was also involved, was designed in part to deter or punish Thai involvement in the Vietnamese conflict. In this respect it failed, for the Thai government not only took an active role in Vietnam but went so far in 1967 as to allow the United States to station B-52s in Thailand. Although these giant aircraft were intended for use in Vietnam, they obviously posed a serious threat to China, and in particular to its western regions, which would be harder to attack with bombers flying out of the Western Pacific. Peking has evidently considered these risks acceptable and has continued to foster insurgency in Thailand, but it has remained confined to outlying areas and minority groups and has had little impact so far on the mainstream of Thai political life. On the other hand, the insurgency might conceivably give Peking something to bargain with if a settlement in Vietnam should lead the Thai government to re-evaluate its international orientation.

Peking regards Malaysia's abundant resources, notably tin and rubber, as interesting and trades with it to a limited extent. On the other hand, it regards the government of Malaysia as a creation of British colonialism and supported in a number of ways, including insurgent activities on the part of leftist Chinese in Sarawak, Indonesia's efforts to "crush" it between 1963 and 1965. This campaign, which may have included a secret agreement to partition the remains of Malaysia between Peking and Djakarta, collapsed with the failure of the PKI's coup in 1965 and the decision of the new Indonesian government to terminate the "confrontation" in the following year. Peking keeps in being, and uses to a limited extent, a guerrilla force in Sarawak and another near the Thai-Malaysian border, but its capabilities for influencing the general course of political events in Malaysia are limited. The government is essentially under Malay control. That government maintains diplomatic relations with neither China and has so far been able to cope with what unrest exists among the Chinese population, which although roughly equal in numbers to the Malay and substantially wealthier per capita has little political power. It is doubtful whether Chinese communism presents more of a threat to the political stability of the present order in Malaysia than does the influence of the small but dynamic state of Singapore.

During the brief period (1963–65) when Singapore belonged to Malaysia, its dynamic Prime Minister Lee Kuan Yew made an energetic effort to build political support for himself in the rest of Malaysia as well. Had he been allowed to do so, he might have led a successful effort to make the Chinese rather than the Malay community the leading one. It was mainly on account of this effort that Singapore was expelled from Malaysia in 1965 and resumed an independent, if economically rather precarious, existence. Lee's forceful leadership and progressive policies had already reduced Communist political activity, which has been under both Chinese and Indonesian influence, to almost negligible proportions, whereas in the 1950s it had been a serious problem. An economic collapse of the island, which is heavily dependent on foreign trade, might revive Communist influence, but it appears that Peking will not be in a position for some years to take advantage of such a revival if it should occur.

In Indonesia, China confronts a country so large and remote as to be almost invulnerable to direct Chinese pressures. The Indonesians have ambitions for regional leadership in at least the insular portions of Southeast Asia and are not much afraid of China, partly because they know that they hold in their hands as hostages some 3 or 4 million persons of Chinese extraction. In spite of some problems presented by the citizenship of many of these overseas Chinese, Sino-Indonesian relations began to warm up after 1956 as President Sukarno conceived a warm admiration for Chinese domestic and foreign policies. After he intervened in 1960 to bring about a settlement of the citizenship dispute, Sino-Indonesian relations began to grow much closer. Peking saw in Indonesia a valuable partner in Asia and the Third World against the despised Indians in particular, as well as an arena within which to combat the influence of the Soviet Union and promote the political growth of the PKI to the extent that its overriding interest in preserving its friendship with Sukarno permitted. Still more obvious, Peking and Djakarta felt a common interest in expelling Western (Dutch, British, and American) influence from Southeast Asia. In the process of cooperating with Sukarno and the PKI, Peking became dependent for its influence in Indonesia on their political fortunes and therefore suffered heavily in the common disaster inflicted by the army and other anti-Communist Indonesians in late 1965. For Peking to regain a significant degree of influence in Indonesia, one would have to assume a shift to the left on the part of Djakarta or a shift to the right on the part of Peking beyond anything now in prospect, or else an improbable outbreak of large-scale "people's war."

In spite of its seemingly strategic location and sizable rice surpluses, Burma does not appear to present many strategic attractions to China and, apart from the controversial but not really very significant presence of occasional bands of "KMT irregulars" (former Chinese Nationalist soldiers) near the Sino-Burmese border, presents no threat to it. Ever since attaining independence in 1948, Burma has been troubled, although mainly in its outlying regions, by revolts on the part of a number of ethnic minorities and Communist groups. Probably because of the lack of unity among the insurgent elements and Peking's greater concern with other areas, it has by and large not given much support to these revolts. It did become somewhat concerned when the military government of General Ne Win, who had overthrown the ineffectual Prime Minister U Nu the year before, launched an intensified military campaign in late 1963 against the most serious dissident minority groups and against the mainstream of the Burmese Communist movement, which was under strong Chinese influence. Peking was even more concerned when Ne Win began about 1966 to show signs, mainly for economic reasons, of abandoning the self-defeating policy of virtual economic isolation that he had adopted to please China among other reasons. Accordingly, the volume of Chinese political support for and military aid to Burmese insurgent movements has tended to increase somewhat. Northern Burma apparently serves as a route for small numbers of dissident Nagas who pass between their homes in northeastern India and Southwest China in search of arms and training, which they have been receiving. In 1967 and 1968, presumably under the impression that it was doing what Peking wanted, the Burmese Communist Party launched its own version of the Cultural Revolution, in the course of which a large portion of the leadership killed itself off. In late June 1967, when the phase of Red Guard diplomacy was at its height, the long-suppressed objections of the Maoists to Ne Win, who seems to have been on good terms with Liu Shao-ch'i, erupted in a series of Chinese student demonstrations in Rangoon that brought violent Burmese official and popular reprisals and touched off a furious Chinese propaganda campaign against Ne Win. Although this cooled off somewhat in late 1967 as Red Guard diplomacy faded away, Peking appears to possess little capacity at present for building a significant political influence in Burma.

During Nehru's lifetime at any rate, India was China's most serious rival for influence among the states of Asia. Even if this had not been the case, an eruption of hostility between them sooner or later was guaranteed by the Maoist view of India. Judging by all the available evidence, this was and probably still is to the effect that India is a creation of British colonialism, the prime example of an Afro-Asian country that gained its independence by methods other than the approved one of revolutionary warfare, an opportunistic seeker after American and Soviet aid and support, and an unviable state torn by powerful centrifugal forces. Although China found it useful to cultivate Nehru briefly in the early and mid-1950s as a form of anti-American insurance and a way of enhancing Chinese influence in the Third World, the basic hostility remained throughout, at least on the part of the more Maoist-minded members of the Chinese leadership. This attitude seems to include a hope, perhaps an expectation, that India will break up sooner or later into separate linguistic units, in which case the political prospects of the militant pro-Chinese Communist machines in some areas would presumably be greatly improved. Peking has greatly resented the closeness in Indo-Soviet relations since the mid-1950s, Moscow's apparent tendency to build India up as a counterweight against China, India's manipulation of Soviet and American interest in its survival, and India's interest in minimizing direct Chinese influence not only in the Himalayan states but in Tibet. In part at least, Peking surfaced its border dispute with India in the mid-1950s as a means of deterring or punishing an assertion of Indian interest in the fate of Tibet. When, following an outburst of fighting on the border and in the hope of preventing Soviet diplomatic gains in India at Chinese expense, Peking offered New Delhi what it regarded as a reasonable compromise settlement of the border dispute only to be rejected, Chinese hostility toward India could no longer be suppressed. The Indian Army was attacked in late 1962 not only to keep it away from the approaches to Tibet but also to humiliate India in the eyes of the world, Afro-Asia in particular. The political costs and military risks of this drastic step were such, however, that China shifted to less direct methods. Chief among these was a close relationship with Pakistan; among the others were increased activity in the Himalayan states and occasional support for insurrection or subversion in such areas as Nagaland and West Bengal. China continues to hope for a disruption of Indian political unity, but in spite of India's serious political problems, including the substantial influence of the supposedly pro-Chinese Communist elements in West Bengal, this hope appears doomed to disappointment at least for a good many years to come. Among the factors limiting China's ability and willingness to exert direct pressures on India is a realization that New Delhi might feel compelled to abandon neutrality or seek nuclear weapons, or both, with potentially very serious results for both China and Pakistan.

The keystone of the Sino-Pakistani relationship is obviously an intense common hostility to India. For about a decade, the benefits of the relationship were relatively slight and largely negative; Pakistan, for example, experienced no political difficulties with China as a result of joining SEATO. In 1959, when tension along the Sino-Indian border became serious, Pakistan secretly approached China with a view to reaching an agreement on the border between Sinkiang and the Pakistani-held portion of Kashmir. In spite of the absence of a significant response at that time, Pakistan's interest was whetted by disenchantment with the United States after 1961 because of the Kennedy administration's preference for India and was symbolized by Pakistan's voting for the first time for Peking's admission to the United Nations in the autumn of 1961. The Sino-Indian border war of late 1962 precipitated a border agreement and other manifestations of closer relations between China and Pakistan, including the establishment of air connections that considerably simplified travel between China and many other parts of Asia. China probably helped to incite, and certainly sympathized with, Pakistan's attempt in 1965 to strengthen its weak hand in Kashmir by military means. Although China was the only power to support Pakistan in this conflict, the crude and rather ludicrous pressures that Peking brought to bear on New Delhi were insufficient to prevent President Ayub from calling off the war and accepting Soviet mediation in a settlement that gained him nothing with respect to Kashmir. His dismissal of his pro-Chinese Foreign Minister Bhutto represented another setback for Peking. On the other hand, suspension of American military deliveries to Pakistan as well as India opened the way to a substantial program of Chinese military aid to Pakistan, including heavy tanks and jet fighters, after 1966. To Peking's disgust, Pakistan began about two years later to receive economic and military aid from the Soviet Union as well. For this among other reasons, Peking probably regarded the Pakistani political crisis of the late winter of 1969, which led to Ayub's decision not to run for President again and to Bhutto's reemergence as a major political figure, with some satisfaction. Peking's stock with student militants and leftist politicians in East Pakistan, who played a prominent part in the agitation against Ayub, stood fairly high, but there was a serious problem. If leftist activity in East Pakistan, which included strong opposition to the dominant political position of West Pakistan, should go so far as to lead to union with West Bengal, where pro-Chinese influence is also considerable, the result would be a major triumph for Chinese influence in that important area, but presumably a disaster for Chinese influence in West Pakistan, a region of far greater utility to Peking from the standpoint of the struggle against India.

In Afghanistan, China has in essence adopted a low posture. Apart from the small urban population, the country offers few opportunities for political penetration and receives economic aid from the United States and the Soviet Union which China is in no position to match. China's main advantage in dealing with the Himalayan states is not so much its proximity, which is partly nullified by the barrier of the Himalayan ridgeline, as the substantial residue of anti-Indian feeling. China has exploited this in the case of Nepal, which is an independent state, by means of a substantial aid program, which has included the construction of an important highway linking Katmandu with Lhasa. Except for a time during the heyday of Red Guard diplomacy, Peking has managed to preserve at least polite relations with the Nepalese government and yet to remain a major influence on the local Communist Party, whose importance is considerable. Presumably for the sake of its larger interests, China has tolerated the presence in northern Nepal of a sizable population of Khamba refugees from Tibet, some of whom conduct occasional armed raids back into Tibet. The degree of Chinese political activity and influence in Nepal is debated. Indian sources tend to rate it highly, and in fact to exaggerate it, presumably in order to gain Western support for the Indian side of the Sino-Indian dispute in the Himalayas. Reports by Americans who have visited Nepal without first being briefed in New Delhi suggest that the Chinese role looks less impressive when not viewed through Indian spectacles. China's problem in Sikkim and Bhutan is that these small states are under Indian protection and are not legally entitled to conduct their own foreign relations. Their governments, furthermore, are essentially pro-Indian, although they are not averse to trying to enlarge their area of maneuver by largely indirect and secret dealings with China.

China enjoys some influence on the Ceylonese left, which although badly divided was in power from 1956 to 1965. Apart from political appeals, a major source of what influence China possesses is the willingness it has shown since the early 1950s to sell badly needed rice to Ceylon at good prices in exchange for rubber. On balance, however, the island hardly looks like one of the most promising fields for the practice of Chinese foreign policy and diplomacy.

CHAPTER X

Peking and the
Third World

AT VARIOUS TIMES Chinese pronouncements have referred to the developing countries, including Asia except for Japan, as the "first intermediate zone" between American "imperialism" and the "socialist camp," or (in a phrase borrowed from the now dead Indonesian Communist leader D. N. Aidit) as the "world countryside." The enormous significance of this vast region (minus Asia, which has already been treated) in Chinese foreign policy is the theme of the present chapter.

GENERAL CONSIDERATIONS

It is clear that Peking seeks with both the national and the revolutionary components of its foreign policy some of the same rewards that were the object of the traditional Chinese tributary system, notably prestige and a feeling of acceptance, in particular acceptance as a model of revolutionary strategy and "socialist construction." Rather vague and largely psychic gains of this kind are not enough for Peking today, however, as they generally were in earlier times. Current Chinese foreign policy seeks concrete influence, the more the better as long as serious risk or prohibitive cost, as defined by some standard that can be approximately inferred but has never been explicitly stated, is not involved. Practically speaking, the overriding Chinese objective with respect to the Third World has been since 1949 to combat and minimize the influence of the United States, and since about 1960 that of the Soviet Union as well.

Chinese policy toward the Third World has always seemed to be of two minds as to whether Chinese interests and those of the anti-American (and later anti-Soviet) struggle could best be served by the promotion of chaos through the energetic incitement of revolution on the part of virtually any oppositionist forces (the "united front from below," in classical Communist parlance) or by the cultivation of nationalist governments and statesmen, including possibly influential regional leaders, whose outlook was compatible with at least the anti-American and/or anti-Soviet aspects of Chinest policy (the "united front from above"). It has already been suggested that, at least by the early 1960s, these two lines corresponded roughly with the views, respectively, of Mao Tse-tung and the non-Maoist (or less Maoist) component of the Chinese leadership.

Before about 1953 the Maoist line was in the ascendant, but Chinese foreign policy during that period had little practical significance except in Asia. The Korean and Indochinese crises, among other things, evidently convinced Peking that Chinese security, as well as the extension of Chinese national (if not necessarily revolutionary) influence from Asia to the rest of the Third World, required a shift to primary reliance to the approach "from above." A number of considerations, apart from the obviously persisting influence of Mao Tse-tung, argue that this shift was one of strategy and tactics, not of principle, and that Peking tacitly reserved to itself the freedom to reverse the emphasis and revert to a strategy stressing "armed struggle" and the "united front from below." Among the indications that favor this belief is the fact that the Chinese never gave more than passing endorsement to the idea expounded by Khrushchev at the Soviet Twentieth Congress that local Communist parties (mainly in the West, but by implication elsewhere as well) should stress political methods rather than "armed struggle."

As Peking raised its eyes from Asia to the rest of the Third World and considered what region offered the most promising field for the application of the approach "from above," it must have seen at once that Sub-Saharan Africa and Latin America were too geographically remote and politically difficult of access (in the sense of being still under overwhelming Western influence) to be of much immediate interest. The Arab countries of the Middle East, on the other hand, were seething with anti-Western feeling, and the previously dominant positions of Britain and France in the region were in serious danger. The lead in the Arab struggle against Western influence and Israel clearly belonged to Egypt. Accordingly, with Nehru acting as a helpful go-between, Chou En-lai began to cultivate Nasser at the Bandung Conference. To a large extent because of the relationship established in this way, Peking soon succeeded in gaining a highly influential role in the Afro-Asian People's Solidarity Organization, which was formed at the end of 1957 with headquarters in Cairo. The initial overwhelming Chinese emphasis at the meetings of this organization on the "liberation" of Taiwan did not prove an especially effective ploy, but it does indicate the high priority that Peking placed at that time, in its dealings with the Third World, on its own national interest as against the promotion of revolution for its own sake. It also suggests the priority that, as already pointed out, Peking accorded to its interests in Asia over those elsewhere. During this period, both to capitalize on the "spirit of Bandung" and to compensate for its limited capabilities and interest in the field of economic aid giving as compared with the United States and the Soviet Union, Peking laid enormous emphasis in its propaganda on the mythological beast of "Afro-Asian solidarity" and on the alleged (and usually nonexistent) history of its own traditional friendship with the countries of the Third World.

The successes of the Chinese approach "from above" to the Third World for a brief period after the Bandung Conference were modest but real. Apart from a second round of diplomatic recognitions and the launching of Chinese aid on a small scale in non-Communist Asia, the main progress for reasons already indicated was in the

Arab world. A major example was Nasser's diplomatic recognition of Peking in 1956, which probably contributed along with his arms deal with Czechoslovakia of the previous year to bringing the United States to withdraw financial support for the Aswan Dam, a step that in turn led to the Suez crisis. Another major example was the establishment of a Chinese presence, consisting of a diplomatic mission and aid program, in the poor but strategic state of Yemen in 1958.

But by 1958 the factors that were to lead Peking to change its line and give the approach "from below" equal, and perhaps greater, emphasis were already becoming apparent. The resurgence of the most militant form of Maoism in Chinese domestic politics, represented by the Great Leap Forward, necessarily exerted a strong influence on Chinese foreign policy. For one thing, on the rationale that "the East wind has prevailed over the West wind" Peking urged a more militantly anti-"imperialist" strategy on the Soviet Union, and China could hardly help taking a more negative line toward the non-Communist, "national bourgeois" leaders of the Third World, China's self-selected arena of struggle against "imperialism," because Mao had always regarded the "national bourgeoisie" everywhere as insufficiently anti-"imperialist." By the latter part of 1959 this last point was being made explicitly in Chinese theoretical statements.

More specifically, during the period when Peking was following primarily the approach "from above" in its dealings with the Third World, there had arisen a close relationship among three leaders, Nehru, Nasser, and Tito, who regarded themselves as neutral in the Cold War and in fact as spokesmen for the neutral or nonaligned states and peoples of the world. In its new mood of militancy after 1957, Peking came to regard them as not only pretentious but as unreliable in their opposition to "imperialism," and later as tending to be pro-Soviet. By 1958 China's relations with each of the three were under serious strain. The reasons for this in the case of Nehru, which of course included his interest in Tibet, have already been discussed. Tito had already come to symbolize to Mao the kind of "modern revisionism" whose allegedly corrupting influence on the "socialist camp," and on Khrushchev in particular, he (Mao) deplored. In Nasser's case, Peking's disenchantment was less obvious, but still real; one of its causes was his repressive policy toward his own Communists, for which among other things the Chinese allowed a leading Arab Communist, Khalid Bakdash, to rebuke him publicly in Peking in 1959. Nasser's motives in forming the United Arab Republic through union with Syria in early 1958 included a desire to check the growth of Communist influence in Syria and must have appeared highly suspect in Peking. By that time, furthermore, a more militant alternative to Nasser had appeared within the Arab world in the form of the Algerian National Liberation Front, which was fighting for independence from France. From 1958 the Front became the model that Peking held up for the emulation of the Third World, and after the attainment of Algerian independence in 1962 Algeria became for a time a significant base for Chinese activity in the rest of North Africa and even Sub-Saharan Africa.

Probably the most important, and certainly the most durable, of the forces that drove Peking to shift its emphasis in dealing with the Third World from the approach "from above" to the approach "from below" was its growing rivalry with and hostility toward the Soviet Union. In 1959 the two parties contrasted clearly, and even debated openly, their varying positions on policy toward the Third World. To a large extent no doubt because of his general reluctance (subject to occasional exceptions) to risk a direct confrontation with the United States, Khrushchev stressed peaceful economic and technological competition on the Soviet Union's part with the United States in the Third World, a willingness on the whole to give "national bourgeois" regimes, the more leftist of which he classified after 1960 as "national democracies," the benefit of the doubt, and a continued preference for political action over "armed struggle" on the part of local Communist parties. Soon afterward, to be sure, a number of developments, including the seeming opening up of revolutionary opportunities in Africa after 1960 and his desire not to be left astern by the Chinese, led him to intervene actively in the Congo and Laos and, mainly it would appear to impress the incoming Kennedy administration as well as Peking, to make a seemingly belligerent speech on January 6, 1961, in which he promised active Soviet support to "wars of national liberation." Steps such as these, however, even when reinforced by his occasional toughness on Berlin and his effort to emplace offensive missiles in Cuba, were too erratic to refute, at least in the eyes of the extreme left in the Third World, the Chinese charge that his anti-"imperialism" was more a matter of expediency than of principle.

As developed in theory and practice after about 1958, the more militant, "from below" version of Chinese strategy toward the Third World has of course claimed to be based on principle, whereas Peking has asserted the opposite of Soviet strategy. To a considerable extent, this claim is probably genuine in the minds of its most ardent proponents. To the objective observer, however, the Chinese claim to a strategy founded on pure principle is likely to appear as an exercise in self-deception, if not partial falsification. For one thing, Chinese incitement of revolution in the Third World, usually at modest risk and expense to Peking, undoubtedly is intended among other things to distract the United States, and perhaps the Soviet Union as well, from the immediate periphery of China and so reduce the risks and obstacles to Chinese policy in Asia; in this respect, as in several others, Chinese policy has not been notably successful. Peking's actual efforts in the Third World, especially as compared with its theoretical formulations and propaganda, seem rather modest when it is recalled that China enjoys a significantly higher threshold of action with respect to the United States than does the Soviet Union, in the Third World at any rate. In other words, apart from Khrushchev's occasional aberrations the Soviet Union's great strategic military power renders it more liable to American attention and counteraction and tends to generate a stronger sense of caution on the part of its leadership where operations outside its recognized sphere of influence are concerned.

As Chinese strategy toward the Third World evolved after 1958, it continued to stress and try to take advantage of China's undoubted status as a genuinely Afro-Asian power, something that the United States and the Soviet Union are not, but without consciously going so far in this respect as to diminish Chinese effectiveness in other quarters such as the "socialist camp" and the "second intermediate zone" (the developed countries other than the United States). But more openly than before, good relations on the part of other Afro-Asian countries with China were now proclaimed to be conditional not only on opposition to American "imperialism" but on opposition to Soviet "revisionism," an issue of little interest in the Third

World except to the extreme left. In the vain hope of counteracting the attractiveness of American and Soviet aid, Peking began to preach that Afro-Asian countries should be economically "self-reliant," as it claimed to be itself, in the sense of not accepting aid from non-Afro-Asian sources; it can hardly have escaped either Peking or a number of its hearers that such a policy on the part of a poor developing country would tend to condemn it to economic stagnation and promote political unrest, perhaps to Communist advantage. Peking increased its own efforts in the field of economic aid after 1960, as though to balance its increasing political assertiveness and militancy, but the chosen recipients were relatively few in number and were carefully selected on ideological grounds. Although not above opportunistic collaboration with some of its leaders, Peking displayed with growing clarity a distaste for the "national bourgeoisie" that provided most of the ruling elite of the Third World. It refused to use the Soviet term "national democracy," with its strong overtones of approval of those Third World states that took an anti-"imperialist" line, restricted private enterprise, and allowed freedom of political action to the local Communists, and used instead the term "national democratic movements," which placed the emphasis on parties and revolutionary processes rather than on established states. Where a Communist Party existed, as it often did not and does not in the Third World, in a formal sense at least, Peking strongly encouraged it to retain its organizational independence at all costs, as against the occasional Soviet preference (as in Algeria) for a merger with a stronger leftist nationalistic movement in the hope of practicing what has been called "licensed infiltration." Over and above the mere fact that this approach was a Soviet one, Peking objected to it because it was reminiscent of the strategy forced on the Chinese party by the Comintern in the years leading up to the disaster of 1927. Where there existed a movement, Communist or not, that was militantly opposed to "imperialism" and to its real or alleged local agents (often including the government of the country in question), Peking would often provide aid and advice of various kinds calculated to lay the groundwork for—and when the time was considered ripe launch—an "armed struggle" or "people's war" against the purported "imperialist" enemy. Peking considered, and still does, that these movements should be "self-reliant," in the sense that they should make their own political decisions to the extent possible and that Chinese aid should be kept limited and covert on the whole, with the advantage that China can if it chooses disclaim any direct responsibility for the fate of the movements. This has proven a convenient option on those occasions when Chinese incitement has led or at least contributed to a premature showing of its hand on the part of a Third World revolutionary movement and a resulting setback or disaster.

This general Chinese line, which was substantially more militant and "from below" than the one prevailing in the era of Bandung, was already becoming evident by 1960, and its ascendancy in Peking was strengthened by a series of seeming opportunities and challenges that began at about that time. One of these was the wave of decolonization in Sub-Saharan Africa after 1960. Another was China's increasingly bad relations with India, and the border war of late 1962 in particular. Another was Peking's friendship, after 1961, with a militant Sukarnoist Indonesia, which seemed to promise improved Chinese access not only to Southeast Asia but, via the traditional tie between Indonesia and Madagascar, perhaps to Sub-Saharan Africa as well. Another, of course, was the escalating Sino-Soviet dispute.

In the early 1960s Chinese policy toward the Third World suffered from a curious combination of liabilities, apart from Peking's inherent limitations as a wielder of influence outside Asia. One was the unseemly wrangle with Moscow, which bored and wearied Afro-Asians, by no means all of them Communists, who were expected to take sides in it and which deprived Peking of what might have been the advantages of Soviet aid and cooperation. Another was the fact that, in spite of this dispute, Peking was in no political position to espouse or even endorse nonalignment in the Cold War, because of its commitment to the "socialist camp" and to the principle of active hostility to American "imperialism." It could and did cooperate with left-wing, anti-"imperialist," nominal neutrals like Indonesia and use them to combat the influence of genuine neutrals like India, but it could not take part in the gatherings of nonaligned statesmen of which Nehru, Nasser, and Tito were so fond, such as the Belgrade Conference of 1961. On these occasions Peking had to rely on its leftist friends like Indonesia to present its case for it. Understandably, China opposed and deprecated the second conference of nonaligned countries, which convened at Cairo in 1965, as much as appeared prudent, and stressed instead the Second Afro-Asian Conference (in succession to the Bandung Conference), which was to meet at Algiers in June 1965 and at which China could be represented by right, regardless of its aligned status. But as we have seen, Chinese obtrusiveness in insisting that the conference adopt its position on the exclusion of the Soviet Union, the condemnation of the United States over Vietnam, the exclusion of Malaysia, and the repudiation of economic aid from non-Afro-Asian countries led to the cancellation of the conference, with a coup in Algeria serving as the initial pretext.

In spite of this setback and others, or perhaps partly because of them, Chinese assertiveness in and toward the Third World grew even greater during the Cultural Revolution. Chinese propaganda and subversive activity, as well as occasional demonstrations by Chinese diplomats and students, brought on diplomatic crises with a number of Third World countries, such as Tunisia. As in their discussions of the American threat to China itself, the extreme Maoists seemed to be urging a strategy of provocation by leftist elements calculated allegedly to provoke "imperialist" armed intervention and thus teach the "revolutionary people of the world" a lesson by "negative example" and spur them to greater efforts. The activities of the Boxers in China at the beginning of the century, when they unquestionably provoked an armed intervention by the "imperialist" powers of the day, were sometimes cited as a model of sorts.

The limited trend toward moderation in Chinese domestic and foreign policy that began in the late summer of 1967 seemed to have had the effect, where the Third World was concerned, of restoring something resembling a balance between the approaches "from above" and "from below," without producing anything like a clear-cut priority for the former. There was increased emphasis on friendly relations with and aid to leftist Third World states, notably Tanzania, but little reduction of interest in and support for armed anti-"imperialist" movements, such as the Fatah in the Middle East.

On the whole, China's record to date in the Third World beyond Asia is one of much noise, limited efforts, and still more limited successes. It seems likely that the record will remain substantially the same as long as Mao and his "thought" continue to be the predominant political influences in Peking. Chinese prospects for influence could of course be favorably affected by the adoption of a Chinese strategy that was less loud in word and more effective in deed (and hence probably more "from above"), presumably after rather than before Mao's death, or by a drastic worsening of economic and political conditions in the Third World or some significant part of it.

CHINA AND THE MIDDLE EAST

China's most obvious assets in seeking to expand its influence in the Middle East are the Arabs' dislike of Western "imperialism" and their hatred of its alleged agent Israel, as well as the unrealizability of the dream of Arab unity, so that Peking is able to deal with a number of relatively weak states rather than with some powerful union. Apart from its own objective limitations, China's most important liabilities in the Middle East are probably its inablity to dispel entirely the justified suspicions of some Arabs that the Moslem community in China is repressed, and the weakness of the Communist parties throughout the Middle East. China's massive propaganda to and its commercial contacts with the Middle East have been greatly facilitated by its possession of broadcasting facilities and its access to port facilities in Albania. As yet, China has shown no great interest in Arab oil; its demand is limited, and in any case it would have difficulty in competing in this field with the powerful Western and Japanese interests.

On the political side, China has displayed enough opportunism in its Middle Eastern policy to detract from its claim that it more than any other major power acts on principle, but not enough to achieve significant practical successes. It gave the Algerian National Liberation Front earlier and more effective support than did the Soviet Union, in the form of *de facto* diplomatic recognition in 1958 and substantial military aid, since unlike the Soviet Union it did not then care about having good relations with France. The latter became possible and desirable in Peking's eyes only after France conceded independence to Algeria in 1962. Although China cultivated the leftist Ben Bella government of Algeria with some success, it made unseemly haste to recognize the Boumedienne government after Ben Bella was overthrown by a coup in June 1965. Peking's motive was to salvage the Afro-Asian Conference, but this proved impossible, and Chinese failure was compounded by a display of indifference to principle at least in this case.

As we have seen, Peking has managed to keep its dislike of Nasser's pro-Soviet tendencies and his repression of his local Communists under reasonable control, presumably because of its continuing realization of his political importance in the Middle East. There have been occasional rumors that Peking has offered some sort of nuclear aid to Nasser, but confirmation has never been forthcoming. Certainly it has given him some conventional military aid and following an agreement of 1965 supplied some, but not very much, aid and training to the Palestine Liberation Organization, which was under Nasser's influence.

Elsewhere in North Africa, Peking established diplomatic relations with Morocco in 1958 and has remained on reasonably good terms with it since. China sells green tea to Morocco and buys cobalt, which is used in nuclear experimentation, from it. Chinese hostility to the allegedly pro-"imperialist" Bourguiba, plus obtrusive behavior during the Cultural Revolution, resulted in a suspension of Sino-Tunisian diplomatic relations in 1967.

China has generally enjoyed good relations with the leftist, unstable government of Syria and has provided it with economic and military aid. Among the countries of the Arabian Peninsula, China has had significant relations to date only with Yemen. Having established diplomatic relations with the government of the Imam in 1958 and launched a program of roadbuilding, Peking continued this policy after the Imam's government was challenged and ultimately displaced by the Yemeni Arab Republic, which was under the influence of Nasser.

The Middle Eastern war of mid-1967 provided China with an excellent opportunity to proclaim, if not necessarily to put into effect, its support for Nasser and the Arab "people" and its opposition to Western "imperialism" and Israel. In addition to extending some aid to the United Arab Republic, it issued a number of loud progaganda blasts and detonated its first thermonuclear bomb on June 17, almost at the moment when Soviet Premier Kosygin reached the United States, as though to dramatize its opposition to the settlement of Middle Eastern or any other problems through the United Nations and through Soviet-American discussions. The Palestine Liberation Organization having largely collapsed as a result of the June war, Peking now began to extend aid to the more active and effective anti-Israeli terrorist organization, the Fatah.

CHINA AND AFRICA

Peking can be assumed to have been long aware of Africa's natural resources and of the desirability of denying these if possible —as it is not—to the West, but there were few opportunities for Chinese diplomatic or revolutionary activity there until the wave of decolonization that began in 1960. Stimulated no doubt by the Congo crisis and a strong tendency toward increased Soviet involvement in the region, Peking apparently then proceeded to overestimate the revolutionary potential of the region and its own opportunities for making major gains. It launched an intensive propaganda effort in Africa and began to give aid and support to a variety of allegedly anti-"imperialist" movements and insurgencies, as well as outright tribal revolts in some cases. Neither this activity nor Peking's effort at more conventional diplomacy in the region was outstandingly successful. The Sub-Saharan states divided their diplomatic recognitions about equally between Peking and Taipei, the more leftist as would be expected generally opting for Peking, since it was impossible to have relations with both.

Ever since 1960 Peking seems to have considered the former Belgian Congo, reasonably enough, as the most important country of Sub-Saharan Africa from the standpoint of resources and location. But direct Chinese influence on the Congo has been limited by the uncongenial political orientation of its government, the failure of viable revolutionary movements to materialize, intervention by other external powers or forces (notably the United States, the Soviet Union, and the United Nations), and the general confusion and unmanageability of the situation. Nor have Peking's efforts to establish revolutionary bases around the edges of the Congo, from which Congolese exiles and other chosen friends of Chinese-style revolution could hope to penetrate the adjacent provinces of the Congo, achieved much better results. In 1965 and early 1966 China lost all or most of its presence in Burundi and the Central African Republic, which border on the Congo, as well as in Dahomey and Ghana, as a result of revolutions or coups. In another country contiguous to the Congo, Congo Brazzaville (the former French Congo), Chinese influence stood high after a leftist revolution in 1963, but this influence appeared to be jeopardized by a military coup that occurred some five years later.

Among the other francophone states, China has long enjoyed considerable influence in, and extended aid to, the two leftist states of Guinea and Mali. But since about 1964 Peking appears to have considered them less important than Tanzania, which has an excellent strategic location on the Indian Ocean and in relation to the states of the White Redoubt (Angola, Mozambique, Rhodesia, and South Africa), as well as the Congo. It is here that China has been making its greatest effort in Africa since 1965. It has benefited from a congenially leftist political climate, especially in Zanzibar. It has maintained an active and generally successful diplomacy, including a treaty of friendship signed in 1965. It has extended very substantial economic aid, and in particular has agreed to take the main responsibility for surveying and construction of the Tan-Zam (Tanzania-Zambia) railway, which when completed should facilitate not only Zambia's economic access to the outside world but its exploitation as a revolutionary base. China is evidently involved, together with some other external states and agencies, in providing training to African revolutionaries in Tanzania for later use against the White Redoubt. Other African revolutionaries have received training in China itself.

Except for the progress it has made in Tanzania, China's record in Africa has been none too brilliant in recent years. In more countries than not, it has acquired a formidable reputation as a troublemaker, and it has shown little enthusiasm and in fact some hostility for the sacred cause of African unity. Its opportunities for the future, however, appear impressive, since Sub-Saharan Africa is of all the regions of the Third World the one where the Western or "imperialist" presence is the most obtrusive. But the challenge and risks seem proportional to the opportunities, for a prolonged Chinese failure to provide genuinely effective support to the struggle against the White Redoubt might prove disastrous to Peking's hopes for influence in the region. And it has not escaped the attention of African revolutionaries that China trades fairly extensively with Rhodesia and South Africa.

CHINA AND LATIN AMERICA

Latin America possesses obvious attractions for Peking in the form of its natural resources and the widespread opposition to the influence of the "colossus of the North." On particularly favorable occasions, such as the crisis in Panamanian relations with the United States at the beginning of 1964 and the American intervention in the Dominican Republic in 1965, China has made strenuous efforts through propaganda to take credit for being at least as anti-"imperialist" as anyone in Latin America. On the other hand, China has no diplomatic relations with any Latin American country but Cuba, although it enjoyed some influence on the leftist Goulart government of Brazil before it was overthrown by a military coup in 1964, and although the New China News Agency has offices in ten Latin American countries apart from Cuba. Chinese influence on the intellectuals of the region is not nonexistent, but it is not great.

Another problem for Peking is the fact that the Communist parties of Latin America are without exception weak, ineffective, and pro-Soviet. Virtually ignoring their unsuitability as instruments for revolutionary action, Peking has concentrated since the early 1960s on trying to use them in connection with the Sino-Soviet dispute. After failing to win over the entrenched leaderships, Peking tried after 1963 to create reliable splinter parties where possible. It succeeded to varying but not very impressive degrees in Brazil, Peru, Colombia, Chile, and Haiti. Its failure with the orthodox parties was indicated by its successful insistence, at the Tricontinental Conference held at Havana early in 1966, that the Afro-Asian

People's Solidarity Organization maintain its separate identity rather than be merged in an Afro-Asian-Latin American People's Solidarity Organization where the pro-Soviet Latin American Communist parties would play an important role.

Peking showed considerable interest in Castro as soon as he came to power at the beginning of 1959, because his rise had taken place via guerrilla warfare, he was known to be leftist, and he seemed likely to exert some influence on revolutionaries elsewhere in Latin America. Cuba, furthermore, possessed very considerable symbolic importance in the context of the anti-"imperialist" struggle because of its closeness to the United States and the latter's historically significant role in its affairs. China succeeded in establishing diplomatic relations and beginning an aid program with Cuba in 1960. Sino-Cuban relations were warm for a time, especially in late 1962 when Peking exploited Khrushchev's performance in the missile crisis for all it was worth. But here again the Sino-Soviet dispute came to overshadow Peking's other interests. Chinese resentment of Castro's willingness to curry favor with Moscow to a degree in return for aid became increasingly obvious, and Castro began to seem insufficiently revolutionary in the struggle against "imperialism," as compared for example with the more congenial Guevara, in Peking's eyes. By late 1965 Chinese efforts to propagandize the Cuban regime, including the army, on behalf of Peking's side of the Sino-Soviet dispute had aroused Castro's objections. China then reduced its imports of Cuban sugar and its exports of rice to Cuba on the stated ground that it would be better for Cuba to be self-sufficient in rice. Castro responded by denouncing the Chinese, and Mao Tse-tung in particular, publicly in the early months of 1966. The death of Guevara some two years later seemingly completed the process of cutting Peking off from effective contact with the most promising stream of revolutionary activity in Latin America. It is hard to imagine China ever gaining the leadership of the mainstream of revolutionary movements in Latin America except in the improbable contingency of the conjunction of three circumstances: the collapse of the Castroites (or their acceptance of Chinese influence), massive failures or changes of orientation on the part of the Latin American governments, and major policy blunders by the United States.

CHAPTER XI

Peking and the West

IN JANUARY 1964, when Sino-French diplomatic relations were in the process of being established, Peking formulated its then view of the world in an editorial that declared that between the "imperialist" United States and the "socialist camp" lay two "intermediate zones," of which the first was made up of the developing countries and the second of the developed ones (including Japan). This chapter deals with Chinese policy toward the second of these "intermediate zones," except that Japan is omitted, since it has already been treated under Asia, and the United States is included.

In reality, the idea of the second "intermediate zone" if not the term dates from about 1961, when an agricultural crisis and a sharp reduction in Sino-Soviet trade forced Peking to turn primarily to the countries of the "zone" for capital equipment (subject to the limitation that the United States discouraged the governments of the "zone" from guaranteeing long-term industrial credits to China), technical information of many kinds, and grain imports amounting to several million tons a year, while refusing an American offer to sell grain.

From the national or diplomatic standpoint, there are obvious reasons why Peking should cultivate an active policy toward the countries of the second "intermediate zone." A superpower, actual or aspiring, tends to feel a need for involvement in all major sectors of the international system, and in the Chinese case there is a compulsion to seek influence at the expense of Washington and Moscow. This line of approach is in tension, however, with the strong Maoist desire for leftist revolutions in the developed as well as in the developing countries, a desire whose manifestations tend to alienate the governments and responsible elements of the developed countries. Mao Tse-tung, who has more in common with the anarchist Bakunin than with the scholarly Marx, claims that proletarian risings along the lines of the famous Paris Commune of 1871 are the wave of the future for the West. Increasingly ignoring or denouncing the orthodox Communist parties as "revisionist" and pro-Soviet, he has encouraged the emergence of radical "Marxist-Leninist" parties and splinter groups and has given some aid and support to student demonstrations. His name and "thought," which is often badly misunderstood as holding that unorganized violence is sufficient to produce a genuine revolution, stand high with some elements of the radical left in the West, in spite of or rather because of the Cultural Revolution.

THE UNITED STATES

The Chinese Communist leadership clearly decided after 1945 that there was a need for an adversary or devil figure in succession to Japan. The requirements of Maoist revolutionary strategy, Marxist-Leninist ideology, and political mobilization of the Chinese people all pointed to the United States, the leading "imperialist" power, as the logical candidate. The choice was all the easier because the United States did in fact intervene in the Chinese civil war after 1945 on the Nationalist side, short of the commitment of its own forces. As the leaders of a would-be superpower, Mao and his colleagues have undoubtedly taken great satisfaction from measuring themselves, not like other Asian countries against a hostile neighbor, but against the strongest power in Asia and indeed the world.

Late in 1949, when it became clear that in spite of articulate

Republican opposition the State Department was actively considering diplomatic recognition of the new regime in Peking, such a step was abruptly put out of the question by calculated mistreatment of American diplomatic and consular personnel then remaining in China. To this promising but still incipient adversary relationship, the Korean War made a huge contribution, among other reasons because a son of Mao Tse-tung was killed in combat. The United States proceeded to put into effect a strategy of military containment and attempted political isolation of China. This consisted mainly of denying diplomatic recognition and encouraging others to do the same; extending military protection and other forms of support to the Nationalists on Taiwan, a step that Peking has since charged constituted American "occupation" of Taiwan, a charge that appears implicitly to invoke the Sino-Soviet alliance but has never evoked a corresponding response from Moscow; excluding Peking from the United Nations and gaining from that body (in early 1951) a condemnation of China as an aggressor in Korea and an embargo on "strategic" trade with it by most of its non-Communist members; maintaining a total embargo on American trade with China; and the strengthening of existing American bases and forces in Asia and the Western Pacific, the giving of military aid to a number of anti-Communist Asian governments, and the conclusion of alliances directed actually or potentially against China. Of these alliances there were four bilateral ones (with Japan, the Philippines, South Korea, and Nationalist China) and two multilateral ones (the Anzus Treaty with Australia and New Zealand and the SEATO treaty with the same two countries plus Britain, France, Pakistan, the Philippines, and Thailand, the most important of these countries being Thailand since it was the one most directly threatened and the only one not covered by some other treaty with the United States).

The events of the Korean War showed that direct Chinese military action aimed at frustrating or defeating the American containment strategy would be unsuccessful and far too risky, especially in view of the inadequacy of Soviet support, which tended to decrease after Stalin's death. Indirect military action, meaning armed revolutionary activity, would also be difficult to orchestrate, as the history of efforts along these lines between 1948 and 1951 had shown, and in any case would be countereffective since it would tend to drive the Asian governments affected closer to the United States.

The only possible strategy, for the time being at least, was to cultivate at least the majority of the Asian governments rather than trying to subvert them. The inauguration of an effective diplomacy along these lines was made possible by the Korean and Indochinese armistices and was encouraged by the Soviet Union, at least until the Bandung Conference (at which the Soviet Union was not represented) suggested that Chinese Asian diplomacy might have an effect, even if not a purpose, adverse to Soviet interests. India was the key to Peking's policy in Asia during that period for several reasons, among them the fact that Nehru disliked the policy of the United States toward Asia in general and China in particular. During the months following the Geneva Conference he and U Nu of Burma tried, although with few concrete results, to mediate or at least mitigate the Sino-American conflict.

Of probably greater importance was the fact that the Geneva Conference led directly to the beginning of Sino-American diplomatic talks, at the ambassadorial level, over a number of issues such as the prospective release of prisoners held on both sides. The atmosphere was also improved by the withdrawal of some, but by no means all, American troops and Chinese "volunteers" from Korea. In August 1955, as a direct result of the four-power summit conference of the previous month, and in a sense to compensate for China's exclusion from it, Sino-American ambassadorial talks began at Geneva on a more formal and regular basis. In September the talks produced the only public agreement yet to have emerged from them in the form of an "agreed announcement" to the effect that all prisoners would be released on both sides. The Chinese released some American civilian and military prisoners they were holding but continued to detain others, while loudly and with little justification accusing the United States of not fulfilling its part of the bargain. Apart from the prisoner question, the main American demand was for a mutual "renunciation of force," and the main Chinese demand was for an end to the American "occupation" of Taiwan. No agreement on these points was possible, but the talks went on. In 1956, realizing apparently that American pressures on China, such as Secretary Dulles's famous "brink of war" statement of January 1956, were tending to create sympathy for the Chinese side, Peking began to try to bring pressure of its own to bear by issuing propaganda appeals to the Nationalists for an accommodation and by announcing in August 1956 that it would allow American correspondents to visit China.

By the time Washington, which at first was considerably embarrassed by this last move, agreed to it, the climate in Peking had begun to change, and virtually no American newsmen have actually succeeded in getting to China. An especially Cold War-like speech by Secretary Dulles at San Francisco on June 28, 1957, may have contributed to the change of climate, but far more important was the general radicalization of Mao Tse-tung's thinking and behavior in the second half of the year, under the rubric "the East wind has prevailed over the West wind." Early in 1958 Peking suspended the Sino-American talks, which Washington was then trying to hold at a level below the ambassadorial. But the Taiwan Strait crisis of August–October 1958, which Mao initiated as an external manifestation of his current radicalism, produced indications that the United States would take whatever action might be necessary to prevent the Nationalists from being pushed off the offshore islands. The situation was a dangerous one, and contact had to be reestablished with the adversary to avoid a possible disaster. On September 6, accordingly, Chou En-lai proposed that Sino-American ambassadorial talks be resumed, this time at Warsaw. Since then, the revived talks have again tended to deadlock on matters of substance, but they have provided each side with a valuable means of communicating its views on important questions of common interest to the other.

In the last years of Secretary Dulles's tenure, Peking was considerably worried by what it regarded as an aggressive American policy in Asia, notably in Laos. It is worth asking why his resignation and death in the spring of 1959, which was followed by a display of greater American interest in travel to and other contacts with the mainland of China, did not lead to any significant mellowing of Peking's policy toward the United States. The main reason apparently was that Mao Tse-tung was still in a highly militant mood and was smarting over his setback at the paws of the American "paper tiger" in the Taiwan Strait the previous year. Secondly,

Khrushchev, who was able to suspend his penchant for making an issue of Berlin much more easily than Mao was able to suspend his for making an issue of Taiwan, launched himself in the summer of 1959 into an energetic campaign of summit diplomacy which brought him to the United States; it was unthinkable for China to do anything that would remotely suggest an intent to imitate this performance. Finally, the crisis in Laos continued and indeed grew more acute in the last months of 1960. There was one possible sign that China was now somewhat less afraid of the United States now that Dulles was dead. Peking, which when most afraid had cultivated India, initiated a major dispute with it in the late spring and summer of 1959 over the Tibetan and border issues. Another likely consideration was that, as he was to do again in 1962, Mao consoled himself at India's expense for his inability to make headway against stronger opposition in the Taiwan Strait. In the spring of 1960 the downfall of Syngman Rhee and the riots in Japan over the renewal of the security treaty with the United States apparently generated some hope in Peking that the American position in Northeast Asia was weakening, but this mood soon passed.

Although a few aspects of the Kennedy administration's Asian policy, notably its announcement in 1962 that it would not support a Chinese Nationalist attack on the mainland, met with Chinese approval, on balance the verdict was strongly unfavorable. Peking regarded with the deepest misgivings the doctrine of "flexible response" and the associated emphasis on counterinsurgency, and in particular the growing American involvement in South Vietnam after October 1961. Increasing American economic military support for India also met with Chinese disfavor. For a variety of practical and ideological reasons, including the role of the Soviet Union, Peking regarded the test ban treaty, signed in the summer of 1963, as the unkindest cut of all. A few weeks later Mao issued the first of a series of eight personal statements of an anti-American kind on a variety of issues, this one dealing with racial unrest in Alabama. The news of President Kennedy's assassination was greeted in China by organized displays of public rejoicing, no doubt to the horror of Khrushchev among others, who seemed sincerely shocked at the tragedy. Peking largely ignored a conciliatory speech by Assistant Secretary of State Roger Hilsman on December 13, 1963, in which he expressed a cautious hope that in time a more pragmatic leadership, one easier to deal with, would come to power but indicated that the United States hoped to be able to improve its relations with China in the meantime.

Sino-American relations during 1964 and 1965 were dominated by growing tension over Vietnam. Peking's fears for its own security were apparently eased somewhat, although not entirely, when the United States resumed bombing North Vietnam in late January 1966, after a "bombing pause," without escalating the war, and a few months later an informal understanding appears to have been reached at Warsaw to the effect that as long as China did not intervene in Vietnam it would not be attacked, and vice versa.

Although pleased by such manifestations of American discontent with official policy toward China as the Senate Foreign Relations Committee's hearings on China and Vietnam in the spring of 1966, Peking was evidently embarrassed by the ensuing tendency of the Johnson administration to endorse the slogan "containment without isolation" and by President Johnson's speech in July advocating "reconciliation" with China. Acrimonious debate in the United States over China policy was one thing; actual overtures were another. The time evidently seemed right to Mao, especially in view of the requirement of increased militancy imposed by the Cultural Revolution, to make a dramatic but riskless demonstration of his continued determination to struggle against "imperialism" and all its works. On September 7 the Chinese delegate to the ambassadorial talks at Warsaw not only made but published a statement strongly repudiating all American gestures toward better relations on the ground that the United States was still aggressively hostile to China and was giving abundant evidence to that effect in Vietnam.

In the spring of 1968 a number of developments, including the approach of an election campaign, produced a new round of conciliatory statements on China policy by American officials, including an invitation to send observers during the campaign. Peking's response, in late May, was to announce that it would hold no more talks at Warsaw until after the election and to ignore all overtures. On November 25, at a time when Mao appears to have been ill or at any rate not actively in charge in Peking for some reason, China invited the United States to resume discussions at Warsaw on

February 20, 1969, when the Nixon administration would have had a month to get its bearings. This is one of a number of indications that the relative moderates in the Chinese leadership, such as Chou En-lai, probably favor some sort of more stable relationship or détente with the United States, although it is doubtful whether even they would accept indefinitely a continued denial of Taiwan. In late January Mao resumed the helm, and on January 27 a propaganda campaign against the Nixon administration began that culminated on February 19 in a withdrawal of the earlier invitation to resume the ambassadorial talks. It appears, then, that Mao basically dislikes official contacts of any sort with the United States. Certainly he is encouraged by the growth of racial and student unrest in the United States, which his propagandists portray as the beginnings of revolution. The latest of personal anti-American statements was issued in April 1968 on the occasion of the murder of Dr. Martin Luther King, whose devotion to nonviolence the bellicose Mao did not mention.

Among the objections raised to American China policy, it is sometimes said that the United States has allowed itself to be drawn so deeply into Asia by its preoccupation with China that it has weakened its position in Europe to the advantage of the Soviet Union. There is some truth in this assertion, but it is only one aspect of an immensely complex problem. Through its development of nuclear weapons, its role in Vietnam, its fostering of the Sino-Soviet border dispute, and so on, China has exerted a significant distracting influence on the Soviet Union as well as on the United States although to a lesser degree. In the Soviet Union, as in the United States, China policy is a controversial subject. Moderates among the leadership, including apparently some of the military, tend to stress the Chinese threat and the need for long-term measures to meet it, while in some cases advocating a softer line toward Europe, both East and West. The hardliners, on the other hand, including many leaders of the party apparatus, claim to believe that Maoist chauvinism, as they regard it, is a passing phase, that "healthy forces" like themselves will prevail in China in time, and that the Soviet Union must continue to devote its main attention to strengthening its influence over European affairs.

It is unlikely that China will ever willingly accept the United

States as a major power in Asia. Whether it will have to do so unwillingly is impossible to say, but the current trend is clearly toward a somewhat lower level of American involvement in Asia. This trend appears to create openings for increased Chinese influence, especially since China will presumably improve its nuclear capability with time. But limits will probably be set to such increases not only by continuing American strategic superiority but by the growing stability of most Asian countries, to which American policy has made a significant contribution.

THE BRITISH COMMONWEALTH

Peking appears to regard Britain as a country whose government in the last analysis follows the lead of the United States, as it certainly has on a number of issues of importance to China such as the Korean War and the nuclear test ban treaty. On the other hand, it preserves enough freedom of action so that it can be useful to China on occasion as a means of contact with and even restraint on the United States. The main reasons why Peking did not allow the raising of its diplomatic mission in London and the British mission in Peking to embassy status were that Britain still holds a piece of what is regarded on the mainland as Chinese territory, Hong Kong, and maintains a consulate on Taiwan. Peking also undoubtedly resents Britain's rather negative policy toward the large Chinese community in Malaysia during the colonial era and the crucial British role in coping with Indonesia's effort to "crush" Malaysia between 1963 and 1966.

Before the Second World War, Britain and Japan were by far the leaders in foreign trade with and investment in China. The war of course cost Japan its investments on the mainland, among other things, but British like some other foreign investors returned after the war and made some headway in putting their operations back together. The British attitude, official and unofficial, toward the Nationalists was generally unfavorable, and correspondingly favorable toward the Communists by the time they came to power. There was some hope that this attitude might be rewarded by immunity from nationalization for British investments, but if there ever was any such possibility—as seems unlikely—it soon disappeared when Britain supported the United States in the Korean War. British, like other foreign investments, were taken over, and their former owners were often assessed large sums for alleged back taxes and back pay for Chinese employees. British trade with China was inevitably at a low level during that period, since Peking by conscious choice was doing three-quarters of its foreign trade with the rest of the Communist bloc. Since 1960 this latter situation has ceased to exist, and British trade with China has benefited correspondingly, although not to the same extent as that of some other powers such as Japan and West Germany.

On the whole, the main issue between Britain and China is Hong Kong. Peking regards the whole of the Crown Colony as having been wrongfully seized in the nineteenth century and as therefore still Chinese territory. Britain, on the other hand, is legally correct in maintaining that the island of Victoria, with its magnificent harbor, was ceded outright to Britain by China in 1842 and that the area known as Kowloon, which is situated directly across the harbor from the island, was ceded in 1860. Britain acknowledges, however, that the larger area to the north of Kowloon, known as the New Territories, was acquired on a ninety-nine-year lease in 1898 and must therefore revert to China in 1997, except in the unlikely event that the Chinese government should then agree to extend the lease. Although most of the population of nearly 4 million and of the industry is located in the island and Kowloon, the New Territories are considered essential to the viability of the Crown Colony because of their food production. There thus appears to be no future for Hong Kong as a British Crown Colony after 1997, and a substantial number of young residents are demonstrating their appreciation of this fact by emigrating. It is universally realized that the colony is indefensible against a serious attack, and if one occurred it is unlikely that the small British garrison would try to defend it, as was done without success against the Japanese at the end of 1941.

Since China regards Hong Kong as Chinese territory, the question naturally arises why it has not tried to take it. There appear to be several compelling reasons. In the first place, even if there were no serious British resistance, and even though the United States has made no formal commitment to defend Hong Kong, an attack on it would constitute a major international incident, and the United States Seventh Fleet is not far away. Secondly, and perhaps even more important, China earns $600–$700 million a year by trading with Hong Kong, the trade consisting mainly of the export of food and water from the mainland. Hong Kong also serves the mainland as a useful point of commercial and financial contact with the outside world. Thirdly, it is clear that no one in China except perhaps some of Mao's most militant followers has any desire to assume the onerous and chaotic responsibility of administering Hong Kong under present conditions. It is very suggestive that in the summer of 1967, when Red Guard violence in Hong Kong was at a fairly serious level, the Chinese Army units at the border gave no trouble and in some cases restrained militant civilians who wanted to take action against the colony. Hong Kong remains a sore point for Maoists at all levels, however, as Peking's detention of the Reuters correspondent Anthony Grey from July 1967 to September 1969, in retaliation for the suppression of three Communist newspapers in Hong Kong, shows.

As the fact that it can afford such a large unfavorable balance of payments in its dealings with the mainland indicates, the economy of Hong Kong is in a highly prosperous condition by Asian standards. The government of Hong Kong deposits its assets in the Bank of England, where although not under the British government's control they form an important part of the financial support for the pound. For economic reasons such as this, and because of its sense of responsibility for the welfare of the overwhelmingly Chinese population of the colony, Hong Kong is the only area where Britain expects to maintain a military presence and a colonial dependency of significant size "east of Suez" after 1971. By 1997 it hopes that the political situation in China will have improved and that some sort of reasonable relationship between Hong Kong and the mainland can be negotiated at that time, if not sooner.

When it decided its policy toward Chinese recognition about the beginning of 1950, Canada chose to follow the American rather than the British lead and to maintain relations with Nationalist China while withholding it from Peking. The Korean War, in which Canada contributed troops to the United Nations side, and the hardening of American policy toward China at that time prevented any serious consideration of change. China and Canada began to become important to each other in 1961, when China inaugurated grain imports and Canada was in a position to supply wheat. This it did on such a scale that it reportedly had to refill its stockpiles from American sources, so that American wheat apparently flowed to China indirectly. Prime Minister Pierre Elliott Trudeau visited China in 1960, several years before becoming Prime Minister, and was apparently favorably impressed. Probably in part for this reason, and because in recent years China has shown a tendency to favor Australia over Canada when making grain purchases, Canada began about the end of 1968 to explore the possibility of establishing diplomatic relations with Peking without breaking them with Taipei. To judge by past experience, the probabilities were overwhelmingly in favor of failure, so that Canada would have to choose one or the other. In that case, its choice would be Peking. On the other hand, if Peking should change its previous practice to the extent of tolerating a Canadian "two Chinas" policy, this would be a development of major importance even if Taipei refused to cooperate.

There is considerably more fear and antagonism in Australia toward China than in Canada. The White Australia policy is thought to be imperiled by China, and Australian security appears threatened by Communist subversion in Southeast Asia. The Chinese nuclear weapons program has created some alarm in Australia. There is a feeling that China may have been antagonized by Australian military action in Malaysia and Vietnam. And yet, in spite of all this nervousness, there has been surprisingly little Chinese propaganda or other activity that could be considered directly hostile to Australia. It is possible that this forbearance is related to Chinese purchases of Autralian grain, but there is probably a deeper and more serious reason. In 1942, when Southeast Asia had been overrun by the Japanese, Australia served as a major American military base, and something of the same sort might happen again. More specifically, Peking may see reason to fear that as the American military presence elsewhere in Asia is presumably reduced "after Vietnam," the United States might decide to seek Australian permission to emplace intercontinental missiles to help contain China. Sites in Australia would have the important advantage over sites in the United States from the American viewpoint that the missiles would not have to overfly Soviet territory on the way to their targets. It is sensible for Peking to do nothing to unnecessarily increase Australian antagonism.

New Zealand is of course much less important to China than Australia, except that its Communist Party has a pro-Chinese leadership. To many New Zealanders, however, China seems as great a threat for the future as it does to Australians.

WESTERN EUROPE

For obvious ideological reasons, Peking feels a basic hostility toward the governments of Western Europe and expresses it whenever the latter take some "reactionary" step at home or abroad. On the other hand, Peking keeps this hostility within some bounds because it is even more concerned to combat American and Soviet influence in Western Europe. Any effort by the United States to strengthen Western European unity, revive NATO, or the like is met with Chinese accusations that American domination of Europe is the object. China's major embassies in Western Europe are those at Bern, The Hague, and Paris, and much of its diplomatic activity in the region is conducted from these centers. Since 1961, as already indicated, China has regarded Western Europe as an important source of capital equipment and technological contacts. In party matters, Peking has to face the fact that the orthodox Communist parties of Western Europe are pro-Soviet with respect to the Sino-Soviet dispute, in spite of the shock administered by the Soviet invasion of Czechoslovakia. Since about 1963, therefore, Peking has encouraged and supported the emergence of pro-Chinese "Marxist-Leninist" parties and splinter groups; the only one of any real importance, however, has been the one in Belgium, and it has largely lost its standing in Peking's eyes since the beginning of the Cultural Revolution because its leader, Jacques Grippa, was considered sympathetic to Liu Shao-ch'i. At present, a more promising avenue for Chinese revolutionary activity is the more loosely organized student protest movements. In addition to propaganda incitement, Peking gave some financial and other support to the student demonstrations in Paris in May 1968, which had the specific attraction that they seriously embarrassed the French government at a time when it was sponsoring the talks between the United States and North Vietnam, to which the Maoists in Peking strongly objected.

In 1962, after President de Gaulle had established at least a minimal political respectability in Chinese eyes by conceding independence to Algeria, Peking began to propose the establishment of diplomatic relations. This was a time shortly before the Cuban missile crisis, when it appeared that the United States and the Soviet Union might be about to reach a test ban agreement; China was probably interested in establishing relations with a power whose leader had similar ideas on the subject of nuclear weapons to its own. The actual signing of the test ban treaty in the summer of 1963 intensified de Gaulle's "Yalta complex" (France had not been represented at the Yalta Conference) and consequently his interest in relations with China as a counterweight. Another motive was his irritation at Soviet objections to his dealings with West Germany and his desire to annoy Moscow in retaliation. Finally among his major probable motives, he wanted to play a prominent role in working out a settlement in Indochina and considered that Chinese cooperation would be essential in that connection. He hoped to be able to maintain his diplomatic relations with Nationalist China as well. Peking refrained from making an issue of this, probably because it reasoned that Taipei would break relations with Paris. But when French recognition of Peking was announced on January 27, 1964, Taipei hesitated, apparently because of American advice against hasty action. Peking then had to make it clear that France could not have relations with both Chinas and thus maneuvered de Gaulle into breaking relations with Taipei.

Apart from giving China a valuable diplomatic and political base in Paris, Sino-French diplomatic relations have not produced much in the way of results. Trade between them, for example, has not grown as fast or to the level reached by China's trade with West Germany, with which it has no diplomatic relations. The responsibility for this state of affairs seems to lie on the Chinese side, and the corresponding disappointment on the French. The main reason is probably the radicalization of Chinese policy during the last few years, which tended to make de Gaulle's basic political objectionability seem more serious than before. In addition, Peking is probably irritated at his occasional overtures to the Soviet Union, his ineffectiveness in Vietnam since the American escalation, and his role in francophone Africa.

The only other Western European country whose relations with China seem worth discussing here is West Germany, and this is a case well worth discussing. Peking is well aware of West Germany's actual economic strength and its potential military power, as well as its enormous political importance as a source of preoccupation and distraction to the Soviet Union. It appears that it is not necessary for China to do much more than it has done in order to derive benefit from West Germany's existence, unless the Soviet Union should begin to devote its primary attention to China rather than to West Germany, and that there are obstacles in the way of doing so. For one thing, Peking naturally objects to the "bourgeois" and at least formally pro-American orientation of the Bonn government. For another, diplomatic relations with Bonn, whether East Germany then broke relations with Peking or not, would tend to impair the validity of the Chinese argument that no country can have diplomatic relations with both Chinas.

On the West German side, there is some feeling, mainly on the right, that a political and diplomatic relationship with China would help in coping with the Soviet Union and promoting the reunification of Germany, to which the Soviet Union is the main obstacle. There is a still wider realization that China can have value to West Germany as a source of preoccupation and distraction to the Soviet Union; this seems to have happened, for example, in 1964, when Khrushchev was preparing to improve his relations with Bonn, apparently as a preliminary to devoting his main attention to his Chinese problem. To many West Germans, it seems advisable not to irritate the Soviet Union by making a major overt move in China's direction as long as there appears to be any chance of improving relations with Moscow; such was the thinking during the heyday of the West German Ostpolitik, which until the invasion of Czechoslovakia aimed at improving West German relations with Eastern Europe as a future bridge to the Soviet Union. Another important consideration is the attitude of the United States, but if Washington should try seriously to establish diplomatic relations with Peking Bonn, which lacks the complication of relations with Taipei, would probably be glad to follow suit.

Early in 1964, following three years of rapid growth in Sino-German trade, representatives of both sides met for secret talks at Bern. The Germany side was interested mainly in a formal trade and consular agreement, to include the Berlin clause (in other words, a recognition of West Berlin as a part of West Germany for the purposes of the agreement). The Chinese side was basically willing not only to meet these desires but, according to some (non-West German) sources, to go so far as to establish diplomatic relations. If so, the German side reserved judgment on the latter proposal; loud East German complaints, during the spring of 1964, of betrayal by China in favor of West Germany suggest that Peking may in fact have offered Bonn a diplomatic relationship, perhaps to punish Ulbricht for his support of Khrushchev in the Sino-Soviet dispute. In any case, Bonn dropped the whole idea a few months later, to the disappointment of some industrial interests in West Germany, when it became clear that the United States objected to any sort of agreement between Bonn and Peking, especially in an election year. The only new development that might have been considered an outcome of the Sino-German talks was the establishment of a New China News Agency office in Bonn at the end of 1964.

Trade between China and West Germany continued to grow, and early in 1966 it was announced that a German consortium called Demag would build a large steel plant in China. The German answer to American criticisms was that the plant would produce steel suitable only for civilian, not military, purposes. The project soon ran into serious difficulties because of American objections to the guaranteeing of a long-term credit by the West German government to enable China to pay for the equipment, and still more on account of the confusion caused by the Cultural Revolution. By 1967, a year in which China's trade with West Germany as well as with other countries fell off slightly, it appeared that the Demag project was dead. It is not clear whether recent reports of its revival have any foundation.

In recent months, and especially since the setback to the Ostpolitik administered by the Soviet invasion of Czechoslovakia, Moscow has been alleging with apparent seriousness that West Germany and China are colluding against it. Some of the specific Soviet charges, like the one that West German scientists are helping China with its nuclear weapons program, are almost certainly false. What probably lies behind the Soviet concern is a fear that West Germany might benefit, at least indirectly, from a growing Soviet preoccupation with China resulting from such things as the Chinese nuclear weapons program and the Sino-Soviet border dispute. West Germany, for its part, may be trying to salvage something from the setback of 1968 to its *Ostpolitik* by extracting concessions from Moscow through hints of willingness to deal with China, among other things. It is an interesting fact that since about the end of 1968 Moscow has shown a more conciliatory attitude toward Bonn in some respects. It is not yet clear, however, how much credit China can reasonably claim for this development, or what benefits if any it may be able to extract for itself by playing some sort of West German card in its dealings with the Soviet Union. It is not likely to get very much unless NATO begins to dissolve or for some other reason West Germany becomes convinced that it cannot count on American protection. In that case Bonn, which has far more reason to fear a war with the Soviet Union than does Paris, might well follow the French example by trying to establish a diplomatic and political relationship with Peking.

PART THREE

CHAPTER XII

Foreign Policy Since the Cultural Revolution

IN FOREIGN POLICY as well as in domestic affairs, it was a fortunate thing for Peking that the Cultural Revolution came to an end in the second half of 1968. The virtual paralysis of creative policy making that it entailed would have been a serious drawback under the external conditions that arose at that time. Those conditions were not among the original causes of the decision to terminate the Cultural Revolution, but they probably accelerated the process of termination. In turn, the end of the Cultural Revolution opened the way to some dramatic and important shifts in Chinese foreign policy, of which the most spectacular symbol to date has been President Nixon's visit (February 21–28, 1972). It is not true that, as Peking has characteristically insisted, China's policy has remained constant and it is only others who have changed.

THE END OF THE CULTURAL REVOLUTION

The termination of the Cultural Revolution stemmed from a series of decisions taken by Mao and his advisers, beginning in late

July 1968, to eliminate the Red Guards as a political force and to restore the party and its apparatus as the leading element of the political system. It was to be a party, however, that differed from its pre-Cultural Revolution forerunner in being even more loyal to Mao's "thought" (outwardly, at least) and in being to a great extent under the control of military commanders at the regional and provincial levels. Accordingly, the list of provincial Revolutionary Committees (new model provincial governments) was completed in early September 1968, the Red Guard units were forcibly broken up at about the same time, and two years later the formation of new provincial Party Committees was begun.

Near the beginning of this shift, which was far more important and complex than this necessarily brief summary suggests, there was a traumatic external development in the shape of the Soviet invasion of Czechoslovakia (August 21, 1968) and the proclamation soon afterward of the so-called Brezhnev Doctrine, which seemed to assert a Soviet right to intervene forcibly in any other "socialist" country if "socialism" as defined in Moscow was judged to be endangered.

As the time for the repeatedly postponed Ninth Party Congress, which was to legitimate the political order bequeathed by the Cultural Revolution, approached, a policy debate evidently took place in Peking over the proper method of coping with the Soviet threat. One side, probably led by Chou En-lai, apparently argued that ambassadorial contacts with the United States (which had been suspended since May 1968) should be re-established, and that ambassadors should be sent back to at least some of the countries with which China had diplomatic relations, as a political restraint on Moscow. The other side, probably led by Lin Piao, argued that the classic Maoist dual adversary strategy of simultaneous political and ideological struggle, with military overtones, against both American "imperialism" and Soviet "revisionism" (or "social-imperialism") must be maintained and would suffice on both fronts; there was no need for diplomatic gestures, toward the United States at any rate. With Mao's ultimate support, the second viewpoint prevailed, and a session of the Sino-American ambassadorial talks that had been scheduled for February 20, 1969, was cancelled almost at the last minute. More important, Lin Piao seems to have decided to dramatize the dual adversary strategy and create what he regarded as an appropriately militant atmosphere for the forthcoming Ninth Party Congress, at which he (the first military man to gain a comparable distinction in any Communist Party) was scheduled to be proclaimed Mao's heir as party leader, by means of a staged incident. Annoyed by an intensification of Soviet patrolling along the Manchurian border but apparently convinced that Moscow was effectively distracted by a "minicrisis" then in progress over West Berlin, he arranged, on March 2, 1969, an ambush of a Soviet patrol on a disputed island (known to the Chinese as Chenpao, to the Russians as Damansky) in the Ussuri River, which flows between Manchuria and the Maritime Province of the Soviet Far East. Overwhelming Soviet retaliation on the same island, on March 15, led to a final postponement of the Ninth Party Congress to April 1, by which time a shift in Soviet policy had produced indications that Moscow preferred negotiation to fighting and would therefore not try to pre-empt the Chinese Ninth Party Congress by force as it had pre-empted the Czechoslovak Fourteenth Party Congress by the invasion of the previous year. In retrospect, it appears that March 15, 1969, marks the beginning of Lin Piao's decline, a process that was to require two and one-half years.

This result was not immediately apparent, however, for Lin delivered the main report at the Ninth Party Congress (April 1–28, 1969) and was named as Mao's heir in the new party constitution adopted by the congress. The foreign policy section of Lin's report was a ringing reaffirmation of Maoist fundamentalism, including the dual adversary strategy, but it did indicate that Peking was not seriously demanding the return of all territory allegedly taken by Russia from China (actually, the Manchu Empire). It would have been dangerous to leave this important point in the obscurity that earlier Chinese statements on the Sino-Soviet territorial dispute had thrown over it.

THE NORMALIZATION OF EXTERNAL RELATIONS

The end of the Cultural Revolution alone would have been sufficient to produce a trend toward normalization of China's external relations—the sending of ambassadors back to countries with which

Peking already had diplomatic relations, for example. But given the Soviet threat and other new developments discussed below, Peking has capitalized on the good will toward China present nearly everywhere to push normalization far beyond the pre-Cultural Revolution stage. The most important and difficult aspect of the process, the improvement of relations with the United States, is a matter of such significance that a separate section will be devoted to it.

The return of ambassadors—different individuals in nearly every case from those recalled during the Cultural Revolution—to Peking's embassies abroad began in mid-May 1969, shortly after the end of the Ninth Party Congress. They went first to countries with which China's relations were either close (as with Albania) or important (as with France, given its key role from March 1969 as intermediary between China and the United States). A few non-Communist countries with which China's relations were strained, notably India and Indonesia, were not sent ambassadors. Nor was the Mongolian People's Republic (Outer Mongolia), alone among the Communist countries, presumably because it not only supported the Soviet Union strongly in the Sino-Soviet dispute but provided bases for Soviet forces threatening China.

More important, Peking succeeded in establishing diplomatic relations (by the end of 1971) with about thirty Western and Third World countries beginning with Canada (in October 1970). In none of these cases did Peking permit the other country to continue any formal relationship with the Republic of China on Taiwan, but it was somewhat flexible as to the degree to which it insisted on recognition by the other country of its sovereignty over Taiwan.

One of the main features of Peking's normalization campaign has been an increased, and ultimately successful, interest in entering the United Nations, again without essential compromise on the question of the Republic of China's representation. In this connection the establishment of diplomatic relations at the latter's expense was a useful ploy that was reflected in increased votes for Peking at the United Nations. After much maneuvering, in the course of which the United States shifted to support for Peking's representation while continuing to oppose expulsion of the Republic of China, Peking was voted in, and Taipei out, by slightly better than a two-thirds vote on October 25, 1971. Peking thus acquired an important and prestigious forum from which to propagate its post-Cultural Revolution foreign policy.

Formally and in terms of propaganda, this policy is one of continuing the dual adversary strategy of struggle against the two "superpowers" and of trying to enlist the support of the "small and medium states" by playing on their resentment of the superpowers, while continuing to support revolutionary movements anywhere that are regarded by Peking as popular and progressive. In reality, Peking has subordinated its support for revolution (without abandoning it, because it is a sacred cause and China wants to keep this option open) to its cultivation of other governments with a primarily anti-Soviet purpose—obviously in order to build political support for China against Soviet pressures and competition. In fact, although not in theory or in its propaganda, Peking has begun to climb down from the dual adversary strategy and has begun to "tilt" in the direction of the United States as the best potentially available counterweight to the Soviet Union.

The reality, as distinct from the appearance, of the new policy evidently reflects the external aspect of Premier Chou En-lai's "game plan." The latter's domestic aspect, which may be even more important both in his eyes and in fact, has involved the elimination of Lin Piao, an effort to reduce the political influence of the army (and in particular of Lin's faction within it), the modernization of the conventional forces along lines suitable for territorial defense in addition to their partial depoliticization, and the strengthening of the new (post-Cultural Revolution) party and state machinery under Chou's personal guidance. For his purpose Chou finds the Soviet Union, with its massive conventional power (about 40 divisions) poised near China's borders, a more appropriate and useful threat than the United States, whose threat to China has been largely nuclear. But that is not to say that, either in Chou's eyes or in reality, the Soviet threat is not a real one or that Peking's improving relations with the United States do not serve an authentic and important external purpose as well as a domestic one.

THE SINO-SOVIET CRUNCH

During the months following the Ussuri clashes of March 1969, the Soviet Union rapidly built up its forces along and near the

Chinese border, staged a series of border incidents, and strongly implied in both overt and covert statements that unless Peking agreed to hold formal talks on the territorial issue it might be subjected to invasion or the destruction of its nuclear installations, or both. On the Chinese side, the management of this formidable threat rested largely with Chou En-lai, who appears to have been under considerable political pressure from Maoist fundamentalists (although not necessarily from Mao himself) not to negotiate with the "social-imperialists." The external pressures proved stronger than the domestic, and on September 11, 1969, two days before the expiration of a June 13 Soviet ultimatum of sorts on the question of border talks, Chou held discussions at the Peking airport with Premier Kosygin. Partly as a sop to the Maoist fundamentalists, the Chinese public was prodded into a prolonged and intensive campaign of "war preparedness" (stockpiling of supplies, contstruction of air raid shelters, etc.), which would unquestionably be useful in the increasingly unlikely event of a Soviet or other foreign attack and would therefore presumably help to deter such an attack.

Beginning on October 20, 1969, and at intervals since, Sino-Soviet talks on the border question have been held at the Deputy Foreign Minister level in Peking. In late 1970, ambassadors were exchanged and a trade agreement was signed, as at least an indirect result of the border talks. Apart from occasional, rather implausible, leaks by each side designed to prove its own reasonableness and the other's unreasonableness, the border talks have proceeded in strict secrecy. As far as can be determined from the outside, there has been some progress toward an agreement on certain disputed sectors of the border (Peking claims that in certain areas the Soviet Union has inherited or occupied territory beyond what was conceded by the original "unequal treaties" imposed by tsarist Russia in the nineteenth century). On the other hand, there appears to be a deadlock over the Chinese demands for a formal cease-fire and a mutual troop withdrawal from the de facto border, as well as complete evacuation by both sides of disputed areas, and for the incorporation into the hypothetical boundary treaty of a Soviet admission in principle that the original treaties were "unequal" and therefore basically invalid, even though Peking is not claiming the return of the territories conceded under them to Russia.

Although the Soviet Union would like a formal acceptance by Peking of essentially the current de facto border, it also appears to see some advantage in keeping the issue alive under an umbrella of superior Soviet military power. This is particularly so since the announcement in July 1969 of the Nixon Doctrine, which strongly implied a progressive American decontainment of China. For the Soviet Union, as it has boasted informally on occasion, has been trying to keep Peking pinned to the Sino-Soviet border, so to speak, as a means of distracting it from any possible effort to fill the partial vacuum being created in Asia by American disengagement from the area. Moscow seems to intend to fill that vacuum itself if possible, although it has some serious handicaps to overcome, and it is competing vigorously with Peking for influence in virtually all parts of Asia, with emphasis naturally on the more important areas such as Japan, Indochina, and the South Asian subcontinent. In June 1969, in an obvious bid for influence of this kind, Brezhnev rather vaguely proposed a collective security system for Asia, including China. As yet this trial balloon has won very little support in Asia, and like any other initiative by Brezhnev, who is especially obnoxious in Chinese eyes, it has been loudly denounced in Chinese propaganda. Peking claims to see, and probably does see to a considerable extent, Soviet activity anywhere in Asia as aimed at "encircling" China; as already suggested, there is some truth in this perception. There is little doubt that managing the Soviet threat along the border and Soviet competition in third areas, notably Asia, remain the most urgent preoccupations of Chinese foreign policy. It is for this reason, although not for this reason alone, that Peking has sought to improve its relations with the United States.

THE OPENING TO THE UNITED STATES

The recent striking developments in Sino-American relations would almost certainly have been impossible before 1969, that is, before Peking became seriously alarmed by the Soviet threat and before the United States made a firm and formal decision to reduce its military role in Asia, Indochina in particular. Both these points deserve further elaboration.

The substantive aspect of the Soviet threat has already been discussed, but it should be added that Peking has not been in a position to talk about the problem in this way in public, or for that matter even in its private talks with American officials. For one thing, pride forbids an acknowledgment of such fear. Secondly, acknowledgment would confer undesirable bargaining leverage on the United States. Thirdly, such talk might alarm Moscow sufficiently to precipitate the very Soviet attack that Peking is seeking urgently to avoid. Peking does not want, and would not get if it did, an anti-Soviet alliance or nuclear guarantee from the United States; a political relationship sufficient to give Moscow pause is what seems to be desired, and it appears to be in process of achievement. It is true, however, that in 1969 Moscow privately asked the United States what its reaction would be to a Soviet destruction of China's nuclear installations and was strongly discouraged; the American attitude probably played a part in Moscow's decision not to attack China.

As a matter of principle, and on account of its delicate relations with Hanoi and its own concern over the presence of American forces near its southern border, Peking has felt that it had to insist that any real improvement of Sino-American relations was contingent on a prior indication of firm and sincere American intent to de-escalate the war in Indochina and withdraw American forces. Since it was President Nixon's intention, on assuming office in January 1969, to do exactly that, as well as to seek a better relationship with China, Peking eventually became convinced. The main setback, the intrusion of American ground forces into Cambodia in the spring of 1970, proved to be a temporary one. The conclusive argument in Peking's eyes seems to have been the willingness of the United States to accept a defeat of South Vietnamese forces in southern Laos in February–March 1971 rather than inject its own ground forces into the struggle there. When Chou En-lai went to Hanoi in early March, he undoubtedly hoped to take credit for China for having deterred such an escalation, but he also probably told the North Vietnamese that Peking now regarded Nixon's performance regarding Indochina as sufficiently acceptable so that it would now begin to reciprocate openly to the overtures that he had been making for the previous two years.

Since before the beginning of his administration, President Nixon had regarded an improvement of relations with China as highly desirable and as an essential concomitant to his parallel objective of reducing American involvement in Indochina and the rest of Asia. He believed, correctly, that there had been a tendency in the United States to overestimate Chinese "expansionism" and therefore the Chinese "threat" to Asia. But even if that had not been so, it would still have seemed advisable to seek a better relationship with Peking, if only to discourage it from trying to fill whatever vacuum the United States might leave in Asia as it disengaged and from increasing the level of its support to Asian "people's wars." One of the assumptions underlying the Nixon Doctrine was that Asian countries are basically capable of handling internal threats to their security on their own, as Indonesia had done in 1965. Accordingly, Nixon communicated privately to Peking through a variety of intermediaries, beginning in March 1969 with President de Gaulle, his desire to visit China and otherwise improve Sino-American relations. From the middle of 1969 he began, and continued over a period of about two years, to reduce almost to zero restrictions on travel to and nonstrategic trade with the mainland of China by American citizens. At the end of 1969 he suspended the Seventh Fleet's Taiwan Strait patrol, an act of no military importance but of considerable symbolic significance in Peking's eyes.

For reasons already indicated, Peking gave few overt signs of reciprocation at first. In mid-December 1969, however, it indicated an interest in resuming the suspended ambassadorial talks at Warsaw, two sessions of which were accordingly held, on January 20 and February 20, 1970. There is reason to believe that during these sessions Peking indicated an interest in having President Nixon visit China. The timetable of Sino-American rapprochement was thrown into disarray for a time, however, by the Cambodian crisis; an ambassadorial session in Warsaw scheduled for May 20, 1970, was cancelled by the Chinese side, and on that date Mao issued a strong personal statement denouncing the United States and urging intensified revolutionary struggle against it by the "people" everywhere. After the withdrawal of American ground forces from Cambodia at the end of June, the rapprochement got under way again, once more with the help of intermediaries from third countries. Around the end of the year, Mao indicated to the American journalist Edgar Snow a definite willingness to receive Nixon. The invitation, still controversial in China, was made sufficiently firm during the celebrated secret visit to Peking by presidential adviser Henry Kissinger (July 9–11, 1971) so that it was announced by both sides shortly after Kissinger's visit. Meanwhile, Peking had characteristically moved to parallel these formal contacts with a campaign of "people's diplomacy" aimed at easing fundamentalist reservations in China about the U.S. contacts and at impressing American public opinion and thereby putting pressure on the United States government. In April 1971 Peking invited an American table tennis team to visit China and began to play host to a series of American journalists, radical student groups, etc.

Apart from gaining propaganda advantages in these and similar ways and securing at least indirect support from the United States against the Soviet Union, Peking hoped to exploit American eagerness for help with a political settlement in Vietnam and a release of American prisoners, preferably before the American election of November 1972. Peking had to be careful not to let its relations with the United States develop in such a way as to produce an open dispute with the perennially suspicious leadership in Hanoi. Even if it had wanted to, which it did not, Peking would have been in no position to "deliver" Hanoi in exchange, say, for American concessions on Taiwan. Like Hanoi, Peking wants all American forces out of Indochina, an end to Vietnamization, and leftward changes in the composition of the currently non-Communist Indochinese governments. Where Peking differs from Hanoi is that it feels little enthusiasm for the idea of the unification of Vietnam under Hanoi's control, probably because such an outcome would make a more powerful rival in mainland Southeast Asia out of what is already in some ways a troublesome partner.

Of greater real importance to Peking than Indochina, as long as the latter does not become the source of a direct threat to Chinese security, is the continuing issue of Taiwan. The essence of Peking's demands on the United States in this connection has long been an insistence on complete American military withdrawal and on repudiation of the concept of "two Chinas" through the recognition of the Taiwan question as an internal Chinese one in which neither the United States nor any other foreign power (Japan in particular) should interfere. In addition, Peking demands that the United States give no support to any movement for independence for the indigenous Taiwanese (or Formosans). It was well understood in Washington that at least token, and probably more than token, concessions to Peking's stand on Taiwan would have to be made if the Nixonian opening to Peking was to bear useful fruit. And yet it was hoped to find a way to do so without seeming to betray the Republic of China or further weakening the confidence of the United States' other Asian allies, already somewhat shaken by the Nixon Doctrine. In reality, such a feat was to prove impossible. The Republic of China was of course greatly alarmed, and the Japanese government was outraged at not being consulted in advance on this major shift in American China policy, as Washington had earlier promised to do.

Japan is a problem of enormous importance in Sino-American relations as well as in many other contexts; a separate section is devoted below to Peking's current policy toward it. Here it is sufficient to say that Peking wants to give Washington a higher sense of stake in good relations with China than in good relations with Japan and to discourage the United States from promoting in any way any trend toward Japanese rearmament or Japanese self-assertion in Asia. The importance of these problems is only slightly more obvious than the difficulty for Peking of working out any effective arrangement with the United States for their solution.

Korea is important to Peking as an area lying between China and Japan. As with Indochina, Peking wants American forces and military aid programs removed. But in this case Peking loudly supports the unification—peaceful, it insists—of the country under North Korean control. Probably the reason is that a Communist Korea would not be a serious rival for Peking, and that a non-Communist South Korea abandoned by the United States would be a vacuum that Japan would probably tend to fill.

Such appear to be the major items of concern to Peking in its recent and current dealings with the United States.

THE REPERCUSSIONS

Of the powers whose reaction to the Sino-American rapprochement could be troublesome to the two parties, the most important is obviously the Soviet Union. The Soviet reaction has been a complex affair, but it can be said in brief that Moscow has felt concern and has intensified its anti-Chinese program while somewhat moderating its behavior toward the United States. This Soviet behavior in turn has created concern in Peking and appears to have played a part in recent domestic Chinese political developments. Two aspects of the intensive and widespread program of Soviet diplomatic activity that occurred during the summer and autumn of 1971 seem to have been of special concern to Peking: the Soviet-Indian friendship treaty of August 9, which was clearly designed among other things to deter possible Chinese intervention in the escalating crisis between India and Pakistan; and the four-power agreement of September 3 on West Berlin, which seemed to free the Soviet Union from preoccupation in the west to devote greater attention to its China problem. Parallel with this diplomatic offensive went a series of high-level and unusually strong Soviet propaganda attacks on China, one of whose themes was anger at alleged Chinese obstructionism in the border talks.

If Moscow was concerned over the impending Nixon visit to China, elements within China were hardly less so. Chief among these appears to have been Lin Piao, who evidently clung to the dual adversary strategy and opposed the opening to the United States. As already indicated, Lin was probably scheduled already by Chou En-lai for elimination on domestic grounds. Lin's objections to the opening to the United States strengthened the case against him, since it could be plausibly argued that he was endangering the country by trying to obstruct its best chance for security against the Soviet menace in its seemingly enhanced current form. In addition, Lin was personally objectionable to Moscow for a number of reasons, one of them being his alleged responsibility for the clash of March 2, 1969, on the Ussuri River; his removal, it could be argued, would help therefore to defuse Sino-Soviet tension. It was probably on the basis of some such case as this that Chou En-lai succeeded, after careful preparation and with Mao's approval, in ousting Lin from his various posts, evidently on September 11–12, 1971. The plausibility of this analysis is not necessarily impaired by the fact that the rather esoteric official propaganda case against Lin since his fall has included the charge that he was pro-Soviet, as well as anti-Mao; such charges, however implausible, have been made against most high-level candidates for the memory hole in China in recent years.

Further preparations for the Nixon visit could then proceed; Dr. Kissinger visited China again for this purpose in late October. On the Chinese side, the slight advance publicity given the Nixon visit was one of the signs that the visit remained controversial. On the American side, the enormous publicity for the visit reflected an official desire to make the greatest possible favorable impact on the American voter.

The fact that the presidential visit occurred at all was in itself bound to improve the climate of Sino-American relations and pave the way for future contacts; this was probably its most important achievement. More concrete gains were hard to find, at least on the American side. The Chinese side had skillfully enhanced President Nixon's sense of stake in the outcome, and thereby probably increased his willingness to make concessions (in addition to quieting criticism of the visit in China) by giving him an early and unscheduled interview with Mao Tse-tung. For reasons already indicated, the American side was fairly forthcoming on Taiwan. It committed itself in the final communiqué eventually to withdraw all its forces from Taiwan and indicated elsewhere that it would meanwhile maintain only about 2,000 men on the island (as leverage on Peking to confine itself to peaceful approaches to both Taiwan and Indochina). The United States also stated that it did not "oppose" the Chinese view that Taiwan is a part of China, and refrained from inserting in the communiqué a reference to its defensive obligations to the Republic of China. In short, the American side went a considerable distance toward accepting Peking's position on Taiwan. Other portions of the communiqué appear to be of minor importance, except as atmospherics, by comparison with those just mentioned. It appears to be true that, as both sides have insisted, no secret agreements were reached during the presidential visit. After their conclusion, the negotiations were treated in the Chinese media as a great success for Peking's diplomacy and a personal political triumph for Chou En-lai.

PEKING AND JAPAN

Since the end of 1969 Peking's anti-Japanese propaganda, much of it for American consumption, has reached levels rarely if ever attained before. The charges center on an alleged rapid revival of Japanese "militarism" and "imperialism" that is in fact not occurring and does not seem likely to occur. What is the explanation?

Most Chinese have an understandable dislike of Japan based on the history of Japanese aggression against China. Since past phases of Japanese expansion have tended to begin with moves against Korea and Taiwan, Peking was angered and somewhat alarmed when in November 1969, in an important statement issued jointly by President Nixon and Japanese Premier Eisaku Sato, Japan acknowledged an interest in the security of South Korea and Taiwan. This statement indicated nothing more than Japanese willingness to cooperate, logistically for the most part, with the United States if the latter should have to fulfill its treaty commitments to the defense of those areas, but it was bound to have a sinister ring in Peking's ears.

Even though Japan spends less on armaments than China does, and even though it is currently planning to acquire no strategic weapons systems with which it could attack China even if it wished, the Chinese elite in varying degrees is concerned over Japan's remarkable economic resurgence and the growth of its Self Defense Forces. In some of his recent interviews with foreigners, Chou En-lai has showed, however, that he understands that if there is a Japanese threat it is a matter for the future rather than a present reality.

Whether or not a Japanese threat to China actually exists, it may be that Peking would have to allege one in any case. For the Chinese Communists have long built their domestic and foreign propaganda, and to a considerable extent their policies as well, around a foreign demon figure. It was mainly Japan until 1945. By 1949 it was already becoming the United States, which was joined after 1960 by the Soviet Union. Since 1969, however, the United States has tended to lose its credibility as a demon, and it has appeared prudent, at least to Chou En-lai although not to all his colleagues, to avoid provoking the Soviet Union unnecessarily by denouncing it in ways capable of evoking a response more damaging than propaganda blasts. Under these circumstances, Japan is virtually the ideal candidate for the role of principal demon. In addition, Chou has tried to justify the opening to the United States to doubting colleagues by arguing that the opening will help to split the United States from Japan, which is alleged to be in the process of becoming the main threat to China. In reality, Chou is trying to use the United States to balance and restrain the Soviet Union more than to help cope with Japan, but as already indicated it would be risky to say so publicly.

China and Japan have long been rivals in Asia, and they are likely to remain so. Chinese anti-Japanese propaganda is intended among other things to capitalize on the widespread anti-Japanese feeling in Asia, especially in North Korea, and to help weaken Japan by tending to split it from the United States and the Republic of China. To a considerable extent, Peking's current strategy of carrot and stick, with emphasis on the latter, in dealing with Japan appears to be aimed at convincing Tokyo of the unwisdom of trying to extend its influence as the United States retreats under the Nixon Doctrine, and to emphasize the advantages of preferring good relations with Peking on Chinese terms. Among the likely future issues between China and Japan are predominance over the East China Sea continental shelf and its possibly large oil deposits, and sovereignty over the disputed Tiao Yü T'ai Islands (known as the Senkaku by the Japanese), which are on the continental shelf but are claimed by Japan as part of the Ryukyus (which are not on the continental shelf). There might also be a serious dispute over Taiwan itself, in the event that its government, in an effort to remain separate from the mainland and in view of American disengagement, either sought or accepted protection from Japan.

Peking is clearly trying to take advantage of the growing unpopularity of Premier Sato, who is due to leave office during 1972, and by denouncing him and cultivating other Japanese factions and parties to contribute to a more pro-Peking policy on the part of his successor. Success in this is practically assured, for a time at least, particularly now that the United States has set an example of sorts for Japan, since virtually all major Japanese political figures favor trying to achieve a better relationship with Peking. On the basis of Chinese statements, it appears that Peking wants a reduction of Japanese ties with the United States and of Japanese trade with Taiwan and South Korea, a cancellation of Tokyo's peace treaty of 1952 with the Republic of China, and of course no further rearmament. In return, Chou En-lai has held out the lure of a Chinese forgoing of reparations from Japan (Peking has not actually been claiming any) and the signing of a nonaggression pact and an agreement on mutual nonuse of nuclear weapons. Sino-Japanese trade has reached an annual level of about US$1 billion, both ways, a figure that is a much higher percentage of China's total external trade than of Japan's. Accordingly, China has less economic leverage on Japan than the other way round, but Peking has been allowed by various private and semiofficial Japanese negotiators to get away with attaching political conditions, sometimes of an insulting nature, to trade agreements. It is possible that if Peking continues to take a haughty line as Japan seeks friendlier relations with it, Japanese pride will reassert itself with unfortunate results for China.

PEKING'S OTHER PROBLEM AREAS

Peking's Indochina policy seeks to avoid any genuine risk of a clash with the United States while engaging in political and propaganda pressures toward American military withdrawal from Asia. There is still political rivalry with Hanoi for influence in Indochina, but Peking is determined not to allow this rivalry to escalate to the level of an open dispute, especially while Hanoi enjoys the prestige that its conduct of the war has won for it in many quarters. Peking had a major windfall as a result of the Cambodian crisis in the spring of 1970. The deposed Prince Sihanouk sought and was granted asylum in China, where he remains to this day as the nominal head of a leftist government in exile. With him as a pawn, Peking managed to play host somewhere in China (probably at Canton) on April 24–25, 1970, to a "summit conference of the Indochinese peoples" at which North Vietnam and the left wing movements of South Vietnam (the National Liberation Front) and Laos (the Pathet Lao) were represented in addition to Sihanouk's regime. Peking's position was especially strong at that time because North Vietnam was virtually at war with the new Lon Nol government of Cambodia, largely because the latter was playing on popular hostility to Vietnamese influence (mainly due to the Vietnamese community living in Cambodia and to North Vietnamese military bases near the South Vietnamese border) as a means of countering the popularity of the deposed Prince Sihanouk among the masses. Peking accordingly stepped into the breach by undertaking secret negotiations with the Lon Nol government for continuation of the North Vietnamese bases, for which in the past all major figures in the Cambodian elite, Lon Nol as well as Sihanouk, have been liberally paid by Hanoi. The invasion of the base area by American and South Vietnamese troops at the end of April rendered any such deal impossible and led on May 5 to Chinese recognition of Sihanouk's regime, rather than Lon Nol's, as the government of Cambodia. At that time the new government in Phnom Penh closed the routes by which Chinese supplies had been moving from the Cambodian coast to the bases and into the hands of the Viet Cong in the Mekong delta. Peking's independent access to the revolutionary movements in Cambodia (as distinct from Sihanouk's government in exile) and South Vietnam having thus been considerably reduced, it has had to cooperate somewhat more closely with North Vietnam on the ground; by the end of 1970, Chinese military advisers had entered Cambodia, evidently from Laos and by arrangement with the North Vietnamese military authorities in that area. In Laos itself, Chinese military engineers have been building the so-called China Road across northwest Laos in the direction of the northern tip of Thailand, presumably to balance North Vietnamese and American influence in Laos as a whole and to facilitate pressures on Thailand; the road has not been extended to the border beyond the Mekong, however, probably in order not to alarm the Thai government unduly at a time when Peking is trying to exploit its concern over the implications of the Nixon Doctrine to promote a shift toward neutralism.

By all odds the most important crisis in Asia in 1971 was the Indo-Pakistani confrontation over Bangla Desh (formerly East Pakistan). Peking was anxious not to see a breakup of Pakistan as a result of internal "fissiparous tendencies" (a favorite South Asian term) intensified by external pressures, because this would reduce Pakistan's value as a counterweight to India and might set a tempting precedent for Soviet intervention in China's border areas. Although Peking clearly disapproved of the appalling behavior of the Pakistani army in Bangla Desh after March 1971, it regarded this as an internal Pakistani issue in which no outside power had any right to intervene; as it indicated in a statement of April 11, it considered the obvious Indian sympathy for Bangla Desh and Soviet support for the Indian stand as amounting to such intervention. Peking itself rejected some private approaches from the Bangla Desh leadership. Alarmed by the anti-Chinese overtones of the Soviet-Indian friendship treaty of August 9, paralyzed by fear of Soviet counterpressure along the Sino-Soviet border, and later largely sealed off from the subcontinent by snowfilled passes, Peking gave the Pakistani government little beyond fresh commitments of economic and (probably) military aid and propaganda support. Even the latter was timed and tailored in such a way as not to dangerously provoke the Soviet Union. The major Chinese statement on the crisis, as well as an unpublished "ultimatum" to India reminiscent of the one of 1965, was issued on December 16, when a cease-fire had just been agreed on between India and Pakistan. With little consolation beyond the thought that it had the United States as a silent partner in its defeat, Peking seemed content to wait for President Bhutto of Pakistan to give the lead on policy toward Bangla Desh.

Peking has been cultivating the leftist government of Mme. Bandaranaike in Ceylon for a number of reasons, including an anti-Indian purpose and the island's strategic location in the Indian Ocean. On the other hand, Peking has also maintained contact with various left wing revolutionary groups that oppose her government. When a "Guevarist" student rising occurred in Ceylon in April 1971, Peking was confronted with a choice between these two approaches. It promptly supported the government, denouncing the revolt, and denying any part in it. The government for its part absolved Peking of complicity and contented itself, apart from suppressing the rising with considerable severity, with expelling the recently established North Korean diplomatic mission on the ground that it had been involved in the rising. It seems possible that there had been some Chinese involvement, if not in the actual revolt then with the groups that participated in it, but if so Peking bought forgiveness through its public stand in favor of the government and a promise of further economic aid.

In the Middle East, Peking has encountered a number of recent problems and setbacks: continuing strong American and Soviet influence, an anti-Communist crackdown by the Nimeri government in the Sudan (July 1971), and the poor performance of the Palestinian guerrillas against the Jordanian army (especially in the crisis of September 1971), to say nothing of the Israeli army. In any case, the guerrillas seem to be growing somewhat disillusioned with Peking, owing to a gap between promise and performance, and Peking for its part detests hijacking, a practice to which the guerrillas are addicted. But Peking is not without assets and achievements in the region. Its support of Pakistan has given it a useful geographical and political entree. Its militantly anti-Israeli line and its opposition to any sort of negotiated settlement persist, at least overtly, in spite of an apparent Israeli desire for better relations with Peking, and make a good impression on most Arab governments and political movements. Widespread resentment of American and Soviet influence redounds to Peking's advantage on occasion. China loudly supports the demands of petroleum-producing Middle Eastern countries for higher royalties from Western oil companies. The recent wave of diplomatic recognitions by Arab countries has greatly increased the number of Peking's Middle Eastern listening posts, of which that in Beirut looks likely to become one of the most important. Egyptian President Anwar Sadat has shown just enough of a tendency toward independence of Soviet influence to give Peking some hopes in that direction. Diplomatic recognition by Turkey (August 1971) has led to a valuable Chinese air link with the Balkans. To keep its revolutionary hand in, Peking continues to support with arms and some training the guerrilla movements in the Persian Gulf area.

In Africa, Peking continues to support revolutionary movements in opposition to the governments of the White Redoubt (the Portuguese colonies, Rhodesia, and South Africa) but otherwise subordinates revolutionary activity to the cultivation, reasonably successful, of indigenous governments. A turning point in this direction appears to have been the collapse in 1968 of Biafra, which Peking supported to the best of its limited ability against the Nigerians. In East Africa, Peking's activity and influence are greatest in Tanzania, where it continues to construct the Tan-Zam Railway and missile tracking facilities on the island of Zanzibar. (It has not yet conducted a full-fledged ICBM test, however, either over the Indian Ocean or anywhere else, for a number of reasons, which apparently include a desire to avoid provoking the Soviet Union;

instead, the discrete components of the program are being tested individually within China, except when they were used to launch the two earth satellites orbited by Peking in April 1970 and March 1971.) In West Africa, the main centers of Chinese activity, including arms and training for revolutionaries from White Redoubt countries, appear to be Guinea and the tiny state of Equatorial Guinea.

In Latin America, Peking continues to focus its anti-"imperialist" propaganda on dislike of the "colossus of the north" and tries also to promote distrust of its own colossus of the north, the Soviet Union. With an eye to China's own continental shelf, Peking's propaganda endorses the claim of several Latin American countries, notably those on the Pacific side, to a 200-mile limit on their territorial waters. Peking has somewhat improved its once chilly relations with Cuba since the end of the Cultural Revolution, at least to the extent of sending an ambassador to Havana. Peking approves of the Marxist Allende government of Chile, with which it has established relations and from which it has reportedly begun to buy copper.

In Eastern Europe, Peking naturally tries to plan on anti-Soviet feeling, with much greater success in the Balkans than in the Northern Tier countries (Poland, East Germany, and Czechoslovakia). It has reminded the East Europeans, however, that it cannot give them effective support against the Soviet Union in the event of a real crunch. Although Chinese economic and military aid to Albania continues, Peking's once warm political relationship with Tirana has cooled somewhat in keeping with the decrease in Chinese militancy since the end of the Cultural Revolution and Albania's fear of a Sino-Soviet deal at its expense since the beginning of the Peking talks in October 1969. In November 1971 the Chinese party was unprecedentedly unrepresented at an Albanian party congress. Peking has encouraged Rumania and has supported that country's efforts to resist Soviet attempts to integrate it more closely into the Warsaw Pact structure and into Comecon (the Council of Economic Mutual Assistance, the rough Soviet and East European equivalent of the Common Market). Bucharest has rejected the Soviet view that the Warsaw Pact would come into operation in the event of a Sino-Soviet war. President Ceausescu was one of the intermediaries between the United States and China during the two years prior to the

Kissinger mission of July 1971. Ceausescu was evidently much impressed, during his visit to China in June 1971, with Chinese social discipline, and tried to introduce something like it into his own country. Moscow has especially resented this pro-Chinese activity on Romania's part because Rumania, unlike Yugoslavia or (since 1968) Albania, is a member of the Warsaw Pact. Peking's relations with Yugoslavia have warmed considerably since the end of the Cultural Revolution, mainly because Yugoslavia has been the object of intensive Soviet attention of the carrot-and-stick variety; in June 1971 Yugoslav Foreign Minister Mirko Tepavac paid a visit to Peking. China's relations with the Soviet-oriented regimes of the Northern Tier countries are generally chilly. In December 1970, at the time of the downfall of the Gomulka regime in Poland, Peking loudly denounced the incoming leadership of Edward Gierek as "revisionist" and as an oppressor of the Polish working class; whatever view one takes of the first of these charges, the second is clearly untrue, by East European standards at any rate.

One of the signs of post-Cultural Revolution moderation in Chinese foreign policy has been a considerably increased flexibility in dealing with the international Communist movement. This trend has been associated with the reconstruction of the Chinese party since the Cultural Revolution and with the atmosphere surrounding the celebration of its fiftieth anniversary (July 1, 1971). One of the departments of the Central Committee's Secretariat known to have been revived since the Cultural Revolution is the International Liaison Department, which deals with foreign Communist Parties and is headed by Keng Piao, a man with military and foreign affairs experience who evidently enjoys the confidence of Chou En-lai. Increased flexibility has taken the form of greater reserve toward the formerly pro-Chinese "Marxist-Leninist" splinter parties (of which there are about thirty) and friendly contacts with those "revisionist" parties (such as the Spanish Communist Party) that have repudiated Soviet leadership. In the course of these contacts, the Chinese have denied any desire to provide a model or leadership for the international Communist movement. As in other aspects of Chinese foreign policy, there is a strong anti-Soviet thrust, and Communist Parties like the French that maintain close Soviet ties still encounter Chinese hostility. Peking appears to be trying to counter Soviet efforts, such as the international conference of Communist Parties (other than pro-Chinese) held at Moscow in June 1969, to maintain some sort of hegemony over the international Communist movement; to neutralize the negative effects on many foreign Communists of certain Chinese policies such as support for Pakistan during the Bangla Desh crisis; and to explain its sensational and controversial opening to the United States.

Peking's feelings about the New Left abroad are decidedly mixed. It privately deplores the luxuriant "fissiparous tendencies" present even among the elements of the New Left that are called Maoist. It realizes that, for this reason among others, the New Left has not been very effective politically. It also appears to see an unpleasant resemblance between the New Left and various ultraleftist tendencies in China that began to be curbed in the summer of 1967 and that since the end of the Cultural Revolution have been referred to collectively and pejoratively in the Chinese press as the May 16 Group; it is likely that the case against the purged Lin Piao includes the charge that he headed this movement. On the other hand, Peking sees some value in the New Left as a source of pro-Chinese and anti-Soviet and anti-American pressures on the governments concerned. In the case of the United States in particular, Peking has been happy to benefit from the New Left's sense of affinity with it on the Indochina question.

In Western Europe, Peking tries to exploit dislike of the United States and the Soviet Union, the latter being rather widely feared as a probable source of long-term pressures. To this end Chinese propaganda has begun to endorse the Common Market as a means toward West European economic self-reliance. The country in Western Europe with which Peking has the friendliest relations is France; President de Gaulle served as the first intermediary for American overtures to Peking (March 1969), and Mao wrote an extremely sympathetic letter to Mme. de Gaulle at the time of her husband's death (November 1970). Relations with Britain, which were in a state of crisis in 1967, have improved gradually since the end of the Cultural Revolution; in March 1972 Peking agreed that each side should raise its diplomatic mission to embassy status, in return for the closing of the British consulate on Taiwan, in addition to British recognition of Taiwan as part of the CPR. West Germany continues to trade extensively with China and would probably like to establish diplomatic relations with it, but there are a number of obstacles in the way, including a German desire not to get ahead of the United States. In addition, Peking likes to curry favor with East Germany by occasionally appearing more anti-Bonn than Moscow is, and it is considerably disturbed by Moscow's efforts at détente with West Germany (notably the treaty of August 1970 and the four-power agreement of September 1971 on West Berlin), which evidently appear to Peking as an attempt to tidy up the German situation as a likely preliminary to more intensive pressures on and competition with China.

CHAPTER XIII

The Balance Sheet and the Outlook

To EVALUATE the past and estimate the future of a phenomenon as complex and rapidly changing as the foreign policy of China is a difficult if not impossible task. But it is one that the writer of a book like this can hardly avoid. For if he does not tackle it, he abandons the field to others even less qualified.

ACHIEVEMENTS

No one can reasonably deny that China's international record displays significant achievements. No century that had not displayed these would be so widely discussed, and to be discussed in this way is itself a distinction of a sort.

There is no doubt that the unity and integrity of China's national territory have been established to a degree unmatched since the late eighteenth century. The exception of Taiwan, significant though it is, weighs far more lightly on the scales than the massive fact of the relative unity of the mainland. To the extent that there is a threat to the unity and viability of the China mainland, and there is, it comes much more from domestic than from external causes.

The main threat appears to come from the aftereffects of the Cultural Revolution. But until that titanic phenomenon at any rate, China was not only united but was developing, economically, militarily, and so on, at an impressive although uneven rate. In the process, it was becoming not only a significant dispenser of aid to Third World countries but also something of a model of development, even if one that was unique and not fully imitable. In these respects, it resembled the Japan of half a century ago. The general resemblance was enhanced by the fact that China like Japan had managed to develop without incurring a significant long-term foreign debt; to be more accurate, after the withdrawal of Soviet aid in 1960 China rapidly repaid the debt to the Soviet Union that it had accumulated up to that time.

In the process of being united and developed under Communist rule, China has eliminated all significant direct foreign influence within its borders. It seems unlikely that ever again will China contain, as it did in the late nineteenth and early twentieth centuries, large foreign spheres of influence. To be sure, not all the credit, if that is the right word, for the elimination of foreign influence can be given to the Chinese Communists; Japanese influence was eliminated in 1945 by Japan's defeat in the Pacific War, which was largely the work of the United States. But the Chinese Communists can justify claim to have eliminated all residual Western influence shortly after the outbreak of the Korean War and all significant direct Soviet influence through the dissolution of the Sino-Soviet joint stock companies in 1955.

China has succeeded not only in uniting its national territory (again, apart from Taiwan) but in establishing to a degree the principle that its borders must not be closely approached by large, hostile military forces. The main episodes that established this principle were of course the Korean War and the Sino-Indian border fighting in 1962. The main exception, and it is a very important one, is the Sino-Soviet border, on the Soviet side of which Moscow appears to do what it pleases. But elsewhere Indian, American, and other foreign forces approach the Chinese border only in small numbers and with great circumspection, although the United States has committed occasional individual violations of Chinese territorial waters and airspace in order to keep alive a challenge to Peking's claim to *de jure* sovereignty over the mainland of China.

In its Asian policy, China has been fairly successful in exploiting certain quarrels among states of the region. In particular, it has gained considerable benefit, of a national rather than revolutionary kind, through supporting Pakistan and Nepal in their controversies with India, and Cambodia in its quarrel with all its neighbors (including North Vietnam).

China has also succeeded fairly well in projecting, except in strongly anti-Communist quarters, the image of an essentially non-expansionist power. As regards the ability and intent to conduct aggressive military operations on foreign soil, the image is basically correct, although it must be conceded that Peking gave Stalin roughly as much cooperation as he desired during the preliminaries and early stages of the Korean War. Another relevant development during the years just preceding the consolidation of the American containment policy was the clear demonstration that the Chinese Communists intended to engage in a kind of revolutionary, as contrasted with conventional, expansionism by inciting and supporting armed Communist revolution elsewhere in Asia. Peking's reputation for nonexpansionism, therefore, although basically justified, is not entirely so.

At times, and especially during the period between the launching of the Great Leap Forward in 1958 and the dramatic developments of 1965 in Asia, China has succeeded to a significant degree in projecting the image of an Asian wave of the future, or in other words an expectation, on the part of Prince Sihanouk for example, that local Communist parties supported by and subservient to China were likely to come to power in Asia. This image tended to fade after 1965, and still more after the onset of the Cultural Revolution, but it might revive after the United States withdraws militarily from South Vietnam, especially if it also does so from other parts of Asia such as Thailand and Japan.

To a considerable extent China has succeeded in exploiting anti-American feeling in various parts of the world and in getting China's partial international isolation, much of which is due to Peking's own behavior, attributed to the policy of the United States.

While portraying itself with some success as an injured, innocent victim in its relationship with the United States, China has also managed to gain widespread acceptance for its claim to be a far more revolutionary power than the Soviet Union. To a high degree, this acceptance is based on purely verbal belligerency. In practice, China has shown itself hardly more willing, and less able, to take serious risks in confronting "imperialism" on behalf of some revolutionary cause or other.

Finally, Peking has been effective in exploiting the feeling, which is especially widespread in Asia and the United States, that China is an intrinsically important country. Again with the exception of strongly anti-Communist quarters, it is generally taken for granted that it would be desirable to establish better relations with China, for the sake of peace and trade as well as for other reasons. Perhaps the main exception to this generalization at present is the Soviet regime, which tends to regard China as a Yellow Peril and is apparently disturbed by Peking's admission in October 1971 into the United Nations and also by the establishment of diplomatic relations with it by such countries as Canada.

FAILURES

As might be expected, some of China's failure in foreign policy, or at least the causes of some of its failures, have been self-inflicted. The China-centeredness and auto-isolation of elite and populace alike, which have been both manifested in and reinforced by the Cultural Revolution, have led to numerous errors of perception and action, as when Peking broke off trade relations with Japan in 1958 in the hope of achieving a significant political effect. The Cultural Revolution led directly to at least three developments that decreased Peking's effectiveness in international politics: the virtual suspension of high-level state visits by Chinese leaders to other countries and by foreign statesmen to China and the withdrawal of almost all Chinese ambassadors from their posts; the temporary upsurge of Red Guard diplomacy, which antagonized many foreign governments and harmed China's image around the world, without achieving any countervailing gains; and the deep involvement of the armed forces in domestic politics and provincial administration, which clearly reduces their military effectiveness.

Peking has had no significant success since 1950 in recovering any of China's "lost" territories, and with the possible exception of Taiwan it seems very unlikely to have any real success in the future. Most of these territories either lie in Soviet Asia or (in the case of Outer Mongolia) are under Soviet protection, and it appears virtually certain that Peking is well aware not only of the Soviet Union's superior military power but of its determination to prevent Chinese expansion in its direction or at its expense. In fact, Peking for these reasons probably does not entertain any serious designs on its "lost" territories in Soviet Asia, but if it does not, this fact in itself represents a setback, since the issue is taken fairly seriously by the politically conscious section of the Chinese public.

Peking has not achieved, and indeed has never thought it wise formally to proclaim, its apparent objective of acquiring a sphere of influence embracing all or most of Asia, or at any rate Southeast Asia. Nor has it succeeded in gaining acceptance for the idea that it should be conceded such a sphere, except on the part of some Western political scientists like Professor Hans Morgenthau. At present, the trend is if anything in the opposite direction. China lost a very promising partner, Indonesia, in 1965. American containment is still a problem for Peking. In Asia, as in other parts of the world, the small states, whether Communist or not, are tending to behave in an increasingly independent fashion, whatever the attitude of the larger powers. China has been effectively ignored in the course of many, although not all, recent international transactions in Asia in which it has had an interest; an example is the agreement between Indonesia and Malaysia to end the "confrontation" between them in the spring of 1966. Asian regionalism, a phenomenon basically distasteful to Peking, has been on the increase in recent years, South Korea and Thailand being two of the countries most active in promoting it. Worse still, perhaps, from Peking's point of view, and to a considerable extent on account of China's policies, the list of countries playing major international roles in Asia has been enlarged to include not only the United States and China but also the Soviet Union, and perhaps in the fairly near future Japan and India as well.

Although Mao Tse-tung has badly hampered the working of Peking's otherwise fairly effective version of conventional diplomacy, his own favorite techniques have generally not worked very well. Except in Vietnam, an unusual situation in almost every way, "people's war" has not been notably successful and shows few signs of being about to become so, save perhaps in the immediate vicinity of Vietnam. It has tended to feed on the grievances of backward tribal peoples in remote areas, who have little access to or influence on the governments of their countries or on the areas where the ethnically different majority groups live. With the partial exception of Vietnam, there has been no overriding issue like the Japanese invasion of China in 1937 to galvanize into being a popular resistance to the "imperialists" that is capable of being diverted under Communist leadership into an assault on the indigenous government. Nor have Mao's occasional personal statements on international questions, or China's nuclear tests, achieved the anticipated effect of "encouraging the revolutionary people of the world" in their hypothetical struggle against "imperialism." It is conceivable, however, that this situation may change when China begins to test missiles of intercontinental range.

China to date has not even come close to gaining the leadership of the world's left, to which it evidently aspires. Mao's arrogance and radicalism, which appear even greater than they actually are, have repelled nearly all the orthodox Communist parties, whether in power or not. Chinese influence is generally greater, and sometimes predominant, on the various "Marxist-Leninist" parties, radical student movements, and so on, but these groups, while more active and sometimes more influential than the corresponding Communist parties, are usually not very well organized or effective. A massive and widespread increase in social discontent would probably be required for Maoism, or some other form of Chinese revolutionary influence, to acquire major worldwide importance. At present, as a result of the Cultural Revolution, Maoism seems to have become equated in the minds of many foreign radicals with anarchism, which in reality it is not.

If China's influence on Asia has been less than overwhelming, its influence on regions other than Asia has been generally minor, except in selected individual countries like Albania and Tanzania where China has concentrated its efforts in order to capitalize on some local situation that appears promising. China's current stock in trade of anti-Americanism and anti-Sovietism is insufficient to compensate for the deficiencies in Peking's other means of promoting its influence in remote areas.

The future evolution of Chinese foreign policy will almost certainly be influenced if not determined by domestic developments. In the foreign as in the domestic field, a strong Maoist flavor is likely to be preserved for the sake of legitimacy, unity, and continuity. There will probably be continued lip service, and perhaps more, to the cause of revolutionary violence abroad, notably "people's war" in the Third World and civil unrest in the Western countries.

On the other hand, this Maoist component is likely to be held at a level that does not interfere seriously with what will probably be the mainstream of Chinese foreign policy. This is an increased reliance on state action, including pressures as well as conventional diplomacy, rather than on revolutionary militancy. For example, Peking is likely to accept at least passively any settlement to which Hanoi may agree, (except perhaps in the unlikely event that Hanoi appears to be abandoning entirely its interest in the revolutionization of South Vietnam). The main form of Chinese pressure on Japan to reduce its security ties with the United States will probably be a manipulation of commercial relations rather than Maoist efforts to incite a "people's war" to be waged by the Japanese Communists. Peking seems likely to continue to normalize its relations with the United States, short of the establishment of diplomatic relations, with the main purpose of counterbalancing Soviet pressures and encouraging the United States in its tendency toward military disengagement from Asia and the Western Pacific. Presumably, Peking hopes to work out some sort of acceptable settlement of the Taiwan question in the context of such an American disengagement.

As for Sino-Soviet relations, at least during the remainder of Mao Tse-tung's lifetime Peking seems likely to avoid both dangerous provocation of the Soviet Union and a general political agreement with it. Since the Soviet attitude is rather similar, a Sino-Soviet war appears improbable, although of course one could result from accident or miscalculation. The situation after Mao's death is hard to predict, in this as in all other respects. The most plausible forecast would probably be one of a trend toward improving Sino-Soviet relations, although not to the level of cooperation attained during the heyday of the relationship (roughly 1950–55).

Peking denies any ambition to become a superpower, in the sense of a state with not only the power but the desire to impose its will on other countries. What this probably means is that Peking intends to curb the desire because it knows that its power will always be limited. There is very little chance that Peking will acquire the economic and military strength to put it in the same class with the United States and the Soviet Union, although it will probably have enough to deter an attack by either of them. Accordingly, Peking is likely to pursue its quest for political influence (as distinct from economic and military power) along present lines, by posing as the friend and champion of the "small and medium states" (other than those aligned too closely with one of the two "superpowers") and of revolutionary movements around the world, insofar as the latter can be supported without excessively antagonizing governments whose good will is important to Chinese interests.

SOME THOUGHTS ON AMERICAN CHINA POLICY

The question of Sino-American relations has appeared repeatedly in these pages, but always from the Chinese point of view. Since the perspective is now to be reversed, it may be useful to begin with some historical remarks, just as the treatment of Chinese foreign policy was introduced by a summary of the relevant historical background.

Since the rise of significant great-power rivalries in eastern Asia at the end of the nineteenth century, American policy toward the region has been essentially one of trying to maintain a balance of power, even though that policy often masqueraded under other labels such as the preservation of "orderly processes." In the process of trying to maintain a balance of power, usually in the face of Japanese pressures and always by means short of force until attacked by Japan in 1941, the United States developed three guiding principles for its Asian policy. The first was the centrality of China and the necessity to prevent its coming under foreign domination. This principle, which came into being about 1898, is of course the basis of the Open Door Doctrine. It was assumed that if left to itself China would develop in time into a modernizing state that was constitutional if not democratic and not only peaceful but friendly to the United States. The shock was correspondingly great when in 1949 China fell under the control of a regime that was not only anti-American but explicitly proclaimed its orientation toward Stalinist Russia, with which the United States was then locked in a massive Cold War in Europe and the Middle East. The second and third principles emerged about 1940, with the fall of Western Europe to a German state both able and willing to develop nuclear weapons and in other ways to pose a direct military threat to the United States, and with pressures on Southeast Asia and its vast resources by a Japan rendered oil-hungry by the American "moral embargo" imposed in retaliation for its invasion of China. The second principle was the strategic and political importance of the Malay Barrier (Malaysia and Indonesia) to Western Europe and Australia, and therefore indirectly to the United States. The third was the strategic priority of Europe over Asia, in view of the limits on American resources, the greater cultural and political claims of the European countries, and the overarching threat posed by Nazi Germany.

It took a Japanese attack to bring the United States to fight for these principles, all three of which were involved in the complex diplomatic crisis leading up to Pearl Harbor. Concern for China's fate and reluctance to see it dominated by Japan led Washington to refuse to underwrite in advance a Sino-Japanese settlement that would leave Japanese troops in China, as Tokyo demanded. The United States would neither lift its moral embargo nor tolerate Japanese efforts to secure oil in large amounts through pressure on the Dutch authorities still controlling Indonesia (then the Netherlands Indies). When the Japanese military occupied northern Indochina in September 1940, the move was tolerated reluctantly in

Washington because it was correctly viewed as a step in the strategic encirclement of China, which the United States was not prepared to break by force. But when the Japanese military, in violation of commitments made to the French authorities, occupied southern Indochina in July 1941, Washington rightly interpreted the step as one aimed at Southeast Asia, and the Malay Barrier in particular. Japanese assets in the United States were promptly frozen, and this action turned out to be the diplomatic point of no return on the way to Pearl Harbor. Throughout this period, as well as after its entry into the war, the United States was more active in promoting its interests in Europe than in Asia, even though Japan was much more disposed than Germany to seek a direct quarrel with the United States.

There is no need to summarize the involved history of American efforts, after Pearl Harbor, to aid and support the Chinese Nationalists against the Japanese and as a theoretically major power in the postwar period and to help them stay in power by working out a political settlement between them and the Communists. Despite enormous disappointment in the Nationalists' performance and shock at Mao Tse-tung's open proclamation in mid-1949 of an anti-Western and pro-Soviet orientation, the State Department began from the spring of 1949 to explore actively the possibilities of diplomatic relations with the new Communist China. The idea foundered by the end of the year before the opposition of Communists in China and Republicans at home, and Washington then adopted an attitude of wait-and-see, or in Secretary Acheson's famous phrase, "letting the dust settle."

There was not long to wait. The outbreak of war in Korea, followed by Chinese intervention in the autumn of 1950, transformed Sino-American relations. In Washington's eyes there appeared to be an imminent threat of Soviet domination of mainland Asia, with the Chinese as well as the North Koreans among Moscow's principal agents. The Chinese Nationalists, who had been treated rather cavalierly since the American election of 1948, suddenly became again the important allies that they had been during the war against Japan, and military aid and protection were extended to them in their bastion on Taiwan. In the early stages of the Sino-American fighting in Korea the United States proceeded to construct its containment policy toward China. As developed by about 1955, it consisted of sizable American bases and forces in Asia (mainly Japan and Okinawa, South Korea, and the Philippines), a series of security treaties or defensive alliances (with Japan, South Korea, the Philippines, and Nationalist China, as well as the multilateral Anzus and SEATO treaties), the withholding of diplomatic recognition from Peking and strong political support for Taipei, a complete embargo on American trade with the mainland of China, economic and military aid to several Asian countries that appeared or claimed to be threatened by China, and efforts to isolate China diplomatically by such means as working against its admission to the United Nations. Undoubtedly a major reason for the rigor and vigor with which first the Truman and then the Eisenhower administration proceeded to contain and isolate China was the huge and unsavory domestic debate over "Who lost China?" After the "loss" of China in 1949 and the rise of Senator Joseph McCarthy in 1950, no American official or politician could afford to appear less than resolutely opposed to Chinese communism and all its works.

During this period General MacArthur, curiously enough, although of course strongly hostile to Peking, was almost the only prominent American to see China as a threat in its own right and not as a mere satellite of Moscow. In general, the myth of the Sino-Soviet relationship as a monolith dominated from Moscow persisted in high official circles in Washington until about 1961, when the evidence of Sino-Soviet discord had become too obvious to be ignored any longer. By that time, Washington's attitude toward Peking had begun to mellow somewhat for reasons essentially unconnected with the Sino-Soviet dispute. The process was related to the death of John Foster Dulles and the subsequent warming of Soviet-American relations symbolized by Khrushchev's visit to the United States in the late summer of 1959.

Even under the Kennedy administration, which was well aware of the Sino-Soviet dispute, the thawing of policy toward Peking did not go beyond a greater willingness to countenance travel to China by Americans and to consider trade with it. One reason was the lack of interest on the part of Peking, which was then loudly accusing Moscow of being soft on "imperialism"; in 1961

China rejected an informal offer by President Kennedy to sell it grain. Another was the continuing influence of Nationalist China, which in 1961 succeeded in vetoing even so innocuous a modification of American policy as the establishment of diplomatic relations with Outer Mongolia. Another reason was the obvious fact that the Sino-American quarrel had developed a rationale and history of its own, quite apart from the question of Soviet-American or Sino-Soviet relations. Finally, in the light of a number of developments such as the Laos crisis and Peking's militantly anti-"imperialist" stance in the Sino-Soviet polemic, China was seen as even more hostile and dangerous to the United States in some respects than was the Soviet Union itself.

It began to seem increasingly urgent to find some new, more stable, basis for Sino-American relations as it became clear by about 1962 that China was not only determined to develop its own nuclear weapons but would have some fairly soon, and by 1963 that it would not be a party to any practical international agreements to limit the testing and use of nuclear weapons. The first Chinese nuclear test in October 1964 emphasized the seriousness of the problem without making its solution any easier.

Sino-American relations acquired an aura of increased tension and urgency as the Vietnam war escalated in early 1965. The United States government based its increased involvement largely on the essentially incorrect theory that Hanoi was acting as China's agent, yet this assumption was more than outweighed by the fact that both Washington and Peking were anxious to avoid another Sino-American war like the one in Korea. Paradoxically, this mutual fear opened the way to a trend toward improved Sino-American relations. For American congressional and public opinion inclined increasingly toward a softer China policy, with the minimum purpose of avoiding a collision over Vietnam. The Johnson administration moved somewhat with the tide in its public statements on China, but more important it designed its military strategy in Vietnam so as not to create a serious threat to the survival of North Vietnam or to Chinese security, so that Peking might not feel compelled to react as it had in Korea. In other words, the United States avoided, among other things, posing a credible threat of invasion of North Vietnam, with the result that Hanoi was effectively free to send as much of its army as it liked into South Vietnam, where the United States felt compelled to cope with it through a costly "search and destroy" strategy. With this important exception relating to Vietnam, American China policy remained largely frozen during the Johnson administration.

As already indicated (in Chapter XII), President Nixon came into office committed, in his own mind if not fully in public, to a serious effort to improve relations with China. His main concern was domestic: to improve his political standing and chances of reelection in 1972 by reducing American military involvement in Asia, and especially in Vietnam. An improvement in relations with China was thought to be helpful, and perhaps indispensable, to that end. At the minimum, China might be persuaded to avoid trying to exploit American disengagement from Asia for its own advantage. Perhaps Peking might be induced to cooperate in a political settlement for Vietnam that would enable the United States to get its forces out and its prisoners back and yet would give the Saigon government a reasonable chance of survival. It was hoped that improved Sino-American relations would help both parties in their difficult dealings with Moscow. It was known in Washington that Peking was seriously worried by Soviet pressures, and this fear has been viewed officially as virtually the sole reason for Peking's positive response to the American overtures that have been made to it since 1969. This is a comforting view, since it implicitly denies that Peking is trying to take advantage of vulnerabilities in the American position, but it is an oversimplification, since Peking has been playing on the urgent American desire for help toward a Vietnam settlement to get concessions for itself, notably on Taiwan.

As already suggested, the Shanghai communiqué did in fact include some American concessions on Taiwan, notably the commitment in principle to withdraw all American military personnel from the island as tension in the region diminishes. Inasmuch as most of the 8,000-odd American military personnel on Taiwan are there in connection with logistical operations in support of the effort in Vietnam, Peking obviously has acquired an incentive for favoring an early Vietnam settlement, something that it has tended to oppose in the past. Peking's relationship with the United States has become in effect more important to it than its relationship with

North Vietnam, a trend that has angered Hanoi and led to a gain for Soviet influence on North Vietnam at Chinese expense. The North Vietnamese offensive in South Vietnam that began at the end of March 1972, with what degree of Soviet support is not clear, was probably designed among other things to test and if possible to wreck what Hanoi seems to regard as an emerging Sino-American understanding adverse to its own interests. Hanoi may even have hoped to produce the defeat of President Nixon in the 1972 election, much as the Tet offensive of 1968 contributed to the defeat of the Democrats. Peking, on the other hand, has acquired a substantial interest in President Nixon's re-election, because although the Democrats generally also favored an improved relationship with China they tend, at least in Peking's eyes, to be "softer" on the Soviet Union than Nixon is.

While not exactly friends, the United States and China have become each other's most important partner in at least one respect, to the point where their emerging relationship has survived the serious vicarious setback inflicted by the defeat and dismemberment of Pakistan by India supported by the Soviet Union, as well as the 1972 increase in the level of American military action in Vietnam. The major common interest is the need to manage the problem presented to both by the Soviet Union's increasingly activist behavior. The extreme difficulty and sensitivity of this task accounts for much of the extraordinary secrecy with which both the parties have surrounded the substance, as distinct from the atmospherics, of their relationship. Another reason is that on each side the policy of Sino-American détente has been controversial. The White House would have encountered endless bureaucratic delays and objections, as well as some prodding from congressional quarters to move faster, if it had not kept its plans and moves to itself. On the other side, Chou En-lai has had to proceed with great care if the domestic opponents of the opening to the United States were to be denied an opportunity to wreck his plan. This disaster, which would have had serious effects on Chou's personal political position, was prevented when Mao Tse-tung agreed to receive Nixon on the first day of his visit, without advance publicity, and thereby put his stamp of approval on the visit, and by implication on the opening to the United States as well.

Peking has carefully avoided arousing great expectations of improved Sino-American relations in the minds of its own people. On the American side, where fortunately the government cannot influence public opinion to an equal degree, an imposing euphoria has emerged in many quarters. It is widely believed that nothing but an unreasonable official American attitude toward China and American policy toward Vietnam prevents, or has ever prevented, good relations between China and the United States. This is a gross distortion. In addition to Taiwan and Vietnam, Chinese and not only official American ideology have operated until recently to keep Peking and Washington apart. Before an American president could visit China, not only did the United States have to come to a decision to disengage militarily from the mainland of Asia and from Taiwan, but Peking had to become sufficiently worried about the Soviet Union to abandon the decade-old Maoist dual adversary strategy for a "tilt" in favor of Washington and against Moscow. There is an obvious danger that American euphoria over China may be succeeded, in one of the pendulum swings in which public opinion in the United States so often indulges, by undue disillusionment if, as seems entirely possible, the new Sino-American relationship fails to measure up to the current great expectations.

Even if the relationship makes life easier for both parties in the Far East, the same is not necessarily true of their allies.

On the American side, the ally most directly affected is of course the Republic of China on Taiwan. The United States, having already made some concessions to Peking at its expense, is likely to make more. The result has been a serious crisis of confidence in Taipei intensified by expulsion from the United Nations. For the time being, Taipei is trying to broaden its options by expanding its international contacts, including (informally) those with India and the Soviet Union. In the long run, two main alternatives appear to be open. One is to reach an agreement with Peking that each will abandon its claim to the other's territory and that both will live separately and more or less amicably as "one China, one Taiwan." The other is to reach an agreement with Peking for some form of unification, with Taiwan presumably having an autonomous status. Either of these arrangements would be acceptable to the United States in the current stage of its China policy, which insists merely that Taiwan not be coerced (something that Peking is probably not yet in a position to do in any case, even if the United States abrogates its defense commitment to Taiwan). There is no sign yet of progress toward either type of agreement. Of the two, one on unification seems slightly more probable, or at least more viable, in the long run. For a separate arrangement, and still more a perpetuation of the status quo (a separate Taiwan under threat from the mainland), would run the risk that Taiwan might move or drift under some form of Japanese protection, a situation that would be totally unacceptable to Peking and would raise tension in the Far East to a possibly dangerous level.

Another American ally greatly affected by the Nixon China policy is Japan. Here the objection is not really a substantive one, since any successor to Premier Sato is likely to use the American opening to Peking as a welcome occasion for improving Tokyo's own relations with Peking, if possible without sacrificing Japan's important economic relationship with Taiwan. The objection is rather that the United States violated a previous commitment to Tokyo, which on the strength of that commitment had been aligning its China policy rather closely with Washington's, by undertaking a major new initiative toward Peking (the Kissinger visit of July 1971 and the arrangement for President Nixon to visit China) without informing, much less consulting, Tokyo in advance. This "shock," as the Japanese call it, has contributed along with the trend toward American disengagement from Asia to a feeling that Japan can no longer rely on the United States but must make its own international arrangements, including perhaps an improved relationship with the Soviet Union and China. There is, of course, the possibility that Japan might decide to rearm on a major scale in order to be able to stand alone if necessary, but at present such a development, which would have serious repercussions, does not seem likely.

American efforts at accommodation with China have intensified a tendency on the part of the smaller Asian governments allied with the United States to accommodate with China and other Communist states and have evoked criticisms of the governments in question from their opposition politicians and intellectuals for not moving faster. These criticisms appear to have contributed, along with other issues, to the crackdowns in late 1971 by the military elites in Thailand and South Korea, which presumably want to be in full control of whatever moves they may decide to make to improve their relations with China.

The current official American hope is to replace the Sino-American confrontation in the Far East with a four-power balance (the United States, the Soviet Union, China, and Japan) under whose umbrella the region as a whole would find peace and stability. Ideally, none of the four parties would fight any of the others or combine with another to the detriment of a third. A system of this kind gave Europe a long period of relative peace after the Congress of Vienna (1814–15). But in addition to the scarcity of common interests among the four parties there is the fact that the United States, unlike the other three, is not geographically a Far Eastern power and has created by its recent behavior considerable doubt as to whether it wants to be one. From excessive containment of China and excessive military involvement in Vietnam the United States is in danger of shifting, in characteristic pendulum fashion, to an unduly rapid shuffling off of the burdens it has assumed. If so, it is distinctly possible that the major beneficiary will be the Soviet Union, the United States' greatest international problem. In any case, the Nixon Doctrine and the concomitant American military disengagement from Asia accompanied by the opening to China appear to have started a chain of events whose future links cannot be clearly foreseen but are likely to be momentous and beyond the power of the United States to control.

Sources and References

CHAPTER I
The Legacy of China's Past

This chapter is intended as a brief introduction to pre-1949 China for the general reader and cannot hope to satisfy the specialist, because of the breadth of the subject and the brevity of the treatment. The writer's understanding of traditional and modern China was formed to a large extent during his graduate school days and under the tutelage of Professor John K. Fairbank, the dean of American historians of modern China. This is not to say, of course, that Professor Fairbank would necessarily agree with all the interpretations given in this chapter, let alone in the rest of the book. The reader could not do better, if he wishes to pursue the subject further, than to read Professor Fairbank's excellent book, *The United States and China* (3rd ed. revised, Harvard University Press, 1971), which contains much valuable and readable material on pre-1949 China as well as on the history of Sino-American relations. A much more extended treatment can be found in the chapters on China of the masterly historical text, Edwin O. Reischauer and John K. Fairbank, *East Asia* (2 vols., Boston: Houghton Mifflin, 1960 and 1965).

Within the broader area of pre-1949 China, the most important subject for the purposes of this book is of course the rise of the Chinese Communist movement. This is a field in which much important research and writing are being done, but much remains to be done. The brief interpretation given here is therefore advanced in a highly tentative spirit. In addition to the writings on this subject listed elsewhere (under Suggestions for Further Reading), mention should be made of the work of William F. Dorrill, which has appeared so far in "Transfer of Legitimacy in the Chinese Communist Party: Origins of the Maoist Myth," *The China Quarterly*, no. 36 (October–December 1968), pp. 45–60 (also available in John Wilson Lewis, ed., *Party Leadership and Revolutionary Power in China* [Cambridge University Press, 1970], Ch. 2); "The Fukien Rebellion and the CCP: A Case of Maoist Revisionism," *The China Quarterly*, no. 37 (January–March 1969), pp. 31–53.

On the question of Chinese political attitudes, a recent book well worth consulting is Richard H. Solomon, *Mao's Revolution and the Chinese Political Culture* (University of California Press, 1971), which owes a good deal to the work of Lucian Pye.

CHAPTER II

Stalinism and Armed Struggle (1950–53)

There is little good published analysis of China's foreign policy and foreign relations during the early years of the Communist regime. This chapter accordingly is based mainly on the writer's own analysis of original Chinese and other (principally Soviet and American) sources, as well as contemporary journalism. The main exception is the Korean War, which is comparatively well covered in secondary sources. The best general book on it is David Rees, *Korea: The Limited War* (New York: St. Martin's Press, 1964). Some valuable light is shed by a participating statesman in Dean Acheson, *Present at the Creation: My Years in the State Department* (New York: W. W. Norton, 1969). The Chinese side, to the end of 1950, has been covered by Allen S. Whiting (see under Suggestions for Further Reading).

In the account given here, the most controversial aspect is the version of American and Soviet policy around the time of Stalin's death; a documented version appears in the writer's *Communist China in World Politics* (Boston: Houghton Mifflin, 1966), pp. 220–229. Evidence for the American nuclear threat against China appears in the Eisenhower and Sherman memoirs (Dwight David Eisenhower, *Mandate for Change, 1953–56* [New York: Doubleday, 1963], p. 181; Sherman Adams, *Firsthand Report* [New York: Harper, 1961], pp. 48–49, 102). The Soviet side is more difficult to reconstruct. Indications of a bellicose mood on Stalin's part may be found in Boris I. Nicolaevsky, *Power and the Soviet Elite* (New York: Praeger, 1965), pp. 170, 247–249; and K. P. S. Menon (the Indian ambassador to Moscow at the time), *The Flying Troika* (London: Oxford University Press, 1963), pp. 26–29. A comparable indication of a bellicose mood on Mao's part appears in Chow Chingwen, *Ten Years of Storm: The True Story of the Communist Regime in China* (New York: Holt, Rinehart and Winston, 1960), p. 82.

CHAPTER III

The Road to Bandung (1953–55)

Little analytical work has been done on Sino-Soviet relations in the late Stalin and early post-Stalin periods (down to the Soviet Twentieth Party Congress of February 1956). The main general work on this topic is the good one by Howard L. Boorman and others, *Moscow-Peking Axis: Strengths and Strains* (New York: Harper, 1957). Some important information may be found in the valuable monograph by Uri Ra'anan, *The USSR Arms the Third World: Case Studies in Soviet Foreign Policy* (Cambridge, Mass.: M.I.T. Press, 1969).

The most comprehensive work on the preliminaries to and the course of the Geneva Conference of 1954 is Robert F. Randle, *Geneva 1954: The Settlement of the Indochinese War* (Princeton University Press, 1969). There is also a useful study by Melvin Gurtov, *The First Vietnam Crisis: Chinese Communist Strategy and United States Involvement, 1953–54* (Columbia University Press, 1967).

There is little of value by way of published analysis of the Taiwan Strait crisis of 1954–55. On the American aspect, see Stewart Alsop, "The Story Behind Quemoy: How We Drifted Close to War," *The Saturday Evening Post*, December 13, 1958, pp. 26–27, 86–88.

The Chinese transition from an "armed struggle" to a "peaceful coexistence" strategy toward Asia (especially southern Asia) has not been sufficiently studied. On the Bandung Conference see George McT. Kahin, *The Asian-African Conference: Bandung, Indonesia, April 1955* (Cornell University Press, 1956).

CHAPTER IV

The Challenge to Mao and His Response (1956–58)

A good analysis of Chinese intraparty differences in the aftermath of the Soviet Twentieth Party Congress may be found in Richard H. Solomon's book cited under Chapter I.

Sino-Soviet differences during the period after the congress are brilliantly treated in the standard work by Donald S. Zagoria, *The Sino-Soviet Conflict, 1956–61* (Princeton University Press, 1962). Peking's own summary account is "The Origin and Development of the Differences Between the Leadership of the CPSU and Ourselves," *People's Daily* and *Red Flag*, September 6, 1963 (reprinted in *The Polemic on the General Line of the International Communist Movement* [Peking: Foreign Languages Press, 1965]., pp. 55–114).

On the Chinese aspect of the Taiwan Strait crisis of 1958 see Tang Tsou, "Mao's Limited War in the Taiwan Strait," *Orbis*, vol. III, no. 3 (fall, 1959), pp. 332–350. The Soviet aspect is perceptively analyzed in John R. Thomas, "Soviet Behavior in the Quemoy Crisis of 1958," *Orbis*, vol. VI, no. 1 (spring, 1962), pp. 38–64 (reprinted in Raymond L. Garthoff, ed., *Sino-Soviet Military Relations* [New York: Praeger, 1966], Ch. 7).

CHAPTER V

The Struggle Against Khrushchev (1959–64)

The Sino-Indian crisis of 1959 is covered from the official Chinese viewpoint in *Concerning the Question of Tibet* (Peking: Foreign Languages Press, 1959) and *Documents on the Sino-Indian Boundary Question* (Peking: Foreign Languages Press, 1960). For the Indian side see *Notes, Memoranda and Letters Exchanged Between the Governments of India and China* (New Delhi: Ministry of External Affairs, 1960, n.d.). In 1963 Peking described the Soviet stand on this crisis as "the first instance in history in which a socialist country, instead of condemning the armed provocations of the reactionaries of a capitalist country, condemned another fraternal socialist country when it was confronted with such armed provocations" ("Whence the Differences?" *People's Daily*, February 27, 1963).

On the P'eng Te-huai affair see David A. Charles (pseud.), "The Dismissal of Marshal P'eng Te-huai," *The China Quarterly*, no. 8 (October-December 1961), pp. 63–76; J. D. Simmonds, "P'eng Te-huai: A Chronological Re-Examination," *The China Quarterly*, no. 37 (January-March 1969), pp. 120–138.

On the Laotian crisis see A. M. Halpern and H. B. Fredman, *Communist Strategy in Laos* (The RAND Corporation, RM-2561, June 1960); Brian Crozier, "Peking and the Laotian Crisis: A Further Appraisal," *The China Quarterly*, no. 11 (July-September 1962), pp. 116–123; Arthur Lall, *How Communist China Negotiates* (Columbia University Press, 1968); *Concerning the Situation in Laos* (Peking: Foreign Languages Press, 1959); Alexander L. George and others, *The Limits of Coercive Diplomacy: Laos, Cuba, Vietnam* (Boston: Little, Brown, 1971); Chae-Jin Lee, *Communist China's Policy Toward Laos: A Case Study, 1954–67* (University of Kansas: Center for East Asian Studies, 1970).

The best analysis of early Chinese policy toward Africa is Richard Lowenthal, "China," in Zbigniew Brzezinski, ed., *Africa and the Communist World* (Standford University Press, 1963), Ch. 5. See also Charles Neuhauser, *Third World Politics: China and the Afro-Asian People's Solidarity Organization, 1957–67* (Harvard University: East Asian Research Center, 1968).

On the Sino-Indian border war of 1962, see *The Sino-Indian Boundary Question* (Peking: Foreign Languages Press, 1962); later volumes of the Indian white paper on the border question (cited under Chapter V, at the beginning); the strongly pro-Chinese account by Neville Maxwell, *India's China War* (New York: Doubleday, 1972); and the writer's analysis in *Communist China in World Politics*, Ch. 11.

The Sino-Indonesian alliance of the early 1960s and its disastrous termination in 1965 are well treated in Justus van der Kroef, "The Sino-Indonesian Partnership," *Orbis*, vol. VIII, no. 2 (summer, 1964), pp. 332–356; John O. Sutter, "Two Faces of *Konfrontasi:* 'Crush Malaysia' and the *Gestapu*," *Asian Survey*, vol. VI, no. 10 (October

1966), pp. 523–546; Uri Ra'anan, "The Coup That Failed: A Background Analysis," *Problems of Communism*, vol. XV, no. 2 (March-April 1966), pp. 37–43; Sheldon W. Simon, *The Broken Triangle: Peking, Djakarta, and the PKI*, (Johns Hopkins Press, 1968).

Chinese policy toward the intensifying crisis in Vietnam in the early 1960s is treated by the writer in *Communist China in World Politics*, Ch. 13, which, however, he now believes to overstate the eagerness of both Peking and Hanoi to revive insurgency in South Vietnam. For a valuable corrective see George McT. Kahin and John Wilson Lewis, *The United States in Vietnam* (New York: Dial Press, 1967), especially Ch. XI.

Sino-Soviet relations in the late Khrushchev period are well covered, with extensive documentation, in William E. Griffith, *The Sino-Soviet Rift* (Cambridge, Mass.: M.I.T. Press, 1964); and William E. Griffith, *Sino-Soviet Relations, 1964–65* (Cambridge, Mass.: M.I.T. Press, 1967). See also the Chinese and Soviet articles collected in *The Polemic on the General Line of the International Communist Movement* (Peking: Foreign Languages Press, 1965).

CHAPTER VI

The Foreign Policy of the Cultural Revolution (1965–68)

A detailed and valuable analysis of the Cultural Revolution has been published recently: Thomas W. Robinson, ed., *The Cultural Revolution in China* (University of California Press, 1971). The important contribution by Melvin Gurtov, "The Foreign Ministry and Foreign Affairs in the Chinese Cultural Revolution" (Ch. 5), originally appeared in *The China Quarterly*, no. 40 (October-December 1969), pp. 65–102.

On Sino-Soviet relations during the Cultural Revolution see Maury Lisann, "Moscow and the Chinese Power Struggle," *Problems of Communism*, vol. XVIII, no. 6 (November-December 1969), pp. 32–41. Sheldon W. Simon has written a valuable article on a related topic: "Maoism and Inter-Party Relations: Peking's Alienation of the Japan Communist Party," *The China Quarterly*, no. 35 (July-September 1968), pp. 40–57.

The Chinese strategic debate of 1965–66 is treated in a brilliant and controversial paper by Uri Ra'anan, "Peking's Foreign Policy 'Debate,' 1965–66," in Tang Tsou, ed., *China's Policies in Asia and*

America's Alternatives (University of Chicago Press, 1968), Ch. 2. Two other studies on related topics are David P. Mozingo and Thomas W. Robinson, *Lin Piao on 'People's Wars': China Takes a Second Look at Vietnam* (The RAND Corporation, RM 4814-PR, 1965); and Harry Harding and Melvin Gurtov, *The Purge of Lo Jui-ch'ing: The Politics of Chinese Strategic Planning* (The RAND Corporation, R-548-PR, February 1971).

CHAPTER VII
The Making of Foreign Policy

Little good work has been done on the making of Chinese foreign policy. Valuable material by a perceptive observer on the underlying cultural and political attitudes may be found in Ross Terrill, "The 800,000,000, Part II: China and the World," *The Atlantic*, vol. 229, no. 1 (January 1972), pp. 39–62. A useful analysis of the Maoist external outlook and strategy is Tang Tsou and Morton H. Halperin, "Mao Tse-tung's Revolutionary Strategy and Peking's International Behavior," *The American Political Science Review*, vol. LIX, no. 1 (March 1965), pp. 80–99.

A thoughtful series of articles has been written by A. M. Halpern, largely on the basis of content analysis: "Communist China and Peaceful Coexistence," *The China Quarterly*, no. 3 (July-September 1960), pp. 16–31; "The Chinese Communist Line on Neutralism," *The China Quarterly*, no. 5 (January-March 1961), pp. 90–115; "The Foreign Policy Uses of the Chinese Revolutionary Model," *The China Quarterly*, no. 7 (July-September 1961), pp. 1–16; "Communist China's Foreign Policy: The Recent Phase," *The China Quarterly*, no. 11 (July-September 1962), pp. 89–104.

On the availability to the Chinese elite of unslanted information on the outside world, see Henry G. Schwarz, "*The Ts'an-k'a o Hsiao-hsi:* How Well Informed Are Chinese Officials About the Outside World?," *The China Quarterly*, no. 27 (July-September 1966), pp. 54–83.

The best single work on Chinese nuclear doctrine and strategy is Alice L. Hsieh, *Communist China's Strategy in the Nuclear Era* (Englewood Cliffs, N.J.: Prentice-Hall, 1962). There is no comparable adequate work on Chinese conventional military doctrine and strategy, but see the two important policy statements (by Lo

Jui-ch'ing and Lin Piao) in Samuel B. Griffith, ed., *Peking and People's Wars* (New York: Praeger, 1966).

CHAPTER VIII
Peking and World Communism

Several major works on Peking and world communism (including of course Sino-Soviet relations) are cited elsewhere (under Chapters III, IV, and V, and under Suggestions for Further Reading). In addition to these, it is worth consulting G. F. Hudson and others, *The Sino-Soviet Dispute* (New York: Praeger, 1961); Isaac Deutscher, *Russia, China, and the West: A Contemporary Chronicle, 1953–1966* (Baltimore: Penguin, 1970); and Richard Lowenthal, *World Communism: The Disintegration of a Secular Faith* (London: Oxford University Press, 1964).

CHAPTER IX
Peking and Asia

In addition to works on China and Asia cited under other chapters and under Suggestions for Further Reading, the reader may wish to consult the original documents in G. V. Ambedkar and V. D. Divekar, eds., *Documents on China's Relations with South and South-East Asia, 1949–1962* (Bombay: Allied Publishers, 1964).

CHAPTER X
Peking and the Third World

In addition to the works on Peking and the Third World cited in Suggestions for Further Reading, it is worth mentioning a valuable study by Ernst Halperin, "Peking and the Latin American Communists," *The China Quarterly*, no. 29 (January-March 1967), pp. 111–154.

CHAPTER XI
Peking and the West

There are few good studies on Peking's policy toward the West (including the United States). A brilliant analysis of some ideological and attitudinal problems on both sides is Michael Lindsay, *China* and the Cold War: A Study in International Politics (Melbourne University Press, 1955). Some Chinese documentation appears in Yuan-li Wu, *As Peking Sees Us* (Stanford University: Hoover Institution, 1969). Some recent documents and reflections on Chinese policy toward the United States, as well as vice versa, are contained in *United States Relations with the People's Republic of China* (Washington: U. S. Government Printing Office, 1972).

CHAPTER XII

Foreign Policy Since the Cultural Revolution

A. M. Halpern has written a good analysis of the post-Cultural Revolution phase, "China's Foreign Policy since the Cultural Revolution," in Roderick MacFarquhar, ed., *Sino-American Relations, 1949–71* (New York: Praeger, 1972), except that his heavy reliance on content analysis has led him to minimize Peking's "tilt" (in its behavior, not in its propaganda) in favor of the United States as against the Soviet Union. The Sino-Soviet aspect of the post-Cultural Revolution period is treated in the writer's *The Bear at the Gate: Chinese Policymaking under Soviet Pressure* (Washington: American Enterprise Institute, and Stanford University: Hoover Institution, 1971). The statement regarding the Soviet query to the United States on the possible destruction of China's nuclear facilities rests on several well informed American press sources.

CHAPTER XIII

The Balance Sheet and the Outlook

Some of the recent books on American China policy are listed in Suggestions for Further Reading. Others of value are: Foster Rhea Dulles, *American Policy Toward Communist China, 1949–1969* (New York: Crowell, 1972); A. Doak Barnett and Edwin O. Reischauer, eds., *The United States and China: The Next Decade* (New York: Praeger, 1970); Jerome Alan Cohen and others, *Taiwan and American Policy: The Dilemma in U. S.–China Relations* (New York: Praeger, 1971); *China and U. S. Foreign Policy* (Washington: Congressional Quarterly, 1971); and Earl C. Ravenal, ed., *Peace with China? U. S. Decisions for Asia* (New York: Liveright, 1971).

SUPPLEMENT

SINCE THE FIRST EDITION of this book was written, the publication of useful works relevant to its topic has of course continued. There is space to mention only a few.

Three other general works on Chinese foreign policy have been published recently in the United States. The writer will avoid the suspicion of bias by simply listing them and inviting the reader to determine his own preference. They are: Ishwer C. Ojha, *Chinese Foreign Policy in an Age of Transition: The Diplomacy of Cultural Despair* (Boston: Beacon, 1969); Arthur Huck, *The Security of China: Chinese Approaches to Problems of War and Strategy* (New York: Columbia University Press, 1970); and J. D. Simmonds, *China's World: The Foreign Policy of a Developing State* (New York: Columbia University Press, 1971).

A good deal of information, along with some second-rate analysis, on the United Nations aspect may be found in Byron S. J. Weng, *Peking's UN Policy: Continuity and Change* (New York: Praeger, 1972).

A similar comment can be made on the largest recent book on Sino-Soviet relations, which devotes only about one-third of its space to the period since 1949: O. Edmund Clubb, *China and Russia: The "Great Game"* (New York: Columbia University Press, 1971). Harold C. Hinton, *The Bear at the Gate: Chinese Policymaking under Soviet Pressure* (Washington: American Enterprise Institute, and Stanford University: Hoover Institution, 1971) analyzes the Chinese side of the Sino-Soviet tension since 1969 over the border issue.

A collection of thoughtful essays on Sino-American relations by a leading authority can be found in A. Doak Barnett, *A New U. S. Policy Toward China* (Washington: Brookings Institution, 1971). An excellent collection of essays and documents covering recent developments through the announcement (July 15, 1971) of the Chinese invitation to President Nixon is Roderick MacFarquhar, ed., *Sino-American Relations, 1949–71* (New York: Praeger, 1972).

Peter Van Ness has written a reflective and useful book on an important aspect of Chinese foreign policy: *Revolution and Chinese Foreign Policy: Peking's Support for Wars of National Liberation* (University of California Press, 1970).

A detailed and valuable work on Chinese policy toward Southeast Asia, with special reference to Thailand, Cambodia, and Burma, is Melvin Gurtov, *China and Southeast Asia—The Politics of Survival: A Study of Foreign Policy Interaction* (Lexington, Mass.: D. C. Heath, 1971. Neville Maxwell has written a controversial, excessively anti-Indian book on the Sino-Indian border fighting of 1962: *India's China War* (New York: Doubleday, 1972).

The most detailed and informative book on Peking's African policy yet published is Bruce D. Larkin, *China and Africa, 1949–1970: The Foreign Policy of the People's Republic of China* (University of California Press, 1971).

Suggestions for Further Reading

EVER SINCE the time of Marco Polo, China's remoteness, uniqueness, and undeniable achievements have tended to fascinate thinking Western man, who has often attributed to it virtues lacking in his own civilization while overlooking its faults. This tendency was largely suspended in the early nineteenth and twentieth centuries, in view of China's obvious weakness and the plethora of accounts by Western travelers who saw it warts and all. But the trend toward ecstatic works both of description and of analysis has resumed since 1949, for China is strong once more and has impressed many moderates and men of the left in the West favorably, by contrast not only with "imperialist" and "bourgeois" West but with the overbureaucratized Soviet Union. There is probably no other country on which the general level of public discourse in the West so willingly suspends elementary standards of critical judgment and lapses into massive wishful thinking, or rather wishful feeling. Factual information on China is undeniably scanty, largely because of Peking's determination to impose its own propaganda on the world to the exclusion if possible of objective analysis. But enough reasonably "hard" information is available to make possible a far higher level of writing and discussion than now exists, if it were not for the subjective problems already mentioned.

This is not to say that all available writings on China are bad. A great deal of good work has been done on various aspects of China and from various points of view. It is becoming more and more widely recognized that more of this work has been done in the United States, during the period since the end of World War II, than in any other single country. For this reason, and also because this book is intended primarily for the American reader, suggestions given below stress works written and published in the United States. To save time and space and spare feelings, no examples will be cited from the numerous category of works to avoid. On the other hand, it should not be assumed that merely because a particular work is not cited it falls into this category. This is a highly selective list, so much so that no citations of individual periodical articles are given, even though much of the best writing on recent and above all contemporary subjects appears in this form rather than books. References to especially useful periodical articles and more extensive bibliographies can be found in a number of the works mentioned.

Although an "area" knowledge of China is not absolutely essential to an understanding of China's role in the world of today, it is distinctly helpful and most interesting in its own right. Someone wishing to take this approach would be well advised to imagine himself as a prospective tourist and study the superb and recent *China* (Paris: Nagel Publishers, 1968), which contains valuable information on practically all aspects of contemporary China except the political and on its traditional background. Be warned, however, that the orthography employed is the current official Chinese one and different from the one used in this book and in most Western language writings; the differences, however, can be mastered without undue effort. Next our budding China area specialist ought to read the invaluable selections from the best Western writing on modern and contemporary China (the traditional period is regrettably slighted) in Franz Schurmann and Orville Schell, eds., *The China Reader* (3 vols., New York: Random House, 1967). The choice of selections, and still more the commentaries, are somewhat colored by the editors' noticeable Maoist sympathies, but the effect is not so serious that a sophisticated reader cannot make the necessary allowances.

A logical next step would be to broach the history of the Chinese Communist movement. Probably the best place to begin would be Benjamin Schwartz's classic *Chinese Communism and the Rise of Mao* (Cambridge: Harvard University Press, 1951), which deals with the early years with the greatest penetration and wisdom. Another valuable work, especially good on the period before about 1940, is Conrad Brandt, John K. Fairbank, and Benjamin Schwartz, eds., *A Documentary History of Chinese Communism* (Cambridge: Harvard University Press, 1952). It should be pointed out that many of these relatively early post-World War II works are available in later, including paperback, editions. Shanti Swarup, *A Study of the Chinese Communist Movement, 1927–1934* (Oxford: Clarendon Press, 1966), is valuable mainly for its objective and intelligent analysis of the early politico-military strategy of Mao Tse-tung. Edgar Snow's classic, *Red Star Over China*, first published in 1937 and since then in editions too numerous to mention, contains a wealth of authentic and fascinating information on the Chinese Communist movement, precisely because the author displayed a bias in favor of the Chinese Communists so transparent and sincere that they invited him to North Shensi in the summer of 1936; the reader can easily make allowances if he chooses. An important and controversial interpretation of the Chinese Communists' rise to power, stressing the role of Japanese atrocities in rallying the peasantry behind the Communists, is Chalmers A. Johnson, *Peasant Nationalism and Communist Power: The Emergence of Revolutionary China, 1937–1945* (Berkeley: University of California Press, 1962). A very valuable American military intelligence study compiled in 1945 has been reprinted in Lyman P. Van Slyke, ed., *The Chinese Communist Movement* (Stanford: Stanford University Press, 1968). First-rate journalism and political analysis dealing with various aspects of the late civil war period may be found in A. Doak Barnett, *China on the Eve of Communist Takeover* (New York: Praeger, 1963).

Mao Tse-tung and his "thought" stand by themselves as a separate subject of immense importance. It is one that can be usefully approached through the sympathetic works of Stuart Schram (*Mao*

Tse-tung, New York: Simon and Schuster, 1966; and *The Political Thought of Mao Tse-tung*, rev. ed., New York: Praeger, 1968) and the unsympathetic one of Arthur A. Cohen (*The Communism of Mao Tse-tung*, Chicago: University of Chicago Press, 1964). Regardless of his own viewpoint, the student ought not to excuse himself from direct contact with Mao's writings. The standard source is of course *Selected Works of Mao Tse-tung* (4 vols., Peking: Foreign Languages Press, 1961–65), which covers up to 1949. The major writings should be read with the greatest care, preferably more than once. As to the question of which are the major writings, Peking itself has been of some help by reprinting the principal works on strategy in *Selected Military Writings of Mao Tse-tung* (Peking: Foreign Languages Press, 1963) and some of the main political works (with important omissions, but with the inclusion of some dating from later than 1949 and therefore not to be found in the *Selected Works*) in *Selected Readings from the Works of Mao Tse-tung* (Peking: Foreign Languages Press, 1967). A still briefer, and more propagandistic, sampler is the famous Little Red Book (*Quotations from Chairman Mao Tse-tung*, Peking: Foreign Languages Press, 1966 and subsequently).

On domestic affairs since 1949, the section on China (by Harold C. Hinton) in George McT. Kahin, ed., *Major Governments of Asia* (rev. ed., Ithaca: Cornell University Press, 1963) may be recommended as an introduction. Every serious student ought to read Lucian W. Pye's stimulating and controversial *The Spirit of Chinese Politics: A Psychocultural Study of the Authority Crisis in Political Development* (Cambridge: The M.I.T. Press, 1968), which is at its best in dealing with Chinese politics and less satisfactory when trying to apply Western psychological theory of dubious validity to Chinese behavior. Another difficult and highly important book is Franz Schurmann, *Ideology and Organization in Communist China* (rev. ed., Berkeley: University of California Press, 1968), which is as thoughtful and analytical as is possible within the context of a basically sympathetic view of the subject. A detailed and objective study of the workings of the Communist Chinese political system, based largely on interviews with refugees, is A. Doak Barnett, *Cadres, Bureaucracy, and Political Power in Communist China* (New York: Columbia University Press, 1967). An extremely valuable collection of original documents in translation dating from the period of the Great Leap Forward is *Communist China, 1955–1959: Policy Documents with Analysis* (Cambridge: Harvard University Press, 1962).

Probably the best introduction to military matters in China is John Gittings's scholarly study, *The Role of the Chinese Army* (London: Oxford University Press, 1967). A somewhat more specialized work that requires and will repay careful reading is Alice Langley Hsieh, *Communist China's Strategy in the Nuclear Era* (Englewood Cliffs, N. J.: Prentice-Hall, 1962). Valuable essays on various aspects of the subjects named in the title can be found in Morton H. Halperin, ed., *Sino-Soviet Relations and Arms Control* (Cambridge: The M.I.T. Press, 1967).

Among general works on Chinese foreign policy, the patriarch is A. Doak Barnett, *Communist China and Asia: Challenge to American Policy* (New York: Harper, 1960). A more recent and rather detailed study is Harold C. Hinton, *Communist China in World Politics* (Boston: Houghton Mifflin, 1966). Some valuable essays can be found in *China Briefing* (University of Chicago: Center for Policy Study, 1968), especially that by David Mozingo, which, however, goes rather far in explaining most of Chinese policy as a reaction to actual or assumed American initiatives or threats. Herbert Passin has written an excellent analysis of Chinese "people's diplomacy" in *China's Cultural Diplomacy* (New York: Praeger, 1962). Two useful studies of Chinese diplomacy, the first of which, however, proceeds from a somewhat too favorable and optimistic set of apparent assumptions about Chinese policy, and the second of which makes some mistakes in interpreting its data, are Arthur Lall, *How Communist China Negotiates* (New York: Columbia University Press, 1968); and Kenneth T. Young, *Negotiating with the Chinese Communists: The United States Experience, 1953–1967* (New York: McGraw-Hill, 1968).

Some good studies have been published on China's policy toward Asia. Two are collections of essays: Alastair Buchan, ed., *China and the Peace of Asia* (New York: Praeger, 1965); and Tang Tsou, ed., *China in Crisis* (2 vols., Chicago: University of Chicago Press, 1968), vol. 2, *China's Policies in Asia and America's Alternatives*. An important pioneering study, containing a wealth of valuable information, which, however, is not always clearly interpreted, is Allen S. Whiting, *China Crosses the Yalu: The Decision to Enter the Korean War* (New York: Macmillan, 1960). A valuable analysis applying the latest in international relations theory and methodology to an important aspect of China's Asian policy is Sheldon W. Simon, *The Broken Triangle: Peking, Djakarta, and the PKI* (Baltimore: The Johns Hopkins University Press, 1968).

Some of the best writing dealing with China's foreign relations has been evoked by the Sino-Soviet dispute. The standard work is Donald S. Zagoria's masterly *The Sino-Soviet Conflict, 1956–1961* (Princeton: Princeton University Press, 1962). The story is continued in two important studies by William E. Griffith, each of which contains original documents as well as analysis: *The Sino-Soviet Rift* (Cambridge: The M.I.T. Press, 1964) and *Sino-Soviet Relations, 1964–1965* (Cambridge: The M.I.T. Press, 1967). A valuable recent work is John Gittings, *Survey of the Sino-Soviet Dispute* (London: Oxford University Press, 1968), in which the author's anti-American sympathies sometimes lead him astray.

Little of value on the Cultural Revolution has yet appeared in book form. A useful chronological survey may be found in Keesing's Research Report, *The Cultural Revolution in China: Its Origins and Course* (New York: Scribner, 1967).

Of the enormous volume of writing on American China policy, little has appeared in book form and even less is of real value. Apart from studies of largely historical interest relating to the pre-1949 period, one might begin with a book presenting penetrating analyses of the policies of selected other countries toward China: A. M. Halpern, ed., *Policies Toward China: Views from Six Continents* (New York: McGraw-Hill, 1965). A recent and highly sophisticated book on American policy, past, present, and future, toward Asia as a whole is Bernard K. Gordon, *Toward Disengagement in Asia: A Strategy for American Foreign Policy* (Englewood Cliffs, N. J.: Prentice-Hall, 1969). A briefer and somewhat more dovelike prescription may be found in Edwin O. Reischauer's contribution, "Transpacific Relations," in Kermit Gordon, ed., *Agenda for the Nation,* (Washington: Brookings, 1968). Of great value as a reference work on events, major statements, etc., is *China and U. S. Far East Policy, 1945–1967* (Washington: Congressional Quarterly,

1967). The 1966 Senate hearings on China are digested in Akira Iriye, ed., *U. S. Policy Toward China* (Boston: Little, Brown, 1968).

At or before this point, the student ought to begin his own independent study of original Chinese sources, presumably in English translation. The Foreign Languages Press publishes in pamphlet form many although by no means all official Chinese statements (speeches, editorials, etc.) relevant to policy. These may be ordered from China Books and Periodicals, 2929 24th Street, San Francisco, California 94110; and China Publications, 95 Fifth Avenue, New York, N. Y. 10003. Much fuller translations, usually available only in major research libraries, are prepared in Hong Kong by the American Consulate General (principally under the title *Survey of the China Mainland Press*) and the Union Research Institute (under the title *Union Research Service*).

Periodicals of particular value on contemporary China are *The China Quarterly* (London), *Asian Survey* (Berkeley), *The Far Eastern Economic Review* (Hong Kong), *China Topics* (London), *Current Scene* (Hong Kong), *Problems of Communism* (Washington), and *China News Analysis* (Hong Kong).

For more detailed research, a number of valuable aids are available. One is the annual bibliography of works on Asia in Western languages published by the *Journal of Asian Studies* (Ann Arbor). Another is Peter Berton and Eugene Wu, comp., *Contemporary China: A Research Guide*, (Stanford: Hoover Institution, 1967). Raw biographic data may be found in *Who's Who in Communist China* (Hong Kong: Union Research Institute, 1966). Far better is Donald W. Klein and Anne B. Clark, *Biographic Dictionary of Chinese Communism* (two vols., Harvard University Press, 1971).

Index

Abdullah, Sheik, 150
Acheson, Dean, 42, 315
achievements of foreign policy, 306–9
Adenauer, Konrad, 216
Afghanistan, 112, 193, 226, 246–47
Africa, 110–12, 151–52, 186, 195, 255, 259–61, 301–2
Afro-Asian Conference, 77, 132, 139, 147–48, 193–94, 239, 256–58
Afro-Asian People's Solidarity Organization, 152, 194, 250, 261–62
Afro-Asian-Latin American People's Solidarity Organization, 152, 194, 261–62
agriculture, 2–6, 40, 172, 263
Aidit, D. N., 144, 248
Akahata, 187
Aksai Chin region, 97–98, 112
Al Fatah, 186, 256, 259
Albania: Chinese aid to, 160, 195, 197, 215; Chinese support of, 104–7, 159; chrome exports, 105; Communist power seizure, 196; and Sino-Soviet dispute, 215, 217–19; and World Federation of Trade Unions, 103
Algeria, 50, 250–58
American China policy, 313–22: history of, 313–19; and Japan, 321; outlook for future of, 322;

and Soviet, 319–20; and Taiwan, 320–21; *see also* United States
Angola, 111, 151, 197, 260
Anzus Treaty, 265
armed struggle strategy, 35–56, 73–75, 146, 225, 249
Asian policy of China, 38, 73–79, 231–47, 308–11
Asian policy of U.S., 268, 314
Aswan Dam, 251
attitudes of the Chinese, 30–32
Australia, 237, 265, 274–75
Ayub Khan, Mohammed, 150, 246

Bakdash, Khalid, 252
Bakunin, Mikhail, 264
Bandaranaiko, Mme., 300
Bandung Conference, 68–69, 72, 77, 132, 147, 193, 232, 250, 266
Belgian communism, 228, 275
Belgrade Conference, 255–56
Ben Bella, Achmed, 147, 258
Beria, Lavrenti, 60–61
Berlin, 41–42, 59–60, 218
Bhutan, 98, 112–13, 247
Bhutto, Zulfikar, 151, 246, 300
Borneo, 118
Boumedienne, Henri, 147, 258
Bourguiba, Habib, 258
Boxer Rebellion, 12, 256
Brazil, 261
Brezhnev, Leonid, 128, 217, 289

Brezhnev Doctrine, 159, 284

British Commonwealth, 271–75

British East India Company, 10

Brunei, protectorate of, 118

Bulganin, Nikolai, 61

Burgess, Guy, 48

Burma: border region of, 112, 199; Communist Party of, 39, 227, 244; KMT irregulars in, 109, 243; leftist insurgency, 161, 243–44; mentioned, 7, 36, 51, 76, 174, 182, 196, 238, 239; people's wars, 200, 244; Rangoon demonstrations, 203; treaty of friendship, 193

Burundi, 37, 111, 151–52, 260

Cairo Conference, 172

Calcutta Youth Conference, 29, 49, 50

Cambodia: antagonism to Chinese in, 198; economic aid to, 195; Communist Party in, 226; Liu Shao-ch'i tour of, 182; rivalry for influence in, 239–40; treaty of friendship, 193; U.S. intrusion in, 290, 291; Viet Minh in, 65–66

Canada, 273–74

Canton Province, 13

Castro, Fidel, 115, 152, 228, 262

Ceausescu, 302–3

Central African Republic, 111, 152, 260

Ceylon, 76, 226, 247, 300

Chang Hsueh-liang, 14–15, 23–24

Chang Kuo-t'ao, 23

Ch'en Po-ta, 189, 191

Chen Tu-hsiu, 20

Chen Yi: at Geneva Conference, 193; mentioned, 109, 117, 120, 144, 168; Red Guard criticism of, 153–54, 202; on transferring nuclear aid, 187–88; on war without boundaries, 185

Chen Yun, 188, 189

Chiang Ching. *See* Mao Tse-tung, Mme.

Chiang Kai-shek: and Eisenhower, 55, 67; at Kiangsi soviety, 22; mentioned, 173; Northern Expedition of, 14, 19–20; Sian Incident, 23–24; Soviet aid to, 15, 23, 24

Chile, 261, 302

Ch'in dynasty, 2

China: Communism's rise in, 18–20; history of, 1–32; inherited attitudes in, 30–32; modern, 8–32; traditional, 2–8

China, People's Republic of (Communist): American policy on, 289–95, 313–22; as Asian power, 231–33; first people's commune of, 90; history of, 18–20; Mao as senior in, 59–62, 94–95; Red Guard diplomacy, 153–56; and Soviet, 35–36, 102–5, 120–26; Taiwan Strait crisis, 67–69, 74, 89–94, 114, 200, 267; territorial water limit, 92; Third World setbacks, 146–53, 177; *see also* Communist Party of China, Cultural Revolution, foreign policy

China, Republic of (Nationalist): American policy on, 233, 292–95, 317–21; and Canada, 273; and France, 276; and normalization campaign, 286; proclaimed, 12, 14; Quemoy issue, 91, 93; reconnaisance aircraft, 170; security treaty with U.S., 68; Taiwan to be "liberated"? 172–74; Taiwan Strait crisis, 67–69, 74, 89–94, 114, 200, 267; to be unified with Red China?, 320–21; and United Nations, 17, 42, 174, 286, 320; in World War II, 16, 17, 27

Chinese Eastern Railway, 19

Chinese People's Association . . . , 202

Chou En-lai: Albania tour, 153; on ambassadorial talks, 267; Bandung Conference, 77, 193; Burma trip, 76; Cultural Revolution sup-

Chou En-lai (*cont.*)
port, 189; Eastern European tour, 82; foreign policy strategy, 201–2, 287; Geneva Conference, 64–65; and India, 76, 97, 98, 112; and Japan, 296–97; and Lin Piao, 294; mentioned, 86, 109, 136, 141, 147, 155, 190, 191, 270, 303; Moscow visit, 128; North African tour, 111–12; on Politburo, 188; Rumania tour, 153; and Sino-Soviet relations, 288, 296; Stalin funeral delegation, 58, 59; at Twenty-first Congress, 95; at Twenty-second Congress, 106–7; and the U.S., 284, 290, 295
Chu Teh, 101, 188, 189
Cierna Conference, 216–17
civil war, 17–18, 24
collective mobilization, 215
Colombia, 261
Comintern, 19, 20, 27, 52, 254
communism, international, 205–30, 303–4
Communist Party of China (CPC): anti-Japanese campaign, 23; Central Committee, 90, 94–95, 99, 188–91; coalition government proposal, 28–29; Eighth Congress, 80–84, 188–89, 208; formation of, 19; inherited attitudes of, 30–32; and Kuomintang, 13–14, 19; land reform measures, 25; membership growth, 25; Military Committee, 90; Moscow meeting of 1928, 20; Ninth Congress, 189, 191, 219, 284, 285; opposition to détente, 71; peaceful coexistence strategy, 73–77; Politburo, 188–91; rise of, 18–30; Seventh Congress, 28, 84; and Sino-Japanese War, 24–26, 29; Stalin on, 84; Standing Committee, 188–89, 191; and World War II, 16, 17, 26–27; *see also* China, People's Republic of
Confucianism, 4–5, 10

Congo, Republic of, at Brazzaville, 111, 193, 252, 260
Congo, Republic of, at Leopoldville, 110, 111, 151, 259–60
Cuba: guerrilla warfare in, 262; mentioned, 114, 166, 276; relations with China, 115, 152, 228, 261–62; Soviet aid to, 228; U.S. quarantine of, 116
Cultural Revolution: against intellectuals, 140, 145; Albanian approval of, 215; Army intervention, 141; attacks on foreigners, 154–55; and Burma, 244; causes of, 137; end of, 156, 283–85; and foreign policy, 127–62, 309; Great Leap Forward, 137; launching of, 137–41; militancy of, 269; polemics against Soviet, 128–37; and policy formulation, 188–90; purges, 140; recall of overseas diplomats, 153, 155; results of, 156, 171; supervision of, 133; Third World setbacks, 146–53, 177, 256; and Vietnam War, 141–46; *see also* Red Guard movement
Czechoslovakia: arms deal with Egypt, 251; Cierna Conference, 216–17; reaction to de-Stalinization, 80; Soviet invasion of, 159, 175, 178, 209, 211, 216–18, 225–29, 275–78, 284

Dahomey, 152, 260
Dairen, 40, 54–55
Dalai Lama, 52, 97–98
Dang Las Dong Party, 51
de Gaulle, Charles, 124, 276, 277, 291, 304
Demag, 278
Democratic Centralism, 203
détente, 71, 100, 122, 160, 270
Dienbienphu battle, 62, 63, 75
Dillon, C. Douglas, 100
diplomatic relations, return to, 285–87

Dominican Republic, 142
dual adversary strategy, 287, 320
Dubcek, Alexander, 158, 217
Dulles, John Foster, 63, 75–76, 93, 98, 168, 214, 266–67, 316

East Berlin, 60
East Germany, 125, 214, 219, 278
"East wind over West wind," 85–90, 267
Eastern Europe: CPC and, 212–19; current problems, 302–3; de-Stalinization in, 80–82; Huang Yung-sheng tour of, 193, 217–18; and Sino-Soviet dispute, 212–19
Eden, Sir Anthony, 64
Egypt, 72, 250–52, 258–59
Eighth Route Army, 26
Eisenhower, Dwight D., 55, 56, 67, 100, 103, 316
Eisenhower Doctrine, 107
Europe, CPC policy toward, 272–75
European Defense Community, 64, 65
evaluation of foreign policy, 306–22

failures of foreign policy, 309–12
Finland, 125
Five Year Plans, 61, 71, 85–86, 171
Foreign Languages Press, 182
foreign policy: achievements of, 306–9; on Africa, 259–61, 301–2; on Algeria, 250–58; on Asia, 231–47; and Bandung Conference, 250; on Bangla Desh, 299–300; on Ceylon, 300; concerns and goals of, 165–79; of the Cultural Revolution, 127–62; and differences in leadership, 179–82; diplomatic relations resumed, 285–87; on Eastern Europe, 302–3; economic aid programs, 194–96; evaluation of, 306–22; failures of, 309–12; formulation of, 188–91; from above approach, 249–52, 257; from below approach, 252–54, 255; and Great Leap Forward, 251; on Himalayan states, 246–47; implementation of, 201–4; and international communism, 303–4; on Japan, 295–98; on Latin America, 261–62, 302; and leftists, 194–96, 304; and legacy of the past, 1–32; making of, 165–204; Mao's "thoughts" on, 192; on Middle East, 257–59, 300–1; and military considerations, 182–88; outlook for, 312–13; propaganda, 191–93; since end of Cultural Revolution, 283–305; Sino-American, 107–9, 185, 289–95, 313–22; Sino-Soviet, 169–78, 205–30, 287–89; during Stalinist period, 35–59; on Taiwan, 320–21; and Third World, 176–78, 227–30, 248–62; on Western Europe, 304–5
Formosa Resolution, 68
France: CPC policy towards, 275–77; Dienbienphu battle, 62, 63, 75; diplomatic recognition of China, 37, 124, 125; mentioned, 121, 237, 263, 265; Nationalist China and, 276; and Vietnam War, 50, 62, 63
French Congo, 111, 193, 252, 260
Friendship Associations, 202–3
future of foreign policy, 312–13

Geneva ambassadorial talks, 72, 167, 266–67
Geneva Conference of 1954, 53, 62–68, 185, 193
Geneva Conference of 1961–62, 109–10, 193, 222–23
Geneva Summit Conference of 1955, 71, 74, 266
Germany, Federal Republic of: CPC policy, on 277–79; consular talks, 169; Grand Coalition, 216; mentioned, 124, 125, 126, 187, 197, 213, 218, 219; *Ostpolitik,*

Germany (*cont.*)
211, 216, 277–79; trade, 197, 272, 276, 278
Ghana, 37, 152, 193, 260
Gierek, Edward, 303
Glassboro Conference, 136
Goldwater, Barry, 125
Gomulka, Wladyslaw, 81, 303
Goulart, Joao, 261
grain imports, 104, 274
Great Britain, 37, 121, 154–55, 237, 271–73
Great Leap Forward, 87–90, 94, 99, 104–6, 137, 139, 188–89, 199, 214, 221, 251
Grey, Anthony, 273
Grippa, Jacques, 228, 275
Guam, 236
guerrilla warfare: communist power seizures by, 196; in Cuba, 262; in Malaya, 51; Mao's, 21–22; in Sino-Japanese War, 24; in Vietnam, 50
Guinea, 193, 260

Haiti, 261
Harriman, Averell, 99
Hilsman, Roger, 268–69
Himalayan states, 246–47
Hitler, Adolf, 1, 125, 166
Ho Chi Minh, 36, 39, 50, 64–66, 118, 222
Hong Kong, 37, 121, 154, 237, 271–73
Huang Yung-shen, 193, 217–18
Hundred Flowers campaign, 83–86, 94
Hundred Regiments Offensive, 26, 27
Hungary, 80–81, 84, 213, 216
hydroelectric industry, 45

imperialism, 166, 177
India: American aid to, 268; and Bangla Desh, 299–300; border dispute with China, 97–98, 111–17, 147, 150, 200, 226, 232, 255;

Communist Party in 39, 51–52; CPC policy towards, 74–77; Dalai Lama's flight to, 97–98; diplomatic recognition of China, 36; Kashmir dispute, 97, 112–13, 150; Khrushchev visit, 112; and Korea, 55, 75; Pakistan dispute, 150–51, 197–98; rivalry with China, 244-45; Soviet policy on, 211
Indochina, 289–90, 298–99, 314–15
Indonesia: antagonism to Chinese in, 198; anti-Malay Federation campaign, 118, 237, 241, 271; anti-Sukarno uprising, 107; Chinese dual citizenship, 77, 117, 198–99, 242; Communist Party, 39, 51, 117–18, 148–49, 224–25, 241; *coup* of 1965, 147–49, 186; diplomatic recognition of China, 36; Five Principles of Peaceful Coexistence, 76; Java raid, 161–62; Khrushchev visit, 112, 117; Liu Shao-ch'i tour, 182; mentioned, 132, 255, 256; military power seizure, 238; treaty of friendship, 193; United Nations walk-out, 147; West Irian dispute, 118; World War II, 314–15
Indo-Pakistani War of 1965, 150–51, 186
industrialization, 45, 60, 85, 95, 103–4, 172, 210, 263
Inner Mongolia, 16, 18, 172, 220
International Control Commissions (ICC), 66
international credit, 172
International Liaison Department, 201
Israel, 215, 250

Jao Shu-shih, 61
Japan: anti-communism in, 233; China's relations with, since 1969, 295–98; Chinese image in, 234–35; Communist Party in, 41, 133, 225; mentioned, 12, 14, 15, 121, 168, 176, 183, 187, 203;

Japan (*cont.*)
  neutrality pact, 16, 21; passivity
  in international politics, 236; security treaty with U.S., 268; and
  Sino-American relations, 293,
  321; Sino-Soviet Alliance on, 39;
  Soviet diplomatic relations, 70;
  Soviet policy on, 211; trade, 234,
  235, 272; U.S. occupation of,
  166–67; and World War II, 16,
  17, 271, 272, 314–15
Java, 161–62
Jesuits, 10
Johnson, Lyndon B., 120, 136, 157,
  192, 269, 317–18
joint stock companies, 40, 70

K'ang Sheng, 138, 155, 189, 191
Kao Kang, 60–61, 71
Kashmir, 97, 112–13, 150, 245
Kazakh tribe, 113–14
Keng Piao, 303
Kennan, George, 41
Kennedy, John F., 104, 109, 115,
  218, 246, 252, 268, 316–17
Khamba tribe, 97–98, 247
Khrushchev, Nikita: on African
  wars of liberation, 252; CPC and,
  96–126; China visit, 70; Cuban
  missile crisis, 262, 276; de-Stalinization, 79–82, 88, 106–7, 180, 201,
  208, 213; disarmament ploys,
  100–1; fall of, 126–28, 189, 192,
  207, 229; Geneva Summit Conference, 71; global strategy, 72–
  73; Indonesia visit, 112, 117;
  mentioned, 94, 131, 132, 138, 139,
  169, 178, 216, 222–23, 238, 249;
  power struggle of, 63–64, 69, 85;
  Quemoy issue, 92; Tito and,
  105, 122, 214, 215; U.S. tour, 268,
  316; Vienna Conference, 109
Kiangsi soviet, 22, 28
Kiesinger, Kurt, 216
King, Martin Luther, 192, 270
Kissinger, Henry, 292, 295, 321
KMT. *See* Kuomintang

Kommunist, 207
Kong, Le, 108
Korea, 6, 40–43, 88, 175, 221, 222,
  226, 233, 236
Korea, Democratic People's Republic of: Chinese troop withdrawal, 221; diplomatic relations with China, 35–36; Liu
  Shao-ch'i tour, 193; military alliances with China, 185; *Pueblo*
  seizure, 156–57; Soviet aid to,
  221–22
Korean War: armistice, 48–49, 53–
  59, 62, 88, 167, 266–67; China
  and, 44–49, 58, 203–4, 265; end
  of, 57–59; results of, 58–59; Soviet role in, 41–42, 48–49, 53–54;
  and United Nations, 45, 47–48,
  53–54, 265; and U.S. policy to
  China, 315–16
Kosygin, Aleksei, 130, 136, 192,
  259, 288
Kowloon, 272
Kozlov, Frol, 107, 122
Kudryavtsev, S. M., 238
Kuomintang (National People's
  Party): beginning of, 12; Burma
  irregulars, 109, 243; Comintern
  alliance, 13–14, 19; and Sino-
  Japanese War, 24–26, 29; troops
  of, 109, 243; *see also* China, Republic of
Kuznetsov, Vasily V., 320

land ownership, 5, 9
land reforms, 25
languages, 4,
Laos: American policy on, 267,
  289–90, 298–99, 314–15; border
  pressures on, 199; Chinese in,
  198; Communist Party, 226, 239;
  election of 1958, 108; Geneva
  agreements on, 65–66, 107–10,
  193, 222–26; international intervention in crisis, 107–10, 114,
  119, 268; rivalry for influence in,
  239–40; Soviet airlift to, 109,

Laos (*cont.*)
132; Soviet support of, 238; Viet Minh in, 62
Latin America, 228, 261–62, 302
Lenin, N., 19, 57, 102, 106, 166
Leninism. *See* Marxism-Leninism
Li Fu-ch'un, 189, 190
Li Hsien-nien, 312
Li Li-san, 20, 22
Liaotung Peninsula, 40
Liberal Democratic Party in Japan, 234
Liberation Army Daily, 201
Lin Piao: and Cultural Revolution, 140–41, 189; decline of, 285; as Defense Minister, 100; dual adversary strategy of, 284–85, 294; elimination of, 287; foreign policy of, 188–91; mentioned, 155; people's war statement, 140, 192, 195–96; on thermonuclear war, 183; and U.S. relations, 284; and Vietnam War, 143–44
Liu Shao-ch'i: chairmanship, 189; and Cultural Revolution, 140, 179, 190; disagreement with Mao, 84–85, 134, 137–38; elected Chief of State, 94–95; Hanoi visit, 119; Moscow Conference of, 104; North Korea tour, 193; on Politburo, 188; political downfall, 180; Red Guard opposition, 179; Southeast Asia tours, 153, 182, 193
Liu Shao-ch'i, Mme., 137, 138
Lo Jui-ch'ing, 133, 140
Lon Nol, 298–99
Long March, 22–23, 28
"lost territories," 310
Louis, Victor, 219

Macao, 121, 154–55
MacArthur, Douglas, 41, 44–49, 59, 316
McCarthy, Joseph, 316
Maclean, Donald, 48

McMahon Line, 98, 114
Madagascar, 255
Magsaysay, Ramon, 51
Malay Barrier, 314–15
Malay states, 6–7
Malaysia, Federation of: Australian military action, 274; and British, 51, 237; Chinese in, 198, 271; Communist Party, 39, 227; expulsion of Singapore, 242; guerrilla, 51; and Indonesia, 118, 237, 241, 271; mentioned, 118, 148, 241, 242: terrorist movement, 198; United Nations, 147
Malenkov, Georgi M., 60–64, 69, 71, 85
Mali, 193, 260
Manchuria: history of, 7–17; hydroelectric industry, 45; industrialism, 60, 61; mentioned, 42, 166, 172, 182; Soviet flights over, 217
Manchus, 7–12
Mandarin, 4
Mao Tse-tung: anti-Western orientation, 315; background, 21; and border clashes, 288; and Castro, 262; cult of, 78, 83, 95, 229–30; death's possible effects, 312–13; and de Gaulle, 304; and de-Stalinization, 82–85; diplomatic failures, 310–11; domestic challenges to leadership of, 78–95; "East wind over West wind," 85–90, 267; ends Cultural Revolution, 283–84; and Great Leap Forward, 87–90; launches Cultural Revolution, 137–41; and Lin Piao, 285, 294; Long March of, 22–23, 28; and making of foreign policy, 170–82, 189–91; and Nixon's visit, 291, 295, 319; radicalism of, 85, 311; rise to power, 22–30; Secret Speech of 1957, 84–85; as senior Communist, 59–61, 79–80; and Sino-Soviet quarrels, 208–10;

348   *Index*

Mao Tse-tung (*cont.*)
  "thought" of, 27–28, 83, 172, 178,
    192, 228–33, 257, 264; U.S. policy
    of, 30, 93, 156–57, 315
Mao Tse-tung, Mme. (Chiang
    Ching), 137–38, 141, 155, 190–91
Marshall, George C., 17
Marx, Karl, 89, 264
Marxism-Leninism, 102, 178, 207–
    9, 229
massive retaliation doctrine, 63,
    168
Matsu Islands, 68
May Fourth Movement, 13
medium-range missiles (MRBMs),
    169
Mendès-France, Pierre, 65
Menon, Krishna, 113, 114
Middle East: Al Fatah movement,
    186, 256, 259; anti-Western feel-
    ing in, 250, 257; communism in,
    228, 229; crisis of 1958, 90–91;
    crisis of 1967, 136, 192, 258;
    Eisenhower Doctrine on, 107;
    recent problems in, 300–1; Third
    World strategy toward, 257–59;
    see also individual countries
military policy and strategy, 182–
    88
Ministry of Public Security, 202
Molotov, Vyacheslav, 62–66, 85
Mongolia. *See* Inner Mongolia;
    Outer Mongolia
Mongolian People's Republic, 286
Morgenthau, Hans, 310
Morocco, 258
Moscow Communist Party Con-
    ferences: of 1960, 104–8, 122,
    210; of 1965, 130–31
Moslems in China, 257
Mozambique, 111, 151, 197, 260
Multilateral Nuclear Force (MLF),
    125, 216

Naga tribe, 200, 244
Nagy, Imre, 81, 213

Nanking, 12–15; *see also* China,
    Republic of
Nasser, Gamel, 77, 152, 228, 250–
    52, 255
National Liberation Front, 141,
    161, 227, 241
National People's Congress, 94, 101
Nationalist China. *See* China, Re-
    public of
Nehru, Jawaharlal, 36, 37, 52, 72,
    75–76, 97–98, 112–14, 244, 250–
    51, 255, 266
Nepal: Communist Party in, 226;
    Gurkhas in, 7; Khamba refugees,
    247; mentioned, 98, 112, 119;
    treaty of friendship, 193
Netherlands, 37, 181
New China News Agency, 202,
    261, 268
New Left, 304
New York Times, 80
New Zealand, 189–91, 237, 265, 275
Ngo Dinh Diem, 107, 119–20, 143
Nixon, Richard M.: China policy,
    290–91, 318–21; and Japan, 296;
    Mao's campaign against, 270;
    Mao's reception of, 319; and of-
    fensive weaponry, 160–61; visit
    to China, 282, 294–95, 319; and
    West Berlin crisis, 218
Nixon Doctrine, 289, 291, 293, 322
Nkrumah, Kwame, 152
North Atlantic Treaty Organiza-
    tion (NATO), 42, 63, 69, 71,
    211–13, 215, 275, 279
North Borneo, 118
North Korea. *See* Korea, Demo-
    cratic People's Republic of
North Vietnam. *See* Vietnam,
    Democratic Republic of
Northern Expedition of 1926–27,
    14, 19–20
Nu, U, 76, 243, 266
nuclear weapons: aid to Egypt,
    258; Albanian ore for, 105; and
    attack fears, 167–69, 183–85; be-
    ginning of, 56; cobalt imports,

nuclear weapons (*cont.*)
258; effect of, 311; pledge on use of, 186–87, 192–93; research reactor, 87–88; and Sino-American relations, 317; Soviet aid and, 70, 87–89; Soviet nervousness over, 211–12; surface-to-surface, 88; testing of, 126, 136, 145, 160, 259; "thought" of Mao on, 192

Okinawa, 168, 174, 233
On Coalition Government, 166
Open Door Doctrine, 314
Opium War of 1839, 10
Outer Mongolia: border agreement with China, 112; border dispute, 211; defense treaty with Russia, 169; diplomatic relations, 35–36; distrust of China, 220; Hundred Regiments offensive, 26, 27; mentioned, 70, 125, 172; and Moscow Conference of 1960, 104; Russian influences, 12, 19, 220; and Sino-Soviet disputes, 211, 219–20
outlook for future foreign policy, 312–13
overseas Chinese communities, 75, 76, 153–54, 198–99, 201, 242

Pakistan: American aid to, 150; and Bangla Desh, 299–300; Chinese aid to, 186, 195, 246; diplomatic recognition of China, 36; India dispute, 150–51, 197–98, 246; and Kashmir, 112–13, 245; mentioned, 117, 193, 226; military regime, 238; SEATO, 76, 237, 245; Soviet aid to, 238
Palestine Liberation Organization, 258
Panama crisis of 1964, 261
Pant, Pandit, 112
Paris peace talks, 146, 157, 161, 224
Paris Summit Conference, 102–3
Pathet Lao, 107–10

peaceful coexistence strategy, 73–77
Peking: Kuomintang occupation, 14; sack of British compound, 155; student demonstration in, 13; *see also* China, People's Republic of
P'eng Chen, 132–34, 140
P'eng Te-huai, 99–100, 139
People's Daily, 82–84, 114, 123, 132, 201
People's Liberation Army, 99, 202
People's Republic. *See* China, People's Republic of
people's wars: in Burma, 200; Chinese support to, 174–75, 191; failure of, 311–12; Maoist theory on, 195–96; in Thailand, 139, 149–50
Peru, 261
Philby, Kim, 48
Philippines: antagonism to Chinese in, 198; anti-American feelings, 233; anti-communism, 233; Communist revolts, 39; Huks, 51, 227; SEATO, 76, 237, 265
Phouma, Souvanna, 107–8, 110
Poland, 80–81, 125
Polaris submarines, 236
polemics, policy of, 102–5, 120–37
population: density, 184; growth, 3, 8; of Hong Kong, 272; of overseas Chinese, 76; ratio with resources, 171; of Singapore, 198
Port Arthur, 54–55, 70
Portisch, Hugo, 120
Pueblo incident, 156–57, 222
Pye, Lucian, 30

Quemoy, 67, 91–93, 173

Radio Peace and Progress, 136
Rann of Cutch, 150
Red Flag, 201
Red Guard movement: criticism of Chen Yi, 153–54, 202; demonstrations by, 134–36, 154–55; di-

Red Guard movement (*cont.*)
plomacy of, 153–56, 203, 244, 247; end of, 284; and Liu Shao-ch'i, 179; Mao rallies, 140–41; Sino-Soviet border incidents, 135, 170; violence of, 273

Republic of China. *See* China, Republic of

Returned Students clique, 21–22

Rhee, Syngman, 44, 58, 268

Rhodesia, 111, 151, 197, 260–61

Ridgway, Matthew B., 47, 49

Rumania, 103, 125, 153, 159, 193, 197, 215–19

Russo-Japanese War, 12

Sabah, 118

Sadat, Anwar, 301

Sananikone, Phoui, 108

Sarawak, 118, 241–42

Sarit, Marshal, 240

Sato, Eisaku, 296–97

SEATO, 75–76, 109, 237, 240, 245

Selected Military Writings of Mao Tse-tung, 119, 182

Shang dynasty, 4

Sian Incident, 23–24

Sihanouk, Prince, 155, 193, 240, 298–99

Sikkim, 151, 155–56, 199, 247

Singapore, 118, 198, 242

Sinkiang: establishment of joint companies, 40; Kazakh tribe, 113–14; mentioned, 70, 97, 126, 160, 172, 183, 245; Russian influences in, 12; tribal unrest, 169

Sino-American relations. *See* United States' China policy

Sino-Indian border dispute, 97–98, 111–17, 200

Sino-Indian relations. *See* India

Sino-Japanese War, 24–29

Sino-Soviet Alliance of 1950, 37–40, 54–56, 59–60, 79, 94–102, 122–23, 185, 210, 265

Sino-Soviet Nonaggression Pact of 1937, 15, 24

Sino-Soviet relations. *See* Soviet Union

Snow, Edgar, 25, 120, 127, 141, 172, 291

Somalia, 186

South Africa, 111, 151, 197, 260–61

South Vietnam. *See* Vietnam

Southeast Asia Collective Defense Organization, 75–76, 109, 237, 240, 245

Soviet Union: agriculture exploitation, 40; aid to Chiang Kai-shek, 5, 23; aid to Cuba, 228; arms race, 59; border clashes, 218, 285–88, 307; concentration camps, 206; and CPC, 205–30; Cultural Revolution polemics against, 128–37; Czechoslovakia invasion, 159, 175, 178, 209, 211, 216, 225, 228–29, 275–78; de-Stalinization, 80–85, 106–7, 180, 201, 208, 213; dispute with China, 205–30, 287–89; German invasion, 26; Hungarian invasion, 81, 84, 213, 216; India policy, 211; Indo-Pakistani mediation, 151; Japan policy, 211; Korean War role, 41–42, 48–49, 53–54; Laotian airlift, 109, 132; Manchuria overflights, 217, 218; and nuclear weapons, 211–12; Outer Mongolia influence, 12, 19, 169, 220; Security Council walk-out, 42; and Sino-American rapprochement, 293–95, 319–20; Stalinist period, 37–40; Third World strategy, 252–53, 255, 261–62; Ussuri River clashes, 218, 285, 287–88

Spirit of Chinese Politics, The, 30

Sputnik, 86

Stalin, Joseph: aid to Chiang, 15, 23, 24; CPC on, 82; Comintern control, 20, 52; concentration camps, 206; death of, 56, 79, 177–78, 206, 208–10, 213, 265; funeral delegation, 57–60; men-

Stalin, Joseph (*cont.*)
tioned, 1, 16, 17, 36, 73; and Sino-Soviet negotiations, 38–39; and Tito, 89; views on Korea, 45
Starlinger, Wilhelm, 206
Suez crisis, 72, 107, 160, 251
Sukarno, Achmed: Bandung Conference, 77; Malaysia campaign, 118; political decline of, 149; popularity, 148; West Irian dispute, 118
Sukarno, Mme. Hartini, 137
Sun Yat-sen, 12–14
Sung, Kim Il, 42, 45, 221–22
Supreme State Conference, 92
Switzerland, 37
Syria, 86, 252, 258
Szechuan, 22–23

Taipei. *See* China, Republic of
Taiwan. *See* China, Republic of
Taiwan Straits, 67–69, 74, 89–94, 114, 200, 267, 291
Tanganyika, 111–12
Tan-Zam Railway, 260
Tanzania, 111–12, 151, 195, 256, 260
Tao Chu, 189–90
Taoism, 5
Tashkent talks, 151
Tass, 92, 96
Tatu, Michel, 159
Taylor, Maxwell D., 120
Teng Hsiao-p'ing, 84, 134, 140–41, 188–90
Tepavac, Mirko, 303
Thailand: Communist Party in, 227; fear of China, 240; Johnson's visit, 192; mentioned, 3, 7, 109, 161, 197, 237; military regime, 238; Patriotic Front, 149, 227; people's war, 139, 149–50; SEATO, 76, 237, 240, 265; U.S. troops in, 114; Vietnam War and, 135, 150, 241

Third World strategy: on Africa, 259–61; Algeria base, 250; and Cultural Revolution, 146–53, 177, 256; economic aid, 195; from above approach, 249–52, 257; from below approach, 252–54, 255; on Latin America, 261–62; on Middle East, 257–59; military aid, 186; self-reliant movement, 254–55; setbacks, 146–53, 256
Tibet: border clash with Sikkim, 155–56, 199; British influences in, 12; Dalai Lama's flight from, 97–98; Khamba revolt, 97–98; mentioned, 7, 18, 45, 113, 151, 172, 245, 247; Sino-Indian discussions on, 75
tributary system, 7, 10, 248
Truman, Harry S., 17, 37, 42, 44, 47, 316
Truong Chinh, 161, 224
Tun, Than, 227
T'ung Meng Hui, 12
Tunisia, 37, 256, 258
Twentieth Soviet Party Congress, 79–82, 87–88, 232, 249–50
Twenty-first Soviet Congress, 95
Twenty-One Demands, 12–13
Twenty-second Soviet Congress, 106–7
Twenty-third Soviet Congress, 134

unification of China, 172–74
Union of Soviet Socialist Republics. *See* Soviet Union
United Arab Republic, 72, 250–52, 258–59
United Front Work Department, 201
United Nations: India-Pakistan cease fire, 151; Indonesia walkout, 147; and Korean War, 42, 45, 47–48, 53–54, 256; mentioned, 17, 40, 42, 58, 68, 100, 124, 147, 174, 246, 259; Middle East crisis of 1958, 90–91; two Chinas in,

United Nations (*cont.*)
286; West Irian administration,
118
United States: arms race, 59; China
policy of, 55, 67, 289–95, 313–22;
CPC policy towards, 264–71;
Dulles and China policy, 63, 75–
76, 93, 98, 168, 266–67; and Japan, 314, 321; and Laos, 107–9;
massive retaliation theory, 63,
168; and nuclear warfare, 185;
occupation of Japan, 166–67;
outlook for future, 322; Panama
crisis of 1964, 261; *Pueblo* crisis,
156, 157, 222; Senate hearing on
China policy, 134; U-2 incident,
103; Yugoslav military aid, 55
United States Seventh Fleet, 44,
59, 67–68, 92, 170, 273
U.S.S.R. *See* Soviet Union
Ussuri River border clashes, 218,
285, 287–88
U-2 incident, 103

Victoria Island, 272
Vienna Conference of 1961, 109
Viet Cong, 120, 141, 145, 146, 157,
161, 181, 215, 224
Viet Minh, 50, 62–66, 75
Vietnam: antagonism towards Chinese population, 198; Geneva
conference on, 66–67; Johnson's
1966 tour, 192; mentioned, 6,
107, 109, 197
Vietnam, Democratic Republic of:
Chinese aid to, 118–19, 186;
Communist power seizure, 196;
first diplomatic recognition of,
36, 39, 50; Liu Shao-ch'i tour of,
182; mentioned, 65, 181, 197, 239;
relations with China, 317–19; and
Sino-Soviet dispute, 222–24; Soviet aid to, 238
Vietnam War: American China
policy and, 317–19; Australian

commitment, 274; China and,
141–46, 158; disengagement, 204;
Paris peace talks, 146, 157, 161,
224; Senate hearings on, 269;
South Korean troops, 222; Soviet
military shipments, 131, 135, 136,
142, 146, 158; Tet offensive, 157,
161, 224; Thailand and, 135, 150,
241; Warsaw ambassadorial talks,
269
Vlore naval base, 215

Wang En-mao, 160
Wang Kuang-mei, 137–38
Wang Ming, 83
war-lordism, 13–14, 18, 22
Warsaw ambassadorial talks, 92,
161, 167, 267–70
Warsaw Pact, 81, 88, 213
Washington Conference of 1922,
13
Wei-hsing people's commune, 90
West Germany. *See* Germany,
Federal Republic of
West Irian, 118
Western Europe, 304–5
Win, Ne, 156, 196, 243, 244
World Federation of Trade
Unions, 103, 194
World War I, 12–13, 18
World War II, 16–17, 26–30, 125,
175, 314–15
Wuhan incident, 156

Yalta Conference, 276
Yao Teng-shan, 155
Yemeni Arab Republic, 193, 258
Yew, Lee Kuan, 227, 242
Yuan Shih-k'ai, 12–14
Yugoslavia, 36, 55, 73, 105, 159,
196, 197, 213–19

Zambia, 195
Zanzibar, 111–12